DATE			

The Texts of Keats's Poems

Jack Stillinger

The Texts of Keats's Poems

Harvard University Press
Cambridge, Massachusetts
1974

1|12|77

© Copyright 1974 by the President and Fellows of Harvard College
All rights reserved

Publication of this book has been aided by a grant from the
Hyder Edward Rollins Fund

Library of Congress Catalog Card Number 73-86940
SBN 674-87511-7
Printed in the United States of America

1691S

Preface

In this study of all the holograph MSS, transcripts, and early printings of Keats's poems I have attempted to determine—as far as the evidence permits, and I hope not too much further—the relationships among the extant MSS (who copied what from whom), the sources of the earliest published versions (how the poems first got into print), and the relative authoritativeness of the various texts that might have claims to be the standard (which versions are "the best"). The book contains a great deal of information of a specific and limited usefulness. I am concerned in the first place with the question of which words Keats actually wrote, as opposed to those that have been added or substituted by transcribers, printers, and editors from his own time to the present; and in the second place with the purity or wholeness of his texts—I urge the adoption of versions made up of words that all existed together in a single MS or printed text, as opposed to the combining of readings from two or more discrete texts, whatever their individual degrees of authoritativeness. A third concern is the question of which text of any given poem best represents Keats's intentions in the work, the text that in theory he would have approved for publication in a standard edition.

I do not interpret any poems here, nor do I give attention (any more than Keats did) to the minutiae of spelling, punctuation, and capitalization. Textual work on Shakespeare, Hawthorne, and a number of other writers has reached such a point of refinement that the accidentals of a text can be the subject of many pages of discussion. Textual work on Keats, by comparison, is still in its infancy. In each of the two best modern editions, H. W. Garrod's *The Poetical Works of John Keats,*

2nd ed. (1958), and Miriam Allott's *The Poems of John Keats* (1970), the texts of approximately one-third of the poems have one or more wrong words in them, and therefore it seems appropriate at this point to focus on substantive matters. Though I have occasionally made use of accidentals, where it seemed a defensible procedure, as evidence to establish or support a relationship between two texts, my principal interest has been in the words of the texts—I wish to get rid of the wrong ones, and to suggest how to go about constructing texts with a greater proportion of right ones. My thesis, insofar as the study has one, is that we can do a better job than we have in the past in establishing texts for a standard edition.

I first thought of doing this study at the end of the summer of 1971, while reviewing Miriam Allott's new edition for the *Keats-Shelley Journal.* I had published articles on the texts of *Ode on a Grecian Urn, The Eve of St. Agnes,* and *Ode on Indolence,* but it was in going through her edition, and especially in pondering her choices of base-texts for the poems first published after Keats's death, that I became interested in a number of questions which (in my innocence) had not seemed important earlier when I was primarily engaged in critical work on the major poems —such simple and fundamental questions as how many poems Keats wrote, how long several poems of disputed length really ought to be, and which, in the many hundreds of places where seemingly authoritative texts differ from one another, ought to be considered the best readings. I began checking into these matters and found a great many things to worry about: (the modern editors sometimes base their texts on inferior holograph or transcript or printed versions; sometimes combine readings from separate states of text; in places retain words first introduced into the poems by R. M. Milnes, his copyists, his printer, or later editors; and in other places add independent errors of their own.) Garrod's edition especially is full of wrong information in his headnotes and textual apparatus, and Allott's edition, while much improved textually over Garrod's and a genuinely significant work in other aspects besides textual, also has, owing to her dependence on Garrod, too many mistakes. As a consequence of the accumulation of errors in texts and apparatus, no scholar working on Keats these days—at least on the posthumously published poems, which make up about two-thirds of the canon—can, without consulting the MSS and earliest printings himself, fairly assess the probability that any given word or line in a Keats poem was actually written by Keats.

In the last four months of 1971 I was able to collate all but one or two of the extant holographs and transcripts, thanks largely to the existence in the University of Illinois Library of several hundred photostats collected in the 1930's by the late Claude Lee Finney, when he was on the faculty here, and thanks also to the cooperativeness and generosity of libraries and individuals who sent me photographs, microfilms, xeroxes, and a good deal of supplementary information. From my collation notes I wrote a "history" of each text, as far as I could reconstruct it from the available evidence, and then on the basis of my histories wrote the more general introductory Sections I–III, fed the generalizations of the introductory sections back into a revised version of the histories, and finally added the brief conclusion that forms Section V.

At one time or another I have seen and handled the originals of most of the documents that I list and describe, and I have accumulated a considerable mass of data concerning paper and watermarks, but the present work is based almost entirely on photocopies of the MSS. This procedure has its inherent dangers, as everyone knows. I had finished my first draft before Father George Traub, now of Xavier University, made me aware of the existence of a sheet with Charles Brown's inscription on it wrapped around Woodhouse's clerks' transcripts of *The Fall of Hyperion* and some shorter poems at Harvard. I had never heard of this sheet before and therefore had not known enough to ask Harvard to send me a reproduction of it; were it not for this last-minute piece of information—a lucky chance—I would still be wondering why Woodhouse had these poems recopied and how Milnes got the copies. There are undoubtedly other such matters of which, because I have been working with photocopies and through the mails, I am still entirely ignorant. Nevertheless, the only possible way to compare unique MSS that often are physically separated by hundreds or thousands of miles is to put photocopies side by side, and this is what I have spent a great many hours doing in the past several months.

There are a number of problems that cannot be solved definitively and a number of relationships that cannot be worked out from the evidence at hand. For the rest, I confess that I think I am only about ninety-percent right in the various connections that I have set down and diagramed. The principal virtue of the present study is its comprehensive view of the transcribers' and early printers' and editors' practices. If a scholar is working on, say, the relationship between Woodhouse's and Charlotte Reynolds' transcripts of *The Fall of Hyperion,* he gets one sort of impression from confining his data to the two MSS in question (they differ in about ninety-five details of spelling and punctuation and therefore, he might conclude, they probably were made independently from a lost original) and another sort of impression from examining the two

MSS in the larger context of all the transcribers' activities (the better view is that, in comparison with other pairs of transcribers, Woodhouse and Charlotte are so much alike in their details that one *must* have copied the other's transcript). In the instance at hand, I may be wrong about Charlotte's copying Woodhouse: in actual fact she may have sat on Keats's knee and written all of her transcripts from his dictation; but we have no evidence for this latter possibility, and we do have evidence to establish a probability that she copied Woodhouse. Evidence can be misleading of course—one would say that H. B. Forman certainly took his text of O *blush not so* from Brown's extant transcript, except for the fact that Brown's MS was not available to him, and therefore he had to have acquired the poem from some other source. No doubt there are similar instances in which we lack the external facts that would correct the probabilities seeming to result from internal evidence.

Much of the work rests on just such probabilities rather than on factual certainty, and much has to do with simple logic: for example, X transcript has five substantive variants from a holograph version, while Y transcript has the same five variants and three others besides; if either X came from Y or Y came from X, the probability is that Y came from X (because the transcriber of X could not have got the additional three authoritative readings from the variants in Y). I do not claim to have superior logical powers, but nevertheless offer the findings in this study as provisionally definitive. I should like for them to stand until someone else does a more thorough job on the existing evidence or until new facts and MSS are discovered that change the findings.

Though I owe a great deal to institutions and individuals who have helped me at various stages of this project, I must first acknowledge special obligations to the late Professor Garrod and to Dr. Allott and express my discomfort in having to comment on errors in their work. Garrod's first edition of the *Poetical Works,* in 1939, was excellent for its time, and he was almost eighty years old when he and an assistant revised the work for the second edition of 1958. Possibly his chief disservice to Keats scholarship, though an entirely innocent one, was to lend his name as editor to the 1956 Oxford Standard Authors edition of Keats's poems, which is a slightly corrected reprint of H. B. Forman's O.S.A. edition dating from 1906, but which, because of the addition of Garrod's name, has frequently been taken to be as reliable a work as his larger Oxford English Texts edition. Dr. Allott's more recent edition with modernized texts is a considerable improvement over Garrod's work. Her scholarship in chronology and her critical and biographical annotations are first-rate. While the student still must consult Garrod for original spelling and punctuation and also for a fuller account of variants in MSS and early printings, in every other respect her work deserves to be the current standard edition of Keats's complete poems. Most of the flaws in her texts derive from earlier scholars' errors—in about equal proportions from Forman, one of whose editions seems to have served her as a base-text for checking and emending, and from Garrod's faulty apparatus. They are a good illustration of my contention that Keats scholars are seriously hampered in their work by the present state of knowledge about Keats's texts. Dr. Allott has made major contributions to the critical understanding of Keats's poems, and also has been most helpful in replying to my queries about the whereabouts of some MS materials. I do not wish to seem ungrateful, or to be finding fault with her work more generally, in pointing out specific errors in her texts.

This work has been collaborative from the beginning, and I have incurred a widespread indebtedness in the course of doing it. My most considerable obligations are to the Harvard and Pierpont Morgan libraries, which between them possess four-fifths of all the extant Keats MSS and transcripts, and to W. H. Bond, Rae Ann Nager, and Paul Needham. Professor Bond, Librarian of the Houghton Library, and Miss Nager, Curator of the Harvard Keats Collection, were constantly generous in supplying xeroxes and films of Harvard holdings that I did not have among Finney's photostats. Professor Bond gave me a draft copy of his comprehensive index to the Keats Collection, which proved immensely useful especially in the early stages of the work. Miss Nager answered scores of queries with precision, promptness, and—what became increasingly remarkable as the correspondence went on week after week—unfailing good spirits. Mr. Needham provided similarly essential and friendly help with films and information about MSS in the Morgan Library.

Stuart Sperry, of Indiana University, lent me his microfilm of Woodhouse's interleaved copy of *1817* in the Huntington Library. Mrs. C. M. Gee sent xeroxes and information from Keats House, Hampstead, and Vera Cacciatore corresponded about MSS at the Keats-Shelley Memorial House in Rome. Marjorie G. Wynne had photographs made of MSS at Yale, June Moll arranged for films of the draft of *Otho the Great* and some fragments at the University of Texas, and Lola L. Szladits supplied xeroxes of Woodhouse's interleaved *1818* and a photostat of Keats's fair copy of *To Sleep* in the New York Public Library. Ann D. McDermott reported on the MSS at Texas Christian University, and Wanda M. Randall and Thomas V. Lange on MSS in the private collection of Robert H.

Taylor at Princeton. Dorothy Withey, of Stratford-upon-Avon, sent me photographs of her fair copy of *Welcome joy and welcome sorrow*; the Buffalo and Erie County Public Library, the National Library of Scotland, and the Victoria and Albert Museum all supplied photocopies of holograph sonnets in their collections; the Free Library of Philadelphia provided a xerox of a draft fragment of *I stood tip-toe,* and the Trinity College Library both a xerox and an enlarged photograph of the holograph of *Give me women, wine, and snuff.*

W. S. Haugh, City Librarian of Bristol, sent xeroxes of the Reynolds-Hood Commonplace Book, and also put me in touch with George W. Traub, S.J., then a Ph.D. student at Cornell writing on *The Fall of Hyperion,* with whom I entered into a lengthy and enlightening correspondence. Father Traub and several other people —among them Leonidas M. Jones, of the University of Vermont, Paul Kaufman, of the University of Washington, Leslie A. Marchand, of Englewood, Florida, and Peter F. Morgan, of University College, Toronto (who also gave me copies of some pages from his forthcoming edition of Thomas Hood's letters)— contributed information toward identifying the writer of the transcripts in the Reynolds-Hood Commonplace Book, a problem that was not solved until A. E. J. Hollaender, Keeper of Manuscripts in the Guildhall Library, came through with a photocopy of the registration of Hood's marriage to Jane Reynolds. Basil Cottle, of the University of Bristol, Robert Gittings, of Chichester, Willard B. Pope, of the University of Vermont, Joanna Richardson, of London, Donald H. Reiman, of the Carl H. Pforzheimer Library, and the Very Reverend J. H. S. Wild, Dean of Durham, all answered requests for specific information. Eugene Quirk, of the University of Hartford, went to some trouble to secure a xerox of a late printing of the first sonnet *On Fame* in the *Odd Fellow,* and my son Tom Stillinger dug out a text of *This pleasant tale is like a little copse* from the files of the *Morning Chronicle* at Yale. Enid Nixon did some last-minute research for me in the collections of sale catalogues at the British Museum.

Daniel Alpert and the Graduate College of the University of Illinois provided a year's leave of absence from teaching, committee work, and administrative duties. If this study is well thought of, I hope it will be taken as evidence in support of the continuation of sabbatical leaves, for I calculate that the work would have required as many as twelve or even fifteen years to carry out amid the various demands of ordinary academic life. Mary Ceibert, Louise Fitton, and the rest of the staff of the Rare Books Room at the University of Illinois were wonderfully efficient and genial all the year long, and the Library's Reference Department performed some minor miracles in locating out-of-the-way items through interlibrary loan. My colleagues Charles Shattuck and Scott Bennett helped solve specific problems—Professor Shattuck with information about performances of *The Heart of Midlothian* in April 1819 (for the dating of *La Belle Dame* and *Song of Four Fairies*), and Professor Bennett with criticisms of some of my wording in the final pages of Section I. My colleague-wife Nina Baym was a constant source of wisdom and practical advice throughout the project.

I am under more general obligation to Arthur A. Houghton, Jr., who has been almost singlehandedly responsible for the present supereminence of the Harvard Keats Collection; to the late Professor Finney, whose volumes of photostats made the preliminary research possible to the point where I saw the need to embark on the complete study; and to the late Hyder Rollins, who, as my teacher two decades ago, was a principal exemplar of the virtue of a strong sense of fact in literary research. I think this is the sort of work that Rollins would have done had he lived a little longer, and he has been, as he was for an earlier book of mine, the spiritual presider over it.

I have included a brief account of certain of my practices in the histories in Section IV.1 and a list of abbreviations at the end of the book. I would add here that line numbers throughout this study are those of Garrod's 1958 edition, which occasionally differ from Allott's; that in references to books the place of publication is given only when it is not London; and that in quoting Woodhouse's variant readings in the transcripts I have silently expanded his "orig^y," "orig^l," and "or^{ly}" to "originally."

J.S.

Contents

"Give him his proof! A camel's load of proofs!"

—*Otho the Great,* III.ii.208

I

Introduction: The Current State of Keats's Texts

In the 1840's, probably specifically in 1846, Charles Cowden Clarke
sent Richard Monckton Milnes, who was gathering facts and unpub-
lished poems for his *Life, Letters, and Literary Remains, of John Keats*
(1848), a copy that he had written out of Keats's *Think not of it, sweet
one, so.* Clarke's source, as he explained to Milnes in a note at the
bottom of his MS, was a transcript made for him by Richard Woodhouse,
who had seen both Keats's original draft (with the draft MS of *Endymion*
when he borrowed it from J. H. Reynolds) and a revised version copied
by Keats "for a Lady." In the now-lost transcript that he gave Clarke,
Woodhouse had written the main text in black ink and then noted can-
celed readings from the draft (i.e., words that Keats had deleted and
replaced in the draft) in red ink. Clarke reproduced Woodhouse's details
by including the draft's canceled readings marginally in parentheses, as
follows:

> **On . . . .**
>
> Think not of it, sweet one, so;—
>   Give it not a tear;
> Sigh thou mayst, and bid it go
>   Any—any where.
>
> ═══
>
> Do not look so sad, sweet one,—
>   Sad and fadingly;
> Shed one drop then—It is gone   (and only one)
>   Oh! 'twas born to die!   (sweetly did it die)

Still so pale? then dearest weep;
  Weep, I'll count the tears;
And each one shall be a bliss   (For each will I
    For thee in after years.   invent a bliss)

━━

Brighter has it left thine eyes
  Than a sunny rill;
And thy whispering melodies
  Are tenderer still.

━━

Yet, as all things mourn awhile
  At fleeting blisses;   (dying)
Let us too; but be our dirge
  A dirge of kisses.

━━

Ap¹ 1817.   J Keats.

    Milnes, too, like Woodhouse, had access to Keats's draft, lent to him by Reynolds in July 1847. But when he was preparing his work for the printer he chose Clarke's transcript as the copy from which the poem was to be set in type. Even without the parenthetical variants, Clarke's MS combined early and revised texts—"and" (3) and "rill" (14) are both draft readings that, as we know from other Woodhouse transcripts, Keats had subsequently changed to "but" and "hill" in the revised fair copy that he wrote out for the lady, while "Let" (19) is a revised reading that replaced the draft's "E'en let." In addition, Clarke's heading for the lines appears in no other extant MS. But Milnes further corrupted the text. He struck through the last four words of 7 (leaving the canceled draft reading to be printed), the parenthetical variant to 8, all of 11 (leaving the canceled draft reading), and the parenthetical variant to 18. He also deleted "tenderer" in 16, writing in "more tender" above the line, and marked out the date and signature at the end, replacing them with "1817" beside the heading. The first published text of the poem, in *1848* (II, 257), which is identical in wording with Clarke's MS as it was thus altered by Milnes, represents a mixture of canceled draft readings (in 7 and 11), uncanceled draft readings (3 and 14), a revised fair copy reading (19), and a substantive change of Milnes's own invention (16).

    Milnes's handling of the poem ought not to raise any eyebrows, especially if we consider the general state of textual knowledge and practices in the middle of the nineteenth century. Either the main text of Clarke's transcript or, if Milnes had taken a copy of it, Keats's draft would have provided a somewhat better text by present-day standards; but Milnes simply printed the readings that he preferred and occasionally rewrote Keats's lines when he thought they needed improving. What may, on the other hand, be surprising is that modern editors of Keats, even the most recent of them, are hardly more precise and consistent than Milnes was in dealing with Keats's texts. In the case of *Think not of it,* both H. W. Garrod, in *The Poetical Works of John Keats,* 2nd ed. (Oxford, 1958), and Miriam Allott, in *The Poems of John Keats* (1970), give the words, if not the punctuation, of Keats's original draft, and thus achieve a consistency of text—they print all the words of a single authoritative version—even if, by setting aside the readings of Keats's later version, they forsake their usual preference for revised over draft states of Keats's poems. But for many other poems the modern editors produce the same sort of mixture represented by Milnes's text of *Think not of it.* If we consider the general state of textual knowledge and practices in the middle of the *twentieth* century, their procedures are rather disturbing.

The fact is that Keats's texts are not in a very healthy condition these days. We do not agree, for example, even on how many poems Keats wrote. If we count the six lyrics of *Extracts from an Opera* as a single piece, Garrod includes 158 poems and fragments in his 1958 edition, plus the non-Keatsian lines *To Woman (from the Greek)* in his Introduction and *Gripus* in an appendix. Allott prints 150 numbered items in the main part of her edition and another seven (the last item including three separate fragments) in a section of "Doubtful Attributions and Trivia." Section IV of the present study discusses the texts of 150 poems and briefly comments on eight others under the heading "Questionable Attributions." But this closeness in numbers—totals of 160, 159, and 158, respectively—disguises the facts that Garrod prints *Hence burgundy, claret, and port* and *God of the meridian* as two poems, while Allott considers them to be a single poem; that Garrod and Allott treat the forty-two lines beginning "Woman! when I behold thee" as three separate sonnets, while I have taken them to be a single piece; that Garrod and Allott regard both *To A. G. S.* and *"The House of Mourning" written by Mr. Scott* as authentically Keatsian, while I have relegated them to the "Questionable" category; that Allott places *Stay, ruby-breasted warbler* among her "Doubtful Attributions," while Garrod and I are inclined to think it genuine; and that I have added in Section IV.3 a poem that is not given or even mentioned by Garrod and Allott—*Love and Folly*— and have omitted altogether (along with some other bits and pieces not worthy of independent status) a fragment that they both include, th two lines beginning "They weren fully glad" (Garrod, p. 554; Allott, p. 753).

Similarly, there are at least half a dozen poems of unsettled length in the Keats canon. *Not Aladdin magian,* the strangest case of all in this respect, is fifty-seven lines long in Keats's first letter copy, W^2, the earliest printing in the Louisville *Western Messenger,* and Garrod's text; fifty-five lines long in Allott's edition; fifty-one lines in the version published in *PDWJ* and *1848*; forty-seven lines in Charles Brown's extant transcript; and forty-two lines in Keats's second letter copy. *The Eve of St. Mark* is 137 lines long in Allott's edition, 135 in Garrod's, 119 in the first published text (*1848*), and 114 in Keats's letter copy. *Hence burgundy, claret, and port* is either forty-one lines long (Allott) or sixteen lines (Garrod), and *Woman! when I behold thee* is either forty-two lines (as in *1817*) or fourteen (Garrod and Allott). Using approximately the same number of words, Allott prints *Apollo to the Graces* as fifteen lines and Garrod as fourteen, while *There was a naughty boy* is variously 118 lines long (Allott), 117 (Keats's letter), and 116 (Garrod), depending on the arrangement of the lines. *Mother of Hermes* is a line longer in Garrod's and Allott's texts than it is in the earliest extant source, a transcript of a lost letter from Keats to Reynolds. At least some of these discrepancies ought to be resolved. Certainly it is an unhealthy situation when such differences are not discussed or even noticed.

For the forty-five poems published in Keats's three original volumes —*Poems* (1817), *Endymion* (1818), and *Lamia, Isabella, The Eve of St. Agnes, and Other Poems* (1820)—our modern editions, except for occasional misprints, are at least adequate, since they invariably accept these authoritative printings as the bases for their texts. But for the nine other poems first published while Keats was alive (in the *Examiner,* the *Champion,* Leigh Hunt's *Literary Pocket-Book,* and the *Indicator*) and the ninety-six pieces first published after his death, our texts are, in general, in bad shape. Garrod and Allott—to focus on the best recent complete editions—take a number of their texts of the posthumously published poems from inferior MS or printed sources, combine states of text, and occasionally rewrite Keats's lines in the same way that Milnes did in *Think not of it.* They often misunderstand the evidence that the various MSS provide and give a great deal of misinformation about the texts. As a result, no one working on Keats these days, unless he does the collating and works out the relationships for himself, can tell how Keats's texts were copied from one MS to another, or in which order the

various texts were written, or from what sources the poems were first
put into print, or which are authoritative and which are corrupt readings
in any particular text.

Let me give three specific examples of the current state of Keats's
texts. *God of the golden bow* exists in two holographs, four transcripts,
and three early printed texts. Collation of the MSS, plus evidence in a
letter to Milnes published by Hyder Rollins in *The Keats Circle,* reduces
the various texts to two basic states, represented by Keats's original draft
(at Harvard) and a revised holograph fair copy (in the Morgan Library).
Milnes's text in *1848* is substantively the same as the revised fair copy
except in title. Garrod prints a version that generally has the wording
and accidentals of *1848,* but replaces Milnes's title with one apparently
invented by Woodhouse and introduces readings from Keats's draft into
the revised text in 6 and 11. In his apparatus he errs seven times, in
the notes to 6, 11, 20, 23, 27, 30, and 32, in recording readings of
1848 (he seems to have mistakenly used H. B. Forman's 1883 text as
the representative of *1848*—at least the seven "*1848*" variants all appear
in Forman and do not appear in *1848*); he fails to record the readings
of Keats's draft for 6 and 11, misrecords the revised fair copy readings
for the same two lines, and gets the Woodhouse transcripts wrong for
11 and 23 and the *Western Messenger* wrong for 20. He also misdates
the *Western Messenger* printing (it was the issue of June 1836, not "1
June 1836"), and there are various inaccuracies in his quotations of
George Keats's inscription on the draft, Woodhouse's notes in W^2 and
W^3, and James Freeman Clarke's introductory note in the *Western
Messenger.*

A number of these mistakes are of no significance, but one could not
reconstruct the wording of either Keats's draft or the revised fair copy
from Garrod's apparatus. Nor could one clearly understand the relation-
ship of any of the MSS to any other or to the early printings. As a case
in point, Allott, intending to print the substantive text of Keats's revised
fair copy, actually gives the draft rather than the fair copy wording of 6,
simply because Garrod failed to report the draft reading and wrongly
reported the fair copy reading for the line. She also repeats erroneous
information from Garrod's apparatus in her notes to 23 and 30.

Garrod's and Allott's texts of *God of the golden bow* fairly exemplify
a number of tendencies in their handling of Keats's posthumous poems
in general. For a more extreme instance, though it merely represents
an aggravation of the same tendencies, I would choose *Before he went
to live with owls and bats,* which exists in Keats's original draft (Hunt-

ington Library), in a transcript by Brown representing a later state of text, and in a copy of the draft made by J. C. Stephens (this last the source of the first published version, by Nicoll and Wise in 1896). Keats's draft and Brown's transcript are the two principal texts, early and revised. Garrod's text combines distinctive substantive readings of the draft (in 1, 3, and 6) with distinctive readings of Brown's MS (in 7, 8, 10, and 14) under a title apparently of his own devising (at least it is one that does not occur in Brown's or any other known MS). He errs in citing a W^3 transcript (none exists), does not record the differences between Keats's draft and Brown's transcript in 1 and 3, and misrepresents Brown in his notes to the title and 6 and 8, and Stephens in his notes to 8, 10, and 13.

The results can again be seen in Allott's text. Taking over Garrod's title and similarly citing the nonexistent W^3, she purports to give the draft text but has Brown's wording in 3, Stephens' in 6 (an error that Stephens made in copying the draft), and readings in 8 and 13 that exist in no MS but are simply mistakes in Garrod's apparatus. In the case of *Before he went to live,* the student of Keats cannot reconstruct the readings of any of the MSS from the modern editions, much less the relationships among the texts that would enable him to decide on an early or later version of any given line.

Getting the words right for *God of the golden bow* and *Before he went to live* may rate rather low on the scale of critical priorities, but the text of *The Eve of St. Mark,* a poem that, unlike the other two, is frequently discussed in interpretive studies of Keats, ought to be another matter. We have two holograph texts—a draft in the British Museum and a fair copy in a letter in the Morgan Library—as well as transcripts by Brown and Woodhouse (W^2). The first fifty lines of a now-lost shorthand transcript by Woodhouse are known in facsimile, and there is in the Morgan Library an additional sixteen-line fragment in Keats's hand that is sometimes associated with the poem. Examination of the MSS reveals that Brown copied the British Museum draft, that W^2 derives from the draft by way of the intervening shorthand transcript by Woodhouse, that Keats in his letter probably also copied the draft, and that Brown's MS was printer's copy for the first published version, the text in *1848.*

We might argue over the relative claims of the draft and the letter copy to be the basis for a standard text (the two differ substantively in eleven lines and in the letter copy's omission of 115–119), but we should not seriously consider basing a text of *The Eve of St. Mark* on Brown's transcript, W^2, or *1848,* since the ultimate source of these texts, Keats's draft, is itself extant. Both Garrod and Allott, however, do take their texts from one or another of these inferior versions, Garrod from *1848* and Allott from W^2. Garrod emends *1848* substantively in two lines, but ends up with a text combining readings of Keats's draft generally, a reading of the letter copy in 59, and readings that occur in neither holograph in 22, 32, and 53. Allott departs substantively from Woodhouse's transcript in several lines, but retains errors from W^2 in 74 and 115 and also includes a couplet following 68 that Keats had canceled in his draft and omitted in his letter (Woodhouse copied the lines without any hint that they were deleted). The worst feature of both Garrod's and Allott's texts is their incorporation of an extra sixteen lines into the poem after 98 (the Morgan fragment beginning "Gif ye wol stonden")— for which there is no precedent or justification in any of the MSS.

Now how, one may ask, is the ordinary student or critic (or even scholar) of Keats supposed to know whether or not the sixteen-line additional fragment belongs in the text of *The Eve of St. Mark*, or whether Allott's incorporation of the extra couplet after 68 is justified, or whether —where they differ—one of the holograph texts is earlier or later than the other? These are the kinds of question that prompted the present study, and the fact is that none of them can be settled on the basis of Garrod's text or apparatus. He does not record several of the substantive differences between the two holographs, for example; his note to 68/69 does not indicate that the couplet following 68 is deleted in the draft; and his note to the sixteen-line additional fragment ("98*a-p om. 1848 T²EL*") does not make clear that the fragment follows the final line of the poem in W^2 and after a half-page of blank space. Allott's text is similarly misleading, although she is more candid about the critical as opposed to textual grounds on which she follows Garrod in incorporating the sixteen-line fragment.

As a random example of the consequences in Keats criticism, David Luke, in a recent article entitled "*The Eve of Saint Mark*: Keats's 'ghostly Queen of Spades' and the Textual Superstition," first says it is "highly questionable" that Keats's letter copy is later than the British Museum holograph, then deems it "nearly certain" that the British Museum MS is the later text, and finally, without qualification, calls the British Museum MS "the last autograph" (*Studies in Romanticism*, 9 [1970], 164, 165 n., 171 n.). Luke is intent on using the sixteen-line additional fragment as part of the poem in his interpretation, and he therefore would like for the letter copy to be the earlier, so that he can construct a progress of expansion from the letter copy (114 lines) through the

British Museum MS (119 lines) to a hypothetical third state that in-
cludes the extra sixteen lines. This cannot, on scholarly grounds, be
done, and Luke's statements just quoted are all wrong, as comparison of
the two holographs will show. The point, however, is that his statements
are possible on the evidence of Garrod's text and apparatus (Allott's edi-
tion, which does make clear the chronological priority of the British
Museum MS, was not yet published when Luke wrote his article).

The reiterated message of these examples is that Keats critics and
scholars cannot, where textual readings, variants, priorities, and questions
of authoritativeness are at issue, operate even at a minimum level of
competence with the modern editions that are currently standard. The
principal causes of this situation are not difficult to identify. One of
them, of course, is the combination of circumstances that almost two-
thirds of Keats's poems were first published posthumously, in texts over
which the poet therefore had no control; that for most of these poems
there exist (or once existed) several different MS versions, and it was
almost entirely a matter of chance whether a better or inferior—that is,
a more directly authoritative or a more remotely derivative—version of
any given poem was the basis for the earliest publication; and that the
earliest printings of these posthumous poems, especially those in 1848,
have had, because of the ordinary human tendency to conserve some-
thing established, a greater influence on Keats's texts subsequently than
the resources and judgments of the first editors and publishers would
warrant. The most obvious general example of this influence is Garrod's
slavish retention of Milnes's and Milnes's copyists' or printer's accidentals
—and frequently also their wrong words—in poems first published in
1848; an extreme specific instance is Garrod's inclusion of the canceled
opening stanza of *Ode on Melancholy* as a separate item among "Shorter
Poems from the Memoir in 'Life, Letters, and Literary Remains' "—
some 230 pages after his text of the ode among the 1820 poems—
merely because Milnes, who did not reprint the ode itself in 1848, gave
the stanza at the end of his first volume.

Another cause is the circumstance that a great deal of *scholarly* work
on Keats—especially by H. B. Forman beginning in the 1880's and also
by M. R. Ridley in the early 1930's and Garrod in the later 1930's—
was done with apparent thoroughness at a relatively early stage both in
the development of textual scholarship in English literature generally and
in the history of the discovery or rediscovery of Keats materials more
specifically. H. B. Forman had a great many MSS to work with, but not
nearly enough to produce the facts and probabilities that are set forth in

Section IV of the present study, and, besides, he frequently did not understand the significance of the MSS he had. The progress since Forman has been mainly to discover new MSS, record new variants, but hardly ever to make much use of the additional information. Indeed, one of the principal faults of Garrod's apparatus is that he treats all texts as having equal status, printing corrupt readings and slips of the pen side by side with variants that directly reflect what Keats wrote.

A third cause is simply everybody's tendency to accept details without checking, and thus to repeat and accumulate error. As one of many available examples, consider the facts that the *1817* text of *Calidore* has a line space marking a paragraph between 72 and 73; that Forman's 1883 text, just by an accident of format, began a new page with 73 and consequently, since *1817* did not indent new paragraphs, lost all record of the division; and that as a result hundreds of subsequent texts based in one way or another on Forman—including those of the Hampstead Keats, Garrod, and Allott—do not mark the paragraph division between the lines. Allott's texts in particular contain a number of such errors deriving from Forman, most probably by way of his Oxford Standard Authors edition, first published in 1906.

A fourth cause lies in the fact that, although many of the MSS have now come to rest permanently in one place—the Harvard Keats Collection—the MSS in general have been widely distributed in the United States and Great Britain, and until the fairly recent development of microfilming and xerography it has sometimes been costly and sometimes quite impossible to do the kind of collating that the serious study of Keats's texts requires. Garrod, for example, never actually saw a great many of the MSS that he reported on, and he had to use some of the others under less than ideal conditions, while American scholars (like Rollins in editing Keats's letters) were similarly distanced from the MSS in Great Britain.

There is the additional fact that almost all of the specific statements in print about the relationship of one Keats text to another or about the significance of some peculiarity of text are, to be blunt about it, wrong. To cite some examples at random over the years—H. B. Forman thinks that the *Annals* texts of the two Elgin Marbles sonnets were reprinted from the *Examiner* (Forman, 1883, II, 219 n.); but they came instead from an independent MS source. Ernest de Selincourt says there "can be no doubt" that Woodhouse's clerk's transcript of *Hyperion* was made from the British Museum holograph (*Hyperion*, p. 4); but actually the clerk copied Woodhouse's transcript. Amy Lowell suggests that Milnes printed *La Belle Dame* from a Woodhouse transcript (Lowell, II, 228 —so also Forman in the Hampstead Keats, IV, 206 n., and Garrod, 1956 Oxford Standard Authors edition, p. 465); but Milnes gave the printer Brown's transcript. Ridley says that Woodhouse's W^1 transcript of *The Eve of St. Agnes* "was certainly made from" the Harvard draft (Ridley, p. 98); this is in a sense true, but there was at least one and probably there were two intervening transcripts by Woodhouse between the draft and W^1. Garrod supposes that both the W^2 and W^1 transcripts of *Isabella* came from Keats's draft (p. xxxvii); but they derive instead from a shorthand transcript of Keats's fair copy. Harold Edgar Briggs thinks that Milnes printed only the first four lines of *Over the hill and over the dale* because the poem was "indecent" (*Summaries of Ph.D. Theses, University of Minnesota*, 5 [1951], 125); but actually the first four lines were the only ones available in Milnes's source. Alvin Whitley says that the W^2 transcript of *In drear-nighted December* is "unquestionably a copy of" the extant Bristol holograph (*HLB*, 5 [1951], 120); but it came instead, as Woodhouse notes, "from J: H: Reynolds" and demonstrably not from the Bristol MS. Hyder Rollins says that Milnes took his text of *God of the golden bow* from J. F. Clarke's transcript (*HLB*, 6 [1952], 172); but the 1848 text clearly derives from another source. Robert Gittings thinks that George Keats's transcripts of *Ode on a Grecian Urn* and *To Autumn* were made from Keats's drafts, and he even prints photographs of George's transcript of the former as "the nearest to Keats's [lost] first draft that we are likely to get" (*Odes*, p. 68); but George copied Brown's transcript in each case. Allott remarks that "in George Keats's undated transcript (British Museum)" *There is a joy in footing slow* "is copied out as quatrains consisting of lines alternately of 4 and 3 stresses" (p. 370); but the transcript is not by George Keats and, because it was copied from the *Examiner* printing of the lines, it has none of the significance as an independent text that Allott's information implies. Such statements—there are others at hand that could have been cited—proceed from the earlier causes mentioned above, but of course do nothing to help the situation and become themselves sources of further errors.

The present study (which does not claim to be free of the sorts of error just detailed, but hopes to have a somewhat smaller proportion of mistakes than previous scholarly work on Keats's texts) aims to remedy this situation by (1) listing and describing the extant holographs, transcripts, and early printed texts of all of Keats's poems; (2) establishing, where there is more than one text at hand, the chronological and so far as possible the direct relationships among the MSS and printed versions of each poem; (3) stating, on the basis of these relationships, which texts or readings are authoritative and which are corrupt; and (4) proposing, where competing texts exist, which version might be the better or best choice as the proper basis for a standard text. Some of these tasks are easier than others. The survey of MSS and printed texts would not even have had to be done again if Garrod's headnotes and apparatus did not contain so many mistakes. The establishment of relationships is for some poems a purely mechanical operation (where the evidence is clear and unmistakable) and for others a matter of educated guessing (where the evidence is either insufficient or ambiguous). For a few poems, relationships simply cannot be determined, and I have had to end up saying that we have X version and Y version, and we do not know which is the earlier. Where relationships can be solidly established, it is reasonably easy to pronounce on the relative authoritativeness of competing versions; where they cannot I have occasionally resorted to coin-flipping. The choice of a "proper basis" is partly a theoretical matter, and in this last endeavor I have sometimes had to be content with making suggestions merely. The problems of selecting a "proper basis" are separately discussed below, in Section IV.1.

Mainly I have been concerned to describe the transmission of Keats's texts, to identify authoritative texts and thereby to get Keats's words as right as possible, and to offer corrections to the current standard editions. Sections II and III provide summary accounts of the transcripts and the early printed texts—the characteristics of each of the principal transcribers, their customary sources, their general importance in the transmission of Keats's texts, the sources of the early printings, and the editorial treatment of Keats's poems by his contemporaries and more recently. The most significant part of the study is Section IV, in which facts and surmises about each of 150 pieces are set down and (where appropriate) a diagram is given to illustrate the relationships among texts, and the texts of the current standard editions are analyzed and if necessary corrected. The brief final section offers suggestions for a new editing of the poems.

Though I do not interpret Keats's poems, and very seldom suggest critical applications of the findings, the critical significance of the work ought to be obvious. It does make a difference in the interpretation of *The Eve of St. Mark* whether the sixteen-line additional fragment is included or omitted; it surely helps, in reading *Ode on Indolence,* to have the stanzas in the right order; and *Not Aladdin magian* is one kind of poem with the satirical lines following 49 and another kind of poem without them. As an example involving just a single word, consider the on-going debate over "lords" vs. "hoards" in the eleventh line of the sonnet *To Sleep*; the evidence of the MSS suggests that "hoards" is Woodhouse's invention but that Keats adopted it in the latest version of the poem that we have in his handwriting. The *1820* quotation marks around "Beauty . . . beauty" at the end of *Ode on a Grecian Urn* have always been a sticking point in critical interpretation; the present study does not permanently resolve the problem of whether they should be retained or omitted, but can point out that the agreement of four transcripts that do not have them is not so significant as it might initially seem, since the second, third, and fourth of these transcripts derive from the first and therefore have no independent authority. In the case of *Ode to a Nightingale*, the evidence of the MSS shows that the Cambridge draft is not the MS that Brown copied, and that consequently Brown's account of rescuing the poem from four or five scraps hidden behind some books has to be set aside—and in turn our notions of the genesis of the poem must be at least slightly revised. In *Ode on Melancholy,* the MSS make very clear that the canceled opening stanza was not a part of Keats's first draft. Though some details are of course more important than others, potentially every single substantive correction of Keats's texts—and even some accidental matters (e.g., the paragraph space mentioned above after *Calidore* 72)—has critical significance.

I have assumed from the beginning two things that philosophically are far from settled: first, that it is desirable to distinguish between words that Keats actually wrote and those that, intentionally or not, have been added or substituted by editors, printers, and scholars in texts over which the poet had no control; and, second, that a standard text of a poem ought to be based on a version that once actually existed whole and intact—in Keats's mind if not in his handwriting—as opposed to a version subsequently made up by others combining substantive readings from different more or less authoritative states of text. I should make clear that I am not here taking a stand against the kind of eclecticism advocated by the current leading theorists of textual criticism. Such eclecticism most often involves a bringing together of early-stage accidentals and late-stage substantives, while the present study is not concerned with accidentals at all (except as an occasional aid in determining relationships among the texts). Part of my attack is directed against what is sometimes called nineteenth-century unprincipled eclecticism— the kind of picking and choosing represented by Milnes's text of *Think not of it.* But when an editor unintentionally mixes substantive readings from a draft version with readings from a revised fair copy, and furthermore takes over corruptions from a faulty transcript or early printed text, the result is not really eclecticism of any sort (for even unprincipled eclecticism implies conscious choice)—it is merely bad editing.

II

The Manuscripts and the Transcribers

For ten of Keats's poems there are no surviving MSS of any sort—
*Written on the Day That Mr. Leigh Hunt Left Prison, Woman! when
I behold thee, To George Felton Mathew, How many bards, Keen, fitful
gusts, To Kosciusko, Sleep and Poetry, To Leigh Hunt, Esq., This mortal
body of a thousand days,* and *What can I do to drive away.* But for the
remaining 140 pieces we have more than 500 MS texts, of which 124
are holographs and the rest transcripts. The number is not even close
to the total that once existed, but the addition of very many more MSS
in the future appears improbable. Among holographs that were seen in
the later nineteenth century or more recently but have since disappeared,
M. B. Forman's fair copy of *To Hope,* the Lyte MS of *O Solitude,* the
Law draft of *In drear-nighted December,* the Townshend Mayer draft
of *Robin Hood,* and the Wilde draft of *Blue! 'Tis the life of heaven* seem
the likeliest to be still extant somewhere. Missing fragments of the
drafts of *I stood tip-toe, Isabella, Otho the Great, Lamia,* and other MSS
that were cut up and given away in small pieces by well-meaning but
unscholarly friends of the poet keep turning up from time to time. But
the rest of the lost holographs—all those in Keats's "book," for instance
(see *Letters,* II, 104)—and a great many transcripts, including some
by Woodhouse and a sizable number by Brown, probably will never be
recovered.

The study of Keats's texts will continue to be based principally on
the MSS that are known today. This means that for certain poems we
shall forever lack the missing links that might establish important rela-

tionships among the texts, and that for certain crucial problems we shall never have the textual facts necessary to solve them. But the extant MSS contain a great deal of evidence concerning sources and connections, and one can arrive at generalizations from them that may be usefully applied where specific, local details are not in themselves sufficient for dealing with a problem at hand. The main purpose of this section is to establish some of those generalizations.

1   JOHN KEATS

While we may not right off think of Keats as a transcriber of his own poems, the fact is that only about half of the extant holograph MSS are original drafts. Some of the remainder represent revised states of text and are properly considered results of further original composition; but others represent no more than a copying out of what was already creatively arrived at. The holographs in this last category theoretically are transcripts that ought to bear the same relation to their sources as Brown's or Woodhouse's or another copyist's transcripts of holograph originals.

It is frequently difficult to decide whether a given holograph is an original draft or some version subsequent to a lost original. The presence or absence of punctuation is no guide to the status of a holograph, because Keats sometimes thoroughly punctuated his drafts (that of *Ode to Psyche,* for example) and also sometimes used very little punctuation in MSS that are known to be fair copies (there are, for example, only five marks in the extant fair copy of *In drear-nighted December*). Nor is the presence or absence of signs of composition much help. Obviously Keats sometimes had a poem—even one with a complex rhyme scheme, as some of his sonnets—well along toward completion in his mind before he wrote down a single line on paper, and one may suspect, conversely, that a number of MSS showing frequent cancellations and revisions are not, as they might appear, original drafts. I do not believe that generalizations are possible in the matter, except perhaps to say that when Keats had a clear idea of what he was doing, and felt good, he probably wrote cleaner drafts than when he was groping around for a structure, theme, and images or was tired or dull. Every writer experiences those lucky occasions when the words flow from the top of the page to the bottom and also bad occasions when he has to work a passage over and over to get it right; and Keats, even though he was an imaginative genius, was not different from others in this respect. What is plainly (for reasons besides appearance) the first draft of *The Eve of St. Agnes* (at Harvard) has deletions and revisions in almost every line, while the earlier of two holographs of *The Eve of St. Mark* (the British Museum MS), which was written down only two or three weeks after *The Eve of St. Agnes*, is a fairly clean MS with relatively few indications of original composition. Yet the earlier MS of *The Eve of St. Mark* is very likely also a first draft (again, for extrinsic reasons), and the differences in appearance between it and the draft of *The Eve of St. Agnes* may lie almost entirely in the fact that the longer poem is written in the complicated rhyme scheme of the Spenserian stanza while the shorter poem is in the relatively undemanding form of octosyllabic couplets.

What I would stress, however, is that decisions of this sort are usually, and necessarily, quite arbitrary, involving subjective judgment in each case rather than any solid textual evidence. The British Museum holograph of *This pleasant tale is like a little copse*, the Harvard holograph of *On First Looking into Chapman's Homer*, and the Yale holograph of *As Hermes once took to his feathers light* are the earliest known versions of the three poems, but I have suggested in Section IV.2 that the first is a fair copy subsequent to a lost original draft while the other two are the original drafts themselves. The point is that some questions concerning Keats's texts can be resolved factually, while others are matters of opinion based on one's overall experience with the materials, and it is a good idea to distinguish between the two kinds of resolution and make clear their quite different bases.

The earliest extant holographs of the following sixty-one poems are probably, but by no means certainly, original drafts (here and throughout the present study, titles are given according to the forms used in Section IV.2):

I am as brisk
Give me women, wine, and snuff
To My Brother George (sonnet)
On First Looking into Chapman's Homer
On Leaving Some Friends at an Early Hour
To My Brothers
I stood tip-toe upon a little hill (incomplete)
Written in Disgust of Vulgar Superstition
God of the golden bow
On a Leander Which Miss Reynolds, My Kind Friend, Gave Me
Unfelt, unheard, unseen
Hither, hither, love
Before he went to live with owls and bats
O grant that like to Peter I

Think not of it, sweet one, so
Apollo to the Graces
Lines on Seeing a Lock of Milton's Hair
On Sitting Down to Read *King Lear* Once Again
Spenser, a jealous honorer of thine
O thou whose face hath felt the winter's wind
For there's Bishop's teign
Where be ye going, you Devon maid
Over the hill and over the dale
To J. R.
Isabella (incomplete)
Give me your patience, Sister, while I frame
Sweet, sweet is the greeting of eyes
Old Meg she was a gipsy
There was a naughty boy
Ah, ken ye what I met the day
All gentle folks who owe a grudge
Of late two dainties were before me plac'd
There is a joy in footing slow across a silent plain
Upon my life, Sir Nevis, I am piqu'd
'Tis the "witching time of night"
Bards of passion and of mirth
Spirit here that reignest
Hush, hush! tread softly! hush, hush, my dear
The Eve of St. Agnes (incomplete)
The Eve of St. Mark
When they were come unto the Fairy's court
Character of C. B.
As Hermes once took to his feathers light
Hyperion
La Belle Dame sans Merci
Song of Four Fairies
To Sleep
Ode to Psyche
On Fame ("How fever'd is the man")
Two or three posies
Ode to a Nightingale
Ode on Melancholy
Otho the Great
Lamia (incomplete)
Pensive they sit and roll their languid eyes
To Autumn
The day is gone, and all its sweets are gone
To Fanny ("Physician Nature"—incomplete)
King Stephen (incomplete)
This living hand, now warm and capable
The Jealousies (incomplete)

Though Keats, as Woodhouse tells us in a well-known note on the poet's methods of composition, was "impatient of correcting, & says he would rather burn the piece in question & write ano[r] or something else" (*KC*, I, 128), there is plentiful evidence, both in the extant holographs and in the transcripts made from lost revised MSS, that Keats more often than not did "correct" his poems in a later version. The remaining sixty-three holographs of the following fifty-six poems (one of them, *O grant that like to Peter I*, on the same sheet with the draft listed above) I judge to be versions subsequent to Keats's original drafts, whether or not the original draft is known or extant:

Fill for me the brimming bowl
To Some Ladies
On Receiving a Curious Shell and a Copy of Verses from the
    Same Ladies
O come, dearest Emma! the rose is full blown
O Solitude! if I must with thee dwell
Hadst thou liv'd in days of old
To a Friend Who Sent Me Some Roses
Happy is England! I could be content
To My Brother George (sonnet)
To My Brother George (epistle)
To Charles Cowden Clarke
On First Looking into Chapman's Homer
To My Brothers (two copies)
Addressed to the Same ("Great spirits"—three copies)
To G. A. W.
I stood tip-toe upon a little hill
On the Grasshopper and Cricket
On Receiving a Laurel Crown from Leigh Hunt
To the Ladies Who Saw Me Crown'd
God of the golden bow
This pleasant tale is like a little copse
On Seeing the Elgin Marbles
To Haydon, with a Sonnet Written on Seeing the Elgin Marbles
Unfelt, unheard, unseen
O grant that like to Peter I
Endymion
In drear-nighted December
To Mrs. Reynolds' Cat
Lines on Seeing a Lock of Milton's Hair (two copies)
On Sitting Down to Read *King Lear* Once Again
Lines on the Mermaid Tavern (two copies)
Spenser, a jealous honorer of thine
Four seasons fill the measure of the year

Isabella
Give me your patience, Sister, while I frame
Old Meg she was a gipsy
To Ailsa Rock
There is a joy in footing slow across a silent plain
Not Aladdin magian (two copies)
Read me a lesson, Muse, and speak it loud
Nature withheld Cassandra in the skies
Fancy
Bards of passion and of mirth
I had a dove and the sweet dove died
The Eve of St. Mark
Why did I laugh tonight? No voice will tell
As Hermes once took to his feathers light
Bright star, would I were steadfast as thou art
Song of Four Fairies
To Sleep (two copies)
Ode to Psyche
On Fame ("Fame, like a wayward girl")
If by dull rhymes our English must be chain'd (1–4 only)
Shed no tear—O shed no tear
Lamia
To Autumn

To this list one would add Dorothy Withey's MS of *Welcome joy and welcome sorrow*, if it were certain that it is a holograph. Fair copies of *To Hope* and *Blue! 'Tis the life of heaven* are known in photostat or facsimile, and the readings of a few other lost holographs have been recorded by H. B. Forman.

Where two or more holographs of a poem exist, it is usually (but not always) possible to order the MSS chronologically, showing that one preceded another. The hard part is determining the status of these MSS subsequent to the earliest drafts. In some of them Keats is still creating the poem; in others he is simply copying out a finished work, as in letters and MSS that he sent to relatives and friends, in MSS for the printers, in ladies' albums, and the like. Sometimes he copied his poems from Woodhouse's or Brown's transcripts rather than from his own MSS. The problem is to know how seriously to take some of the changes that he made in these copies, and it becomes important when we are trying to decide which of two later versions of a poem—say, one in a Keats copy and another in a Brown transcript—to choose as the basis for a standard text. When, for example, Keats recopied *Not Aladdin magian* in a letter to George and Georgiana more than a year after he first wrote the poem, did he leave out 7–8 on purpose, possibly because he had in the interim used a similar couplet in *The Eve of St. Mark*, or just by oversight? Should a standard text include the couplet (as Garrod does, taking his text from an earlier version) or omit it (as Allott does, following the later letter)? In the following hypothetical situation, where a lost holograph has been copied by Keats in an extant letter and by Brown and Woodhouse in extant transcripts—

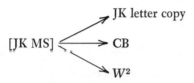

—it is possible that both Brown and Woodhouse would produce more accurate transcripts, and, what it more important, transcripts that better represent Keats's considered intentions in the poem, than Keats himself when he copied out the poem in his letter.

Four poems—*Give me your patience, Sister, There is a joy in footing slow, Not Aladdin magian,* and *The Eve of St. Mark*—deserve special mention in this connection. Each exists in two holograph versions, and for each the later version is a letter copy showing several substantive differences from the earlier version. I have taken Keats's changes in the later texts of *Give me your patience* and *There is a joy* to be considered revisions, and have therefore proposed that the later versions should be the bases for our standard texts. For the other two poems the later texts seem more casually written. In introducing *Not Aladdin magian*, Keats says, "I do not remember whether I have sent the following lines . . . I hope not [for] 't would be a horrid balk to you, especially after reading this dull specimen of description. For myself I hate descriptions. I would not send [it] were it not mine," and after copying *The Eve of St. Mark* he comments, "I hope you will like this for all its Carelessness" (*Letters,* II, 198, 204). "This dull specimen of description" is Keats's prose preceding *Not Aladdin magian* in the letter, and "Carelessness" refers to the original composition of *The Eve of St. Mark*, not the letter copy; but the remarks suggest a degree of detachment that may have carried over into the copying. Keats omits several lines in both copies. I feel that the changes and omissions in these texts are more the product of "Carelessness" than of conscious artistry, and so have recommended other versions as the bases for our standard texts. But again it must be emphasized that such questions are resolved subjectively, pretty much in the same way that one decides whether or not a holograph is an original draft. A good case can be made for preferring the later holographs as the standard for all four of these poems.

Keats cannot be considered the most important transcriber of his poems, but his own MSS provide the best texts for more than a fourth of his 150 pieces and for nearly half of the poems that were published posthumously. In the first list above—the holograph versions that are probably original drafts—twenty-three of the MSS are either the only or the most authoritative texts of the poems they represent. In the second list, a similar number of MSS qualify as the most authoritative versions, though here the figure cannot be given exactly, because in several instances the holographs share claims with other versions to be the best bases for our standard texts. Two of the holographs served as printer's copy for *1817*, the latest MSS of the sonnets *To My Brother George* and *Addressed to the Same* ("Great spirits"); the extant holograph of *Endymion* was printer's copy for *1818*; and the fair copy of *Lamia* was the MS used by the printer for *1820*. One other holograph, the fair copy of *Song of Four Fairies*, was, as Woodhouse says in a note, "Keats's copy for the press." Though the poem was not included in *1820*, this MS is especially valuable for the information that it gives us about printer's copy for the shorter poems in the volume.

2. GEORGE KEATS AND GEORGIANA AUGUSTA WYLIE

George Keats (1797–1841) and Georgiana Augusta Wylie (c. 1797–1879), who were married in late May 1818 and emigrated to the United States a month later, are together responsible for nineteen of the extant transcripts—ten early ones in the so-called Keats-Wylie Scrapbook, recently acquired by Harvard, and nine later ones in George Keats's notebook in the British Museum (MS. Egerton 2780).

The Keats-Wylie Scrapbook, which is described in Sotheby's sale catalogue for 23–24 June 1947 and by M. Buxton Forman in "Georgiana Keats and Her Scrapbook" (*Connoisseur,* 116 [1945], 8–13) and Garrod in his Introduction (pp. xlviii–l), includes the following items, the first four in Georgiana's handwriting and the rest in George's:

> fol.   5r   To one who has been long in city pent
> 6v   Stay, ruby-breasted warbler, stay
> 15r   To My Brother George (epistle—1–31 only)
> 22r   On Receiving a Curious Shell and a Copy of Verses from the
> Same Ladies (1–12 only)

32r   Stay, ruby-breasted warbler, stay
32v   To one who has been long in city pent
33r   To My Brother George (epistle)
34v   To My Brother George (sonnet)
35r   O come, dearest Emma! the rose is full blown
36r   On Receiving a Curious Shell and a Copy of Verses from the
        Same Ladies

The scrapbook also contains Keats's fair copy of the sonnet *To G. A. W.*
(fol. 31v); both Georgiana's and George's transcripts of *Monody on M*^{r}
T. B. Sheridan (fols. 3r and 37r), a poem by Thomas Moore that
Georgiana, as she notes, took "from MSS. of J Keats August—1816"
and apparently thought was written by Keats; and Georgiana's transcript
of *On Death* (fol. 4r), which in the past has sometimes been assigned
to Keats but which ought no longer to be in the canon.

These transcripts of poems that Keats wrote between 1814 and August
1816 were probably made during the latter half of 1816 (the first item
in the above list is dated June 1816 in both Georgiana's and George's
transcripts; the holograph fair copy of *To G. A. W.*, a poem dated De-
cember 1816 in another source, appears to be the latest among the Keats
pieces in the contents). Except for the epistle *To My Brother George*,
which was clearly copied from the extant holograph that Keats sent
George from Margate, nothing is known of the original sources of the
transcripts, though I think it is safe to assume that they invariably derive
from holograph MSS. For the four items that both Georgiana and George
copied, it appears that their transcripts of the epistle to George and *On
Receiving a Curious Shell* were taken independently from the same source
and that George copied *Stay, ruby-breasted warbler* and *To one who has
been long in city pent* from Georgiana's transcripts (Georgiana's partial
copies of the first two show many minor differences from George's,
while the two pairs of transcripts for the latter poems are quite close in
accidentals).

The two transcripts of *To one who has been long in city pent* and
those of *On Receiving a Curious Shell* are the earliest extant versions of
these poems. The transcripts of *Stay, ruby-breasted warbler* represent
one of the two known states of text, though it is uncertain whether this
version is earlier or later than the one that Woodhouse took from his
cousin Mary Frogley's album. George's copy of the sonnet *To My Brother
George* is the intermediate version among three recoverable states of text.
His transcript of *O come, dearest Emma*, in which he rewrote 1 and 11
as "O come Georgiana . . . And there Georgiana," adapts Keats's lines to
his own purposes in wooing his future wife. This last MS was the source

of the earliest publication of the poem when H. B. Forman included it (under the title "Stanzas to Miss Wylie") in his edition of 1883.

George Keats's notebook in the British Museum (on which see Garrod, pp. lix–lx) contains holograph fair copies of *Isabella* (fols. 1r–28r) and *Lines on the Mermaid Tavern* (fols. 29r–30r) and Keats's draft of *The Eve of St. Mark* (fols. 33r–36r)—probably all three, and certainly the last, written in the book before George began copying poems in it—and includes the following transcripts by George:

> fol. 30r   Hence burgundy, claret, and port
> 31r   The Eve of St. Agnes (the first four stanzas before and the remainder following the holograph of *The Eve of St. Mark*)
> 52r   Ode on Melancholy
> 53r   Ode to a Nightingale
> 55r   Ode on a Grecian Urn
> 56v   Welcome joy and welcome sorrow
> 57v   Where's the poet? Show him! show him
> 58r   To Autumn
> 59r   Robin Hood

An unidentified transcript of *There is a joy in footing slow,* taken from the *Examiner* printing of 1822, is bound in at the end of the volume.

Keats reports on 15 January 1820 that "George is busy this morning in making copies of my verses—He is making now one of an Ode to the nightingale" (*Letters,* II, 243), and we can safely assume that George transcribed all of these poems during his three-week visit to England during this January. It is clearly demonstrable that he took his copies of *Hence burgundy, Melancholy, Grecian Urn, Welcome joy, Where's the poet,* and *Autumn* from Brown's transcripts rather than from holograph versions, and on a probability basis we may add *Nightingale* (for which we no longer have Brown's transcript) to the list. Specific details on the relationships of George's transcripts to Brown's are given below in the individual histories of the poems in Section IV.2. In general, the two copyists' transcripts are so close in wording and accidentals (especially in punctuation, where George agrees with Brown about nine out of every ten times) that it is impossible, given Brown's known tendency to add and alter punctuation as he copied, to think that they worked from different sources or even independently from the same sources. The agreement of George's transcripts with Brown's in headings, dates, and such peculiarities as the space left before "e'er" in 40 of *Grecian Urn,* the distinctive readings and misreadings in 6, 8, 17, 18, and 20 of *Autumn,* and the arrangement of the epigraph to *Welcome joy* leaves no doubt that George copied the poems from Brown's MSS. It appears that

George was an unusually precise copyist, one of the few among Keats's family and acquaintance who paid attention to the minutiae of punctuation and spelling as well as to the basic words of a text.

George's transcript of *Robin Hood* (which, in striking contrast to the likenesses observed in the preceding paragraph, varies from Brown's extant transcript both in heading and in accidentals in more than half the lines of the poem) was probably taken from the same lost revised holograph that Brown copied, and his transcript of *The Eve of St. Agnes* was written out from the lost fair copy that Keats or possibly Brown made in September 1819. While the six transcripts deriving from Brown's extant MSS have no independent authority, these last two are quite valuable as our best source of information about the details of the two lost MSS from which they were made. George's copy of *Nightingale* is a help (along with that of C. W. Dilke, who was another faithful preserver of minutiae) in reconstructing Brown's transcript of that poem. George's transcript of *The Eve of St. Agnes* represents the latest recoverable state of the poem before that of 1820.

In addition to these MSS, the unidentified transcript of *O Chatterton* in the Morgan Library may also be by George (in several distinctive letters it resembles George's writing in the Keats-Wylie Scrapbook), and we know of four other transcripts by George that once existed but have since disappeared. Woodhouse preserved in a series of copies a text of *Hadst thou liv'd in days of old* that George wrote out and sent as a valentine to Mary Frogley; and three other poems—*'Tis the "witching time of night,"* *As Hermes once,* and *On Fame* ("Fame, like a wayward girl")—were published, two of them for the first time, in the *Ladies' Companion* (August 1837) from texts that George had transcribed for John Howard Payne (see *KC*, II, 224–225). Payne recopied the three poems from George's texts for Milnes in 1847, and his transcript of *'Tis the "witching time"* was the source of printer's copy for the version in 1848.

3   TOM KEATS

Of the fifteen extant transcripts by Tom Keats (1799–1818), all of which are at Harvard, one is a separate item, *I stood tip-toe*, and the other fourteen are written in a notebook—in H. B. Forman's and Garrod's phrase, "Tom Keats's copybook"—as follows:

> page   1   Specimen of an Induction to a Poem
>   3   Calidore

The copybook also contains on page 22 the transcript of a sonnet by Leigh Hunt—*As one who after long and far-spent years*—first published in the *Examiner*, 14 May 1815.

The earliest of the items in the above list is *Imitation of Spenser* (Keats's first known poem) and the latest is the sonnet *Written in Disgust of Vulgar Superstition*, 22 December 1816, unless Keats wrote *To G. A. W.*, also dated December, after the 22nd. But the poems obviously were not transcribed in chronological order according to composition; *To My Brothers* and the next two sonnets date from October and November 1816, while two subsequent items in the list, including the last, date from June. In general, the copybook texts are substantively very close to those of *1817*, and the arrangement of poems in the transcripts approximates that of the printed volume (the first six items are in the same order in which they appear in *1817*, and the three at the end just before *To one who has been long in city pent* were printed as Sonnets V–VII). The transcripts of *To My Brother George* (sonnet) and *Addressed to the Same* reproduce in each case all but three of Keats's marks of punctuation in the extant holographs that served as printer's copy for *1817*, and they may have been taken from those holographs. (Tom's sources are otherwise unknown, but we may assume, as with Georgiana's and George's transcripts in the Keats-Wylie Scrapbook, that they always derive from holograph MSS.) These circumstances, plus Tom's note following *Calidore,* "marked by Leigh Hunt—1816," suggest that the copybook transcripts were made at the end of 1816, at the same time that Keats was preparing his MSS for the printer of *1817*.

These transcripts (never seen by Garrod, who, however, records some of their readings from H. B. Forman's notes) are relatively important ones. For four of the poems—*Specimen, Calidore, Imitation of Spenser,* and *Had I a man's fair form*—they are the only extant MSS, and for

several others—probably all but *Vulgar Superstition* and *To G. A. W.*—
they represent the latest known MS versions. Tom's copy of *I stood tip-toe*
confirms Keats's intention, maintained at least through the middle of
December 1816, of calling the poem "Endymion" (see *Letters,* I, 121),
and also shows that the lines from Spenser's *Muiopotmos* printed on the
title page of *1817* were originally used as an epigraph for this specific
poem. The transcripts of *Specimen* and *Calidore*, which appear in the
copybook as two parts of a single work, make a connection between the
poems that was not preserved in *1817,* where they are presented, though
consecutively, as separate pieces; and we have here Leigh Hunt's mark-
ings of the two poems, some of which may have influenced Keats's final
revisions. Garrod bases four substantive emendations on the transcripts
of *Specimen, Calidore,* and *Imitation of Spenser*, and probably should
have based a fifth on Tom's *Calidore* 44. A number of other transcripts
have variants that are undoubtedly authoritative (along with some that
are obviously copying errors). Tom's text of *Vulgar Superstition*, the
only one of the fifteen poems not included in *1817,* is the best that we
have for this sonnet.

4   RICHARD WOODHOUSE AND HIS CLERKS

Richard Woodhouse (1788–1834), a nearly lifelong friend and legal
and literary adviser to Keats's publishers Taylor and Hessey, is one of
the two transcribers of major importance. Charles Brown's transcripts
(see below) tend to be more authoritative, because in virtually every
case they derive directly from holographs, and frequently from revised
rather than draft MSS, but Woodhouse's give us more versions that we
would otherwise know nothing about, and a great deal of supplementary
factual and anecdotal information as well. Woodhouse's transcripts con-
stitute the most sizable body of MS material available for the study of
Keats's texts. He made, or directed various clerks in making, no fewer
than 174 of the extant MS copies of Keats's poems, and he was un-
doubtedly responsible for others that are now lost.

Woodhouse is a very attractive character among the members of Keats's
circle, and not least for his early recognition of the poet's greatness.
"Such a genius, I verily believe, has not appeared since Shakspeare &
Milton," he wrote to his cousin Mary Frogley in October 1818, about
the time he was beginning to make his first copies of the poems. In
August 1819, apropos of Keats's financial situation, he again connected
Keats with Shakespeare, telling Taylor, "Whatever People regret that they

could not do for Shakespeare or Chatterton, because he did not live in their time, that I would embody into a Rational principle, and (with due regard to certain expediencies) do for Keats" (*Letters*, I, 383, II, 151). On this latter occasion he offered the publisher £50 to be put at Keats's disposal—one of several such practical kindnesses that we know of. But in the long run, with the same general motivation, he did Keats more good through his scholarly interest in collecting texts and information about the poet for future generations.

A note originally written near the beginning of the W^2 book of transcripts explains some of Woodhouse's aims: "There is a great degree of reality about all that Keats writes: and there must be many allusions to particular Circumstances, in his poems: which would add to their beauty & Interest, if properly understood.—To arrest some few of these circumstances, & bring them to view in connexion with the poetic notice of them, is one of the objects of this Collection—and of the observations —as it is of the notes in the interleaved copies of his published Works. R^{d}W." To this he adds, "How valuable would such notes be to Shakespeares Sonnets, which teem with allusions to his life, & its circumstances, his age, his loves, his patrons &c." In his zeal to do for Keats what "People regret that they could not do for Shakespeare" he copied MSS of poems and letters wherever he could find them, recorded dates, variant readings, circumstances of composition, and added notes concerning sources and similarities in other poets. His collection of "Keatsiana" has been an invaluable quarry for Keats scholars and critics ever since the 1840's, when Taylor, to whom he bequeathed it, turned some of it over to Milnes.

The best sources of information about Woodhouse and his transcripts are Mabel A. E. Steele's "The Woodhouse Transcripts of the Poems of Keats," *HLB*, 3 (1949), 232–256; Hyder Rollins' brief sketches in *KC*, 1, cxliv–cl, and *Letters*, I, 92–93, and of course Woodhouse's letters and other documents in those two works; and Stuart Sperry's fine monograph, "Richard Woodhouse's Interleaved and Annotated Copy of Keats's *Poems* (1817)." Garrod lists some of the material in appendixes to his Introduction, pp. lx–lxv, lxviii–lxxv. Throughout this study I have retained Garrod's symbols—W^3, W^2, and W^1—for the Morgan Library transcripts and two of the books of transcripts by Woodhouse at Harvard. These are unfortunate designations, because in general the W^3 transcripts appear to have been Woodhouse's earliest copies and the W^1 transcripts his latest. But Garrod's symbols are widely known and used, and his numbering of W^2 and W^1 has been taken over both in Mabel Steele's system (where *H2* and *H1* are substituted for W^2 and W^1) and in the current Harvard indexing of the transcripts (where 3.2 and 3.1 are used). I have felt that a new system of symbols would only add to the confusion. Consequently the reader of this study must be prepared to accept W^3—W^2—W^1 as an orderly progress of transmission, even though the numbers themselves would suggest the reverse sequence.

The extant Woodhouse transcripts, including those by copyists under his supervision, fall into seven groups.

(1) Twenty-nine transcripts of Keats's poems in Woodhouse's hand are extant in the Morgan Library (W^3). These once were part of a scrapbook that included not only poems by Keats but a great many letters, poems, and other documents concerning or connected with Keats and transcripts by others as well as by Woodhouse. The scrapbook has been taken apart, and its materials have several times been rearranged. Garrod's list of its poetical contents on pp. lxxii–lxxiii is fairly accurate except that it omits *In drear-nighted December, Nature withheld Cassandra,* and *Gripus,* all in Woodhouse's hand, and does not indicate that three of the items—the third listing of *Fill for me the brimming bowl,* the third listing of *O come, dearest Emma,* and *O Solitude*—are holographs rather than transcripts and that four of the others—*You say you love, On Some Skulls in Beauley Abbey, As Hermes once,* and *O Chatterton* —are in the handwriting of Taylor, Brown, Hessey, and an unknown copyist, respectively (Garrod does include the note identifying the hand of *To Ailsa Rock* as Charles Cowden Clarke's). The three holographs are entered in my list of Keats's revised MSS given above; the transcripts by other hands than Woodhouse's are mentioned later in the present section; and six poems of questionable attribution among his transcripts are discussed in Section IV.3.

(2) The W^2 book of transcripts, which survives intact at Harvard, contains—all in Woodhouse's hand—copies of seventy-three Keats poems and two sonnets by Reynolds, a translation of the Boccaccio story on which Keats based *Isabella,* and (at the end) a table of contents, a record of Keats's changes in *Endymion* between the fair copy MS and the first printed text, and transcripts of the original title page, dedication, and preface intended for that work.

(3) The W^1 book of transcripts, also preserved intact at Harvard, contains thirty-four copies of Keats poems in Woodhouse's hand, copies of four of Reynolds' sonnets also by Woodhouse, and a transcript of *Hyperion* by one of Woodhouse's clerks. Garrod's list on pp. lx–lxi is

reliable, though he does not indicate there that *Hyperion* was copied by a clerk rather than by Woodhouse.

(4) An interleaved copy of *1817* now in the Huntington Library, which Sperry has described in detail, contains transcripts by Woodhouse of six Keats sonnets and also gives us some variants from a lost early version of *To Some Ladies.*

(5) An interleaved copy of *1818* now in the Berg Collection, New York Public Library, contains an exact copy (including cancellations and revisions) of Keats's draft of *Think not of it,* as well as a very full record of variants and canceled readings in the now-lost original draft of *Endymion* Books II–IV—our only source of information about this important MS.

(6) Woodhouse's letterbook, a notebook at Harvard in which Woodhouse and some clerks copied fifty-six of Keats's letters (seventeen of them now known only through these copies), includes as part of the letter transcripts six texts of Keats's poems by the clerks and two more by Woodhouse (as well as part of a third, the first four lines of *Over the hill*).

(7) A small collection of transcripts that Woodhouse made for Brown after he visited Brown in Florence in 1832 is also preserved at Harvard. These are on paper watermarked 1833 and are enclosed in a sheet bearing the inscription in Brown's hand, "Hyperion (remodelled) with minor poems"; Brown passed them on to Milnes with his own MSS in 1841. Two of Woodhouse's clerks copied twenty poems, including *The Fall of Hyperion,* and Woodhouse added two others. The twenty-two items are among the transcripts that Garrod designates *T.* His list on p. lxv (categories B and C) is complete except for the omission of *To Lord Byron.*

(A parenthetical note seems in order here on the various copyists that Woodhouse supervised in making these transcripts. Altogether five or more different hands can be distinguished—that of the W^1 *Hyperion*; at least two others in Woodhouse's letterbook; that of the nineteen shorter poems in Garrod's *T* group plus Canto I of *The Fall of Hyperion*; and still another hand in Canto II of *The Fall of Hyperion.* None of the copyists can be identified, and it is even an assumption that they were law clerks employed by Woodhouse, though they share certain characteristics of handwriting that suggest a similarity of training and occupation, and it is certain that they made the transcripts for Woodhouse, who read over, corrected, and sometimes annotated them. I have not elsewhere in this study distinguished among them, usually referring to each as "one of Woodhouse's clerks.")

In addition to these seven groups, we have Woodhouse's proof-sheets of *Lamia*, at Harvard, which in a sense deserve the same status as a transcript of the poem, since Woodhouse recorded variant readings in them in the same way that he did in the W^2 and other transcripts, and clearly thought of them as a substitute for a transcript. *Lamia* is the only *1820* poem that Woodhouse did not transcribe in the W^2 book.

Among Woodhouse transcripts whose whereabouts are currently unknown, the text of one, a copy of *On Some Skulls in Beauley Abbey*, is available in Colvin, pp. 553–556, and part of the text of another, the first fifty lines of a shorthand transcript of *The Eve of St. Mark*, is given in facsimile by A. Edward Newton, *A Magnificent Farce and Other Diversions of a Book-Collector* (Boston, 1921), p. 121. Joseph Severn's "copies written by Woodhouse" of *After dark vapours, God of the golden bow, On the Sea, Time's sea hath been*, and *Blue! 'Tis the life of heaven* (*KC*, II, 131) have since been lost, and so also have another Woodhouse transcript of *Isabella* (besides the three that are extant) and a transcript of *Otho the Great* (see *KC*, I, 79, and the discussion of *Otho* in Section IV.2).

Because Garrod does not attempt a complete account of the Keats items in the W^2 book of transcripts, which Woodhouse considered the most important single collection among his Keatsiana, the comprehensive list given here follows the order of W^2. "Stated or probable source"— the stated sources are presented as quotations, usually from W^2—refers to Woodhouse's initial source for the earliest of his transcripts in each case, and not necessarily to the immediate source of the W^2 transcript, which sometimes was copied from an earlier Woodhouse transcript.

	W^2	Other Woodhouse transcripts (including clerks')	Stated or probable source
fol.	8r As from the darkening gloom a silver dove	W^3; W^1 (p. 22); clerk (T)	"F," "from Mary Frogley" (lost transcript by Kirkman)
	9r Oh, how I love, on a fair summer's eve	W^3; interleaved *1817*; W^1 (p. 21); clerk (T)	"F," "from Mary Frogley" (lost transcript by Kirkman)
	14r God of the golden bow	W^3; W^1 (p. 36)	"from a M.S. in Keats's writing" (the fair copy in the Morgan Library?)

W^2	Other Woodhouse transcripts (including clerks')	Stated or probable source
15r In drear-nighted December	W^3; W^1 (p. 34)	"from J: H: Reynolds" (lost transcript by Reynolds)
16r Think not of it, sweet one, so	W^3; W^1 (p. 20); interleaved *1818*	"from JK's M.S." (lost holograph; the *1818* transcript from the draft in the Morgan Library)
18r After dark vapours have oppress'd our plains	interleaved *1817*; W^1 (p. 23); clerk (*T*)	"from J.H.R." (lost transcript by Reynolds?)
19r To a Young Lady Who Sent Me a Laurel Crown	W^1 (p. 26); clerk (*T*)	"from J.K's M.S." (lost holograph)
19v This pleasant tale is like a little copse	W^1 (p. 24); clerk (*T*)	"J.K's M.S." (lost holograph)
21r On Seeing the Elgin Marbles	W^3; interleaved *1817*	"from the Examiner"
22r To Haydon, with a Sonnet Written on Seeing the Elgin Marbles	W^3; interleaved *1817*	(same as the preceding)
23r Blue! 'Tis the life of heaven —the domain	W^1 (p. 30); clerk (*T*)	"from K's M.S." (lost holograph "in a M.S. collection of the Poetry of [Reynolds,] Keats & others")
24r To Mrs. Reynolds' Cat	W^1 (p. 27)	(unknown)
25r On Sitting Down to Read *King Lear* Once Again	W^1 (p. 28)	"J.H.R." (lost transcript by Reynolds?)
26r On the Sea	interleaved *1817*; W^3; W^1 (p. 32);	"Champion" (the first clerk's copy, however,

W²	Other Woodhouse transcripts (including clerks')	Stated or probable source
	clerk in letterbook (p. 44); another clerk (*T*)	from Keats's letter to Reynolds)
27r To the Nile	interleaved *1817*; W¹ (p. 31)	"from J.K.'s M.S." (lost holograph)
28r Time's sea hath been five years at its slow ebb	W¹ (p. 29); clerk (*T*)	(unknown)
29r The Gothic looks solemn	W¹ (p. 33)	"a letter to J.H.R." (possibly via a lost transcript by Reynolds)
30r Isabella	W³ (shorthand); W¹ (p. 172)	(Keats's fair copy in the British Museum)
56r Hence burgundy, claret, and port	clerk in letterbook (p. 54)	"extracted from a letter to J.H.R." (lost letter)
56r God of the meridian	clerk in letterbook (p. 54); W¹ (last 13 lines only, p. 11)	(same as the preceding)
58r Robin Hood	W¹ (p. 12)	(lost Keats letter or a transcript by Reynolds)
61r Lines on the Mermaid Tavern	W¹ (two copies, pp. 16, 154)	(lost Keats letter or a transcript by Reynolds)
62r Not Aladdin magian	W¹ (p. 138)	(lost Keats letter or a transcript by Reynolds)
64r When I have fears that I may cease to be	clerk in letterbook (p. 55); W¹ (p. 144)	"From JK's letter to W.H.R. [*sic*]" (lost letter to Reynolds)
65r Dear Reynolds, as last night I lay in bed		(lost Keats letter)
69r Bards of passion and of mirth	W¹ (p. 142)	"from J.H.R." (lost transcript by Reynolds)

W²	Other Woodhouse transcripts (including clerks')	Stated or probable source
71r As Hermes once took to his feathers light	W¹ (p. 156)	(lost holograph?)
72r Ode to Psyche		"Given by J.K. to J.H.R." (lost transcript by Reynolds)
75r And what is love? It is a doll dress'd up		(unknown)
76r La Belle Dame sans Merci	W¹ (p. 146)	(Brown's transcript or a lost holograph)
78r To Homer	W¹ (p. 146)	(unknown)
79r Hyperion	clerk in W¹ (p. 39)	"from J.K's Manuscript," "the original & only copy" (the MS in the British Museum)
110r The Eve of St. Agnes	W¹ (p. 108)	"from J.K's rough M.S." (the draft at Harvard)
125r The Eve of St. Mark	Woodhouse shorthand transcript, 1–50 known in facsimile	"from J.K's M.S." (the draft in the British Museum)
131r Hush, hush! tread softly! hush, hush, my dear	W³	"from C.B."
132r Mother of Hermes! and still youthful Maia	clerk in letterbook (p. 65); another clerk (T)	"from a letter to J.H.R." (lost letter)
133r Welcome joy and welcome sorrow	W¹ (p. 150)	(lost holograph?)
134r Fragment of Castle-builder		(unknown)
137r Extracts from an Opera	W³ (two songs only)	(unknown)

W^2	Other Woodhouse transcripts (including clerks')	Stated or probable source
140r Nature withheld Cassandra in the skies	W^3	(lost Keats letter or a transcript by Reynolds)
142r To Autumn		"sent me at Bath by J.K. in a letter"
144r Spenser, a jealous honorer of thine	clerk (T)	"fm JK's M.S." (the fair copy in the Morgan Library)
145r Ode on Melancholy		"from C.B."
147r Ode on Indolence		"from C.B."
150r Character of C. B.		(lost holograph?)
151r To Sleep	W^1 (p. 158)	(lost holograph?)
152r On Fame ("Fame, like a wayward girl")	W^1 (p. 160)	(lost holograph?)
153r On Fame ("How fever'd is the man")		(lost holograph?)
154r If by dull rhymes our English must be chain'd	W^1 (p. 158)	(lost holograph?)
155r Lines on Seeing a Lock of Milton's Hair	W^1 (p. 160)	(Brown's transcript?)
157r Ode to a Nightingale	W^1 (p. 164)	(lost holograph?)
161r Song of Four Fairies		(Brown's transcript or a lost holograph)
165r The Fall of Hyperion	clerks (T)	(lost holograph)
183r Fancy		'from C.B."

W²	Other Woodhouse transcripts (including clerks')	Stated or probable source
187r I had a dove and the sweet dove died		"from C.B."
187r Where's the poet? Show him! show him		"from CB."
188r Ode on a Grecian Urn		"from C.B."
193r On a Leander Which Miss Reynolds, My Kind Friend, Gave Me	Woodhouse (*T*)	(Keats's draft at Harvard)
194r Apollo to the Graces		"From the orig^l in Miss Reynolds's Possession" (the draft at Harvard or a lost holograph copy)
195r You say you love, but with a voice		"from Miss Reynolds" (Charlotte Reynolds' transcript)
196r The Jealousies		(lost transcript by Brown)
212r The day is gone, and all its sweets are gone	W³; Woodhouse (*T*)	(Keats's draft in the Morgan Library)
213r There is a joy in footing slow across a silent plain	W³	"from K's letter" (to Bailey)
215r Four seasons fill the measure of the year	Woodhouse in letterbook (p. 98); clerk (*T*)	"from K's letter to B.B."
216r O Chatterton! how very sad thy fate	clerk (*T*)	(unidentified transcript in the Morgan Library)
217r To Lord Byron	clerk (*T*)	(unknown)
218r To J. R.	clerk (*T*)	(Keats's MS at Harvard)

W^2	Other Woodhouse transcripts (including clerks')	Stated or probable source
219r Stay, ruby-breasted warbler, stay	W^3 (two copies); clerk (T)	"F," "from Mary Frogley" (lost transcript by Kirkman)
219r O come, dearest Emma! the rose is full blown	W^3 (two copies); clerk (T)	"F," "from Mary Frogley" (lost transcript by Kirkman)
220r On Peace	W^3; clerk (T)	"F" (lost transcript by Kirkman)
221r Ode to Apollo ("In thy western halls")	W^3; clerk (T)	"F" (lost transcript by Kirkman)
222r Fill for me the brimming bowl	W^3 (two copies); clerk (T)	"F," "from Mary Frogley" (lost transcript by Kirkman)
223r Hadst thou liv'd in days of old	W^3 (two copies); W^1 (p. 18)	"F," "the original Valentine . . . now in [Mary Frogley's] custody" (lost copy by George Keats)

The following additional Woodhouse items are not included in the W^2 book of transcripts:

	Woodhouse transcripts	Stated or probable source
Lines Written on 29 May, the Anniversary of Charles's Restoration, on Hearing the Bells Ringing	W^3 (two copies)	"F," "from [Mary Frogley]" (lost transcript by Kirkman)
Unfelt, unheard, unseen	W^3	(Keats's fair copy in the Morgan Library?)
O blush not so! O blush not so	W^3; clerk in letterbook (p. 53)	(the clerk's copy from Keats's letter to Reynolds; W^3 perhaps from a lost transcript by Reynolds)
O thou whose face hath felt the winter's wind	Woodhouse in letterbook (p. 25)	(Keats's letter to Reynolds)

	Woodhouse transcripts	Stated or probable source
Over the hill and over the dale	W^3; Woodhouse in letterbook (1–4 only, p. 113)	"From a letter sent by Keats to Rice"
On Some Skulls in Beauley Abbey, near Inverness	lost transcript printed by Colvin	(Brown's transcript)
Lamia	proof-sheets	

One of the most considerable problems in the study of Keats's texts is determining Woodhouse's sources. We know that he began the W^2 book of transcripts in November 1818 with a series of poems that he took from texts "copied for my cousin [Mary Frogley] into a Volume of M.S. poetry, by Mr Kirkman, and said to be by Keats" (see below); that he borrowed from Taylor "Reynolds's volume of Poetry," a now-lost MS collection that included copies of several Keats poems, also in November 1818 (*KC*, I, 63–64); that Brown's four volumes of transcripts were made available to him through Taylor probably sometime between March 1820 and August 1821 (*KC*, I, 105, 261, 264); that he saw Keats's letters to Benjamin Bailey and the poems in them, again through Taylor, in or shortly after May 1821 (*KC*, I, 243–244); and that at some time or other he had in hand albums belonging to Charlotte Reynolds (*KC*, I, 265) and at least one other Reynolds sister (he took his date for *In drear-nighted December* "from Miss Reynolds' album"; the heading in his Morgan Library MS of the sonnet *To A. G. S.* also mentions "this [Miss Reynolds'] Album"; and his Morgan transcript of some lines beginning "When I percieve the efforts that combine / To grace this honored book, dear Jane, of thine" has the note "written by Mrs. Reynolds in her daughter's album"). At various times in his extant letters and notes he orders the interleaved *1818*, asks Taylor for a copy of a sonnet, gets another sonnet from Reynolds, and hopes to receive two more from C. C. Clarke (*KC*, I, 65–66, 85, 275). Some undated penciled notes at the end of W^2 headed "Poems of J.K. which I have not" suggest the methodical character of his quest for texts to add to his collection:

> Sonnet to Ailsa crag—in Literary Pocket Book
> Ano^r Sonnet in the lit^y P. Book
> Meg Merrilies—(penès C Browne)
> Some o[the]^r Small Poems written dur^g a trip to Scotland (D^o)
> Part of an historical Tragedy on the fall of the Earl of Essex or E^l of
> Leicester

Lines sent in 1816 or thereabouts to Miss [followed, after a space, by
a parenthesis containing several illegible letters—perhaps "GWLy"
for Georgiana Wylie?]
q. The Indicator
A blank verse translation of one of Ronsard's Sonnets—Sent to J.H.R.
Part of a Prologue to "Otho"—
Fragment of a fairy Tale sent to his Brother George—beginning "Now
when the Monkey found himself alone"—

When he made this list he probably already had (without realizing that
it was the other "Sonnet in the lit^y P. Book") the second of these items,
Four seasons fill the measure of the year, and he subsequently got *To
Ailsa Rock* from C. C. Clarke; but he apparently never acquired copies
of the others. The fifth item he perhaps knew of through a letter from
Keats to Taylor that he had twice transcribed (*Letters,* II, 234), though
the entry may suggest that some fragment of the work actually existed
(possibly he was thinking of *King Stephen*). The eighth item is probably
one of "2 translated sonnets" that Woodhouse mentions in a "Tuesday.
Ev^g" letter to Taylor (*KC,* I, 79), but is not Keats's surviving translation
from Ronsard, *Nature withheld Cassandra,* which is in rhyme rather than
blank verse and which Woodhouse almost surely already had when he
wrote this list. The sixth, ninth, and tenth items are unidentified.

Woodhouse very helpfully specifies the source—"from Mary Frogley,"
"from JK's M.S.," "from C.B.," and the like, most often at the end of the
text and at the left—for more than half the poems that he copied.
When he actually uses the word "from," his references to source appear
to be reliable (the designation of source for *Hush, hush! tread softly,*
"from C.B.," is the most questionable among them). Where he does not
provide such notes, his sources can be settled with certainty in some
cases but have to be guessed at in others. I hope I have made a clear
distinction between fact and conjecture in the various histories in Section
IV.2. Woodhouse also dates a great many of his transcripts, and some-
times indicates sources for his dates in notes that have the form "C.B.
1819," again usually at the end of the text and at the left. A point
worth emphasizing (since Garrod and others have not realized the differ-
ence) is that a note like "from C.B." is intended to be a clear indication
of source, written down at the time that Woodhouse made the transcript,
while "C.B. 1819," added to a transcript after Woodhouse saw a Brown
copy with a date on it, merely records the year of composition and the
source of the date. It may be that the texts of some of the later W^2
transcripts with "C.B. 1819" and other dates after them were actually
made from Brown's transcripts (the W^2 items on fols. 150–154 are

instances of this possibility, though in the histories in Section IV.2 I have supposed that the five transcripts were all copied from the same sources that Brown used); but in cases where their texts are substantively very close we can never be certain, since both Woodhouse and Brown took a very casual attitude toward accidentals in their copying.

After the question of sources, the next most difficult problem at hand is determining the relationships among the Woodhouse transcripts when there are more than one for a poem. Most of the stated sources in the above comprehensive list are quoted from the W^2 transcripts, but these, as I have already said, were not necessarily the immediate sources of the W^2 copies. The W^2 transcript of *The Eve of St. Mark*, for example— "from J.K's M.S."—was actually written out from an earlier transcript that Woodhouse made in shorthand, and the W^2 *Isabella* and *The Eve of St. Agnes* were likewise almost certainly made from shorthand copies, though the latter W^2 transcript again has the note "Copied from J.K's rough M.S." Woodhouse's notes refer to his initial source of text in each case, and not reliably to the source of the particular transcript containing the note.

The W^3 transcripts are a miscellaneous lot, in many cases (where there are duplicate Woodhouse transcripts and the chronological order among them can be established) the earliest extant copies made by Woodhouse. In general, though there are a number of exceptions, they seem to be a group of preliminary transcripts that were set aside after Woodhouse recopied the poems in his larger collection, the W^2 book of transcripts, which is the one that he took the most care with, entering variants, sources, dates, and annotations to the extent that it has the character of a variorum edition of the poems. The W^1 transcripts appear to be a partial set of duplicates, perhaps for insurance against the loss of the W^2 copies. It is possible that these were kept by the publishers, for in a letter to Taylor Woodhouse speaks of writing out *Isabella* again in "the Book [at Taylor's] in which she was to be copied" (*KC*, I, 78–79), while in another letter, concerning Keats's revisions in *The Eve of St. Agnes,* he asks Taylor to "turn to it" (*Letters*, II, 163)—and both poems are included in the W^1 book. There are trial layouts in pencil of the 1820 title page near the front and again at the end of W^1.

Originally the W^2 book contained ten poems at the beginning that were prefaced by a note at the top of fol. 1r: "The small pieces marked F. (10 in number) were copied for my cousin into a Volume of M.S. poetry, by Mr Kirkman, and said to be by Keats.—They appear to be so from internal Evidence. They must have been all written before the

year 18   Some of them are perhaps among his earliest compositions.
—They have different degrees of merit.—All are worth preserving; if
merely as specimens of his powers at different times, & his Improvement."
(Kirkman, a cousin of G. F. Mathew, is mentioned three times in Keats's
letters but otherwise is a very shadowy figure among the poet's acquaint-
ance.) Mabel Steele has reconstructed the original contents of these
early leaves in W^2 as follows:

> fol. 1r Stay, ruby-breasted warbler, stay
> 2r O come, dearest Emma! the rose is full blown
> 3r See, the ship in the bay is riding
> 4r Hadst thou liv'd in days of old
> 6r Fill for me the brimming bowl
> 7r On Peace
> 8r As from the darkening gloom a silver dove
> 9r Oh, how I love, on a fair summer's eve
> 10r Ode to Apollo ("In thy western halls")
> 12r Lines Written on 29 May, the Anniversary of Charles's
> Restoration, on Hearing the Bells Ringing

At some later time Woodhouse cut all but two of these leaves (fols. 8
and 9) out of W^2 and transferred them to the W^3 scrapbook. He re-
copied six of the transferred poems at the end of W^2 (on fols. 219–223),
but did not replace the two others, *See, the ship in the bay is riding*
(because Keats told him that he had not written the poem) and *Lines
Written on 29 May* (in this instance, for reasons unknown).

The difficulty of determining the relationships among Woodhouse
transcripts can be illustrated by consideration of some of these ten poems,
eight of which Woodhouse transferred from W^2 to the W^3 scrapbook.
In the original W^2 copies, all ten have "F" at the end, and would seem
obviously to derive from the same source, and at the same time and in
the same way. There are also duplicate W^3 copies of *Stay, ruby-breasted
warbler, O come, dearest Emma, See, the ship, Hadst thou liv'd in days
of old, Fill for me the brimming bowl, As from the darkening gloom,
Oh, how I love,* and *Lines Written on 29 May,* and these all (except
for *Hadst thou liv'd in days of old,* which is accompanied by a more
elaborate note) have "from Mary Frogley" in shorthand at the end. The
"F" transcripts and the "from Mary Frogley" transcripts are clearly, ac-
cording to the forms by which Woodhouse designated the source, two
distinct groups. It seems extremely unlikely that Woodhouse would
have made both groups of copies independently from Mary Frogley's
album. Consequently, one of the groups ought to be the original copies,

and the other group ought consistently to derive from the first. The specific details, however, suggest otherwise.

For several of these poems there is simply no internal evidence on which to establish the priority of one duplicate copy over another; the transcripts lack significant substantive variants, and their differences in accidentals are of no help. But for *Stay, ruby-breasted warbler, O come, dearest Emma, Hadst thou liv'd in days of old, Fill for me the brimming bowl,* and *Lines Written on 29 May* there are at least hints of such evidence, and the tendencies of these hints are not consistent. The "F" transcript of *Stay, ruby-breasted warbler* varies from the "from Mary Frogley" copy in "leafless" for "hapless" in 19; because "leafless" is confirmed as authorial by the extant transcripts of Georgiana and George Keats, one would suppose, since it is difficult to imagine Woodhouse getting a right word by miscopying a wrong one, that the "F" copy was made first. The "F" transcript of *O come, dearest Emma* is headed "To Emma," while the "from Mary Frogley" copy has no title; one might think that Woodhouse would have added, rather than omitted, a title in a later copy, and therefore that the untitled transcript is the earlier. In *Hadst thou liv'd in days of old* the evidence, such as it is, lies in the two transcripts' explanatory headnotes, one of which is either an expanded or condensed version of the other; because the note in the "F" transcript is longer and less pointedly composed than that in the other Morgan copy, it might be thought that the "F" text is the earlier. With *Fill for me the brimming bowl* it is again a question of variants: the "from Mary Frogley" transcript has three substantive variants from the "F" copy (in 8, 9, and 20) that agree with an extant holograph MS, and therefore it ought reasonably to be considered the earlier. The priority of the "F" transcript of *Lines Written on 29 May* is suggested by the presence of a marginal variant to 5 ("originally and"), which could not have come from the other W^3 copy, and also perhaps by its longer and slightly more detailed heading.

Thus one kind of logic (that one of the groups ought consistently to derive from the other) is confounded by another: the specific details make it appear that for three of the poems (*Stay, ruby-breasted warbler, Hadst thou liv'd in days of old,* and *Lines Written on 29 May*) the "F" transcript is the earlier, while for the other two the "from Mary Frogley" copies are the earlier. (In Section IV.2 I have felt obligated to follow the evidence of the specific details, proposing—where there are no competing versions from other sources—whichever seems the earlier transcript in each case as the proper basis for a standard text. I am thus probably wrong in either three or two of my guesses about the order of these transcripts, but it seems a safer course than the risk of being wrong in all five.) But this is only one of a number of oddities in Woodhouse's transcripts. We do not know why he transferred these early poems from W^2 to the W^3 scrapbook, or why he made several copies of some poems and only a single copy of others, or the basis for his selection and arrangement of poems in the W^1 book of transcripts (where, for example, one of the sonnets *On Fame* is included but not the other that is usually elsewhere associated with it) or in the interleaved *1817* or the group that he had his clerks transcribe for Brown. For four poems that Keats composed or copied in his 31 January 1818 letter to Reynolds, Woodhouse appears to have taken two transcripts from the letter itself (*Hence burgundy* and *God of the meridian*), another probably from his clerk's copy of the letter (*When I have fears*), and the fourth possibly from a copy made by Reynolds (*O blush not so*); the first two poems are separated by several leaves from the third in W^2, and the fourth is not in W^2 at all. Some of the details in his transcripts of *Hush, hush! tread softly* are simply incomprehensible.

For the later transcripts the evidence of relationships is somewhat clearer, but only somewhat. Of the six copies of sonnets in the interleaved *1817*, that of *On the Sea* is distinctly different in several respects from the other five and seems to have been Woodhouse's first transcript of that poem. The other five are derivative copies, taken in two cases probably from W^3 transcripts and in the other three probably from W^2 texts. Among the W^1 transcripts, only one (*Hadst thou liv'd in days of old*) can be shown to have been made from another source than W^2. Since nine or ten of the W^1 copies demonstrably or very probably derive from W^2 texts, and there is no instance where W^1 appears to have been the source of a W^2 or any other MS copy, I have regularly assumed, though not always without some discussion of the matter in Section IV.2, that the W^1 transcripts, except for *Hadst thou liv'd in days of old*, were taken from W^2. (There is one other worrisome exception to the W^2–W^1 sequence besides *Hadst thou liv'd in days of old*. The W^2 text of Reynolds' *Sweet poets of the gentle antique line* reads "silver" in 5—perhaps a copying error based on "silver" in 3—while W^1 has the correct word "golden"; Woodhouse could not have taken W^1's "golden" from W^2's "silver." But it is still possible that he copied the W^1 text from W^2, incorporating in W^1 a correction that he learned about in the interim. In any case the W^2 text is written on a verso page facing Keats's *Blue! 'Tis the life of heaven*, and thus has the status of an explanatory note rather than that of a regular transcript.) The late transcripts made by Woodhouse's clerks (Garrod's *T*) are in the same order as the W^2 transcripts (the last nine items follow W^2 fols. 215–222 exactly), and they were obviously copied from that source, with which they agree in most accidental as well as substantive details. A comprehensive diagram of the most frequent relationships among the Woodhouse transcripts would be the following:

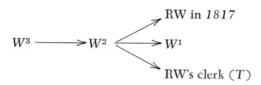

—but many variations are possible.

Woodhouse has rightly been called the most scholarly of Keats's transcribers. He was widely read and knew several languages (he published *A Grammar of the Spanish, Portuguese, and Italian Languages* in 1815), and of course the comprehensiveness and painstakingness of his Keatsiana are evidence of a scholar's instincts. But his scholarliness in the texts of his transcripts must be understood to apply to substantive readings only. Rollins reports that, in transcribing Keats's letters, Woodhouse "felt free silently to correct misspellings, to supply or omit punctuation, to change a capital to a small letter or *vice versa*. . . . But in regard to what seemed to him important he was meticulous" (*Letters*, I, 19). The same description fits his transcripts of the poems, as Sperry has already observed (p. 310, n. 25). There are exceptions—for example, his W^3 copy of *Over the hill* has "water" for his source's "bourn" and "or" for "and," and there are several instances where a suggested improvement that he penciled in the margin of one copy was incorporated in the text, as if it were Keats's own wording, in a later copy. But generally, in transcripts that we can check against known extant sources, Woodhouse was extremely accurate in getting the words right.

His treatment of accidentals is another matter. When Woodhouse made a point of strictly following Keats's punctuation (as in his two copies of *There is a joy in footing slow*), he did it quite faithfully, but usually he did not intend to reproduce original punctuation, spelling, and capitalization. In transcripts where his sources are available for comparison, he changed Keats's accidentals on an average of about once per line. This is perfectly understandable and approvable, because Keats himself was in general very little interested in such details, and expected others to take care of them for him. His texts that we read today *always* to some degree reflect someone else's punctuating and spelling—Reynolds', Taylor's, Brown's, Woodhouse's, Milnes's, and that of other copyists, editors, and printers from his own time to the present. Woodhouse also changed accidentals freely in recopying the poems from one of his own transcripts to another. His later clerks were more scrupulous in minute details, but their superior reliability is of no significance, since their texts simply incorporate the details of the W^2 transcripts that they copied.

Woodhouse's scholarliness perhaps best shows itself in the care and frequency with which he recorded variants marginally and between the lines in various transcripts, especially those in W^2. He sometimes saw and made notes from as many as three or four different versions of a poem. He queried words, suggested improvements, and, as I have already mentioned above, several times followed his own suggestions by incorporating them in later copies of the poems (he also seems to have occasionally penciled corrections, variants, and proposed revisions into other people's MSS that he was copying or collating—see the discussions in Section IV.2 of *You say you love, Lines on Seeing a Lock of Milton's Hair, To the Nile, Hyperion, To Sleep, Ode on Melancholy,* and *To Autumn*). The handwriting in some of the markings and alternate wordings in the transcripts causes a special problem. Woodhouse's shorthand (based on William Mavor's *Universal Stenography,* 1779 and many later editions) is of course unmistakably his in these MSS, but his regular hand is not a highly distinctive one, and it varies according to whether he was writing in haste or was copying carefully and deliberately. Sometimes it looks very much like one of Keats's characteristic handwritings. And many people have gone through and marked Woodhouse's transcripts since his own day. As a consequence, we cannot be certain, when a word is penciled in a blank space or in the margin or above the line, whether it is a variant recorded by Woodhouse, a suggested improvement by Woodhouse or someone else, a revision by Keats, or—if it represents the wording of a text published while Keats was alive—a change made for or taken from the printed version. The short word "very" penciled in a blank space in the eleventh line of the W^1 copy of *To a Young Lady Who Sent Me a Laurel Crown*, for example, may be in Woodhouse's or Keats's writing or someone else's (Keats at one time or another handled both the W^2 and W^1 books of transcripts—W^2 when he copied *To Sleep* from it and W^1 when he prepared *Isabella* for the printer of 1820).

Milnes's substitution of "mighty" in the *1848* text is plainly not authoritative, but we shall probably never know for sure who was responsible for the penciled "very"—and so also in a number of other cases. Some of the pencilings and other markings were probably made quite late, and after Woodhouse's death.

There are also large X's, check marks, and B's above or beside many titles especially in W^2 (the "B" was pretty certainly Woodhouse's indication of poems for one of his later clerks to copy for Brown, since the letter appears by the W^2 titles of all the shorter poems that the clerk transcribed except *Mother of Hermes* and *Spenser, a jealous honorer*, and does not appear by any poem that he did not copy), and frequently the word "Not." Some of these markings seemingly have to do with whether or not a poem was published—the writer of "Not" at one point expands to "Not in Forman," and Sidney Colvin has added a correction, "Yes it is S C"—but in general it is not obvious what the various markings of this sort mean. Some smaller x's beside the first lines in twelve of the late clerk's *T* transcripts are more clearly Milnes's designation of texts that Coventry Patmore was to copy for him.

Taken altogether, Woodhouse's transcripts are a very impressive collection. They represent the only surviving MS texts of seven of Keats's poems and provide distinctive early or revised versions that would otherwise be unknown for about twenty more. And they contain a wealth of information about the texts. Woodhouse's contributions to the final wording of *Isabella*, *Lamia*, and some shorter poems (for example, the addition of "I swear" in *Lines on Seeing a Lock of Milton's Hair* and the substitution of "hoards" in *To Sleep*) are determinable only through the transcripts (or, in the case of *Lamia*, through the proof-sheets), and his lost copy of *On Some Skulls in Beauley Abbey*, via the text that Colvin printed, is our only means of knowing which lines Keats was responsible for in that poem. Two of the W^1 transcripts—*Isabella* by Woodhouse and *Hyperion* by one of his clerks—served as printer's copy for *1820*, and various of the letterbook and W^2 texts, the latter through the late clerks' copies, were Milnes's source for sixteen of the poems that he published in *1848* as well as for *The Fall of Hyperion* in *1857* and two other poems in *1876*. Five additional poems (plus several others in the "Questionable" category) were first published from Woodhouse's MSS in the twentieth century. His transcripts are still the best bases for our standard texts of at least fifteen poems, and possibly for as many as twenty others.

5   JOHN HAMILTON REYNOLDS AND CHARLOTTE REYNOLDS

The MSS of John Hamilton Reynolds (1794–1852) are an important missing link in the sequences of transmission surveyed in this study. Although he was for a while one of Keats's closest friends, we know less about him than we do about many others in Keats's circle, mainly because most of his letters and other papers have been destroyed or lost. Were it not for Woodhouse's transcripts of Keats's letters to Reynolds, we would have very little idea of their relationship, and Reynolds would not figure prominently among the friends of Keats. They were frequent companions and correspondents, and Keats gave or sent him a great many of his poems, often just after he wrote them (some of them in response to Reynolds' own poems), and Reynolds made copies that he lent to various people including Taylor and Woodhouse. But except for Woodhouse's transcripts, a few holographs now at Harvard and in the Morgan Library (MSS that Keats presented to Reynolds), and the record of one transcript that was extant in the 1870's, nothing of this exchange of poetry or Reynolds' copies has survived.

In November 1818 Woodhouse saw "Reynolds's volume of Poetry," a MS collection that apparently contained copies of *God of the golden bow*, the two Elgin Marbles sonnets, *On the Sea*, *In drear-nighted December*, and *To the Nile*, as well as poems by Reynolds and Leigh Hunt (*KC*, I, 63–64). This may or may not be the same "M.S. collection of the Poetry of himself [Reynolds] Keats & others" from which Woodhouse copied the holographs of both *Blue! 'Tis the life of heaven* and the Reynolds sonnet that Keats was responding to (the description is quoted from Woodhouse's headnote to the W^2 text of Reynolds' *Sweet poets of the gentle antique line*). According to his W^2 notes, Woodhouse took *After dark vapours, In drear-nighted December, On Sitting Down to Read "King Lear" Once Again,* and *Bards of passion* "from J: H: Reynolds" or "J.H.R."—in each case either a copy by Reynolds or a holograph in his possession—and he at least saw and recorded readings from "JHR's copy" of *Ode to a Nightingale*. Other poems that Woodhouse may have taken from copies by Reynolds include *The Gothic looks solemn, O blush not so, Robin Hood, Lines on the Mermaid Tavern, Time's sea hath been, Not Aladdin magian, Nature withheld Cassandra,* and *Ode to Psyche.*

In promising to send Milnes the now-lost draft of *Endymion*, Reynolds comments, "I had little to do in revising" (*KC*, II, 178). We do not know what he contributed to that poem, or to others that he may have influenced or helped Keats with. Apparently he was not a careful copyist. If

Woodhouse did take his W^2 transcript of *Ode to Psyche* from a Reynolds copy, it is possible that Reynolds himself made changes of wording in 13, 14, and 67, since the W^2 text has readings that differ from all other extant MSS in these lines. Woodhouse remarks to Taylor, "I see there are a few variations in *his* [Reynolds'] *Edition* of the Sonnets on the sea, & on the Elgin Marbles, from the Copy I had. Perhaps he wrote them from Memory" (*KC*, I, 63). Reynolds' one recoverable text of a Keats poem—a version of *Blue! 'Tis the life of heaven* published by A. J. Horwood in the *Athenaeum*, 3 June 1876, p. 764—has major unique variants that are almost certainly his own alterations or errors in 1, 2, and 6. It would be a great help to our understanding of Keats's texts if we had more of Reynolds' copies and some additional facts concerning his sources and methods. It is conceivable that other changes by him of which we are entirely unaware continue to survive, through Woodhouse's copies, in some of the texts that we consider standard today.

Reynolds' four sisters, Jane, Mariane, Eliza, and Charlotte, were the recipients of several letters and perhaps half a dozen poems by Keats (see the list in Bate, pp. 102–103 n.). At least two of the sisters, as we know from Woodhouse's notes, kept albums that contained poems by Keats, and Jane Reynolds may have been the source for some of the poems that Thomas Hood, whom she married in 1825, published in various annuals and in *Hood's Magazine*.

The one surviving MS collection by a member of the Reynolds family is the Reynolds-Hood Commonplace Book, in the Bristol Central Library (Garrod's *R*, p. lxxvi; for a fuller description see Paul Kaufman, *K-SJ*, 10 [1961], 43–52). This contains, along with poems by Reynolds, James Rice, Benjamin Bailey, Hood, and several others, the following sixteen items by Keats:

fol. 25a God of the golden bow
     26   Think not of it, sweet one, so
     27a Blue! 'Tis the life of heaven—the domain
     28   On the Sea
     28a On Sitting Down to Read *King Lear* Once Again
     29   To the Nile
     29a Time's sea hath been five years at its slow ebb
     30   Not Aladdin magian
     31   When I have fears that I may cease to be
     31a Hence burgundy, claret, and port
     31a God of the meridian
     33   The Fall of Hyperion (I.1–326 only)
     39   You say you love, but with a voice

39a Lines on Seeing a Lock of Milton's Hair
40a Extracts from an Opera (three songs only)
41a Nature withheld Cassandra in the skies

The transcriber of these pieces was Reynolds' youngest sister, Charlotte (1802–1884). Previously she has been identified as Jane Reynolds (by Kaufman, pp. 46, 48), and her handwriting is the same as that in the "Thursday Morn^g" note to Woodhouse beginning "Miss Reynolds' Compliments to Mr Woodhouse—she will feel obliged if he will send by the bearer her Album . . ." (*KC*, I, 265), which has been assigned both to Charlotte (by Lowell, I, 114, and tentatively by Rollins in *KC*) and to Jane (by Finney, I, 346, II, 748, item 36, and 749, item 57). But Charlotte's signature as a witness to Jane's and Thomas Hood's marriage at St. Botolph's, Aldersgate, 5 May 1825 (Register of Marriages, 1813–1829, Guildhall Library, MS. 3857/3, p. 212, entry no. 634)— especially with its quite distinctive capital "R"—proves beyond question that she was the copyist of the poems and the writer of the note to Woodhouse.

These transcripts bear a close relationship to Woodhouse's W^2 copies. They generally have the same headings as those in W^2, the same dates (when Charlotte includes dates), the same arrangement and indention of lines, and for fragmentary pieces the same dashes and x's at the end to indicate incompleteness. In a total of 673 lines, Charlotte's texts differ substantively from W^2 in only twenty variants, more than half of which are obviously her copying errors. In accidentals, especially in punctuation, her transcripts are again very similar to the W^2 texts. In *On the Sea,* for example, she has exactly the same punctuation as Woodhouse; in the three songs from *Extracts from an Opera* she has thirty-nine of his forty marks of punctuation, in *Blue! 'Tis the life of heaven* twenty-eight of his thirty-one marks, and in *Time's sea hath been* fourteen of his fifteen. Her text of *On Sitting Down to Read "King Lear" Once Again* differs in seven accidentals from Woodhouse's in W^2, but the figure is misleading: three of these are very minor spelling variants ("Shaksperian" for "Shakspearian" and "thro'" twice for "through"), and two are instances in which she merely left off or added a dash after an exclamation mark; only her omission of commas in 5 and 13 can be considered significant differences—and against these there are some twenty-five or more agreements in punctuation, distinctive internal capitalization, hyphenation, and the like. In some poems and passages the punctuation is quite conventional, and it would not be difficult to imagine two writers independently pointing the lines in the same way; but in other places—

for example, many long and complicated passages of *The Fall of Hyperion*
—the consistent agreement is quite striking. I think it is safe to assume
as fact for each of the sixteen items that either Charlotte and Wood-
house copied from the same source, or one of them took his text from
the other.

Woodhouse specifically cites Keats's MSS as his sources for *God of*
the golden bow, Think not of it, Blue! 'Tis the life of heaven, To the
Nile, When I have fears ("From JK's letter to W.H.R. [*sic*]"), *Hence*
burgundy and *God of the meridian* (both "extracted from a letter to
J.H.R."); for *On the Sea* he notes "Champion," and for the *King Lear*
sonnet "J.H.R." He also did not take *The Fall of Hyperion* or *Extracts*
from an Opera from Charlotte's transcripts, which are incomplete for
these works, or *Lines on Seeing a Lock of Milton's Hair* (he notes that
37–38 were written as a single line in his source, but they are two lines
in Charlotte's MS). He did not, then, copy at least the preponderance
of these poems from Charlotte's texts. And Woodhouse's known tendency
to add punctuation and otherwise alter accidentals in the process of copy-
ing—especially in copying Keats's frequently erratic and underpunctu-
ated MSS—makes it very unlikely that he and Charlotte worked inde-
pendently, even if always from the same sources: it would be a fantastic
coincidence for both of them to have arrived at the same minute details
in so many lines.

Consequently there is a high probability that Charlotte took at least
some of her texts from the W^2 transcripts. She specifies the source of
only one poem, *When I have fears*, "From J. Keats' letter to J H R"
(which is close to the wording of Woodhouse's W^2 note). Her copies
generally follow the W^2 order (the fourth through seventh items in the
list are the same, and almost in the same order, as W^2 fols. 25–28, and
the eighth and ninth items also occur together in W^2, as do the last
two items), and there are further specific details suggesting W^2 as a
source: her date at the end of *God of the meridian*, for example, "Feb
7 1818," which may be a misreading of Woodhouse's "Feby 1818," and
some peculiarities in her text of *The Fall of Hyperion*—"wrapt" in I.51
(where Woodhouse originally wrote "wrapt" and later deleted the "w")
and "what" in I.298 (where Woodhouse wrote "was" and penciled
"what?" in the margin).

That Charlotte did not copy all of these poems from W^2 is evidenced
by Woodhouse's shorthand note to the W^2 copy of *You say you love*, "from
Miss Reynolds"; by Charlotte's correct reading, "rich," in 4 of *When I*
have fears where W^2 has an erroneous "full"; and possibly also by her

inclusion of a heading to *Nature withheld Cassandra* ("Sonnet translated from Ronsard") where the W^2 transcript has no title. The fact that she grouped together three poems included in a single letter to Reynolds (*When I have fears, Hence burgundy,* and *God of the meridian*) while Woodhouse separated the first from the other two in W^2 would be further evidence, except that Charlotte gives the letter date only to the first ("31 Jan 1818") and assigns the latter two to "Feb 7 1818." The probability, then, is that she took some of these poems from W^2, but not all of them. At this point we have to enter the realm of conjecture.

I think there is a strong likelihood that Charlotte transcribed the first eight poems and *The Fall of Hyperion* from W^2, but that she may have taken at least *When I have fears, You say you love,* and perhaps also *Nature withheld Cassandra* from other sources. In the first and third of these latter pieces her copies have a higher proportion than usual of accidental variants from W^2 (as well as the correct substantive reading in the first and the heading in the third mentioned just above), and I interpret Woodhouse's designation of source for *You say you love* as a reference to Charlotte's extant transcript, which she may have made from a MS given by Keats to her brother. For the rest—*Hence burgundy, God of the meridian, Lines on Seeing a Lock of Milton's Hair,* and *Extracts from an Opera*—there is still a fair chance that her source was W^2, but the matter has to be left unsettled.

If it were known that Charlotte Reynolds always copied the same MSS that Woodhouse did, her transcripts would be a valuable check on Woodhouse's readings, especially in *The Fall of Hyperion,* and they would share with various Woodhouse MSS a claim to be the proper bases for our standard texts of *Think not of it, Blue! 'Tis the life of heaven, Time's sea hath been,* and *God of the meridian.* Given the probabilities arrived at in the preceding paragraphs, however, we must regard her copies as largely derivative. Nevertheless, her text of *You say you love* appears to be the most authoritative available, and it is possible that her text of *Nature withheld Cassandra* ought to be considered equally authoritative with the W^3 transcript of that poem.

6   CHARLES BROWN

Charles Brown (1787–1842), who has connections with several literary figures in addition to Keats, is the other major transcriber of the poems besides Woodhouse. A "Russia-merchant" turned gentleman of leisure, he was Keats's closest associate from December 1818, when the poet moved in with him at Wentworth Place in Hampstead, until the summer of 1820, when he went off to Scotland, not to return until after Keats's departure for Italy. The two collaborated in writing *Otho the Great*—Brown providing "the fable, characters, and dramatic conduct," while Keats "acted as Midwife to his plot" (*KC*, II, 66; *Letters*, II, 157) —and Brown had a hand in other works by suggesting the subjects of *King Stephen*, *The Jealousies*, and a few shorter poems, and by persuading Keats, when he was about to give up poetry, to "try the press once more" with *1820* (*Letters*, II, 121; on Brown generally, see Joanna Richardson, *The Everlasting Spell: A Study of Keats and His Friends*, 1963, pp. 17–109, and my edition of *The Letters of Charles Armitage Brown*, Cambridge, Mass., 1966).

Though his MS "Life of John Keats" contains a famous account of his rescuing *Ode to a Nightingale* in the spring of 1819 (very likely it was *Ode on Indolence* instead) and the statement that "From that day [Keats] gave me permission to copy any verses he might write, and I fully availed myself of it" (*KC*, II, 65), Brown actually began copying Keats's poems during the walking tour that they took together through the Lake District and Scotland in the summer of 1818. By the spring of 1820 he had collected "four MS books in my hand writing of Mr Keats' poems"— each, as he later explained to Milnes, to whom he gave the MSS in 1841, with a poem "of an exceptionable kind . . . written and copied for the purpose of preventing the young blue-stocking ladies from asking for the loan of his MS Poems" (*KC*, I, 261, II, 103). The "exceptionable" poems have not survived (unless *O blush not so* is one of them), and many of the other MSS are also missing, but we do have forty-three texts by Brown, all but one of them extant transcripts. Most of these are included in Garrod's descriptions of Milnes's collections that he designates *T* and *T*², pp. lxiv–lxvii. Because Milnes dismantled the volumes in the 1840's, and the original contents and order cannot be reconstructed, the present list follows the chronological arrangement of Section IV.2:

> On *The Story of Rimini*
> Before he went to live with owls and bats
> The Gothic looks solemn
> Lines on Seeing a Lock of Milton's Hair
> On Sitting Down to Read *King Lear* Once Again
> When I have fears that I may cease to be
> O blush not so! O blush not so
> Hence burgundy, claret, and port
> Robin Hood
> Lines on the Mermaid Tavern

Welcome joy and welcome sorrow
To the Nile
Extracts from an Opera
To Homer
Not Aladdin magian
On Some Skulls in Beauley Abbey, near Inverness
Where's the poet? Show him! show him
Fancy
Bards of passion and of mirth
Spirit here that reignest
Hush, hush! tread softly! hush, hush, my dear (1–20 only)
Ah, woe is me! poor Silver-wing
The Eve of St. Mark
Character of C. B.
Ode on Indolence
As Hermes once took to his feathers light
Bright star, would I were steadfast as thou art
La Belle Dame sans Merci
Song of Four Fairies
To Sleep
Ode to Psyche
On Fame ("Fame, like a wayward girl")
On Fame ("How fever'd is the man")
If by dull rhymes our English must be chain'd
Ode on a Grecian Urn
Ode on Melancholy
Shed no tear—O shed no tear
Otho the Great (not quite complete)
To Autumn
The day is gone, and all its sweets are gone
I cry your mercy—pity—love!—aye, love
King Stephen (I.i.1–ii.19 only)
In after time a sage of mickle lore

These items are at Harvard with the exception of *The Gothic looks solemn,* which is known only through a letter printed by H. B. Forman in his edition of 1883 (IV, 74 n.); *On Some Skulls in Beauley Abbey,* which is among the papers from Woodhouse's scrapbook in the Morgan Library; and *Shed no tear* and *In after time a sage of mickle lore,* both of which are at Keats House, Hampstead. The Harvard transcripts are all from the MS volumes that Brown gave to Milnes except that of *Not Aladdin magian,* which is a recent acquisition from the Very Reverend J. H. S. Wild, Dean of Durham, Severn's great-grandson.

The extant transcripts do not, of course, amount to anything like "four MS books." Brown's volumes probably included the four long poems published in *1820—Lamia, Isabella, The Eve of St. Agnes,* and *Hyperion* —and certainly included *The Jealousies*. From various references to "C.B." in Woodhouse's *W²* book we know that Brown copied *Fragment of Castle-builder, And what is love, I had a dove,* and *Ode to a Nightingale;* and Brown's "Life" of Keats and his publication of poems in *NMM* and the Plymouth newspapers indicate the former existence of transcripts of *Old Meg she was a gipsy, To Ailsa Rock, This mortal body of a thousand days, There is a joy in footing slow, Not Aladdin magian* (a different version from the one extant at Harvard), and *Read me a lesson, Muse.* In the absence of specific information about Milnes's sources for two poems to Fanny Brawne we can conjecture that Brown also transcribed *What can I do to drive away* and *To Fanny* ("Physician Nature"). Doubtless there were other transcripts of which we have no hint.

The most significant fact about Brown's transcripts is that, with a single exception (*On "The Story of Rimini,"* which he may have taken from a copy by Leigh Hunt), his source in every instance was almost certainly a holograph, and more often than not a revised MS—the latest authorial version—rather than an early draft. We know Brown's sources for sure (because we have them available for comparison) for only ten or a dozen poems. But Keats's letters and Brown's "Life" document the fact that Brown constantly had direct access to Keats's MSS: "Brown is coppying a song about Meg Merrilies," Keats writes to his brother Tom on 3 July 1818 ("I took a copy of it at the time," Brown notes in his "Life"); "Brown has been rummaging up some of my old sins—that is to say sonnets. . . . I have just written one on Fame—which Brown is transcribing and he has his book and mine" (Keats to George and Georgiana, 30 April 1819); "Mr Brown is copying out our Tragedy of Otho the gre[at] in a superb style" (to Fanny Keats, 28 August 1819); and of *The Jealousies* Brown remembered "having copied (for I copied as he wrote) as many as twelve stanzas before dinner" (*Letters*, I, 317, II, 104, 149; *KC*, II, 61, 72). Dilke noted in his copy of *1848* (Morgan Library, I, 245), against the passage in which Milnes tells of Brown's rescuing *Ode to a Nightingale* and transcribing other poems, that "Brown had slowly and doubtingly grown into a high admiration of Keats, & began therefore to collect every scrap of his writings"; but Brown did not, as Woodhouse frequently did, copy other people's copies. In the one recorded instance where he acquired texts from someone other than the poet—in a letter to Fanny Brawne of 17 December 1829 he mentions "those poems addressed to you, which you permitted me to copy"

(*The Letters of Charles Armitage Brown*, p. 295)—still his sources were very likely holograph MSS.

It appears that for at least some of the poems Brown's copy became the principal authorial MS version, while Keats's draft was given away, set aside, or discarded as no longer of any importance. Brown's statement to Milnes in October 1840—"most of the originals were scrambled away to America by his brother, after I had made copies of them for the press" (*KC*, II, 37–38)—tends to support this, as does Keats's remark on 12 June 1819 to James Elmes, who wished to publish *Ode to a Nightingale* in his *Annals of the Fine Arts*: "I have but just received the Book which contains the only copy of the verses in question" (*Letters*, II, 118; unless Brown transcribed the poem after this date, the reference is almost certainly to Brown's "Book" rather than to Keats's). There is also the notable fact that, except for a dozen copies that Keats made for acquaintances or sent in letters and two MSS intended for the printer (*Song of Four Fairies* and *Lamia*), the extant holographs written after December 1818 are all drafts rather than fair copies. The presence of Keats's hand in the transcripts of *Lines on the Mermaid Tavern*, *To the Nile*, *To Homer*, *Ode to Psyche*, *Otho the Great*, and *To Autumn* shows that the poet read over and used Brown's MSS for further revision; and it is possible, even likely, that at least one of Keats's late fair copies (*Song of Four Fairies*) and some of the lost MSS given to the printer of *1820* were made from Brown's transcripts rather than from holograph texts.

Rollins observes that "Brown made no special effort at literal accuracy" in his copies of Keats's letters included in his "Life"—"He misread 'best' as 'last,' 'my lungs or stomach' as 'my stomach, or lungs,' 'you' as 'your'. . . . But within his limits he was a good transcriber" (*Letters*, I, 19–20). In texts where we can check him against his sources, Brown seems to have been more careful in poems than in letters concerning substantive matters, although he supplied punctuation and changed accidentals in the poems as freely as Woodhouse did (between Keats's draft and Brown's transcript of *The Eve of St. Mark*, for example, there are seventy differences in accidentals in the first fifty lines—mostly Brown's addition of punctuation). A special problem arises where Brown's transcripts vary substantively from other authoritative sources. His copy of *To Autumn*, for example, was pretty clearly taken from the extant holograph draft, and yet it has "sweet" for the draft's "white" in 8 and "or" for "and" in 29 (there are other variants, but they are explainable as misreadings, as these are not). In another transcriber's MS we might view these changes, both of which were incorporated in the *1820* text, as corruptions, but with Brown's transcripts there is a better probability that such changes are authoritative. "Brown and I sit opposite one another all day authorizing," Keats told George and Georgiana in February 1819 (*Letters*, II, 61). In such a situation, which one supposes was frequent rather than unusual, Keats may have requested changes while Brown was making his copies. At any rate I have, in Section IV.2, in places where there is little or no evidence to go on, tended to prefer Brown's readings over those of other transcribers, and sometimes even over those of earlier holograph versions, simply because of this close relationship at the time that Keats was writing and Brown was copying. Except possibly Tom Keats, none of the other transcribers actually sat across the table from the poet while copying his poems, and Brown is not known, as Woodhouse and Reynolds are, to have "improved" Keats's texts on his own.

Brown's transcripts were seen and copied by Dilke (see below), George Keats, and Woodhouse, among others. Woodhouse in particular made extensive use, taking texts and noting headings, dates, and variants from more than thirty of them, extant and lost. After Keats's death Brown himself published poems from them—fourteen for the first time—in *NMM*, the *Examiner*, *PDWJ*, and the *Plymouth, Devonport, and Stonehouse News*, and he provided his friend E. J. Trelawny with fifty-four extracts, eighteen of them from the unpublished *Otho*, *King Stephen*, and *The Jealousies*, to be used as chapter epigraphs in *Adventures of a Younger Son* (Brown's fair copy of the *Adventures,* which was edited by Mary Shelley and others and then used as printer's copy for the 1831 first edition, has recently been acquired by Harvard, and the extracts there, placed all together at the end of the MS, constitute further partial transcripts of the three works). In 1841, after giving up his attempts to publish the "Life" of Keats and the poems on his own, he turned over his MSS to Milnes, who used them as the basis for the biographical narrative and a major proportion of the texts in *1848*.

Eighteen of the extant transcripts actually served as printer's copy for *1848* (they have the printers' names and other markings on them), and several others now lost were almost certainly used for the same purpose—six poems from the Scottish tour, for example, that Brown intended to quote in his "Life" and that Milnes incorporated into letter texts and his narrative in Volume I, for which almost no printer's copy survives. Some of the other transcripts, both extant and lost, were the source for the copy (rather than the copy itself) given to the printer.

Altogether, through his own publication of poems in periodicals and his gift of MSS to Milnes, Brown was responsible for the first publication of more than thirty of Keats's poems.

Because Brown's transcripts were so frequently copied and drawn upon by others, they cannot be said to give us very many otherwise unknown versions of Keats's poems, and they are our sole MS source for only three pieces, *Ah, woe is me, I cry your mercy,* and *In after time a sage.* But they obviously have been important in the history of Keats's texts (and also in the history of Keats's reputation, which improved rapidly after the publication of *1848*), and they are still the best bases for our standard texts of at least sixteen poems and part of another, and possibly for as many as nine more.

7   CHARLES WENTWORTH DILKE

Charles Wentworth Dilke (1789–1864), schoolfellow of Brown, co-owner of Wentworth Place, and a good friend of Keats until April 1819, when he moved away from Hampstead, transcribed seventeen of Keats's poems on some blank leaves at the end of his copy of *1818* now at Keats House, Hampstead (Garrod's *End.*, pp. li–lii), in the following order:

> When I have fears that I may cease to be
> To Homer
> If by dull rhymes our English must be chain'd
> As Hermes once took to his feathers light
> To Sleep
> On Sitting Down to Read *King Lear* Once Again
> On Fame ("Fame, like a wayward girl")
> On Fame ("How fever'd is the man")
> To the Nile
> Lines on Seeing a Lock of Milton's Hair
> Lines on the Mermaid Tavern
> There is a joy in footing slow across a silent plain
> Fancy
> Ode to a Nightingale
> Ode on a Grecian Urn
> Robin Hood
> Hush, hush! tread softly! hush, hush, my dear (1–22 only)

Following a mistaken inscription by Dilke's grandson on the flyleaf of this volume, scholars in the early decades of the twentieth century took these transcripts to be copies in Keats's own hand, and the error has surely been helped along by a difference in general appearance between the handwriting in the transcripts, which slants to the right, and that in some biographical notes on Keats following the transcripts, which we know from other MSS to be Dilke's own hand and which slants slightly to the left. Apart from this difference, however, both handwritings are the same in the distinctive details of letter after letter, and I think certainly belong to a single writer. We must assume that Dilke had two ways of writing, a regular hand that slanted to the left and a special copying hand that slanted to the right.

There is plentiful evidence that Dilke copied fourteen of these texts— all but *Lines on the Mermaid Tavern, There is a joy in footing slow*, and *Fancy*—from Brown's transcripts (the extant transcripts except for *Ode to a Nightingale*). The first five and the ninth sonnets agree with Brown's texts exactly in every detail of wording, spelling, capitalization, and punctuation, and the other poems differ only in a few minor details (e.g., Dilke's lowercasing of words that Brown capitalized). Brown's headings, dates, and distinctive readings and misreadings are all reproduced here, and, as if this were not enough evidence, Dilke has added a large "CB" flourish—Brown's own signature at the end of many of his transcripts— after each of the poems longer than a sonnet that he copied from Brown's texts (*Hush, hush! tread softly* is an exception, but it lacks the "CB" flourish only because Dilke never finished copying the poem, breaking off after "morning's" in 22). The transcripts of *Lines on the Mermaid Tavern* and *There is a joy* were taken from the extant holographs at Harvard, and that of *Fancy* from a lost holograph.

Dilke made his transcripts fairly early, and they do not always reflect the final revisions in Brown's MSS. In general they are not of much importance, since in all but two instances their sources are extant. But because Dilke was an even more precise copyist than George Keats, his transcripts of *Ode to a Nightingale* and *Fancy* retain some value as our best representatives of two MSS by Brown and Keats that have since been lost.

8   OTHER TRANSCRIBERS

Of the remaining transcripts, a sizable number are of very little significance because they were copied from printed sources. The texts of the two Elgin Marbles sonnets and the first twenty lines of *To Charles Cowden Clarke* written by Thomasine Leigh, of Sidmouth (1796–1883), an early friend of Reynolds, Rice, and Bailey, in a commonplace book now at Keats House, Hampstead (see Clayton E. Hudnall, *K-SJ*, 19 [1970], 11–39), were taken from Reynolds' review of *1817* in the

Champion. The copy of the Chapman's Homer sonnet by Mary Strange Mathew (b. 1802), a sister of G. F. Mathew, in an album owned in the 1940's by T. G. Crump, of Reigate, Surrey, derives from *1817*. The transcript of *Shed no tear* by the poet Frederick Locker-Lampson (1821–1895), in a copy of Keats's *Poetical Works* (1841) now in the Berg Collection, New York Public Library, was made from the text in *1848*. Some of the transcripts listed below by C. C. Clarke, J. C. Stephens, Isabella Towers, and B. R. Haydon, and most of those by copyists who cannot be identified are also from published sources.

Fanny Brawne (1800–1865) transcribed at least two of Keats's poems —*Hush, hush! tread softly* in a copy of Hunt's *Literary Pocket-Book* for 1819 at Keats House, Hampstead, and *Bright star* in a copy of Cary's Dante at Yale. The former is probably our best representative of the latest state of the poem and should be the basis for a standard text. The latter also represents a revised state of text—the same as that of the extant fair copy that Keats wrote aboard ship en route to Italy.

Two of the transcripts among Woodhouse's papers in the Morgan Library are by Keats's publishers John Taylor (1781–1864) and James Augustus Hessey (1785–1870). Taylor's copy of *You say you love,* which, as Woodhouse indicated when he recorded variants from it, derives from a MS that belonged to Isabella Jones, shows several substantive differences from the only other known text, that of the copies by Charlotte Reynolds and Woodhouse. Hessey's transcript of *As Hermes once,* deriving from Woodhouse, seems to have been printer's copy for the version published in the *London Magazine* in 1821.

Woodhouse's brother William Pitter Woodhouse included two of Keats's poems in a commonplace book of July–August 1827 that is now at Harvard. The text of the first, *In drear-nighted December,* incorporates Woodhouse's proposed revision of the entire third stanza (see *KC,* I, 64–65), and obviously was provided by Woodhouse; that of the second, *To G. A. W.,* probably derives from *1817,* from which it varies insignificantly in 12. Neither of the texts can be considered authoritative.

There are two transcripts by Leigh Hunt (1784–1859) of *On "The Story of Rimini,"* both at Harvard—the earlier in a copy of Galignani (1829) and the later on a sheet given to Milnes in the 1840's. Both derive from a holograph written in a now-lost copy of *1817* that Keats presented to Hunt. Though there are no substantive variants among the extant MSS of this poem, one or the other of Hunt's transcripts is theoretically our best source of text for a standard edition.

Charles Cowden Clarke (1787–1877), one of the earliest of Keats's

close friends, is the writer of four of the extant transcripts—a copy of
To Ailsa Rock, now in the Morgan Library, which Clarke made for
Woodhouse from the published text in Hunt's *Literary Pocket-Book,* and
copies of *Unfelt, unheard, unseen* (source unknown), *Think not of it*
(from a lost Woodhouse transcript), and *Welcome joy and welcome
sorrow* (probably from the MS now in the possession of Dorothy Withey),
all three at Harvard, which Clarke made for Milnes. The latter three
served as printer's copy for the first published versions of the poems, in
1848. Clarke also sent Milnes several MSS that have since been lost—
holographs or copies of *Written on the Day That Mr. Leigh Hunt Left
Prison* and *O Solitude,* and copies of *Four seasons, To Ailsa Rock,* and
As Hermes once (*KC,* II, 154–155)—and he published *This pleasant
tale is like a little copse* from the only extant holograph MS in his *The
Riches of Chaucer* in 1835.

Clarke was also responsible for a volume of transcripts, now at Har-
vard, that he had made for his sister Isabella Jane Towers (Garrod's *St.,*
pp. l–li). The volume contains the MS title page, "Poems / by / John
Keats / with several, never / yet published / . . . London / written by
J C Stephens / for I J Towers. / 1828," and an inscription at the front,
"I J Towers. / a little Birth day gift from her Brother / 5 October /
1828." J. C. Stephens, who is otherwise unknown but presumably was
a professional copyist, transcribed the thirty-one poems of *1817* and
then, in a separate section, the following:

> On a Leander Which Miss Reynolds, My Kind Friend, Gave Me
> Four seasons fill the measure of the year
> To Ailsa Rock
> Welcome joy and welcome sorrow
> Written in Disgust of Vulgar Superstition
> Before he went to live with owls and bats

The first three items derive from printed sources (*The Gem* and Hunt's
Literary Pocket-Book) and the last three apparently from MSS then in
Clarke's possession—Miss Withey's fair copy, the Harvard draft, and
the Huntington draft, respectively. None of these transcripts has any
independent authority, but that of *Before he went to live with owls and
bats* was the source of the first published version, by Nicoll and Wise
in 1896. At the end of the volume, after the last of Stephens' tran-
scripts, Isabella Towers copied two additional poems, *This pleasant tale
is like a little copse* (from the extant holograph that Keats gave Clarke)
and *In drear-nighted December* (from Galignani's text).

Except for the final item, the rest of the identifiable transcripts are connected with Milnes and his collection of material for *1848*. John Jeffrey (1817–1881), the second husband of Georgiana Wylie Keats, copied fifteen of Keats's letters and sent them to Milnes in September 1845 (*KC*, II, 123). Six of these letters and part of another are currently known only through his transcripts, now at Harvard. While omitting several other poems in the letters that he copied, Jeffrey included texts of the following:

> On Sitting Down to Read *King Lear* Once Again
> On Visiting the Tomb of Burns
> Why did I laugh tonight? No voice will tell
> Character of C. B.
> As Hermes once took to his feathers light
> If by dull rhymes our English must be chain'd

Jeffrey was perhaps the most unreliable of all the copyists (see *Letters*, I, 20–23), but his transcripts are nevertheless of some importance. They were the bases, via Milnes's or an amanuensis' copies, for the texts of four poems published in *1848*, three of them for the first time. His text of the *King Lear* sonnet represents an otherwise unknown version, and the transcript containing *On Visiting the Tomb of Burns* is our only MS source for that poem.

In November 1845 Benjamin Robert Haydon (1786–1846) gave Edward Moxon, Milnes's publisher, copies of the two Elgin Marbles sonnets transcribed from the printed versions in *Annals of the Fine Arts,* where he had had them published from holograph MSS in 1818 (*KC*, II, 141–142). The two transcripts, at Harvard, have no independent authority, but probably were the source of Milnes's texts of the sonnets in *1848*.

The American actor and playwright John Howard Payne (1781–1852) published three poems, two of them for the first time, in the *Ladies' Companion* for August 1837—'Tis the *"witching time of night,"* As Hermes once, and *On Fame* ("Fame, like a wayward girl")—from texts that George Keats had written out for him from Keats's letters (he also, in the same magazine, included *Hither, hither, love* from a holograph that George had given him). Payne recopied the three poems for Milnes in July 1847 (*KC*, II, 223–225). The transcripts sent to Milnes are extant at Harvard. One of them, 'Tis the *"witching time,"* was the basis for Milnes's text of the poem in *1848*.

Eleven other transcripts at Harvard were made by the poet Coventry Patmore (1823–1896), who in 1847 was employed by Milnes as a copyist. They are the following (Garrod's *T* and *T²*, pp. lxvi, lxvii):

Stay, ruby-breasted warbler, stay
As from the darkening gloom a silver dove
Oh, how I love, on a fair summer's eve
After dark vapours have oppress'd our plains
To a Young Lady Who Sent Me a Laurel Crown
This pleasant tale is like a little copse
On the Sea
Time's sea hath been five years at its slow ebb
Blue! 'Tis the life of heaven—the domain
Four seasons fill the measure of the year
To J. R.

In each case Patmore copied the late transcript by Woodhouse's clerk (Garrod's *T*), as the substantive and accidental peculiarities common to the two sets prove beyond any doubt. Since the clerk's transcripts for these poems have small x's at the left beside each first line—Milnes's designation of the pieces that he wished to have copied—Patmore very likely transcribed a twelfth poem, *Ode to Apollo* ("In thy western halls"), which is similarly marked by a small x in the clerk's MS. Eight of the extant transcripts, and probably the lost transcript of *Ode to Apollo* as well, were used as printer's copy for *1848*, and two others appear to have been the bases of new texts in *1876*. Altogether six poems (or seven, if we include *Ode to Apollo*) were published for the first time from Patmore's copies.

Milnes himself (1809–1885) made at least four transcripts, all extant at Harvard, and probably a number of others that have since disappeared. The four known MSS—*I had a dove* (probably from a lost Brown transcript), *Why did I laugh* (from Jeffrey's transcript), *Shed no tear* (from the extant holograph), and *To Fanny* ("Physician Nature," conjecturally also from a lost Brown transcript)—were used as printer's copy for *1848*, where three of the four poems were published for the first time. Milnes's text of *To Fanny* appears to be the best that we have for that poem.

The latest of the identifiable transcripts, again at Harvard, is a copy of Keats's draft of *Spenser, a jealous honorer of thine* written out by Eliza Reynolds' son W. A. Longmore. Longmore made the transcript in 1870 for Milnes (*KC*, II, 331–332), who included a text based on it in a note to the poem in *1876*.

Most of the transcripts by unidentified hands are of no significance— copies of *There is a joy in footing slow* taken from the *Examiner* (bound into George Keats's notebook in the British Museum), *In drear-nighted December* from the *Literary Gazette* (Keats House, Hampstead), *Ad-*

dressed to Haydon ("Highmindedness") and *Written in Disgust of Vulgar Superstition* from unknown sources (both on the same sheet, at Harvard); a transcript of Keats's letter to Tom of 17–21 July 1818 containing *All gentle folks* and *Of late two dainties* (Harvard); and a transcript of an 1847 letter from Henry Stephens to G. F. Mathew containing the first four lines of *Give me women, wine, and snuff* (Harvard —see *KC*, II, 210). The Harvard transcripts of *Addressed to Haydon* and *Vulgar Superstition* were the bases for printings in *Hood's Magazine* and *1876*, respectively, the latter representing the first publication of the poem. Garrod, p. li, reports unidentified transcripts of *On the Sea* and *Blue! 'Tis the life of heaven* in a copy of *1817* that once belonged to Isabella Towers and in 1932 was in the possession of Douglas Cleverdon, of Bristol, and of *To Autumn* in a scrapbook owned by R. W. Chapman—all three texts apparently taken from printed sources, *1848* and *1820*. The single unidentified transcript of any consequence is that of *O Chatterton* among Woodhouse's papers in the Morgan Library. This may be in George Keats's hand, and in any case probably was Woodhouse's source for his own copy. There are no significant variants among the extant MSS of this poem, but in principle the transcript is very likely our best basis for a standard text.

III

The Publication of the Poems

1 KEATS'S THREE ORIGINAL VOLUMES

In *Poems, Endymion,* and the volume entitled *Lamia, Isabella, The Eve of St. Agnes, and Other Poems*—abbreviated *1817, 1818,* and *1820,* respectively—Keats published forty-five poems short and long, all but five of them for the first time. Numerically these represent somewhat less than a third of the poems that we know he wrote, though the remaining two-thirds, because they are generally short pieces, do not equal the published third in quantity of lines. A few routine facts about the circumstances and the texts of these three original volumes may be set down as follows.

1817, printed by Charles Richards and published by Charles and James Ollier at the beginning of March 1817, consists of thirty-one items, in four principal sections with a half title before each of the last three (the titles here, as in other lists, accord with the headings in Section IV.2):

Dedication: To Leigh Hunt, Esq.

Poems: I stood tip-toe upon a little hill
Specimen of an Induction to a Poem
Calidore
To Some Ladies
On Receiving a Curious Shell and a Copy of Verses from the Same Ladies
Hadst thou liv'd in days of old
To Hope

Imitation of Spenser
Woman! when I behold thee flippant, vain

Epistles: To George Felton Mathew
To My Brother George
To Charles Cowden Clarke

Sonnets: I. To My Brother George
II. Had I a man's fair form, then might my sighs
III. Written on the Day That Mr. Leigh Hunt Left Prison
IV. How many bards gild the lapses of time
V. To a Friend Who Sent Me Some Roses
VI. To G. A. W.
VII. O Solitude! if I must with thee dwell
VIII. To My Brothers
IX. Keen, fitful gusts are whisp'ring here and there
X. To one who has been long in city pent
XI. On First Looking into Chapman's Homer
XII. On Leaving Some Friends at an Early Hour
XIII. Addressed to Haydon ("Highmindedness")
XIV. Addressed to the Same ("Great spirits")
XV. On the Grasshopper and Cricket
XVI. To Kosciusko
XVII. Happy is England! I could be content

Sleep and Poetry

Only *O Solitude*, the Chapman's Homer sonnet, and *To Kosciusko* had been previously published, in the *Examiner* for 5 May 1816, 1 December 1816, and 16 February 1817.

Counting the temporarily disappeared fair copy of *To Hope*, which is known in photostats, we have one or more holograph versions for seventeen of the poems, and transcripts for most of these and six others. There is, however, a direct relationship between the MSS and the printed texts in only two instances. Keats's fair copy of the sonnet *To My Brother George* and the latest of three holographs of *Addressed to the Same* were part of the MS, fols. 53 and 66, respectively, from which the volume was set in type. These two MSS are especially valuable as evidence that Keats himself (rather than Tom Keats or a friend) copied out his poems for the printer and that he could punctuate and spell correctly when he wanted to. On the second of the MSS Keats wrote "Christ Day" below the text, apparently recording the day on which he made the copy, 25 December 1816. We know very little about the printing schedule, but can assume that Keats gave the entire MS to the

Olliers around the beginning of 1817 and read the proofs himself. Leigh Hunt may have influenced small changes in *Specimen of an Induction* and *Calidore* when he marked these poems in Tom Keats's transcripts, and also in the three sonnets that he published in the *Examiner,* but on the slight evidence available it appears that Keats had less editorial assistance in this volume than in the two later ones.

The *1817* texts of *To My Brother George* and *Addressed to the Same* are very close to the extant printer's copy—in the first sonnet lowercasing fourteen words that Keats had capitalized but otherwise only adding a hyphen in 12 and omitting a comma after "sky" in 14, and in the second reducing twelve capitals but otherwise varying only in printing "now," which Keats had underscored in the first line, in roman rather than italic type. In general the *1817* texts seem carefully done. There are misprints in *I stood tip-toe* 22, 39, and 233, *To Kosciusko* 7, and *Sleep and Poetry* 377 ("mispent" in *To Charles Cowden Clarke* 82 and "scism" in *Sleep and Poetry* 181 are probably Keats's archaic spellings rather than misprints). Three other errors—in *Specimen of an Induction* 46, *To Some Ladies* 6, and *To one who has been long in city pent* 5—are almost surely Keats's mistakes in his MSS rather than printing errors.

Keats had several helpers with *1818,* which was printed by T. Miller and published by Taylor and Hessey toward the end of April 1818. J. H. Reynolds apparently read over and marked Keats's now-lost first draft (*KC,* II, 178), Taylor made a number of suggestions on the revised fair copy, which Keats delivered to him a book at a time from 20 January through 21 March, and C. C. Clarke may have read part of the proofs (*KC,* I, 12). It is clear, quite apart from the friendliness, encouragement, and financial assistance they gave the poet, that Keats's new publishers were a decided improvement over the Olliers, who less than two months after *1817* was published had written a surly letter to George Keats, beginning, "We regret that your brother ever requested us to publish his book" (Williamson, p. 47 and plates X–XI). Not the least remarkable fact about the relationship of the new publishers to the poet is that Taylor, agreeing to take on the work probably on Reynolds' advice, ordered the printing of Books I and II before he ever saw the remaining books. Keats received the first proofs in the latter part of February while he was still revising and copying Book III (*Letters,* I, 228, 238–239).

Taylor in particular—it was primarily he who was responsible for the publishing, while Hessey had charge of the retail end of the business —went over Keats's text with an eye for careless and inappropriate diction. His markings of some 130 or 140 lines in the fair copy are characterized in the history of the text in Section IV.2, and there is no need to repeat the details here, except to say that his suggestions frequently resulted in changes for the better. His later handling of John Clare's MSS, for which he has been both blamed and defended (see Eric Robinson and Geoffrey Summerfield, *Review of English Studies*, n.s. 14 [1963], 359–369, and Tim Chilcott, *A Publisher and His Circle: The Life and Work of John Taylor*, 1972, pp. 107–122), ought not to reflect on his influence with Keats's texts, which was much less extensive and was exerted tentatively rather than insistently.

The poem was set in type from the fair copy extant in the Morgan Library. Apart from corrections of Keats's slips of the pen and some changes marked by Taylor, there are substantive differences between the MS and the printed text in eighty or more lines—a number of them presumably authorial revisions, but others that are clearly errors. The first issue of the work contained a single erratum (to III.71), while the second issue listed five errata (to I.940, II.149, 789, III.71, and IV.739); at least another dozen or so would have been in order, but Taylor did not even include all the corrections that Keats sent him before the volume was officially published (*Letters*, I, 272–273), apparently unwilling to call undue attention to faults that escaped the printer. Some of the more obvious uncorrected errors suggest that Keats was not a very careful proofreader.

The final volume, *1820*, printed by Thomas Davison and published by Taylor and Hessey in the last week of June 1820, contains thirteen poems, with a half title before each of the first three items, the section of "Poems," and *Hyperion*:

> Lamia
>
> Isabella
>
> The Eve of St. Agnes
>
> Poems: Ode to a Nightingale
>   Ode on a Grecian Urn
>   Ode to Psyche
>   Fancy
>   Bards of passion and of mirth
>   Lines on the Mermaid Tavern
>   Robin Hood
>   To Autumn
>   Ode on Melancholy
>
> Hyperion

These pieces were all new except for the first two odes, which had earlier appeared in *Annals of the Fine Arts* for July 1819 and January 1820.

Keats had thoughts of "try[ing] the press once more" at least as early as June 1819, and in the middle of December was "very busy . . . in preparing some Poems to come out in the Sp[r]ing." Then came the severe hemorrhage on 3 February 1820 and an attack of "violent palpitations at the heart" on 6 March, and Brown wrote to Taylor on 8 March that "Poor Keats will be unable to prepare his Poems for the Press for a long time." About a week later, however, in a letter to Taylor tentatively dated 13 March, Brown was able to report that Keats "wishes his Poems to be published as soon as convenient to yourself,—the volume to commence with St Agnes' Eve. He was occupied yesterday in revising Lamia" (*Letters*, II, 121, 237, 273–274, 276). By 27 April—and possibly several weeks earlier, since in the last letter just quoted Brown adds the request, "Don't let any one take a Copy of Otho," from which we may infer that Brown's transcripts were at the publisher's —Taylor, as he told John Clare, had "all Keats's MSS. in my hands now to make a Selection out of them for another volume" (Edmund Blunden, *London Mercury*, 4 [1921], 141). This last statement suggests that Taylor, no doubt in consultation with Woodhouse, had a part in determining the contents of the volume, though it does not mean that he was responsible for the final choices or the arrangement of the poems.

We have one or more holograph MSS for each of the *1820* poems except *Ode on a Grecian Urn* and *Robin Hood*, transcripts for all but *Lamia*, and a set of proof-sheets for *Lamia*. Three of the extant MSS served as printer's copy—Keats's revised fair copy of *Lamia*, Woodhouse's W^1 transcript of *Isabella*, and his clerk's W^1 transcript of *Hyperion*— but the evidence concerning the lost MSS from which *The Eve of St. Agnes* and the shorter poems were set is conflicting. On the one hand, there is Brown's remark to Milnes in 1840 that "most of the originals [of Keats's poems] were scrambled away to America by his brother, after I had made copies of them for the press" (*KC*, II, 37–38). This is a puzzling statement, because, except for the three poems that Keats had written in George Keats's notebook now in the British Museum (the draft of *The Eve of St. Mark* and the fair copies of *Isabella* and *Lines on the Mermaid Tavern*) and the drafts of *To Autumn*, *Ode on Melancholy*, and *Otho the Great*, George seems to have "scrambled away" only a very few minor pieces (e.g., the drafts of *God of the golden bow*, *Hither, hither, love*, and *Blue! 'Tis the life of heaven*). Brown's extant transcripts—they survive for all the shorter poems in *1820* except *Ode to a Nightingale*—do not show any signs of having been used by a printer, though his texts are usually closer than other MSS to the wording of *1820* and his transcripts of *Fancy* and *Robin Hood*, both of which have line numbers marked on them, are quite similar to *1820* in accidental details. On the other hand, the holograph fair copy of *Song of Four Fairies*, which Woodhouse calls "Keats's copy for the press," is evidence, along with some of the remarks in his letters quoted above, that Keats himself wrote out at least some of the shorter poems for the printer.

Perhaps the best explanation of these various details is that in saying he "made copies . . . for the press" Brown simply meant that he was responsible for the copies retained as the authoritative versions, and that in preparing his MSS for the volume Keats copied some or all of the poems from Brown's transcripts. Possibly Brown's *Ode to a Nightingale* served as printer's copy—the one Brown transcript of a shorter poem in *1820* that is no longer extant. Woodhouse's report that Keats "had the Eve of S^t A[gnes]. copied fair" (*Letters*, II, 162) suggests, since he does not say that Keats himself copied it, that Brown was the transcriber. This lost fair copy was probably the MS given to the printer for that poem.

Between the extant MSS used as printer's copy and the *1820* texts there are substantive differences in more than fifty lines of *Lamia*, in seven of *Isabella*, and in eighteen of *Hyperion*, and the printed texts of *The Eve of St. Agnes* and the shorter poems show a sizable number of readings—more than seventy, all told—that do not appear in the latest surviving MS versions. Many of these new readings were no doubt suggested by Woodhouse and Taylor, who were the principal editors in the volume. Woodhouse's contributions to *Isabella* and *Hyperion* are traceable through the successive MSS leading to the printer's copy for these poems; Taylor's hand is present in the printer's MS for *Isabella*; and Woodhouse's suggestions and changes in *Lamia* can be seen in the extant proof-sheets (details are given in the separate histories in Section IV.2). Obviously they worked together over *The Eve of St. Agnes*, whose sexual explicitness in the revised version caused them a great deal of anxiety; and one may extrapolate the existing evidence to cover some of the shorter poems as well. Except in *The Eve of St. Agnes*, however, there is no indication that they made changes against Keats's wishes. As with Taylor's markings of *Endymion*, the editorial work in the main seems to have taken the form of queries and suggestions, and Keats was a person who recognized an improvement when he saw one. Both the extant proof-sheets and a letter from Keats to Taylor written in the middle of June 1820 (*Letters*, II, 294–295) are evidence that Keats read proofs of the volume.

1820 is the most carefully printed of the three original volumes. There are no substantive mistakes clearly attributable to the printer ("languid" in *Lamia* I.132 appears to be the likeliest possibility), and only a handful of errors in accidentals—the omission of closing quotation marks in *Lamia* I.377 and II.298 and *The Eve of St. Agnes* 144, the omission of punctuation in *The Eve of St. Agnes* 301 and the erroneous addition of a closing quotation mark in 342 of the same poem, and a misplaced hyphen in *Lines on the Mermaid Tavern* 19 (though this last also appears in Brown's transcript). Two substantive errors in *Hyperion* I.6 and 81 are the result of copying mistakes by Woodhouse (in the latter instance) and his clerk (in the former).

1817, 1818, and *1820* represent the latest authoritative versions of the forty-five poems that they contain. For each of the volumes Keats supplied copy, read proofs, and except in a few minor details of *Endymion* and some major details of *The Eve of St. Agnes* (a special problem that is discussed at length in Section IV.2) approved the resulting printed texts, or at least is not known to have been displeased. The texts of the three volumes are in every case—even that of *The Eve of St. Agnes*, in which some major emendations may be desirable—the proper bases for a standard edition.

2   PERIODICAL AND ANNUAL PUBLICATIONS

During his lifetime, fourteen of Keats's poems were first published in periodicals and an annual.

> In the *Examiner:*
> O Solitude! if I must with thee dwell (5 May 1816)
> On First Looking into Chapman's Homer (1 December 1816)
> To Kosciusko (16 February 1817)
> After dark vapours have oppress'd our plains (23 February 1817)
> To Haydon, with a Sonnet Written on Seeing the Elgin Marbles
>   (9 March 1817—in the *Champion* on the same day)
> On Seeing the Elgin Marbles (9 March 1817—also in the
>   *Champion*)
> This pleasant tale is like a little copse (16 March 1817)
>
> In the *Champion:*
> To Haydon, with a Sonnet Written on Seeing the Elgin Marbles
>   (9 March 1817—also in the *Examiner*)

On Seeing the Elgin Marbles (9 March 1817—also in the
   Examiner)
On the Sea (17 August 1817)

In Leigh Hunt's *Literary Pocket-Book* for 1819 (1818):
To Ailsa Rock
Four seasons fill the measure of the year

In *Annals of the Fine Arts:*
Ode to a Nightingale (July 1819)
Ode on a Grecian Urn (January 1820)

In the *Indicator:*
La Belle Dame sans Merci (10 May 1820)
As Hermes once took to his feathers light (28 June 1820)

Between 1822 and 1845 another twenty-four poems also first appeared
in periodicals and annuals.

In the *New Monthly Magazine:*
On Some Skulls in Beauley Abbey, near Inverness (January 1822)

In the *Examiner:*
There is a joy in footing slow across a silent plain (14 July 1822—
   partially printed earlier in *NMM*, March 1822)

In *The Gem* (1829):
On a Leander Which Miss Reynolds, My Kind Friend, Gave Me

In the *Literary Gazette:*
In drear-nighted December (19 September 1829)

In Thomas Hood's *The Comic Annual* (1830):
To Mrs. Reynolds' Cat

In the *Western Messenger* (Louisville):
God of the golden bow (June 1836)
Not Aladdin magian (July 1836)

In the *Plymouth, Devonport, and Stonehouse News:*
If by dull rhymes our English must be chain'd (15 October 1836)

In the *Ladies' Companion* (New York):
On Fame ("Fame, like a wayward girl"—August 1837)
Hither, hither, love (August 1837)
'Tis the "witching time of night" (August 1837)

In the *Plymouth and Devonport Weekly Journal:*
To the Nile (19 July 1838)
Read me a lesson, Muse, and speak it loud (6 September 1838)
Bright star, would I were steadfast as thou art (27 September
   1838)

The day is gone, and all its sweets are gone (4 October 1838)
To Sleep (11 October 1838)
Shed no tear—O shed no tear (18 October 1838)
Ah, woe is me! poor Silver-wing (25 October 1838)
On Sitting Down to Read *King Lear* Once Again (8 November 1838)
Lines on Seeing a Lock of Milton's Hair (15 November 1838)
Old Meg she was a gipsy (22 November 1838)
In after time a sage of mickle lore (4 July 1839)

In *Hood's Magazine:*
Time's sea hath been five years at its slow ebb (September 1844)
Hush, hush! tread softly! hush, hush, my dear (April 1845)

These lists do not include subsequent printings of poems from independent sources (the two Elgin Marbles sonnets in *Annals of the Fine Arts* for April 1818, *As Hermes once* in the *London Magazine* for November 1821 and the *Ladies' Companion* for August 1837, *In drear-nighted December* in *The Gem* for 1830, *To Ailsa Rock* and *Not Aladdin magian* in *PDWJ* for 13 and 20 September 1838, *Old Meg* and *Addressed to Haydon* ["Highmindedness"] in *Hood's Magazine* for June 1844 and April 1845, and *Bright star* in the *Union Magazine* for February 1846), and they of course ignore reprints from published sources, though a few of these are mentioned in the histories of the texts in Section IV.2.

I think we should assume that Keats himself directly or indirectly furnished copy for the poems published in periodicals while he was alive. He was of course closely associated with Leigh Hunt, who edited the *Examiner,* the *Literary Pocket-Book* for 1819 (the first of an annual series), and the *Indicator,* and was even staying at Hunt's house at the time that *As Hermes once* appeared in the *Indicator.* Haydon thought that the Elgin Marbles sonnets were published in the *Examiner* "by Keats himself" (*KC,* II, 142). The *Champion* acquired its poems through Reynolds, a regular contributor to that newspaper, to whom Keats had given texts of the Elgin Marbles sonnets in a presentation copy of *1817* and *On the Sea* in a letter; the *Champion* texts of at least the first two sonnets appear to derive from these MS versions. Keats sent a copy of *Ode to a Nightingale* directly to James Elmes, the editor of *Annals of the Fine Arts* (*Letters,* II, 118–120), and presumably also made the copy, passed on by Haydon, from which *Ode on a Grecian Urn* was printed; the *Annals* texts of the Elgin Marbles sonnets likewise came from holographs forwarded to Elmes by Haydon (*Letters,* I, 122; *KC,* II, 141–142).

Of the poems that appeared after Keats's death, those in *NMM,* the

Examiner, and the two Plymouth newspapers all came from Brown, who was a writer in these periodicals. The two poems in the Louisville *Western Messenger* were published from the extant draft and the earlier extant letter text, respectively, by its editor, James Freeman Clarke, who acquired the MSS, the first as a gift and the second as a loan, from George Keats (*KC*, II, 139–140). Those in the *Ladies' Companion* were included in an article by John Howard Payne—*Hither, hither, love* from a holograph given him by George Keats and the others from copies made for him by George from Keats's letters (*KC*, II, 224). The sources of the poems that Thomas Hood published—in *The Gem*, *The Comic Annual*, and *Hood's Magazine*, all of which he edited—are harder to pin down. Hood was a close friend of Reynolds, who figures frequently in his various publications (see Peter F. Morgan, *K-SJ*, 11 [1962], 83–95), and after 1825 was the husband of Reynolds' sister Jane. *On a Leander* and *To Mrs. Reynolds' Cat* probably derive from holograph MSS (at least in the first instance from an extant holograph) given by Keats to one or more of Reynolds' sisters; *Hush, hush! tread softly* may likewise have come from a holograph or copy in the possession of one of the Reynoldses; *Time's sea hath been* was sent to Hood, as he told a correspondent, "*copied*, from [Keats's] M.S." It appears that Hood was also responsible for the first two printings of *In drear-nighted December*, which various members of the Reynolds family had in an extant holograph and two lost transcripts that Woodhouse made notes of. In later years Hood had connections with Milnes, who regularly contributed to *Hood's Magazine*. The sonnet *Addressed to Haydon* was, as the heading in *Hood's* indicates, "Communicated by R. Monckton Milnes, Esq., M.P.," and *Old Meg*, too, since the *Hood's* text has certain details in common with what we can reconstruct of Brown's lost transcript, probably came from Milnes.

Though we know in a general way, and sometimes specifically, the sources of these publications, what we too often do not know is the extent to which editors and copyists for periodicals introduced changes in Keats's texts. The striking fact about the periodical and annual versions is the frequency with which they vary from other known texts. While the American periodicals reproduced their sources fairly faithfully, about two-thirds of the texts first published in British periodicals contain unique substantive readings, some of which, especially in Hunt's and Hood's publications, represent considerable changes. The *Examiner's O Solitude*, for example, has a unique ninth line and part of the tenth, and its *After dark vapours* has unique readings in three lines. There are major differences from other known versions in both of the poems that were first published in the *Indicator*, while the *Literary Pocket-Book*'s text of *Four seasons* amounts to an extensive revision of the poem. The *Champion*'s *On the Sea* differs substantively from Keats's letter text in four lines. All of Hood's texts have unique variants, again some of them of major proportions.

In studying these texts, one increasingly gets the idea that editors felt free to tinker with, and sometimes rewrite, the poems they published. *1817*, *1818*, and *1820* also, of course, have readings that do not appear in other known texts, but not nearly so many proportionately as the periodicals have, and Keats did not have control over the periodical texts in the way that, in proofreading and in correspondence and consultation with his publishers, he did in his three original volumes. After his death he of course had no hand even in most of the copy from which his poems were published. The high frequency of unique readings (along with Reynolds' documented habit of treating Keats's texts casually, since Reynolds was an intermediary source for the *Champion*'s and probably some of Hood's printings) suggests that in many cases, though we cannot be certain which ones, the periodical and annual texts are not reliably authoritative. As a consequence, when faced with a choice between differing versions of a poem in MS and periodical sources, I have tended in Section IV.2 to favor the MS as a sounder basis for a standard text. Keats may in fact have been responsible for every word of these periodical texts, but the existing evidence makes it seem unlikely that he was.

3   MILNES'S *LIFE, LETTERS, AND LITERARY REMAINS*

The many intentions and attempts to produce a biography of Keats, beginning with Taylor's announcement of a proposed memoir in the *New Times* for 29 March 1821, five weeks after the poet's death, are well documented in Rollins' *The Keats Circle* (see also the introductory material in Brown's *Life of John Keats*, ed. Dorothy Hyde Bodurtha and Willard Bissell Pope, 1937, and *The Letters of Charles Armitage Brown*, Cambridge, Mass., 1966). Not only Taylor but C. C. Clarke, Reynolds, and Brown, among others, had thoughts of writing Keats's life. Through Reynolds, Taylor sought Brown's help and the use of his papers, but Brown refused both, unwilling to "consent to be a party in a bookseller's job" without the right to approve the memoir (see Sharp, pp. 109–112). Discord among the surviving friends of Keats quickly arose, with Brown,

Dilke, Severn, Hunt, and the information and MSS they possessed on one side, and Taylor, Woodhouse, Reynolds, and their recollections and MSS on the other.

It was not until Milnes brought the sides together—or rather, as one who had *not* known Keats, represented a neutral party to whom both sides could entrust their materials—that anything approaching a comprehensive biography could be written. Milnes met Brown at W. S. Landor's house in Florence in 1833, and they surely talked about Keats, who was always much on Brown's mind. Dissatisfied with Hunt's portrayal of the poet in *Lord Byron and Some of His Contemporaries* (1828), Brown had been sporadically gathering information for a memoir, and had got involved in an extended and increasingly bitter controversy with Dilke over George Keats's financial dealings with his brother. In 1836 Brown finally put the materials together for a lecture at the Plymouth Institution on "The Life and Poems of John Keats." More than four years later, having attempted without success in the interim to find a publisher himself, he wrote to Milnes on 14 March 1841: "as I am on the eve of quitting England for ever, I considered it would be my wiser plan to confide in a true lover of Keats, and place the Life and Poems in his hands, to act in my stead. Such confidence I am ready to repose in you, if you will undertake the task" (*KC*, II, 50). Milnes immediately accepted, and Brown almost by return mail sent him a slightly revised version of his 1836 lecture and, shortly afterward, his transcripts of the poems.

From around the beginning of 1845, Milnes worked assiduously in collecting MSS, facts, and reminiscences. Georgiana Wylie Keats's second husband, John Jeffrey, corresponded from Louisville and made transcripts of Keats's letters; Taylor signed an agreement with Edward Moxon, Milnes's publisher, giving him the right to publish Keats's poems, and he turned over for Milnes's use some of the material that Woodhouse had compiled in his volumes of Keatsiana; Severn, Haydon, and C. C. Clarke all provided information and transcripts; James Freeman Clarke sent from Boston a transcript of *God of the golden bow*; Hunt gave him copies of *On "The Story of Rimini"* and the Nile sonnets (though he chose the wrong poem by Shelley); Dilke sent a parcel of papers that included holographs of *Lines on the Mermaid Tavern* and *There is a joy in footing slow*; Reynolds, after first objecting to the use of Keats's letters to him, finally cooperated, and even lent Milnes the original drafts of *Endymion* and two odes; Edward Holmes and G. F. Mathew wrote reminiscences, and the latter copied out several of his own poems; William

Haslam made Severn's letters in his possession available; John Howard Payne sent three transcripts from Paris; and these and other correspondents answered a great many specific queries about details of Keats's life. Among important members of Keats's circle who were alive at the time, only Fanny Brawne, who was married and living on the Continent, and Benjamin Bailey, who Milnes mistakenly thought was dead, did not contribute. Milnes assembled the work in 1847 and 1848, and it was published around the beginning of August 1848, a date after which Keats has always been "among the English Poets."

Not counting the canceled stanza of *Ode on Melancholy*, which was included at the end of Volume I, the *Life, Letters, and Literary Remains, of John Keats—1848* for short—contains sixty-six complete poems and parts of two others, the first thirty items in the narrative "Life and Letters" and the remaining thirty-eight in the section of "Literary Remains," which begins with a separate half title at II, 109. Forty of the items (as well as the first four lines of *Over the hill*) were published here for the first time. The following list, in order according to volume and page in *1848*, indicates new poems with an asterisk, and gives Milnes's known or probable source for each in parentheses.

> In Volume I:
> 11 *Spenser, a jealous honorer of thine (Woodhouse's clerk's transcript)
> 12 *O Chatterton! how very sad thy fate (Woodhouse's clerk's transcript)
> 13 *To Lord Byron (Woodhouse's clerk's transcript)
> 27 On Seeing the Elgin Marbles (Haydon's transcript?)
> 27 To Haydon, with a Sonnet Written on Seeing the Elgin Marbles (Haydon's transcript?)
> 78 Lines on Seeing a Lock of Milton's Hair (in a letter to Bailey; text of the poem probably from Brown's transcript)
> 81 *Hence burgundy, claret, and port (in a letter to Reynolds, from Woodhouse's clerk's letterbook transcript)
> 82 *God of the meridian (same as the preceding)
> 90 *O thou whose face hath felt the winter's wind (in a letter to Reynolds, from Woodhouse's letterbook transcript)
> 96 On Sitting Down to Read *King Lear* Once Again (in a letter to George and Tom Keats, from Jeffrey's transcript)
> 99 To the Nile (Brown's transcript)
> 113 *Dear Reynolds, as last night I lay in bed (in a letter to Reynolds; source of the lines unknown)
> 119 *Over the hill and over the dale (1–4 only, in a letter to Rice, from Woodhouse's letterbook transcript)

135 *Mother of Hermes! and still youthful Maia (in a letter to
       Reynolds, from Woodhouse's clerk's letterbook transcript)
156 *On Visiting the Tomb of Burns (in a letter to Tom Keats,
       from Jeffrey's transcript)
159 *This mortal body of a thousand days (lost transcript by
       Brown)
160   Old Meg she was a gipsy (in a letter to Tom Keats; text of
       the poem from a lost transcript by Brown)
167   To Ailsa Rock (lost transcript by Brown)
180   There is a joy in footing slow across a silent plain (with a
       letter to Bailey; text of the poem from a lost transcript by
       Brown)
186   Not Aladdin magian (in a letter to Tom Keats; text of the
       poem from a lost transcript by Brown)
189   Read me a lesson, Muse, and speak it loud (lost transcript
       by Brown)
233   'Tis the "witching time of night" (in a letter to George and
       Georgiana Keats; text of the poem from J. H. Payne's
       transcript)
241 *Nature withheld Cassandra in the skies (in a letter to
       Reynolds; source of the poem unknown)
269 *Character of C. B. (in a letter to George and Georgiana Keats,
       from Jeffrey's transcript)
281   In after time a sage of mickle lore (lost transcript by Brown)
282 *Where's the poet? Show him! show him (Brown's transcript?)
283 *And what is love? It is a doll dress'd up (lost transcript by
       Brown?)
283 *Fragment of Castle-builder (24–71 only—lost transcript by
       Brown?)
285 *Welcome joy and welcome sorrow (C. C. Clarke's transcript)

In Volume II:
 34 *What can I do to drive away (lost transcript by Brown?)
111 *Otho the Great (Brown's fair copy)
204 *King Stephen (Brown's transcript and Keats's draft)
215 *The Jealousies (lost transcript by Brown)
252 *Ode to Apollo ("In thy western halls"—lost Patmore copy of
       Woodhouse's clerk's transcript)
255   God of the golden bow (source unknown)
257 *Think not of it, sweet one, so (C. C. Clarke's transcript)
258 *Unfelt, unheard, unseen (C. C. Clarke's transcript)
259   Hush, hush! tread softly! hush, hush, my dear (Brown's
       transcript)
260 *I had a dove and the sweet dove died (Milnes's copy probably
       from a lost Brown transcript)
261   Shed no tear—O shed no tear (Milnes's copy from the extant
       holograph)
262 *Spirit here that reignest (Brown's transcript)

263   Ah, woe is me! poor Silver-wing (Brown's transcript)
264   *Extracts from an Opera (Brown's transcript)
268   La Belle Dame sans Merci (Brown's transcript)
271   *Song of Four Fairies (Brown's transcript)
276   *Ode on Indolence (Brown's transcript)
279   *The Eve of St. Mark (Brown's transcript)
284   *To Fanny ("Physician Nature"—Milnes's copy probably
        from a lost transcript by Brown)
287   *Oh, how I love, on a fair summer's eve (Patmore's copy of
        Woodhouse's clerk's transcript)
288   *To a Young Lady Who Sent Me a Laurel Crown (same as the
        preceding)
289   After dark vapours have oppress'd our plains (same as the
        preceding)
290   This pleasant tale is like a little copse (same as the preceding)
291   On the Sea (same as the preceding)
292   *On *The Story of Rimini* (Brown's transcript)
293   *When I have fears that I may cease to be (Brown's transcript)
294   *To Homer (Brown's transcript)
295   *Blue! 'Tis the life of heaven—the domain (Patmore's copy
        of Woodhouse's clerk's transcript)
296   *To J. R. (same as the preceding)
297   Time's sea hath been five years at its slow ebb (same as the
        preceding)
298   To Sleep (Brown's transcript)
299   On Fame ("Fame, like a wayward girl"—Brown's transcript)
300   *On Fame ("How fever'd is the man"—Brown's transcript)
301   *Why did I laugh tonight? No voice will tell (Milnes's copy
        from Jeffrey's transcript)
302   As Hermes once took to his feathers light (Brown's
        transcript)
303   If by dull rhymes our English must be chain'd (Brown's
        transcript)
304   The day is gone, and all its sweets are gone (Brown's
        transcript)
305   *I cry your mercy—pity—love!—aye, love (Brown's
        transcript)
306   Bright star, would I were steadfast as thou art (the extant
        holograph)

Apart from the printer's copy for *Welcome joy,* the last poem in Volume I, nothing of Milnes's MS for the narrative "Life and Letters" seems to have survived. Of the "Literary Remains" in Volume II, however, we have the printer's copy for *Otho the Great* and for all of the last thirty-three poems (beginning with *Think not of it* at II, 257) except *To Homer* and *Bright star.*

Where his sources can be ascertained, Milnes appears to have taken only *Shed no tear*, *Bright star*, and part of *King Stephen* from holographs; the rest of the texts derive from transcripts, frequently from MSS that are several removes from a holograph version. *Oh, how I love*, for example, was printed from Patmore's copy of Woodhouse's clerk's transcript (T), which in turn was taken from the W^2 transcript that Woodhouse made—possibly via an intervening W^3 transcript—from a copy of the poem by Kirkman in Mary Frogley's album. Though the 1848 text is thus five or six times removed from the lost original (*if* Kirkman's source was a holograph), the only certain evidence of textual corruption is Patmore's intentional omission of a word in 12. *On the Sea* is a more extreme example. If I am right in Section IV.2 about the relationships among Woodhouse's transcripts for this poem, the 1848 text is at least seven removes from a MS in Keats's own hand. An early printed version (in the *Champion*), three Woodhouse transcripts, and a copy by Woodhouse's clerk lie between a lost holograph, at one end, and Patmore's transcript from which the poem was printed in 1848. The text was altered several times in the successive recopyings; yet, owing to the peculiar progress of changes in Woodhouse's transcripts (from the *Champion*'s later readings back to the earlier state of a lost letter to Reynolds), the 1848 version differs in only one word from a text that we know Keats was directly responsible for. (It is perhaps worth noting that, even though five MSS of this sonnet leading up to 1848 are available, Garrod's and Allott's texts, since they both derive from *1848,* are yet one step further removed from the lost holograph than Milnes's text is.)

Milnes has been much criticized for some of his practices in 1848 (he was, says Rollins in *KC*, I, cxiv, "a far from scholarly writer who was careless about reproducing texts and quotations exactly and frequently too lazy to verify dates and other biographical details. [In letter texts] He omits, condenses, or shifts the order of his correspondents' words, phrases, or sentences"). Some of this criticism is justified, but with the materials that he had he did not, especially for his time, do a bad job. We can now see that a few of his choices of copy-text were poor ones —he took the *King Lear* sonnet and *Character of C. B.* from Jeffrey's transcripts when he had better texts at hand in Brown's MSS, and the Elgin Marbles sonnets apparently from Haydon's copies when any of the early printed versions would have been preferable sources. A large proportion of his texts, however, derive directly from Brown's and indirectly from Woodhouse's MSS (Milnes did not have access to the W^2

transcripts, as we know both from the absence of any details in *1848* that can be shown to have been based on the W^2 texts or notes and from the specific evidence of Milnes's remark in *1848*, I, 124, that he "cannot lay hands on the first Preface" to *Endymion*, a copy of which is included at the end of the W^2 book; but he did have Woodhouse's letter-book, from Taylor, and the clerk's late transcripts that Woodhouse gave to Brown). In general these were, and in many instances still are, the most authoritative versions available.

Milnes or his copyists or his printer introduced substantive corruptions in at least thirty-seven (roughly four-sevenths) of the poems included in *1848*. Some of these are intentional alterations and revisions—Milnes's changes in *Think not of it* described in the opening section above, for example, or his rewriting of the beginning line of the fifth stanza of *Ode on Indolence*. A great many are simply copying or printing errors. What is most striking is the extent to which these errors persist in our modern editions of the poems.

Milnes's texts have had a considerable influence on subsequent editors' work. Garrod not only follows Milnes's order in two sections of his edition but bases at least fifty-six of his texts on *1848* wording and accidentals, sometimes emending and correcting *1848* errors but in perhaps half the poems retaining them, occasionally in places where his apparatus indicates that he should have known better (a typical example would be *O Chatterton* 6, for which he records "numbers *1848*: murmurs TW^2W^3" but nevertheless prints "numbers" in his text). Milnes's erroneous readings appear even in texts supposedly taken from other sources. Both Garrod and Allott follow Keats's letter text of *Character of C. B.*, for instance, but both print *1848*'s "swine-head" in 13 (for Keats's and Jeffrey's "swine-herd")—and there are many other examples at hand. The greater availability of MSS and information in the twentieth century has not resulted in a proportional improvement in the texts, and in at least a few cases our modern texts are actually inferior to those of *1848*. Milnes merely rewrote three words of a line in *Ode on Indolence*, while Garrod changed the order of the stanzas. For *Otho the Great,* because Garrod and Allott both in their different ways mix draft and revised readings, Milnes's version is still the best printed text available, and the same is true for *God of the golden bow*. *1848* is our sole source for two poems—*This mortal body of a thousand days* and *What can I do to drive away*—and has a claim (along with other sources) to be the proper basis for the texts of at least two others, *Not Aladdin magian* and *The Jealousies*.

4   SUBSEQUENT PUBLICATIONS

Keats's three original volumes offered forty of his poems to the public for the first time, and periodicals and annuals from 1816 through 1845 another thirty-eight; *1848* added forty more (including the substantial portion of *Fragment of Castle-builder* but not counting the first four lines of *Over the hill*). The remaining thirty-two pieces—to complete the account—were published in the following order (sources are again given in parentheses):

For there's Bishop's teign	Tom Taylor's *Life of Benjamin Robert Haydon,* 1853 (from Keats's letter)
Where be ye going, you Devon maid	Same details as the preceding
The Fall of Hyperion	*1857* (from the transcript by Woodhouse's clerks)
Of late two dainties were before me plac'd	*Athenaeum,* 7 June 1873 (from Keats's letter)
Stay, ruby-breasted warbler, stay	*1876* (probably from Patmore's transcript)
As from the darkening gloom a silver dove	Same as the preceding (probably from Patmore's transcript)
Written in Disgust of Vulgar Superstition	Same as the preceding (from the unidentified transcript at Harvard)
Pensive they sit and roll their languid eyes	New York *World,* 25 June 1877 (from Keats's letter)
Give me your patience, Sister, while I frame	Same details as the preceding
O come, dearest Emma! the rose is full blown	H. B. Forman's edition of 1883 (from George Keats's transcript)
O blush not so! O blush not so	Same as the preceding (from an unknown MS probably deriving from Brown's transcript)
There was a naughty boy	Same as the preceding (from Keats's letter)
All gentle folks who owe a grudge	Same as the preceding (from Keats's letter)
Upon my life, Sir Nevis, I am piqu'd	Same as the preceding (from Keats's letter)
Two or three posies	Same as the preceding (from Keats's letter)
The Gothic looks solemn	Same as the preceding (from a lost transcript by Brown)

Ah, ken ye what I met the day	Same as the preceding (from Keats's letter)
Give me women, wine, and snuff	H. B. Forman's edition of 1884 (from the extant holograph)
When they were come unto the Fairy's court	1–17 in *Macmillan's Magazine,* August 1888, and the lines in full in H. B. Forman's edition of 1890 (from Keats's letter)
Before he went to live with owls and bats	*Literary Anecdotes of the Nineteenth Century,* ed. W. R. Nicoll and T. J. Wise, 1896 (from J. C. Stephens' transcript)
This living hand, now warm and capable	H. B. Forman's edition of 1898 (from the extant holograph)
Fill for me the brimming bowl	*N&Q,* 4 February 1905 (from Woodhouse's clerk's transcript)
On Peace	Same details as the preceding
Apollo to the Graces	*TLS,* 16 April 1914 (from the W^2 transcript)
You say you love, but with a voice	Same details as the preceding
On Receiving a Laurel Crown from Leigh Hunt	*The Times,* 18 May 1914 (from the extant holograph)
To the Ladies Who Saw Me Crown'd	Same details as the preceding
Lines Written on 29 May, the Anniversary of Charles's Restoration, on Hearing the Bells Ringing	Amy Lowell's *John Keats,* 1925 (from the W^3 transcripts)
Over the hill and over the dale	Same as the preceding (from Keats's letter)
Sweet, sweet is the greeting of eyes	Same as the preceding (from Keats's letter)
O grant that like to Peter I	J. M. Murry's edition of 1930 (from the extant holograph)
I am as brisk	Garrod's edition of 1939 (from the extant holograph)

Except historically, for their place in the development of Keats's reputation, almost none of these publications is now of any importance. More than half of them contain substantive errors, a number of which continue to appear in our modern editions. The one textually significant item is Forman's printing of *The Gothic looks solemn,* which represents a slightly different version from that in Woodhouse's transcripts and probably ought to be the basis for a standard text.

I have not systematically investigated the transmission of Keats's texts after the earliest printings discussed in the present section. *The Poetical Works of Coleridge, Shelley, and Keats*, published by Anthony and William Galignani in Paris at the end of 1829—representing the first collected edition of Keats's poems—reprinted the contents of *1817, 1818*, and *1820* and added *Four seasons, To Ailsa Rock* (both from Hunt's *Literary Pocket-Book*), *On a Leander* (from *The Gem*, 1829), and *In drear-nighted December* (from the *Literary Gazette*). The Keats section of this edition, which was frequently reprinted in the United States (sometimes with William Howitt's and Henry Hart Milman's poems substituted for those of Coleridge and Shelley), determined the canon and the texts of the poems for at least the next two decades. The first English collected edition, *The Poetical Works of John Keats* published by William Smith in 1840, has the same contents as the Keats section of Galignani's volume, and so do the first several editions and issues published by Edward Moxon beginning in 1846. The Americans fairly quickly incorporated the new poems from *1848* into their editions, but Moxon seems not to have done so until the 1860's. Milnes's Aldine edition, published by George Bell and Sons in 1876 and reissued at least a dozen times during the next thirty or more years, added to the Galignani and *1848* items *The Fall of Hyperion*, the two pieces published in Tom Taylor's *Life of . . . Haydon*, and three new poems—*Stay, ruby-breasted warbler, As from the darkening gloom*, and the Vulgar Superstition sonnet.

The serious scholarly editing of the poems dates from 1883, when Harry Buxton Forman got out the first of his numerous collected editions. Ernest de Selincourt published a valuable critically annotated *Poems* in 1905 (5th ed., 1926), and Sidney Colvin issued a chronologically arranged edition in 1915, but for a period of more than five decades—almost until the Second World War—the standard texts of Keats's poems were Forman's, even though Forman himself died in 1917. Subsequent editors, including the most recent, have drawn heavily on his work. Forman especially exerted influence through his Oxford Standard Authors edition of 1906 and later years; even Garrod's revised Oxford Standard Authors edition of 1956, which is increasingly used for citation in scholarly work these days, is merely an occasionally corrected version of this earlier O.S.A. text.

Garrod's Oxford English Texts *Poetical Works* of 1939—in its second edition (1958) the work cited as "Garrod" throughout the present study—replaced Forman as the standard, and Miriam Allott's *Poems* of 1970, a modernized and chronologically arranged collected edition, represents a great many improvements over Garrod's work. But in Keats's posthumously published poems both Garrod and Allott, as the details in Section IV.2 show repeatedly, retain a sizable number of errors first introduced by Milnes and Forman. While claiming to base her work "on a fresh examination of the MSS," Allott actually constructs some of her texts from faulty information in Garrod's apparatus; Garrod in turn frequently took his details from Forman's editions; and Forman repeated mistakes made by Milnes and, before Milnes, by the transcribers who copied texts from one MS to another until the poems were first put into print. In general terms, though some progress is discernible, the modern editing of Keats is a patchwork affair resting on rather shaky foundations.

IV

The Histories of the Texts

1 EXPLANATION OF METHODS

Section IV.2, just below, presents the textual "histories"—in some cases a full account tracing the step-by-step transmission of a text from Keats's original draft to its first publication, in others no more than a brief statement of the few known facts—of 150 works that can reasonably be assigned to Keats (including two that he coauthored with Brown, *On Some Skulls in Beauley Abbey* and *Otho the Great*). I have omitted a few fragments (e.g., the two lines beginning "They weren fully glad" in Garrod, p. 554, and the two lines in French in *Letters*, II, 172), and have relegated eight pieces, two of which are currently in the Keats canon (*To A. G. S.* and *"The House of Mourning" written by Mr. Scott*), to Section IV.3, "Questionable Attributions."

The histories are arranged in chronological order according to the known or conjectured dates of composition (or, for poems written over a long period, substantial completion). Many of the poems can be dated quite precisely, even, were it desirable to give the information, to the approximate times on the specific days that Keats wrote them; for a number of others we know only the year, and for a very few we have no clue at all. I have occasionally been skeptical of traditional datings, especially those based on allusions to seasons in the poems. It is quite clear that Keats could describe a May morning on any day of the year, and the datings that depend on such references have usually been put forth by scholars only when there is no other evidence to go on. Gittings and Allott, for example, who sometimes arrive at very precise dates from seasonal allusions, ignore the references to "the humming May-fly" and "The stock-dove . . . hatch[ing] her soft brace" in *Hush, hush! tread softly,* which for other reasons they wish to assign to the winter of 1818– 19 (Gittings, *John Keats,* p. 274; Allott, p. 448). My chronological arrangement now and then differs from Allott's, but has been greatly aided by her work, which in pinning down dates is generally excellent. I have suggested a wider range of dates for some poems—e.g., *La Belle Dame* and *Ode on a Grecian Urn*—but also have sometimes cheated by both questioning the traditional dating of a poem and at the same time including it in its customary place according to that dating (e.g., *Ode on a Grecian Urn* and *Ode on Melancholy,* which *may* have been written in the spring of 1819, are discussed immediately after *Ode to a Nightingale,* the one ode of the spring that can definitely be assigned to May).

For the poems published in Keats's three original volumes I have, in the interests of clarity of reference, changed three titles: "To * * * * * *" and "To * * * *" (both in *1817*) are included here under the headings *Had I a man's fair form, then might my sighs* and *Hadst thou liv'd in days of old,* and "Ode" (in *1820*) under the heading *Bards of passion and of mirth.* For the posthumously published poems I have treated titles more freely, regularly dispensing with the customary headings "To _____," "Lines," "Song," "Faery Song," "Fragment," "Stanzas," and some others in favor of the poems' first lines. Most of these headings were supplied by copyists or early editors rather than by Keats, and none—except possibly those identifying the speakers as fairies—contributes to the understanding or the aesthetic appreciation of a poem.

Each history begins, after the title or heading, with the date of composition, the details of first publication, and page references to the texts in Garrod's 1958 *Poetical Works* and Allott's 1970 *Poems.* What follows after this initial information varies according to the availability of MSS and the complicatedness of their relationships. Where there are no extant MSS, and *1817* or another work is our sole source of text, I say so and go on to the next poem. For most of the poems, however, we do have one or more MSS, and the typical entry lists these, gives the locations of holographs (the locations of the transcripts are included in the various parts of Section II), refers to photographic and other facsimiles and transcriptions of MSS available in printed sources, discusses and frequently diagrams what can be determined of the relationships among the MSS and early printed versions, suggests what might be the best basis for a standard text, and briefly indicates the sources of Garrod's and Allott's texts and, where necessary, points out mistakes that need correcting.

The relationships among MSS and the relationships of MSS to printed texts are, as the histories should make obvious, not always easy to work out. When Woodhouse notes that a W^2 text was taken "from C.B." and Brown's MS has the same wording as W^2, when a Dilke transcript agrees substantively and in a high proportion of accidentals with one of Brown's and moreover has the "CB" flourish at the end, or when a transcript by George Keats has peculiar misreadings that could have come only from a Brown MS, it seems safe to assert as fact in these situations that Woodhouse, Dilke, and George Keats copied Brown. Sometimes there are no such clear indications, however, and comparisons of accidentals are more often than not a waste of time (though I have of course made them), because in general the transcribers and to a lesser extent the early printers did not take pains to preserve the spelling, punctuation, and capitalization of their sources. My main principle of procedure concerning accidentals has been to make what use I could of notable agreements but to ignore the differences; that is, I have tended to view close agreement as evidence for a relationship but have usually not considered the lack of such agreement to be evidence against a relationship.

Apart from extratextual evidence (e.g., Woodhouse's or another transcriber's notes specifying sources), the relationships set forth here mainly rest on the evidence of substantive readings, and I have attached considerable importance to substantive agreements and very little to unique variants. The greatest danger in this sort of work is assuming that the MSS now known are the only ones that ever existed—we have a holograph MS and, say, a Brown transcript that agrees substantively, and are tempted to think *therefore* that Brown copied the extant holograph. In a great many such situations the actual truth can never be determined, and we must operate with degrees of probability that cannot be measured (or stated) very precisely. I have attempted to use my adverbs with some discrimination; "surely," "quite probably," "very likely," "possibly," and the like are not all intended to mean the same thing. As a rule there is more discussion when a relationship is questionable, and much less when I consider a relationship to be certain. Some of my statements in the histories are based on the more general data of Sections II and III (e.g., the connection between Charlotte Reynolds' and Woodhouse's transcripts).

The handwriting in the MSS presents some special problems, both in the reading of known hands and in the identifying of uncertain or un-

known hands. Keats's own handwriting in particular has caused diffi-
culties from his own time to the present. His "where" and "when" are
often almost indistinguishable, as are "there" and "then," "month" and
"mouth," and some other pairs of words. In *The Eve of St. Mark* he
wrote "Aron's" in such a way that Brown read it as "Moses' "; Brown
copied "townwards" as "homewards" in the same poem, and Woodhouse
"homely" as "lonely." Keats often did not cross his "t," and thus we
have misreadings of "sleep" for "steep," "leasing" for "teasing," "lighten'd"
for "tighten'd," and many others, especially in the first printed text of
Endymion, which was set in type from Keats's fair copy. The tran-
scribers' hands (except for Haydon's) are generally much less likely to
be misinterpreted in this way, but combinations like "on" and "ou" are
almost always indistinguishable in their MSS, and create ambiguity where
the difference produces different words (e.g., "month" vs. "mouth" in
After dark vapours 5).

The identification of hands is even trickier. The inscription "Margate
—Sept 1816" written at the top of the extant holograph of *To Charles
Cowden Clarke* may serve as a simple illustration of the problem. H. B.
Forman, who spent a good part of his life working on Keats, states un-
equivocally that this is "in George Keats's hand" (Hampstead Keats, I,
63 n.), while Garrod, who also spent much of his life working on Keats,
says "not in Keats' hand but, I fancy, in that of Woodhouse" (p. 35).
I myself would guess that it is in Keats's own hand. But the point is
that there is no proving the matter, and legal history abounds with ex-
amples in which so-called handwriting experts have made wrong identi-
fications. The question is crucial not so much in entire documents (e.g.,
Dorothy Withey's MS of *Welcome joy and welcome sorrow*) as in the
added pencilings and other markings that appear in various MSS, espe-
cially in Woodhouse's. On any given occasion these may be by Keats,
by Woodhouse or another contemporary, or by a later hand, even one
writing in the present century; and our choice—in deciding whether it
is a revision or correction by Keats, an alteration or suggested revision
by a friend, or the marking by a later hand of a variant from a printed
source—makes a significant difference, or would make a significant
difference if there were, as in many instances there are not, good grounds
for choosing. In both of these matters, deciphering and identifying, I
have been aware of the problems involved and have attempted to main-
tain as much caution as the particular circumstances in each case seem
to call for.

Where they are included, the diagrams are intended to illustrate the *most probable* relationships that can be arrived at with the available evidence. The point needs to be emphasized, since there is of course no room for qualifying adverbs in a diagram. An unbroken line connecting two texts indicates a probable or certain *direct* relationship between them (a later MS copied from an earlier, or a printed text set from a MS). Occasionally I have used a broken line to signify *indirect* derivation (as for some of the early periodical printings), and I have also resorted to the broken line in a few instances where the evidence is not sufficient to establish the probability of a direct relationship (Brown's copy of *Spirit here that reignest*, for example, is related to the extant holograph, but not necessarily directly since there may have been an intervening slightly revised holograph now lost). Bracketed items in the diagrams represent hypothesized or known lost MS texts; the unbracketed are all extant. In addition to the abbreviations given at the end of the book, the following are used for Keats and the various transcribers in the diagrams (this list includes all the identifiable transcribers except Leigh Hunt, Frederick Locker-Lampson, Mary Strange Mathew, and W. P. Woodhouse, who do not appear in the diagrams):

BRH	Benjamin Robert Haydon
CB	Charles Brown
CCC	Charles Cowden Clarke
CP	Coventry Patmore
CR	Charlotte Reynolds
CWD	Charles Wentworth Dilke
FB	Fanny Brawne
GAW	Georgiana Augusta Wylie
GK	George Keats
IT	Isabella Towers
JAH	James Augustus Hessey
JCS	J. C. Stephens
JFC	James Freeman Clarke
JHP	John Howard Payne
JHR	John Hamilton Reynolds
JJ	John Jeffrey
JK	John Keats
JT	John Taylor
RMM	Richard Monckton Milnes
RW	Richard Woodhouse
TK	Tom Keats
TL	Thomasine Leigh
WAL	W. A. Longmore

In determining the "proper basis for a standard text"—the phrase is repeated in most of the histories below—essentially two tasks are involved. The first, and usually easier, is to identify discrete versions that are, according to the probabilities in each case, wholly authoritative. *O Chatterton*, which exists in three transcripts, may serve as an example for illustration. The earliest of the texts is that of an unidentified transcript in the Morgan Library. Apart from heading and an explanatory note, no changes were introduced in the successive recopyings represented by the two later transcripts, by Woodhouse and a clerk, but the *1848* text, deriving from the clerk's transcript, has changes of wording in 4, 6, and 8. Thus we essentially have two states of text—that of the transcripts, of which the earliest is the closest to a lost holograph, and that of *1848*. But clearly, where the two differ, only the former state is authoritative; we know for a fact that the *1848* variants originated with Milnes, his copyist, or his printer, and therefore we can describe *1848*'s 4, 6, and 8 as corruptions (and can call Garrod's 6 and 8 and Allott's 8—all of which follow *1848*'s wording—errors). When there is but a single authoritative source, as with *O Chatterton*, the task is relatively simple.

The second and more difficult task presents itself when two or more wholly authoritative texts exist, and we have to decide which of them theoretically better or best represents Keats's considered intentions in the work. This is sometimes a complicated problem, and in a few instances is impossible to resolve satisfactorily. *Song of Four Fairies* is one of the less complicated examples. We have Keats's draft in a spring 1819 journal letter and a fair copy that he made about a year later. Both texts are wholly authoritative versions, but they differ substantively in ten lines. Brown's transcript, an intermediate and presumably also authoritative version, agrees with the draft in 26, 47, 60, and 77, with the fair copy in 19, 32, 46, 55, and 98, and has readings that occur in neither holograph in 9, 44, 71, and 93. Milnes reproduced Brown's wording without error. Garrod's text generally agrees with the fair copy but has (via *1848*) draft readings in 26, 60, and 77 and Brown's distinctive wording in 9, 44, and 71; Allott also follows the fair copy but has the same three draft readings and Brown's variant in 71. While *1848* can be said to represent a wholly authoritative text, that of Brown's intermediate version, both Garrod and Allott combine readings from different states, and thus produce texts that never existed in any one MS or, so far as we know, in Keats's mind. It would have been a better course to follow one of the three MSS consistently—the draft, Brown's transcript, or Keats's fair copy—and best to have reproduced the fair copy text. For this poem the choice of base-text is not a problem, because Woodhouse has identified the later holograph as "Keats's copy for the press," and it obviously represents his considered intentions and is the version that he would have preferred for publication.

In a number of other instances, however, Keats did not leave us a "copy for the press" or clearly indicate his preference among competing versions. It will not do simply to choose the latest known authoritative text, for Keats sometimes produced seemingly inferior later copies (see Section II.1), and in any event there are at least half a dozen poems for which the chronological order of competing versions cannot be established. It is in these cases that we have to consult the crystal ball, and they cannot be settled definitively. When a holograph text and a transcript or early printed text are in competition and it is not clearly evident that the transcript or printed variants are authoritative, I have usually preferred the holograph as the base-text. But I must add that where a Brown transcript differs substantively from an earlier holograph version, I have (for reasons given above in Section II.6) generally taken Brown's variants to be authoritative. Otherwise I have made my recommendations, as everyone else must also, subjectively.

For the forty-five poems included in *1817, 1818,* and *1820,* and another forty-one pieces for which there exists only a single authoritative source (or just a single source regardless of its authoritativeness), the choice of a base-text presents no problems. For each of the remaining sixty-four poems we have two or more differing authoritative versions. While some thirty-three of these cases are fairly easily resolved, most often by the preference for a revised over a draft text, at least thirty-one others pose real difficulties. The following are the problem cases:

> Lines Written on 29 May, the Anniversary of Charles's Restoration, on
>   Hearing the Bells Ringing
> Stay, ruby-breasted warbler, stay
> Fill for me the brimming bowl
> As from the darkening gloom a silver dove
> O come, dearest Emma! the rose is full blown
> Oh, how I love, on a fair summer's eve
> After dark vapours have oppress'd our plains
> To Haydon, with a Sonnet Written on Seeing the Elgin Marbles
> On the Sea
> You say you love, but with a voice
> In drear-nighted December
> Apollo to the Graces

Lines on Seeing a Lock of Milton's Hair
Welcome joy and welcome sorrow
Time's sea hath been five years at its slow ebb
Four seasons fill the measure of the year
Give me your patience, Sister, while I frame
To Ailsa Rock
There is a joy in footing slow across a silent plain
Not Aladdin magian
On Some Skulls in Beauley Abbey, near Inverness
Nature withheld Cassandra in the skies
I had a dove and the sweet dove died
Hush, hush! tread softly! hush, hush, my dear
The Eve of St. Mark
Character of C. B.
As Hermes once took to his feathers light
La Belle Dame sans Merci
To Sleep
On Fame ("Fame, like a wayward girl")
The Jealousies

In considering Garrod's and Allott's texts I have not, of course, judged their work against my own subjective preferences in these problem cases, but I have noted substantive errors, misprints, and a number of inconsistencies (most often, again, the mixing of discrete states of text). Comprehensive—but surely not complete—lists of the errors and inconsistencies in their texts are given in the final section of this study.

2   THE HISTORIES

Imitation of Spenser

Written probably in 1814 (Brown in *KC*, II, 55–56, calls the poem Keats's "earliest attempt" and places it, on information from Keats's brothers and later from the poet himself, after the completion of "his eighteenth year," i.e., after October 1813; Brown thought Keats was born a year later than he actually was, but his wording suggests that he learned of Keats's age at the time rather than the year in which he wrote the poem, and we have at least one other poem, *Fill for me the brimming bowl*, that is securely dated before October 1814). First published in *1817*. Garrod, pp. 25–26; Allott, pp. 3–5.

The one extant MS text, the transcript in Tom Keats's copybook, varies substantively from *1817* in 12 ("scalés") and 29 ("glassy"). *1817*, which is the proper basis for our standard texts of all its poems, has "scales'" and "glossy." Garrod emends the first word to "scalès" (a plural noun) and the second to "glassy," following Tom's transcript in each instance (with a grave rather than an acute accent in the first), and otherwise reproduces *1817* exactly. Allott has "scalës'" (*1817*'s possessive plural plus a representation of Tom's stress mark) and *1817*'s "glossy." Tom's lack of an apostrophe in the first word is of no significance, since like Keats he frequently omitted apostrophes in possessives. One's choices have to depend on whether "light" in 12 is read as a noun or an adjective (in any event we have to imagine a "ruby glow" caused by "golden scales," light or otherwise), and whether the "tide" in 29 is more likely to be "glassy" or "glossy" (both words make good sense, and "silver sheen" in 25 does not really help). Each seems a toss-up.

On Peace

Written perhaps in April 1814 (Napoleon surrendered on 11 April, and shortly afterward departed for Elba), or possibly somewhat later. First published by Ernest de Selincourt in *N&Q*, 4 February 1905, p. 82. Garrod, p. 527; Allott, pp. 5–6.

The extant MSS are two transcripts by Woodhouse (W^3, W^2) and a late copy by one of Woodhouse's clerks (Garrod's *T*). There are no significant differences among the transcripts (W^2 and the clerk's copy have "chains'" and "chain's," respectively, for W^3's "chains" in 12, but W^2's apostrophe is a slip of the pen and the clerk miscopied the word from W^2). In all three MSS, 13 was initially left unfinished—W^3 ending the line with "uncurbed" and W^2 and the clerk's copy adding "th" and "the" —and in all three the line and the rhyme have been completed in pencil, with "the great" in W^3 (probably by Woodhouse) and "-e great?" and "great?" in the others (possibly by different hands). It is not clear whether this incompleteness reflects a lacuna or some damage in a holograph MS or in Woodhouse's more immediate source. The penciled conclusion of the line would seem to be a good guess rather than an authoritative reading.

This is probably the earliest (in date of composition) of ten poems that Woodhouse took from his cousin Mary Frogley's album, initially copying them at the front of the W^2 book of transcripts and heading the first with a prefatory note that begins, "The small pieces marked F. (10 in number) were copied for my cousin into a Volume of M.S. poetry, by Mr Kirkman, and said to be by Keats." For reasons unknown, Woodhouse subsequently cut out eight of the ten transcripts and transferred them to the W^3 scrapbook, and at the same or a later time recopied six of the eight transferred poems at the end of W^2. For these eight poems, therefore, there are W^3

transcripts (all marked "F") that were originally in W^2, and for six of them there are later W^2 transcripts that were copied from these W^3's (see Section II.4 for more specific details). Thus for this poem W^3 is the earliest extant transcript, W^2 is a copy of W^3, and Woodhouse's clerk (as he always did) transcribed W^2. De Selincourt first published the poem from the clerk's MS. Unfortunately nothing is known of Kirkman's sources for the poems that he copied into Mary Frogley's album. In this and subsequent diagrams I have arbitrarily represented them as holographs.

[JK MS] → [Kirkman in Mary → W^3 → W^2 → RW's clerk → [copy] → N&Q
　　　　　Frogley's album]

W^3 is the proper basis for a standard text, and both Garrod and Allott reproduce this MS substantively (though in the few differences in accidentals Garrod's text, following one of H. B. Forman's, is closer to W^2).

Lines Written on 29 May, the Anniversary of Charles's Restoration, on Hearing the Bells Ringing

Written probably in 1814 or 1815. First published in Lowell, I, 66. Garrod, p. 540; Allott, p. 17.

There are two transcripts by Woodhouse, both in the Morgan Library, one with the title "Lines—written on 29 May.—the anniversary of Charles's Restoration.—On hearing the Bells ringing" (Garrod's w^3) and the other headed "Written on 29 May, the anniversary of the Restoration of Charles the 2^d" (Garrod's W^3). The first has "F" at the end, indicating that it was one of the transcripts Woodhouse took from a Kirkman copy in Mary Frogley's album; it was originally a part of the W^2 book of transcripts, and was later transferred by Woodhouse to the W^3 scrapbook. The second transcript has, partly in shorthand, "from D[itt]°," referring to a shorthand notation, "from Mary Frogley," after the preceding poem on the same sheet. Apart from their titles the two transcripts do not differ substantively (both have "Ah" in 4). Though the overall evidence concerning the relationships among such duplicate W^3 transcripts is ambiguous (see Section II.4), in this instance—because of its more elaborate title and the fact that Woodhouse recorded a variant in it ("originally and" before "Vane's" in 5)—I take w^3 to be the transcript made from the album, and W^3 to be a copy of w^3.

[JK MS] → [Kirkman in Mary → w^3 → W^3
　　　　　Frogley's album]

Contrary to Garrod's headnote, there is no shorthand "G" on either of the transcripts, and very little reason to doubt Keats's authorship (as Garrod does, pp. vii, lxxi). If I am right about the order of the transcripts, then w^3 should be the basis for a standard text. Lowell, printing the poem under the w^3 heading, has substantive errors in 1 ("while" for the transcripts' "will") and 4 ("Oh" for "Ah" and "while" for "when"). Garrod takes his title from W^3 and his accidentals from w^3. He corrects Lowell in 1 and the first word of 4, but keeps the erroneous "while" in 4 (he also retains Lowell's "Russel's" in 5, where both transcripts read "Russell's"). Allott, who does not specify her source, has the same substantive text as Garrod.

Stay, ruby-breasted warbler, stay

Written probably in 1814 ("1814" in Georgiana Wylie's transcript; "Ab^t 1815/6" in a note by Woodhouse originally connected with one of his earliest transcripts). First published in *1876*, p. 6. Garrod, pp. 543–544; Allott, pp. 744–745 (among "Doubtful Attributions and Trivia").

We have seven transcripts—three by Woodhouse (W^2 plus two copies in the Morgan Library that Garrod designates w^3 and W^3) and one each by one of his clerks (Garrod's T), Coventry Patmore, Georgiana Wylie, and George Keats (the last two in the Keats-Wylie Scrapbook—facsimiles of both in M. B. Forman's article in the *Connoisseur*, 116 [1945], 11, 13). All seven of the MSS have some form of the heading "Song. / Tune—Julia to the Wood-Robin." Though the poem has sometimes been assigned to George Keats (on the basis of a "G.K." added at the end of Georgiana's transcript by an unknown hand), it seems best to accept Woodhouse's specific attribution (this is the first of ten poems originally in W^2 that were "copied for my cousin [Mary Frogley] . . . by Mr Kirkman, and said to be by Keats"). Contrary to Garrod's headnote, there is no shorthand "G" on any of the Woodhouse transcripts.

There are two basic texts, one of them represented by Woodhouse's, his clerk's, and Patmore's transcripts and the other by Georgiana's and George Keats's transcripts. Woodhouse's w^3, with "F" at the end, indicating that his source was the Kirkman copy in Mary Frogley's album, was originally on fols. 1–2 of the W^2 book of transcripts, and was later transferred to the W^3 scrapbook. Its distinctive readings are "While . . . thought" in 8, "leafless" (which agrees with Georgiana's and George Keats's transcripts) in 19, "sweet" in 20, "Even" in 21, and "flower" in 22. The

W^3 transcript, with "from Mary Frogley" in shorthand at the end, has these same readings except for "hapless" in 19. Because Georgiana's and George's MSS confirm "leafless" in w^3 as authorial, it might be thought that this is the earlier of the two Morgan Woodhouse transcripts and that he introduced "hapless" by mistake into W^3 in the process of copying the poem from w^3. But the evidence is not perfectly clear in the matter (see Section II.4). Woodhouse transcribed W^2 from w^3 (the two are substantively the same), his clerk took his text from W^2, and Patmore copied the clerk's transcript. Milnes printed the poem in *1876* probably from a copy of Patmore's transcript.

Georgiana's and George Keats's transcripts are identical in wording and very close in accidentals. It would seem that one came from the other, and, since George is known to have been an extremely faithful copyist of minute details in his sources, I suppose that George transcribed from Georgiana's MS rather than vice versa. In place of the readings given above, their transcripts show "Whilst . . . thoughts" (8), "leafless" (19), "soft" (20), "E'en" (21), and "longer" (22).

Unfortunately there is no way of knowing which of the two states of text is the earlier. One might prefer Georgiana's version simply on critical grounds, and if so might like to think that it is the later.

$$
\begin{array}{l}
\qquad\qquad\qquad\qquad\qquad\qquad\nearrow W^3 \\
\text{[Kirkman in Mary} \rightarrow w^3 \nearrow \\
\uparrow\text{Frogley's album]} \qquad\qquad \searrow W^2 \rightarrow \text{RW's clerk} \rightarrow \text{CP} \rightarrow \text{[copy]} \rightarrow 1876 \\
\text{[JK MS]} \\
\qquad\quad\searrow \\
\qquad\qquad \text{[JK revised copy?]} \rightarrow \text{GAW} \rightarrow \text{GK}
\end{array}
$$

Following one or another of H. B. Forman's editions, both Garrod and Allott base their texts on the consensus of Georgiana's and George's transcripts. Like Forman, however, they print Woodhouse's "flower" instead of Georgiana's and George's "longer" in 22.

Fill for me the brimming bowl

Written in August 1814 (so dated in the extant holograph and two of Woodhouse's transcripts). First published by Ernest de Selincourt in *N&Q*, 4 February 1905, p. 81. Garrod, pp. 540–541; Allott, pp. 6–8.

We have a holograph fair copy among Woodhouse's papers in the Mor-

gan Library (see Mabel A. E. Steele, *K-SJ*, 1 [1952], 57–63, for iden-
tification of the handwriting, transcription, and a facsimile of the MS),
three transcripts by Woodhouse (W^2 plus two W^3 copies), and a late tran-
script by one of Woodhouse's clerks (Garrod's T).

This is another of the early poems that Woodhouse took from a Kirk-
man copy in Mary Frogley's album. One of the W^3 copies (here referred
to as W^3x), which is undated and has "from Mary Frogley" in shorthand
at the end, varies substantively from the Morgan fair copy in 1 ("the" for
the holograph's "a"), 6 ("fills the Mind with fond" for "heats the Sense
with lewd"), 13 ("In" for " 'Tis"), 22 ("a" for "one"), and 27 ("Even
so" for "So"). The other W^3 transcript (here W^3y), which has "F" and
"Aug. 1814" at the end, was originally on fols. 6–7 of the W^2 book of
transcripts, and was later transferred to the W^3 scrapbook. This shows the
same readings just given for W^3x, and further varies from the Morgan
fair copy in 8 ("wave" for "waves"), 9 ("heart" for "Breast"), and 20
("or" for "the"). Neither transcript has the fair copy's epigraph from
Terence.

At some later date Woodhouse saw a holograph MS very similar to the
Morgan fair copy and entered variants in longhand and shorthand above
the lines and marginally in both of the W^3 transcripts: in W^3x he noted
the Morgan readings for 1, 6 (the last two words of the variant), and 27;
in W^3y he wrote down the Morgan readings for 1, 6 (the full variant),
and 22, and also marked paragraph divisions after 12, 16, and 20 (just
where they appear in the Morgan fair copy). He did not record a variant
in either transcript for 13 and did not comment anywhere on the differ-
ences between the two transcripts in 8, 9, and 20. That the holograph
he saw was not the Morgan fair copy is evidenced by a variant to "zest"
(18) that he noted from the holograph source in W^3x—"originally *rest*"
—where the Morgan fair copy plainly has "Zest." It is not clear which
of the W^3 transcripts is the earlier. Almost surely one of them was copied
from the other, but the evidence is ambiguous (see the discussion of this
problem in Section II.4). I should guess here that W^3x is the earlier, since
it has three readings (in 8, 9, and 20) that are confirmed as authorial
by the Morgan fair copy. If so, the date on W^3y is probably a later addi-
tion, made at the time that Woodhouse saw the lost holograph from which
he recorded the variants in his transcripts.

Woodhouse transcribed W^2 (dated "Augt 1814") from W^3y, incorpo-
rating the variants "a" and "one" in 1 and 22 and making paragraph di-
visions after 12 and 20 (but not after 16). His clerk copied the poem

from W^2 (changing "woman" to "Women" in 4), and de Selincourt first published it from the clerk's transcript (with a mistaken "happiness" for the MSS' "beaminess" in 15).

If W^3x is the earlier of the two W^3 transcripts, and W^3y was copied from it, then there appear to be three authoritative states of text for the poem—that of the Morgan fair copy, that (very close to the fair copy) represented by the variants entered by Woodhouse in the two W^3's, and that of W^3x (without the variants). Again, the order of these states is not clear. Finney (I, 48) thinks the Morgan fair copy is earlier than the version from Mary Frogley's album, and suggests that the change in 6 was made "by Kirkman, possibly out of a delicate regard for the maidenly sensibilities of Mary Frogley." But it is just as likely (or more likely) that Keats himself revised the line, perhaps out of regard for the critical sensibilities of his readers. In the absence of better evidence, I think we should take the version from Mary Frogley's album as the latest of the three states of text and W^3x (without the variants) as the more accurate representative of its readings and therefore the best basis for a standard text. (Cf. the discussion of *O come, dearest Emma,* however, where in a similar situation I have guessed that the Morgan fair copy is a later version.) My diagram is overly precise concerning the immediate source of the extant holograph, the lost holograph that Woodhouse made notes from, and Kirkman's album copy.

```
          JK fair copy
         ↗
[JK MS]↗→[JK MS that RW saw]
         ↘
          [Kirkman in
          Mary Frogley's →W³x→W³y→W²→RW's clerk →[copy]→N&Q
          album]
```

Garrod's text, initially based on one of H. B. Forman's, which in turn came from de Selincourt's in *N&Q*, is substantively identical with the transcript by Woodhouse's clerk and closest to it in accidentals. Thus he has the clerk's unique "Women" in 4 and the mixture of readings that Woodhouse took over from W^3y and the variants noted there when he wrote out W^2. A text based on W^3x would restore "the" (1), "Woman" (4), "waves" (8), "breast" (9), "the" (20), and "a" (22). Allott takes her text (via Garrod's apparatus) from the Morgan fair copy, but prints "wave" for the holograph's "waves" in 8 (Garrod does not note the variant) and "the" for the MSS' "a" in 25 (a mistake taken over from H. B. Forman). She does not follow the Morgan fair copy's paragraph divisions, and her dash after "with" in 6 is an error deriving from Woodhouse's clerk by way of de Selincourt and Forman.

As from the darkening gloom a silver dove

Written in December 1814 (the poem is dated 1816 in all five of the transcripts, but Keats told Woodhouse in February 1819 that "he had written it on the death of his grandmother [December 1814], about five days afterward"—shorthand note originally opposite the W^2 transcript; see Steele, *HLB*, 3 [1949], 243). First published in *1876*, p. 58. Garrod, p. 531; Allott, pp. 8–9.

We have three transcripts by Woodhouse (W^2, W^3, W^1), a late copy by one of his clerks (Garrod's T), and a copy by Coventry Patmore. The W^2 transcript, which has "F" at the end, indicating that this is one of the poems Woodhouse took from a Kirkman copy in Mary Frogley's album, is the first transcript left in the W^2 book (it is on fol. 8) after Woodhouse removed fols. 1–7, 10–13. W^3, with "from Mary Frogley" in shorthand at the end and *Oh, how I love, on a fair summer's eve* on the reverse side (this sonnet follows *As from the darkening gloom* on fol. 9 of the W^2 book), may have been the source of W^2 or may have been copied from it —the overall evidence is ambiguous (see Section II.4). The principal substantive difference among the MSS occurs in 13, where W^3 and W^1 read "pleasures" against the other MSS' "pleasure's" (W^1 has a unique "which" for "that" in 10, and the clerk miscopied "thy" as "they" in 4). I do not believe the agreement of W^3 and W^1 in 13 is weighty enough to offset the general probability (based on Woodhouse's practice elsewhere) that W^1 was transcribed from W^2. The clerk's copy was made from W^2, and Patmore's from the clerk's MS. Milnes printed the poem in *1876* probably from a copy of Patmore's transcript.

$$[JK\ MS] \rightarrow [Kirkman\ in\ Mary\ Frogley's\ album] \rightarrow \begin{cases} W^2 \overset{\nearrow W^1}{\searrow} RW\text{'s clerk} \rightarrow CP \rightarrow [copy] \rightarrow 1876 \\ W^3 \end{cases}$$

Since their relative priority cannot be determined, both W^2 and W^3 have a claim to be the basis for a standard text. Garrod, taking his accidentals from one of H. B. Forman's editions, generally follows W^2, with "pleasure's" in 13. Allott has the same substantive text as Garrod except that, like Forman, she prefers the W^3-W^1 "pleasures."

To Lord Byron

Written in December 1814 (so dated in both of the extant transcripts). First published in *1848*, I, 13. Garrod, p. 477; Allott, p. 9.

The only MSS are transcripts by Woodhouse (W^2) and one of his clerks (Garrod's T). These do not differ substantively and are very close in accidentals. Woodhouse's source is not known (the poem is copied toward the end of the W^2 book—see the discussion of the next poem). The clerk transcribed W^2, and Milnes printed the poem probably from an amanuensis' copy of the clerk's transcript, the only source certain to have been available to him. The *1848* text has "the golden" for the transcripts' "a golden" in 9.

$$[\text{JK MS}]\dashrightarrow W^2 \rightarrow \text{RW's clerk} \rightarrow [\text{copy}] \rightarrow 1848$$

W^2 is the proper basis for a standard text. Garrod takes his text from *1848*, changing "-ed" verb endings to "-'d" in 4, 5, and 10, but retaining *1848*'s "the golden" in 9. Allott reproduces W^2 substantively. The seventh line of the poem is a foot short, and both H. B. Forman (Hampstead Keats, IV, 14 n.) and Garrod have suggested emendations to fill out the meter.

O Chatterton! how very sad thy fate

Written in 1815 (so dated in all three of the transcripts). First published in *1848*, I, 12–13. Garrod, pp. 476–477; Allott, pp. 10–11.

We have a transcript each by an unidentified copyist (Garrod's W^3, among Woodhouse's papers in the Morgan Library), Woodhouse (W^2), and one of Woodhouse's clerks (Garrod's T). The first of these is in a formal hand very much like that of George Keats in the Keats-Wylie Scrapbook and may in fact have been made by him.

There are no substantive differences among the MSS except in heading ("Sonnet" in the Morgan transcript, "Sonnet. / To Chatterton" in W^2 and the clerk's copy) and in the note to "amate" in 8 ("affright—Spencer" in the Morgan transcript, "amate—to affright—Spenser" in W^2, and " 'amate'. Chaucer—Affright—J.K." in Woodhouse's hand in the clerk's copy). The sonnet appears with *To Lord Byron* toward the end of the W^2 book, between a group of poems generally deriving from holograph MSS and a group recopied from earlier transcripts made from Mary Frogley's album. I take the Morgan transcript to have been Woodhouse's source for W^2. The clerk copied W^2, and *1848* (citing Chaucer instead of Spenser in its note) was almost surely printed from an amanuensis' copy of the clerk's transcript. The *1848* text has substantive errors in 4 ("mildly" for the MSS' "wildly"), 6 ("numbers" for "murmurs"), and 8 ("flow'ret" for "flower").

[JK MS] —→ Morgan transcript —→ W^2 —→ RW's clerk —→ [copy] —→ *1848*

The Morgan transcript would appear to be the proper basis for a standard text. Garrod takes his text from *1848*, emending spelling in 3, 4, and 11, and correcting "mildly" to "wildly" in 4. He mistakenly retains *1848*'s "numbers" and "flow'ret" in 6 and 8. Allott follows "Woodhouse's transcripts" (by which she means the Morgan transcript and W^2), but nevertheless has a form of *1848*'s "flow'ret" in 8. Neither editor includes any version of the MSS' or *1848*'s note to "amate," which in the earliest text may be authorial.

Written on the Day That Mr. Leigh Hunt Left Prison

Written on 2 February 1815 (the day on which Hunt left prison). First published in *1817*. Garrod, p. 40; Allott, p. 11.

C. C. Clarke sent Milnes either a holograph or a transcript of this poem in 1846 (*KC*, II, 154), but no MS has survived, and *1817* is our sole source of text. Garrod reproduces *1817* exactly, and Allott does not depart substantively.

To Hope

Written in February 1815 (the date in the lost holograph and in *1817*). First published in *1817*. Garrod, pp. 23–24; Allott, pp. 12–14.

The only known MS text is a holograph fair copy formerly in the possession of M. B. Forman and since disappeared (facsimile of 1–12 in *K-SJ*, 1 [1952], following p. 60; photostats of the whole at Harvard). This varies substantively from *1817* in 8, 10, 14, 28, 33, and 48. *1817* is presumably a later version, and should continue to be the basis for our standard text. Garrod reproduces *1817* exactly except for adding a hyphen in 45, and Allott does not depart substantively.

Ode to Apollo ("In thy western halls")

Written in February 1815 (so dated in the three transcripts). First published in *1848*, II, 252–254. Garrod, pp. 429–430; Allott, pp. 14–17.

We have two transcripts by Woodhouse (W^3, W^2) and a late copy by one of his clerks (Garrod's T). Both W^3 and W^2 have "F" at the end, signifying that Woodhouse got the poem from a copy by Kirkman in Mary Frogley's album. The two transcripts differ in 4 ("sung" in W^3, "sang" in W^2), but in other particulars are virtually identical. The W^3 copy, which originally formed fols. 10–12 of the W^2 book of transcripts and was later removed by Woodhouse and transferred to the W^3 scrapbook, is the earlier transcript. W^2 is a recopying of W^3, and the clerk made his transcript from W^2. The *1848* text, which was almost surely printed from an amanuensis' (probably Patmore's) copy of the clerk's transcript, changed "There" to "Here" in 7.

[JK MS] $\rightarrow$ [Kirkman in Mary $\rightarrow W^3 \rightarrow W^2 \rightarrow$ RW's clerk $\rightarrow$ [copy] $\rightarrow$ *1848*
           Frogley's album]

W^3, the earliest surviving MS, is the proper basis for a standard text. Garrod reproduces *1848* exactly except for omitting stanza numbers (which appear in all the MSS), and thus includes W^2's and the clerk's "sang" in 4 and Milnes's or his copyist's or printer's "Here" in 7. Allott follows "Woodhouse's transcripts" with W^2's "sang" in 4 and both MSS' "There" in 7. She too omits stanza numbers.

To Some Ladies

Written in the summer of 1815 ("1815" in both the extant holograph and Woodhouse's copy of *1817*, plus the fact noted by Allott and others that the addressees, G. F. Mathew's sisters, were on holiday by the sea). First published in *1817*. Garrod, pp. 18–19; Allott, pp. 18–19.

The three recoverable states of text are not directly relatable, but they can be arranged in chronological order. The earliest is a version that Woodhouse saw perhaps in the possession of Mary Frogley. This can be reconstructed from the variants that he recorded to 9, 24, 25, 27–28 in his interleaved copy of *1817* (see Sperry, pp. 113, 143). The next is that of the sole extant MS, a holograph fair copy headed "To the Misses M_____" (with "at Hastings" added in another hand) in the Texas Christian University Library (facsimiles in A. Edward Newton, *The Amenities of Book-Collecting and Kindred Affections*, Boston, 1918, p. 105; *Rare Books, Original Drawings, Autograph Letters and Manuscripts Collected by the Late A. Edward Newton*, Parke-Bernet sale catalogue, New York, 1941, Part Two, p. 159; and Lyle H. Kendall, Jr., *A Descriptive Catalogue of the W. L. Lewis Collection*, Part One, Fort Worth, 1970, following p. 114—see also H. B. Forman, *Athenaeum*, 16 April 1904, pp. 499–500). This version is considerably closer to *1817* than the preceding, varying substantively in 5 (a copying error), 6, 8 ("In," which Forman took to be a correction and subsequently incorporated into his texts), 27, and 28. In 27 the MS reads "san in," which Garrod records in his apparatus as "san<d> in" and uses as the basis for emending his text to "sand in"; but there is no reason to think that "san" was intended to represent "sand" rather than *1817*'s "span," which Keats presumably allowed to stand in proofs and Woodhouse did not mark. (John Jones, *John Keats's Dream of Truth*, 1969, p. 216 n., would further emend the line to read "To possess but a sand in the hour-glass of leisure," but this is just a logical extension of Garrod's misjudgment.) The latest of the texts is that of *1817* (it has to be the latest—otherwise we must suppose that Keats copied out the poem for the Misses Mathew a year and a half or more after he wrote it). This should continue to be the basis for a standard text.

Both Garrod and Allott change *1817*'s "rove" in 6 to "muse" (Keats's fair copy at T.C.U. shows "rove" canceled in favor of the rhyming word —probably he unconsciously reverted to the earlier reading in his lost MS for the *1817* printer). Garrod further omits a comma in 19 (also following the T.C.U. MS), and emends 27 (see above); Allott does not otherwise vary substantively from *1817*. The syntax of 19–20 would be clarified if 19 were punctuated "And, smiles with . . . ."

On Receiving a Curious Shell and a Copy of Verses from the Same Ladies

Written in the summer of 1815 ("1815" in the extant holograph— and see the discussion of the preceding poem). First published in *1817*. Garrod, pp. 19–20; Allott, pp. 19–21.

For this poem we have, in chronological order, a transcript by George Keats and a partial copy (1–12) by Georgiana Wylie, both in the Keats-Wylie Scrapbook; a holograph fair copy at Harvard (the Sykes MS— facsimile of 1–28 in Sotheby sale catalogue, 23 June 1947); a transcript in Tom Keats's copybook; and the *1817* text.

George Keats's transcript has a title at the end, "Written on receiving a Copy of Tom Moore's 'Golden Chain,' and a most beautiful Dome shaped Shell from a Lady," while Georgiana's partial transcript is headed "Eric, Written on his receiving a Copy of T. Moore's 'Golden Chain' and a dome Shaped Shell from a Lady," with "M.S. by John Keats" added in parentheses beside the first word of the title. In the first twelve lines the two transcripts disagree substantively only in 10 (where Georgiana has a unique "thy" for "thine"), though there are many differences between them in accidentals. It is theoretically possible that Georgiana took her three stanzas from George's copy, but I rather think that the two transcripts were made independently from a lost holograph (and that George's is the more reliable in title and 10). Together they represent the earliest surviving version, varying substantively from *1817* in 6, 7, 9, 10, 17, 19, 23, 29, 31, 37, and 39. The holograph fair copy, with the same title as *1817,* is a revised text that varies from *1817* in 5, 9 (it does, however, read "richly"), 13, 28, 29, 37, and 42. Tom Keats's copy, which has a shortened version of the *1817* title, is closer still to the printed text, differing only in 31 ("wandering" for "wondering" and "are" for "were") and in 43 ("bliss" for "blisses").

1817 is the proper basis for a standard text. Garrod reproduces *1817* exactly except for adding a hyphen in 14, and Allott does not depart substantively.

O come, dearest Emma! the rose is full blown

Written probably in 1815 (the only external evidence, not very helpful, is the presence of the sonnet *O Solitude* on the reverse side of the extant holograph). First published in Forman (1883), II, 211–212. Garrod, p. 542; Allott, pp. 21–22.

We have a holograph fair copy in the Morgan Library (see Steele, *K-SJ,* 1 [1952], 57–63, for identification of Keats's hand and a facsimile of the MS), three transcripts by Woodhouse (*W²* plus two *W³* copies that Garrod designates *w³* and **w³**), a late transcript by one of Woodhouse's clerks (Garrod's *T*), and a transcript by George Keats (in the Keats-Wylie Scrapbook).

There are at least three, and probably four, states of text for this poem. One of them is represented by the Morgan holograph fair copy, which is headed "Song" and has "dearest Emma" in 1, "And the" in 2 and 4, "We will hasten, my Fair, to the opening glades" in 5, "freshening shades" in 6, "There, beauteous Emma" in 11, "So fondly" (the first two words of the line) in 13, "Ah! no" in 15, and "Then why lovely" in 17.

Another is represented by the *W³* transcripts, which derive from a Kirkman copy of the poem in Mary Frogley's album. One of these, Garrod's w^3, with "from Mary Frogley" in shorthand at the end, is untitled and reads "my dear Emma" in 1, "The" in 2 and 4, "Oh! come let us haste to the freshening shades" in 5, "opening glades" in 6, "There, beauteous Emma" in 11, "So softly" in 13, "Yet, no!" in 15, and "Ah! why, dearest" in 17. The other early Woodhouse transcript, Garrod's w^3, with "F" at the end, is headed "To Emma" and has the same substantive text as w^3. One of these was surely copied from the other, but the order is uncertain (see Section II.4). Perhaps the absence of a title in w^3 supports the surmise that it is the earlier.

Subsequently Woodhouse saw a holograph MS with some readings in common with the Morgan fair copy, and he entered variants in w^3 for 1 ("dearest"), 2 and 4 ("And the"), 5 ("opening glades"), 6 ("freshening shades"), 13 ("fondly"), and 17 ("lovely"). He did not note variants for the first five words of 5 or the opening words of 15 or 17, and I think it reasonable to assume that the holograph from which he made his notes was not the Morgan fair copy (even though the Morgan MS at some time or other came into his possession, and was added to the W^3 scrapbook). The text represented by w^3 with the interlined variants is therefore a state differing from those of the two preceding paragraphs just above. Woodhouse copied W^2 from w^3, incorporating the variants for 4 ("And the") and 13 ("fondly"). He also added "Mathews" in shorthand beside the title in W^2, curiously using a large and distinct shorthand symbol for each of the seven letters of the name (in effect, "M-A-T-H-E-W-S") rather than those of the usual abbreviated shorthand form (which would transliterate as "Mthws"). Much later his clerk recopied the poem from W^2.

Still another state is represented by George Keats's untitled transcript, which is addressed not to Emma but to Georgiana Wylie. His text has the same readings as the W^3 transcripts except in 1 ("Georgiana" for "my dear Emma"), 11 ("And there Georgiana" for "There, beauteous Emma"), and 13 ("So fondly" for "So softly"). Forman published the poem in 1883 from George's transcript, adding the title "Stanzas to Miss Wylie."

Unfortunately we do not know which of the versions is the earliest, which is the latest, and, if there were four rather than three states, the order of the two in between. "So softly" in 13 may be earlier than "So fondly" (the change made to avoid the repetition with "softly" later in the same line), but the other variants give no clue as to the order. I should guess—and in this instance it is practically a matter of flipping coins—that the version in Mary Frogley's album represented by the W^3 transcripts is the earliest, and that the lost holograph that Woodhouse saw (if this in fact was a different MS from the Morgan fair copy) is the next version, followed by George Keats's adaptation, and finally the Morgan fair copy. But the order could be exactly the opposite, and I would point out that in my discussion of *Fill for me the brimming bowl,* which exists in a similar group of MSS, I have accepted Finney's suggestion that the Morgan fair copy may be earlier than the others. The only certain relationships are those between w^3, W^2, and the clerk's transcript, and that between George Keats's transcript and the first published text.

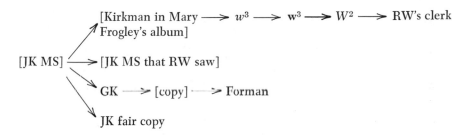

[Kirkman in Mary Frogley's album] → w^3 → w^3 → W^2 → RW's clerk

[JK MS] → [JK MS that RW saw]

GK → [copy] → Forman

JK fair copy

Because their order is so uncertain, each of the different versions has a claim to be the proper basis for a standard text. Garrod follows Forman's wording and generally his accidentals, but restores Woodhouse's title and the W^3-W^2 readings of 1 and 11. Since he retains George Keats's and Forman's "So fondly" in 13 (which also appears in W^2 and the Morgan fair copy), his text is actually closest to that of W^2, from which he varies substantively only in 4 ("The" for W^2's "And the"). Allott bases her text on the Morgan fair copy, but heads the poem "To Emma Mathew" (rather than "Mathews") and prints "Ah" for the holograph's "Then" in 17. Allott's base-text is probably the better choice, although both her title (since Woodhouse knew how to spell Mathew's name, and presumably would have written "Mathew" had he intended his shorthand to refer to one of the Mathew sisters) and her text of 17 are unjustified.

Woman! when I behold thee flippant, vain

Written in 1815 or 1816 (there is no factual evidence for dating; perhaps the best inferential judgments are those of Bate, p. 40 n., and Ward, p. 418, n. 14, who assign the lines to 1815 on the basis of G. F. Mathew's high opinion of them in his *European Magazine* review of *1817*). First published in *1817*. Garrod, pp. 26–27; Allott, pp. 43–44.

There are no extant MSS, and *1817* is our sole source of text. Both Garrod and Allott treat the sonnet-stanzas as three separate poems (like all other nineteenth-century editors, H. B. Forman printed them as a single poem, numbering the lines consecutively, 1 through 42). In the format of *1817* they are clearly presented as stanzas of a single work (cf. especially the headings and arrangement of stanzas of *To Hope* and *Imitation of Spenser,* immediately preceding in *1817*), and should be so regarded by modern editors. Garrod reproduces *1817* exactly except for emending punctuation in the fourth line of the second stanza, and Allott does not depart substantively.

O Solitude! if I must with thee dwell

Written in 1815 or 1816, perhaps in October or November 1815 (almost all writers choose one or the other month, a time shortly after Keats began medical school; but the basis for this dating is rather shaky— mainly J. M. Murry's idea, in *Studies in Keats,* 1930, pp. 1–6, that G. F. Mathew's undated *To a Poetical Friend,* which seems to echo 7–8 of this poem, was written *before* Keats's November 1815 epistle *To George Felton Mathew*). First published in the *Examiner,* 5 May 1816, p. 282 (Keats's first published poem), and then in *1817.* Garrod, pp. 42–43; Allott, pp. 22–23.

In addition to the *Examiner* and *1817* texts, we have a holograph fair copy (Morgan Library, with *O come, dearest Emma* on the reverse side— see Steele, *K-SJ,* 1 [1952], 57–63, for identification of the handwriting and a facsimile of the MS) and a transcript in Tom Keats's copybook. We lack Keats's original draft, his copy sent to the *Examiner,* and his copy made for the *1817* printer. A holograph owned successively by H. F. Lyte, Charlotte Philpotts, and Miss S. Bromley Martin, sold at Sotheby's to A. S. W. Rosenbach on 6 April 1925 and since disappeared, may have been one of these or another fair copy (it was not the extant holograph, which came to the Morgan as part of Woodhouse's scrapbook). The holograph, or a copy of one, that C. C. Clarke sent Milnes in 1846 (*KC,* II, 154) has also not survived.

The four texts are not directly relatable, but can be arranged in chronological order. The Morgan fair copy, which I take to be the earliest, reads "I'd" in 9, "elegant" in 10, and "Pleasure. It certainly" in 12. The *Examiner* text ("To Solitude") has a unique line 9 and beginning of 10 ("Ah! fain would I frequent such scenes with thee; / But . . ."), and *1817* readings in 10 ("innocent") and 12 ("pleasure; and it sure"); the revisions in 9–10 and possibly the others may have been the work of Leigh Hunt. (Woodhouse noted in his copy of *1817* that 9 "was at first written 'Ah fain would I frequent such scenes with thee' "—Sperry, p.

149—but this is surely a wrong assumption based on the *Examiner* text.)
Tom's transcript, which has the Morgan "I'd" in 9 and *1817*'s "innocent"
and "pleasure; and it sure" in 10 and 12, might be thought to precede
the *Examiner* version, but the general evidence that the copybook tran-
scripts were made in late 1816 (see Section II.3) rules out the idea. The
latest version is *1817*'s, which should continue to be the basis for a
standard text.

Garrod reproduces *1817* exactly, and Allott does not depart substan-
tively.

To George Felton Mathew

Written in November 1815 (so dated in *1817*). First published in
1817. Garrod, pp. 28–30; Allott, pp. 24–28.

I have been unable to locate or identify Garrod's "TRANSCRIPT: G. F.
Mathew," from which he records a variant to 68. Except for this, our sole
source of text is *1817*. Garrod adds a hyphen in 9, alters punctuation
in 44, and has tiny errors in 18 (the transposition of a comma and a
quotation mark) and 57 ("Shakespeare" for "Shakspeare"). Allott mis-
takenly prints *1817*'s epigraph for the three Epistles (the lines from
Browne's *Britannia's Pastorals*) as an epigraph specifically for this poem,
but otherwise reproduces *1817* substantively. In his copy of *1817* Wood-
house changed the colon in 89 to a semicolon (Sperry, p. 162).

Had I a man's fair form, then might my sighs

Written in 1815 or 1816 (Finney, I, 97–98, Bate, p. 54 n., Gittings,
John Keats, p. 58 n., and Allott, taking a hint from two Woodhouse notes
connected with *Hadst thou liv'd in days of old*, all suggest that the sonnet
was written as a valentine, perhaps to Mary Frogley, in February 1816).
First published in *1817* (under the heading "To * * * * * *"). Garrod,
p. 40; Allott, pp. 32–33.

Our one extant MS text, the transcript in Tom Keats's copybook, pre-
cedes *1817* but varies from it only in 14 ("incantations," a copying error).
Garrod reproduces *1817* exactly, and Allott does not depart substantively.

Hadst thou liv'd in days of old

Written on or shortly before 14 February 1816 (Woodhouse notes
that the poem was composed for George Keats to send as a valentine to

Mary Frogley, and he saw a copy in George's handwriting that was post-marked 14 February 1816). First published in *1817* (under the heading "To * * * *"). Garrod, pp. 21–23; Allott, pp. 29–32.

In addition to the *1817* text, we have a revised fair copy in Keats's hand (in the Wisbech and Fenland Museum) and four transcripts by Woodhouse (W^2, W^1, and two copies in the Morgan Library that Garrod designates w^3 and W^3).

The first recoverable state of text is that represented by the Woodhouse transcripts, of which w^3 and W^3 are the earliest. The w^3 copy, which has "F" at the end and originally occupied fols. 4 and 5 of the W^2 book of transcripts before it was removed by Woodhouse and transferred to the W^3 scrapbook, has the fullest of Woodhouse's various headnotes: "In page 36 of Keats's poems published in 1817.—are lines, addressed 'to ++++' (Mary).—The published lines were much altered from those originally sent, which were written at the request of Geo: Keats & sent as a Valentine to the Lady in question—The following is a Copy of the original Valentine which is now in the lady's custody—The post-brand bears date the 14 February 1816.—This was one of 3 poetical Valentines written by him at the same time." Each of the other Woodhouse transcripts contains a similar note (see Finney, I, 92–93, who gives the four notes in the order W^3, w^3, W^1, W^2).

For the poem itself, the four transcripts differ substantively among themselves as follows:

	w^3	W^3	W^2	W^1
4	Of	And	Of	And
49	Has	Has	Hath	Has
53	O'er which bend (*a note says that the original had* From the which)	From the which (*in margin*: from which bend)	O'er which bend (*a note says that the original had* O'er the which)	From which bend (*no note*)
57	Moves	Moves (*after deleted* Comes)	Moves (*over deleted* Comes)	Comes
62	Magician's	Magician's (*over deleted* Enchanter's)	Magician's	Enchanter's
63	Enchanter's	Enchanter's	Enchanter's	Magician's

From the progress of changes in Woodhouse's headnotes and the variants given above, it is clear that W^2 was copied from w^3 and that W^1—contrary to what appears to have been Woodhouse's more usual practice of making W^1 copies from W^2—derives from W^3. (I take W^2's 49 to be a copying error, W^1's 53 to be based on the marginal note in W^3, and W^1's 62 and 63 to derive from an error, later corrected, in W^3's 62.) The order of w^3 and W^3 is an open question. One might conjecture that W^3, with a shorter and more considered headnote, is the later of the two, that W^3's 4 is a copying error, and that its 53 is based on Woodhouse's note opposite the text in w^3—but the evidence is very slight, and the reverse order is almost equally arguable (see Section II.4).

$$[\text{JK MS}] \longrightarrow [\text{GK}] \longrightarrow w^3 \begin{cases} W^3 \succ W^1 \\ W^2 \end{cases}$$

Taken as a group, the Woodhouse transcripts vary extensively from *1817* (see Garrod's apparatus for 3–36, 51, 52, 53, 54, 55, 59, 62, 63, 65, 67, and 68).

The second state of text is that of the Wisbech holograph, which I have not been able to examine. This is apparently a revised MS fairly close to the text of *1817*. According to Garrod's notes it has *1817*'s 3–36 (with "never" for "seldom" in 28), "the" for "twin" in 38, "rested" for "nested" in 51 (though Garrod's apparatus, implying that the MS has "rested" in both 51 and 52, may be in error), and "fleur-de-luce's" in 54 (agreeing with the Woodhouse transcripts), and it lacks 65–68.

The *1817* version is the third and latest state, and is of course the proper basis for a standard text. Both Garrod and Allott reproduce *1817* (Garrod exactly except for changing a question mark to a period at the end of 43, and Allott substantively under the title "To Mary Frogley").

I am as brisk

Written probably in 1816 (on the second sheet of the revised holograph MS of *Hadst thou liv'd in days of old*). First published by Garrod in his 1939 edition. Garrod, p. 569; Allott, p. 753.

Keats's MS, in the Wisbech and Fenland Museum, is our sole source of text. I have been unable to check Garrod and Allott, who agree in all details of wording and accidentals.

Give me women, wine, and snuff

Written toward the end of 1815 or during the first half of 1816 (on the cover of a lecture notebook belonging to Henry Stephens, a fellow medical student at Guy's Hospital). First published in H. B. Forman's one-volume *Poetical Works of John Keats* (1884), p. 558. Garrod, p. 554; Allott, pp. 28–29.

The holograph MS is at Trinity College, Cambridge; the version of 1–4 given in *KC,* II, 210 (in an unidentified transcript of an 1847 letter from Stephens to G. F. Mathew), represents a copy of a copy of this MS. Forman printed the lines from the holograph, adding punctuation and making slight changes in spelling. Garrod reproduces Forman's text, and Allott does not depart substantively.

How many bards gild the lapses of time

Written probably in 1816 (Woodhouse's supposed dating of March 1816, however, reported by Ernest de Selincourt in *The Poems of John Keats,* 5th ed., 1926, p. 397, does not appear in Woodhouse's copy of *1817*—see Sperry, pp. 110–111—and it seems unlikely that de Selincourt had access to some other Woodhouse material now lost). First published in *1817.* Garrod, p. 41; Allott, pp. 59–60.

There are no extant MSS of this poem, and *1817* is our sole source of text. Garrod reproduces *1817* exactly, and Allott does not depart substantively.

Specimen of an Induction to a Poem

Written in 1816, probably in the spring sometime after the publication of Hunt's *The Story of Rimini* (in February); a more precise dating is not possible. First published in *1817.* Garrod, pp. 12–13; Allott, pp. 33–36.

The only surviving MS text is the transcript in Tom Keats's copybook, which lacks *1817*'s paragraph or section division between 48 and 49 and varies substantively from *1817* in 8, 9, 10 ("the" for "this" as well as "his" for "its"), 17, 35, 37, 40, 44, 46, 57, and 59. There are lines in the margin beside 1–4, 14, 22–28, 44, 52, 63–68, five check marks at the right beside 17, and a double dagger and a bracket in the left margin beside 18 and a line under "trembling." According to Tom's note at the end of *Calidore,* these marks were made by Leigh Hunt, in 1816. On the relation of this poem to *Calidore* in Tom's copybook see the discussion of the next poem.

1817 is the proper basis for a standard text. Garrod has a misprint ("must" for "muse") in 12, corrects 46 ("steed" for "knight," following Tom's transcript and Keats's correction in several presentation copies of *1817*), and emends the punctuation of 47. Allott also corrects 46.

Calidore: A Fragment

Written in 1816, probably in the spring after the preceding poem. First published in *1817*. Garrod, pp. 14–18; Allott, pp. 36–42.

As with *Specimen of an Induction,* our only MS text is the transcript in Tom Keats's copybook (facsimile of 150–162 in *The Library of the Late George Armour,* Anderson Galleries sale catalogue, New York, 1937, p. 59), in which *Specimen* and *Calidore* are presented as two parts of a single fragmentary work. (All items in the copybook have the author's name at the end except for *Specimen*; all items begin on a new page except for *Calidore*; and Tom's note at the end of *Calidore*, "marked by Leigh Hunt—1816," obviously applies to the whole of *Specimen* and *Calidore*.) The signature at the end of *Calidore* is in Keats's hand (all the others are in Tom's hand). Tom's copy is written continuously from beginning to end—there are no paragraph or section divisions—and varies substantively from *1817* in 6, 8, 10, 16, 28, 29, 38 ("shuttered"), 40, 41, 42, 44 ("window" for "windows" and "its" for "his"), 48, 57, 60, 69, 70, 74 ("along" for "about"), 78, 85, 101, 103, 139, 147, and 158. There are marginal or other markings by Hunt of 2–3, 6–11, 24, 28, 31–32, 34, 40, 42–43, 53–55, 62–63, 65, 68, 77 ("twain" is circled), 79 ("Portcullis" is underlined), 80 ("a Kiss" is underlined), 82–83, 85–86, 88–94, 100–102, 120–123, 138–140, 144–145, and 150–151. Tom's 122, "Tis brave Sir Gondibert the far fame'd," is marked and altered—perhaps also by Hunt, but we cannot be sure—in such a way as to produce *1817*'s " 'Tis the far-fam'd, the brave Sir Gondibert."

1817 is the proper basis for a standard text. Garrod omits *1817*'s paragraph spaces after 33, 37, 41, 45, and 72 (the first four intentionally, though he keeps similar spacings in other poems—e.g., *Sleep and Poetry* after 380, 384, and 388, and *The Eve of St. Mark* after 56, 61, and 66), changes "windows" to "window" in 44 (following Tom's copy), and emends punctuation in 35, 36, 139, and 141. He queries "?his" for "its" in 45, but instead probably should have emended "his" to "its" in 44 (Tom's copy has "its" in both 44 and 45). Allott also omits *1817*'s spaces after 33, 37, 41, 45, and 72, corrects "windows" to "window" in 44, and leaves "his" and "its" in 44 and 45. (The missing space after 72 is a curiosity in the history of Keats's text: H. B. Forman's 1883 edition began a new page with 73, thus losing all record of the division, since *1817* did not indent new paragraphs; and most subsequent texts, including those in Forman's Oxford Standard Authors edition and the Hampstead Keats, have, in following either Forman [1883] or a text deriving from it, inadvertently omitted the space.) In his copy of *1817* Woodhouse inserted "soft" before "affection" in 84—whether an authoritative correction or a suggested improvement is not clear (probably the latter, for the line is metrically short)—and inserted a comma after "they" in 22 (Sperry, pp. 143, 162).

To one who has been long in city pent

Written in June 1816 (so dated in the two earliest transcripts). First published in *1817*. Garrod, p. 44; Allott, pp. 45–46.

In addition to the *1817* text, we have three transcripts—one each by Georgiana Wylie and George Keats, both in the Keats-Wylie Scrapbook (facsimiles in M. B. Forman's article in the *Connoisseur,* 116 [1945], 10–11), and one in Tom Keats's copybook. Georgiana's copy, titled "Sonnet. Written in the Fields June 1816," varies substantively from *1817* in 2, 4, 6, 7, 9, 11, and 14 (it also has "City's" in 1, "of" omitted and later added in pencil in 3, "hearts' " in 5, and "Cloudlets' " in 11, all of which are copying or spelling errors). George's transcript, with "Sonnet" at the beginning and "Written in the Fields—June 1816" at the end, shows the same principal substantive variants. The two MSS represent the earliest known version; since they are quite close in accidentals, I assume that George copied Georgiana's transcript rather than the unknown holograph from which she took her text. Tom Keats copied a revised MS varying from *1817* only in 4.

1817 is the proper basis for a standard text. Both Garrod and Allott correct *1817*'s "hearts"—an error, but probably the reading of Keats's lost MS for the printer—to "heart's" in 5, but otherwise follow *1817* (Garrod exactly). Woodhouse also corrected "hearts" to "heart's" in his interleaved copy of *1817* (Sperry, p. 163).

Oh, how I love, on a fair summer's eve

Written in 1816 (so dated in all six of the transcripts), perhaps in the summer. First published in *1848*, II, 287. Garrod, p. 457; Allott, p. 46.

There are four transcripts by Woodhouse (W^2, W^3, W^1, and a copy in his interleaved *1817*—transcription in Sperry, p. 150), a late copy by one of Woodhouse's clerks (Garrod's *T*), and a copy by Coventry Patmore. The W^2 transcript, which has "F" at the end, signifying that Woodhouse got the poem from a Kirkman copy in Mary Frogley's album, is on fol. 9 of the W^2 book, and is one of the two earliest extant copies. W^3, with "from Mary Frogley" in shorthand at the end and some attempted revisions by Woodhouse in pencil above 9, 12, and 13, is the other earliest transcript. One of these was almost certainly copied from the other, but the overall evidence concerning such duplicates of poems from Mary Frogley's album is ambiguous (see Section II.4). On the basis of general practice elsewhere we can say that W^1 was probably made from W^2, and on the not-very-strong evidence of likenesses in accidentals that the copy in Woodhouse's interleaved *1817* also probably came from W^2. The four Woodhouse transcripts have the same substantive text, except that W^3's "thoughts" (5) appears to have been altered by erasure to "thought."

Woodhouse's clerk copied W^2, and Patmore took his text from the clerk's transcript, omitting "the" (to regularize the meter) in 12. Patmore's MS was printer's copy for *1848*, which followed it in omitting "the."

$$[\text{JK MS}] \longrightarrow \begin{bmatrix}\text{Kirkman in Mary} \\ \text{Frogley's album}\end{bmatrix} \longrightarrow \left\{\begin{array}{l} W^2 \\ \\ W^3 \end{array}\right. \quad \begin{array}{l} \nearrow \text{RW in } 1817 \\ \rightarrow W^1 \\ \searrow \text{RW's clerk} \longrightarrow \text{CP} \longrightarrow 1848 \end{array}$$

Since the authoritativeness of W^3's altered 5 is uncertain, probably W^2 is the safer basis for a standard text. Garrod reproduces *1848* exactly except for restoring "the" in 12. Allott has the same substantive text as Garrod.

To a Friend Who Sent Me Some Roses

Written on 29 June 1816 (the date in Tom Keats's transcript). First published in *1817*. Garrod, p. 41; Allott, pp. 46–47.

The earliest of the three texts we have for this poem is Keats's untitled fair copy in the Morgan Library (facsimile in *Twelfth Year Book . . . The Bibliophile Society,* Boston, 1913, facing p. 75), which begins "As late I wanderd," has "sweet" for *1817*'s "sweets" in 7 and "in" for "on" in 9, and ends (substantively) with the alexandrine printed in *1817*. (Wood-house saw either this MS or another early version, recording in shorthand the variant "wandered" over "rambled" in his interleaved copy of *1817*— Sperry, p. 148.) The transcript in Tom Keats's copybook, titled "To Charles Wells on receiving a bunch of [full blown *deleted*] roses—Son-net," varies from *1817* only in the seven-foot final line, "Whispered of truth, Humanity and Friendliness unquell'd." In the lost MS for the printer of *1817* (or else in proofs) Keats rejected this revised line in favor of the earlier, shorter version in the Morgan MS.

1817 is the proper basis for a standard text. Garrod reproduces *1817* exactly, and Allott does not depart substantively.

Happy is England! I could be content

Written perhaps in 1816 (but there is no real evidence for dating). First published in *1817*. Garrod, p. 50; Allott, pp. 100–101.

The only known MS, Keats's fair copy at Harvard (transcription in Rollins, *HLB,* 6 [1952], 174), has the same wording as *1817*. Garrod reproduces *1817* exactly, and Allott does not depart substantively.

To My Brother George (sonnet)

Written in August 1816 (so dated in George Keats's transcript). First published in *1817*. Garrod, p. 39; Allott, pp. 47–48.

We have, besides the *1817* text, two holograph MSS, both at Harvard —a pencil draft in the so-called Severn pocketbook (facsimile of 1–8 in Parke-Bernet sale catalogue, 4 June 1969) and a fair copy (facsimile in Sotheby sale catalogue, 20 December 1937)—and transcripts by George Keats in the Keats-Wylie Scrapbook and Tom Keats in his copybook. Gar-rod's reference to a W^3 transcript appears to be a mistake (there is none in the Morgan Library, though Woodhouse does quote 1–4 in his notes opposite two transcripts of *Ode to Apollo* ["In thy western halls"], one of which is in the Morgan).

George Keats's transcript, which has readings of the extant original draft in 3, 4 ("That"), and 8, but revised readings in 4 ("from"), 10, and perhaps 13 ("thoughts" may be simply a copying error), is an inter-mediate text between the first draft and the final text, and probably was made from a lost fair copy that Keats wrote and sent to him soon after completing the draft. The later extant holograph was printer's copy for *1817* (there is a "1" between the title and the first line—the poem was

Sonnet I in *1817*—and "53" appearing in the upper righthand corner of the MS is the folio number in Keats's MS for the volume, corresponding to "66" on the latest extant fair copy of *Addressed to the Same* ["Great spirits"], which, as the fourteenth sonnet in *1817,* came thirteen leaves later in the MS). The text of this fair copy is quite close to *1817* in all respects except capitalization. Tom Keats's transcript, which varies substantively only in "curtain" for "curtains" (10), has the same punctuation as the fair copy in twenty out of twenty-three places (the three differences are Tom's omissions), and may have been taken from it.

1817 is the proper basis for a standard text. Garrod reproduces *1817* exactly, and Allott does not depart substantively.

To My Brother George (epistle)

Written in August 1816 (so dated in the extant holograph, George Keats's transcript, and *1817*). First published in *1817*. Garrod, pp. 31–34; Allott, pp. 48–54.

In addition to *1817,* we have Keats's "fair Coppy" sent as a letter (MS at Harvard, text in *Letters,* I, 105–109), and a complete transcript by George Keats and a partial copy by Georgiana Wylie (through "warder" in 31), both in the Keats-Wylie Scrapbook. I have been unable to locate the "second transcript" by George—Garrod's a^2—that H. B. Forman cites for 45 and 77 (Hampstead Keats, I, 58 n., 60 n.) and Garrod cites for 77 and 86.

The earlier of the two known states of text is that of Keats's letter copy, which varies from *1817* in 12, 19, 20, 37, 48, 51, 60, 65, 66, 86, 118, 124, 135, and 139. George's extant transcript and (as far as it goes) Georgiana's partial copy agree with the letter text in all of these; their few variants from the letter—George in 11, 32, 77, and 125, Georgiana in 6 ("lightnings"), 8, and also 11—are not significant, and I think it safe to assume, in spite of their agreement in 11, that both copied the extant letter independently (the two transcripts show many differences from one another in accidentals). The later state is that of *1817,* which should continue to be the basis for a standard text.

Garrod changes *1817*'s "nought" to "naught" in 21 and 32, has a wrong indention in 67, but otherwise follows *1817* exactly, and Allott does not depart substantively. It is possible—but not provable—that *1817*'s "clift" in 124 is a printing error (both the holograph and George's copy read "Cliff").

To Charles Cowden Clarke

Written in September 1816 (so dated in the extant holograph and in *1817*). First published in *1817*. Garrod, pp. 35–38; Allott, pp. 54–59.

The only authoritative MS is the holograph fair copy in the Huntington Library (facsimile in *Books and Letters Collected by William Harris Arnold of New York,* Bangs and Co. sale catalogue, New York, 1901, pp. 105–108); Thomasine Leigh's copy of 1–20 in her commonplace book dated 1 January 1817 was made from an extract quoted in Reynolds' review of *1817* in the *Champion* (9 March 1817, p. 78). The holograph varies substantively from *1817* in 5, 14, 44, 83, 87, 94, 95, 98, 103, 112, and 127. *1817,* set from a later, slightly revised MS now lost, should continue to be the basis for a standard text.

Garrod emends *1817*'s accidentals in 5, 82, 96, and 114, and introduces paragraph or section divisions after 48 and 83 (as in the holograph) but not after 14, where the holograph also has a new paragraph. A word ("a" before "peculiar") is inadvertently omitted from his text in 106. Allott follows Garrod in marking divisions after 48 and 83 (but not after 14); her text has a misprint, "not" for "nor," in 121. For Woodhouse's suggested improvements in wording (94, 97, 110) and punctuation (13, 60, 61, 81, 96) marked in his copy of *1817*, see Sperry, pp. 147, 162.

On First Looking into Chapman's Homer

Written in October 1816 (so dated in the *Examiner*). First published in the *Examiner,* 1 December 1816, pp. 761–762, and then in *1817*. Garrod, p. 45; Allott, pp. 60–62.

We have five sources of text—a holograph MS at Harvard (facsimiles in Lowell, facing I, 180; *K-SJ,* 1 [1952], following p. 60; Bate, p. 87; Ward, following p. 386; and Allott, facing p. 644), a holograph fair copy in the Morgan Library, a transcript in Tom Keats's copybook, and the two early printed versions. The transcript in Mary Strange Mathew's album derives from *1817*; it is an exact copy in all details except for easily explained slips in 6 and 7.

The five texts are not directly relatable, and except for the first and last cannot be chronologically ordered. The earliest is the Harvard MS, "On the first looking into Chapman's Homer," which may well be (as most recent writers have agreed) Keats's first draft, even though it is fairly cleanly written and shows but a single substantive correction ("deep brow'd" for "low brow'd" in 6). It varies substantively from *1817* in 6

("Which"), 7 ("Yet could I never judge what Men could mean"), and 11 ("wond'ring"). The main evidence against its being the first draft is C. C. Clarke's statement that "The original which he sent me had the phrase— 'Yet could I never tell what men could mean' " (*Recollections,* p. 130); but we have no assurance that Clarke's "original" refers to the first draft (there could have been an earlier MS that he knew nothing about) or that he was not simply misremembering the line.

The untitled Morgan MS, on which "To Mariane Reynolds" has been added in another hand (it is surely the "Autograph Verses to Marianne Reynolds . . . 14 lines" in the Towneley Green sale at Sotheby's, 13 May 1901), is a fair copy containing new readings in 6 ("That" for "Which") and 11 ("eagle" for "wond'ring") and what is probably a slip of the pen in 13 ("Look" or possibly "Look' "). Both Tom Keats's transcript ("Sonnet On looking into Chapman's Homer") and the *Examiner* (title as in *1817*) have "But" in 5 and the Morgan readings (except for the Morgan MS's oddity at the beginning of 13) everywhere else. The two texts were probably made about the same time, but there is no way of determining whether they are earlier or later than the Morgan version—I should guess later. *1817,* which should continue to be the basis for a standard text, restores "Oft" in 5, keeps the later readings in 6 and 11, and has an entirely new line 7.

Both Garrod and Allott err in calling the Morgan MS Keats's first draft, but their texts reproduce *1817* correctly (Garrod's exactly). Woodhouse's "of" for "to" (4) in the margin of his copy of *1817* (Sperry, p. 150) is either an explanation or a suggested change, but in any case is not an authoritative reading.

Keen, fitful gusts are whisp'ring here and there

Written in October or November 1816 ("Very shortly after [Keats's] installation at . . . [Leigh Hunt's] cottage," says Clarke, *Recollections,* p. 134; Keats first met Hunt in October). First published in *1817.* Garrod, p. 44; Allott, p. 63.

There are no extant MSS, and *1817* is our sole source of text. Garrod reproduces *1817* exactly, and Allott does not depart substantively.

On Leaving Some Friends at an Early Hour

Written in October or November 1816 ("shortly after" the preceding poem—Clarke, *Recollections,* p. 135). First published in *1817.* Garrod, p. 46; Allott, p. 64.

Our only extant MS is Keats's draft in the Morgan Library (facsimile, according to Hampstead Keats, I, cxiii, in *Illustrated Catalogue of Unique Grangerized Books . . . on Sale by Henry Sotheran & Co.,* 1904; transcription in Hampstead Keats, I, 88–89 n.), which has an early version of *I stood tip-toe* 25–28 and 151–156 on the reverse side. The draft shows much cancellation and revision, but finally produces the *1817* text except in 4, where it has "palm" for "hand." Since the MS contains a note by C. C. Clarke identifying the handwriting as Keats's, it was undoubtedly once in Clarke's possession, and probably he should have been named as the third of the "Friends" in Woodhouse's shorthand explanation above the title in his copy of *1817*—"Reynolds Hunt and [blank] in a hackney coach" (Sperry, p. 150—Woodhouse did not meet Clarke until 1823).

1817 is the proper basis for a standard text. Garrod reproduces *1817* exactly, and Allott does not depart substantively.

To My Brothers

Written on 18 November 1816 (the date in one of Keats's fair copies, Tom Keats's transcript, and *1817*). First published in *1817*. Garrod, p. 43; Allott, pp. 65–66.

In addition to *1817,* we have Keats's pencil draft of 1–8 in the so-called Severn pocketbook (Harvard—facsimiles in Parke-Bernet sale catalogues, 25 April 1945 and 4 June 1969; transcription in Hampstead Keats, I, 81 n.), two fair copies by Keats (both also at Harvard—facsimile of Garrod's H^1 in *The Renowned Library of the Late John A. Spoor,* Parke-Bernet sale catalogue, New York, 1939, Part I, p. 169, and of 1–5 in *K-SJ,* 1 [1952], following p. 60; facsimile of Garrod's H^2 in *Catalogue of the Collection of Autograph Letters and Historical Documents Formed . . . by Alfred Morrison,* III, 1888, 4; transcriptions of both in Rollins, *HLB,* 6 [1952], 161–163), and a transcript in Tom Keats's copybook. Garrod's "MS. in the possession of W. T. Spencer" is the same as his H^2.

The pencil draft is obviously the earliest of the five surviving texts. The order of the two Harvard fair copies, both of which have *1817*'s title, cannot be determined. One of them, dated "Novr 18—" (Garrod's H^1, Rollins, pp. 162–163), has a unique substantive variant in 3 and another variant from *1817* in 13 ("the" for "this"). The other fair copy (Garrod's H^2, Rollins, pp. 161–162), which has the draft of *I stood tip-toe* 231–235 on the reverse side, shows unique variants in 2, 5, and 8, and the same variant from *1817* that H^1 has in 13. (Charles Ollier, one of the publishers of *1817*, wrote at the top of this MS, "1817 This was copy for the press," but he was surely mistaken; I suppose that he saw or rediscovered the MS, glanced at the title and first line, and wrongly assumed that it had been printer's copy.) H^1 is closer than H^2 to *1817*, but since their principal variants are unique in each case it is theoretically possible for either to have been made before the other. Tom Keats's transcript, titled "Sonnet Written to his Brother Tom on his Birthday," is apparently the latest of the MS texts, varying from *1817* only in 14 ("place" for "face," perhaps a copying error).

1817 is the final version, and should continue to be the basis for our standard text. Garrod reproduces *1817* exactly, and Allott does not depart substantively. In his copy of *1817* Woodhouse inserted a comma after "gods" in 3 (Sperry, p. 163).

Addressed to Haydon ("Highmindedness")

Written in 1816 (there is no evidence for a more precise dating, and biographers and editors vary widely in their guesses). First published in *1817*. Garrod, p. 47; Allott, pp. 66–67.

The single extant MS text is a transcript in an unidentified hand at Harvard (the sonnet *Written in Disgust of Vulgar Superstition* is in the same hand on the reverse side). This is titled "High Mindedness" (there is, however, a line through the title) and shows a substantive difference from *1817* in 7 ("Which" for "That"). The source of the transcript is not known, but I should guess that it was made quite late, from some text in Milnes's possession, and perhaps by a professional copyist. It was the basis (either as printer's copy or, more probably, as the source of printer's copy) for the publication of the poem in *Hood's Magazine,* 3 (April 1845), 352, under the heading "Sonnet. By the Late John Keats. (Communicated by R. Monckton Milnes, Esq., M.P.)." None of the six substantive variants in *Hood's* is authoritative: "Adoring kindness" (2), "when" (5), and "sky" (12) are easily seen as misreadings of the transcript; "Which" (7) follows the transcript; and "Dwell" (3) and "So when" (11) appear to be emendations.

1817 should of course be the basis for a standard text. Garrod transposes a comma and a quotation mark in 6, adds a hyphen in 8, but otherwise reproduces *1817* exactly, and Allott does not depart substantively. In his copy of *1817* Woodhouse inserted a comma after "What" in 11 (Sperry, pp. 150, 163).

Addressed to the Same ("Great spirits")

Written on 20 November 1816 (Keats's date at the end of the earliest extant holograph). First published in *1817*. Garrod, p. 48; Allott, pp. 67–69.

For this poem, besides the *1817* text, we have three holograph fair copies (all at Harvard) and a transcript in Tom Keats's copybook. Keats's first copy, in a letter to Haydon of 20 November (*Letters,* I, 117— facsimile following I, 114), varies substantively from *1817* in 9 and 13. His second copy, sent to Haydon on the following day to be forwarded to Wordsworth (*Letters,* I, 118–119), has the same variant in 9 but the *1817* ellipsis in 13 (suggested by Haydon). Tom Keats's transcript ("Sonnet") is substantively identical with *1817*.

Keats's final MS (facsimile in A. S. W. Rosenbach, *Books and Bidders: The Adventures of a Bibliophile,* Boston, 1927, p. 41) was printer's copy for *1817*. It is headed "14"—the poem was Sonnet XIV in *1817*—and "Addressed to the Same," and has "66" in the upper righthand corner, the folio number in Keats's MS for the volume. The presence of "Christ Day" below the text of the poem appears to give us a specific date for part of the copying for the volume: Keats wrote down this poem (and perhaps, if he worked straight through in the order of *1817,* had got as far as the fourteenth sonnet) on 25 December 1816. The text of the MS is substantively the same as *1817*'s ("now" is underlined in 1).

1817 is the proper basis for a standard text. Garrod reproduces *1817* exactly (except that he fails to indent 3), and Allott does not depart substantively.

To G. A. W.

Written in December 1816 (so dated in Tom Keats's transcript). First published in *1817*. Garrod, p. 42; Allott, pp. 98–99.

We have, in addition to *1817,* a holograph fair copy in the Keats-Wylie Scrapbook (Harvard—facsimiles in *Literary Anecdotes of the Nineteenth Century,* ed. W. Robertson Nicoll and Thomas J. Wise, II, 1896, facing p. 281; the *Connoisseur,* 116 [1945], 9; and Sotheby sale catalogues, 23 June 1947 and 21 May 1968), a transcript in Tom Keats's copybook, and a late transcript by Woodhouse's brother W. P. Woodhouse. Garrod's reference to a W^3 transcript appears to be a mistake (there is none in the Morgan Library, and Garrod gives no readings from it).

Keats's fair copy, headed "To Miss Wylie," has the same substantive text as *1817*. Tom Keats's transcript ("Sonnet / To a Lady")—perhaps from a slightly earlier MS, though except in lowercasing several capitals it is very close to the extant holograph—varies only in 13 ("what" for "which"). W. P. Woodhouse's transcript ("Sonnet"), which he presumably took from *1817* or else from some now-lost copy in his brother's possession, has a variant of no significance in 12 ("which" for "what").

1817 is the proper basis for a standard text. Garrod reproduces *1817* exactly except for capitalizing "Grace" in 13 (Keats's MS has the capital), and Allott does not depart substantively.

To Kosciusko

Written in December 1816 (so dated in the *Examiner*). First published in the *Examiner*, 16 February 1817, p. 107, and then in *1817*. Garrod, p. 50; Allott, pp. 99–100.

There are no extant MSS. The *Examiner* reads "Are changed" in 7 and "around" in 8; *1817* has "And changed" in 7 and "and round" in 8. *1817* should be the basis for a standard text, but emendation of some sort is required in 7. In his copy of *1817*—whether authoritatively or as a matter of interpretation—Woodhouse designated "burst" in 6 as a verb and altered "changed" in 7 to "change" (which he also designated as a verb), producing "The names . . . burst . . . And change to harmonies" (Sperry, p. 152). Garrod prints the *Examiner*'s "Are changed" (but otherwise reproduces *1817* exactly), while Allott follows Woodhouse's alteration, omitting the comma after "heroes" in 6.

Sleep and Poetry

Written sometime during October–December 1816 (after meeting Hunt, and before the MS for *1817* was put together). First published in *1817*. Garrod, pp. 51–61; Allott, pp. 69–85.

There are no extant MSS, and *1817* is our sole source of text. Garrod emends *1817*'s punctuation, capitalization, and spelling in 11, 38 (though *1817* does have a hyphen in "up-springs"), 74, 126, 181, 323, 350, and 355, and corrects *1817*'s misprint in 377. He also queries "?smooth" for "sooth" in 180, and records *1876*'s insertion of "me" after "reach" in 274 (the line is metrically short). Allott has substantive errors in 51 ("around" for "round"), 134 ("the" for "a"), 218 ("long" for "lone"), and 222 ("yet" for "ye"), and omits the paragraph spacings after 84 and 154. For Woodhouse's interpretive comments (including the query "cubs" for "clubs" in 234) and some forty additions and changes of punctuation in his copy of *1817*, see Sperry, pp. 152–157, 163–164. (Woodhouse also added half a line to the poem's epigraph; 1 disagree with Sperry's idea, pp. 117–118, 119, that Woodhouse was correcting "a mistake of the printer or some other error.")

I stood tip-toe upon a little hill

Completed in December 1816 (the date at the end of Keats's draft, his fair copy, and Tom Keats's transcript—and see *Letters*, I, 121); possibly begun several months earlier, though the elaborate datings in Ward, pp. 420–421, n. 32, and Gittings, *John Keats*, pp. 70, 77, 92, 93, 106, 109, are too speculative (and Leigh Hunt's statement in *Lord Byron and Some of His Contemporaries*, 2nd ed., 1828, I, 413, that the poem "was suggested to [Keats] by a delightful summer-day, as he stood beside the gate that leads from the Battery on Hampstead Heath into a field by Caen Wood" cannot be based on his own observation, since it refers to a time before he knew Keats personally; Keats could have given him some of these details, but if "delightful summer-day" was inferred from the poem itself then it is of course no help in dating). First published in *1817*. Garrod, pp. 3–11; Allott, pp. 85–96.

There are four known states of text, represented by the original draft (of which somewhat more than half is extant), a holograph fair copy (complete), Tom Keats's transcript, and *1817*. What has survived or been recorded of Keats's draft, which once belonged to C. C. Clarke and was given away by him in fragments of a few lines each, can be listed (with the help of Garrod, pp. lxxxv–lxxxvi) as follows:

1–27	Harvard (facsimiles and transcriptions of 1–5 and 19–23 in *K-SJ*, 10 [1961], 12–13; facsimile of 11–18 in Sotheby sale catalogue, 27 March 1929)
25–28	Morgan Library (transcription in *TLS*, 6 August 1938, p. 519)
28–34	Formerly owned by W. T. Spencer
38–48	Harvard (facsimile in *Scribner's Magazine*, 3 [1888], 299)
53–64	Harvard
70–80	Berg Collection, New York Public Library (transcription in *TLS*, 10 December 1938, p. 786)
81–86	Scottish National Portrait Gallery (transcription in *TLS*, 13 August 1938, p. 531)

87–106   Formerly owned by Stefan Zweig (transcription in *TLS,*
            27 August 1938, p. 555)
107–114   Harvard
116–122   Berg Collection (facsimile in *The Library of Jerome Kern,*
            Anderson Galleries sale catalogue, New York, 1929,
            p. 254; transcriptions in *TLS,* 17 July 1937, p. 528,
            and 10 December 1938, p. 785). Four additional lines
            following 122 are in the Scottish National Portrait Gal-
            lery (transcription in *TLS,* 17 July 1937, p. 528)
123–150   Formerly owned by Stefan Zweig (transcription in *TLS,*
            27 August 1938, p. 555)
151–156   Morgan Library (transcription in *TLS,* 6 August 1938,
            p. 519)
157–173   Owned by Dallas Pratt, of New York
181–195   Owned by Dallas Pratt
215–230   The Free Library of Philadelphia
231–235   Harvard (facsimile in *Catalogue of the Collection of Auto-
            graph Letters and Historical Documents Formed . . . by
            Alfred Morrison,* III, 1888, 4)
231–242   Formerly owned by W. T. Spencer (said by Garrod, p.
            lxxxv, to have been reproduced in the *Sunday Times,*
            12 December 1933 [a Tuesday], and transcribed in a
            John Grant sale catalogue of May 1933; part of this may
            be the same as the preceding item)

Garrod has an excellent note, pp. lxxxiv–lxxxviii, on the relationship of
these fragments and what they reveal about the stages of composition.
The extant fair copy, given by Keats to Haydon (facsimile of 183–226
in Sotheby sale catalogue, 7 June 1937), and Tom Keats's transcript are
both at Harvard (as is W. H. Prideaux's exact copy of the draft version
of 61–64, 111–114, which he sent to Milnes in the 1840's—see *KC,*
II, 219–220).

Since the draft, the fair copy, and Tom Keats's transcript are all dated
December 1816 ("Decr eve 16—" in the fair copy, which I take to mean
"a December evening in 1816"), and we know that Keats was preparing
copy for the printer during this month, the four texts that we have belong
to a very short period. The draft and the fair copy are the earliest of the
four. Tom Keats's transcript, which Garrod knew about but did not col-
late, is headed "Endymion" and contains after the title the lines from
Spenser's *Muiopotmos* that were used on the title page of *1817.* It omits
27–28, marks a new paragraph at 107, and shows substantive variants
from *1817* in 22 ("embower"), 49 ("of" for *1817*'s "from"), 60 ("in"
for "with"), 93 ("would"), 109 ("the mind"—a copying error—for "it
well"), 142 ("winds"), 192 ("the divine" for "thee, divine"), and 224

("To sooth"). (It also, by agreeing with *1817*'s "Homer," answers Garrod's query concerning 217, "?Honor.") Because it is considerably closer in wording to *1817* than the extant fair copy (which varies substantively from *1817* in at least thirty-three lines), we may say that Tom's transcript represents an intermediate text between the fair copy and *1817*. There is a chance that it derives from the same lost MS that was used as printer's copy for *1817,* but we have no way of knowing for sure; it is also not a certainty that the extant fair copy was made directly from the draft. The best we can do in this case is to list the texts in chronological order:

(1) Keats's draft given to Clarke
(2) Keats's fair copy given to Haydon
(3) Tom Keats's transcript based on a lost MS later than the preceding
(4) *1817* (possibly set from the same MS that Tom copied)

1817 is of course the proper basis for a standard text. Garrod corrects *1817* in 22, 39 (*1817* has "brethen"), and 233, and emends punctuation in 94 and 168. He errs in omitting a final period in 176 and in not marking a new paragraph at 181, and departs from his usual practice in printing *1817*'s "Phœbus" as "Phoebus" in 212. Allott has mistakes in 112 ("aye," her systematic spelling for the affirmation, where "ay" meaning "ever" is called for), 129 (perhaps her "stayed" is an erroneous emendation rather than a misprint, though her note gives meanings for "staid"), and 173 ("water" for "watery"); like Garrod she misses *1817*'s paragraph division between 180 and 181. For Woodhouse's half-dozen emendations of punctuation in his copy of *1817*, see Sperry, p. 162.

Written in Disgust of Vulgar Superstition

Written on 22 December 1816 (dated "Sunday Evening Decr 24 1816" in Tom Keats's transcript; the Sunday closest to this date in 1816 was 22 December). First published in *1876,* pp. 58–59. Garrod, p. 532; Allott, p. 97.

We have Keats's untitled draft on the back of an August 1816 letter from George to John and Tom Keats (Harvard—facsimile in *The Renowned Library of the Late John A. Spoor,* Parke-Bernet sale catalogue, New York, 1939, Part I, p. 149) and transcripts by Tom Keats, J. C. Stephens, and an unidentified copyist (Garrod's *T,* also at Harvard— transcriptions of the first three MSS and variants from the last in Rollins, *HLB,* 6 [1952], 167–169).

The first three MSS differ substantively only in 11, where the draft and Stephens' transcript read "going" and Tom Keats has "dying." Because C. C. Clarke told Milnes that Keats wrote the poem "one Sunday morning as I stood by his side" (*KC*, II, 154), possibly Tom's date ("Sunday *Evening*") indicates that Keats revised 11 and Tom copied the poem later on the same day on which it was originally composed—though Clarke's statement comes long after the event, and it is more likely that he was simply misremembering the time of day. Tom gives a title in his transcript ("Sonnet / Written in disgust of vulgar superstition"), and he has added "J Keats / Written in 15 Minutes" at the end of Keats's draft. Stephens, transcribing the draft, which was then in Clarke's possession, also noted "written by J K in 15 minutes" at the end.

The unidentified transcript, with the sonnet *Addressed to Haydon* ("Highmindedness") on the reverse side in the same hand, was probably made by a professional copyist working for Milnes. It is headed "Written on a Sunday Evening," is dated 23 December 1816, and has Tom's "dying" in 11 but also "as" for "ere" in 12. The source of the transcript is unknown; one assumes that it was some now-lost MS in Milnes's possession. It is unlikely (mainly because of the difference in date and the fact that *Addressed to Haydon* is not among Tom's transcripts) that the transcriber worked from Tom's MS. Milnes published the poem in *1876* from a copy of this unidentified transcript. *1876*'s title ("Written on a Summer Evening") and variants in 1 ("toll'd"), 6 ("To some blind"), 8 ("Fond converse"), and 12 ("as") can all be seen as deriving—in every instance but the last by hasty copying or printer's error—from peculiarities of the transcript.

$$\text{JK draft} \begin{cases} \nearrow \text{[revision]} \begin{cases} \nearrow \text{TK} \\ \searrow \end{cases} \\ \searrow \text{JCS} \end{cases} \text{unidentified} \longrightarrow \text{[copy]} \longrightarrow 1876$$
$$\text{transcript}$$

Tom Keats's transcript, with a presumably authoritative title and the revision in 11, is the proper basis for a standard text. Garrod follows this transcript (with "dying"), while Allott takes her title from the transcript but has the draft's "going" in 11.

On the Grasshopper and Cricket

Written on 30 December 1816 (the date on the extant holograph and in *1817*). First published in *1817*. Garrod, p. 49; Allott, pp. 97–98.

Keats's fair copy in the Forster Collection, Victoria and Albert Museum, is titled "On the Grasshopper & the Cricket" but otherwise has the same wording as *1817,* which is the proper basis for a standard text. Garrod reproduces *1817* exactly, and Allott does not depart substantively.

After dark vapours have oppress'd our plains

Written on 31 January 1817 (the date in all five of the transcripts). First published in the *Examiner,* 23 February 1817, p. 124, and then in *1848,* II, 289. Garrod, p. 458; Allott, pp. 101–102.

We have three transcripts by Woodhouse (W^2, W^1, and a copy in his interleaved *1817*—transcription in Sperry, p. 161), a copy by one of his clerks (Garrod's *T*), and a copy by Coventry Patmore. Another transcript by Woodhouse that Severn possessed in 1845 (*KC,* II, 131) has not survived.

There are no substantive differences among the MSS. W^2, "from J.H.R." (i.e., from a holograph that Reynolds had or, much more probably, from a Reynolds copy of a holograph), is almost surely the earliest of the extant transcripts, and the others may be assumed to derive from W^2 (this is questionable only in the case of Woodhouse's transcript in his *1817,* which does, however, have the general appearance—difficult to pin down exactly—of a duplicate rather than an initial copy). One supposes that Keats furnished a MS for the *Examiner,* but we do not know whether this was the same MS that Reynolds had (or copied) or a different one. The *Examiner* text has substantive variants in 5 ("of" for the MSS' "from"), 9 ("The" for "And"), and 12 ("smiling" for "sleeping"), some or all of which may have been the result of Hunt's editing. Patmore's transcript (from the clerk's MS) was printer's copy for *1848,* whose unique variant in 5 ("mouth, relieved" for "month relieving") represents a misreading of Patmore's MS and an alteration made in proofs. (Patmore's "month," just as in the earlier transcripts, can be read as "mouth," but "on" and "ou" in these transcripts everywhere look alike; Garrod's note to the line is misleading and, concerning the *1848* reading, wrong.)

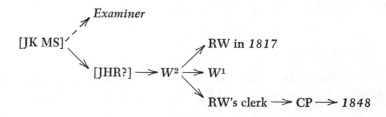

We appear to have two perhaps equally unreliable texts in this instance —that of W^2, probably deriving from a Reynolds copy, and that of the *Examiner*. In the face of ignorance concerning their relative authoritativeness, I suggest that we arbitrarily prefer W^2 as the basis for a standard text. Garrod generally follows *1848* in wording and accidentals, but corrects 5 to "month, relieving" and prefers the *Examiner*'s "The" in 9. Allott's text (from "the transcripts and also *1848*") is similarly a mixture, with "month, relieved of" in 5—combining the *Examiner*'s and transcripts' "month," *1848*'s "relieved," and the *Examiner*'s "of"—and the *Examiner*'s "The" in 9.

To a Young Lady Who Sent Me a Laurel Crown

Written perhaps in 1816 or 1817 (but there is no real evidence for dating). First published in *1848,* II, 288. Garrod, p. 457; Allott, p. 108.

There are two transcripts by Woodhouse (W^2, W^1), a copy by one of his clerks (Garrod's T), and a copy by Coventry Patmore. W^2, "from J.K's M.S." (possibly in the possession of a Reynolds sister, if one of them was the "Young Lady" of the title), is the earliest extant transcript, and the other MSS all derive from W^2. There is one substantive difference among the MSS—W^1 has "own" in 10, while W^2 has "own" altered to "high" (the clerk and Patmore follow W^2 in "high")—and one peculiarity in that all four transcripts have a blank space between "This" and "moment" in 11 into which, in W^1 only, someone has penciled "very." We do not know Woodhouse's authority for the change of "own" to "high" (which he made in W^2 after he had taken the W^1 copy from it), and the handwriting in "very" cannot be certainly identified—it is probably Woodhouse's, but there is an outside chance that it is Keats's. Patmore's transcript (from the clerk's MS) was printer's copy for *1848,* and Milnes added "mighty" in proofs to fill up the blank in 11.

$$[\text{JK MS}] \longrightarrow W^2 \begin{array}{l} \nearrow W^1 \\ \searrow \text{RW's clerk} \longrightarrow \text{CP} \longrightarrow 1848 \end{array}$$

W^2 is the proper basis for a standard text, and probably we should, in the face of ignorance, accept "high" in 10 and adopt W^1's penciled "very" in 11. Garrod reproduces *1848* exactly (except for moving punctuation outside the closing quotation marks in 9 and 11), and thus includes Milnes's "mighty" in 11. Allott does not specify her source, but prints "high" in 10 and "very" in 11.

On Receiving a Laurel Crown from Leigh Hunt

Written at the end of 1816 or early in 1817 (Hunt's sonnet to Keats ending "I see, ev'n now, / Young Keats, a flowering laurel on your brow" is dated 1 December 1816 in a transcript, and his two sonnets on receiving a crown of ivy from Keats are dated 1 March 1817 in the holograph MS; possibly none of these refers to the incident of Keats's poem, but they give an idea of when this sort of activity took place—see Garrod's headnote, p. 2, and Bate, pp. 138–139 n.). First published in *The Times,* 18 May 1914, pp. 9–10. Garrod, p. 529; Allott, p 109.

The single extant MS, a holograph fair copy written in the copy of *1817* that Keats presented to Reynolds (Harvard—facsimiles in *The Times* [above] and in *TLS,* 21 May 1914, p. 242), is our sole source of text. Garrod prints "unmortal" in 4, and Allott "immortal." The word in the MS can be read either way, but critical considerations, plus the fact that Keats used "immortal" in twenty-five or more lines elsewhere but never "unmortal," decidedly favor "immortal."

To the Ladies Who Saw Me Crown'd

Written at the end of 1816 or early in 1817 (dating the same as for the preceding poem). First published in *The Times,* 18 May 1914, pp. 9–10. Garrod, p. 530; Allott, p. 110.

As for the preceding poem, the single extant MS, a holograph fair copy written in the copy of *1817* that Keats presented to Reynolds (Harvard—facsimiles in *The Times* [above] and in *TLS,* 21 May 1914, p. 242), is our sole source of text, and both Garrod and Allott reproduce this substantively.

God of the golden bow

Written at the end of 1816 or early in 1817 (Woodhouse in W^2 says "shortly after" the incident of the two preceding poems). First published in the *Western Messenger,* 1 (June 1836), 763, then in the *Harbinger,* 2 (21 March 1846), 234, and in *1848,* II, 255–256. Garrod, pp. 430–432; Allott, pp. 110–112.

We have two holograph MSS—Keats's original draft at Harvard (transcription in Rollins, *HLB,* 6 [1952], 170–171) and a revised fair copy in the Morgan Library (with *Unfelt, unheard, unseen* written on the first page of the same sheet)—as well as three transcripts by Woodhouse (W^3 —transcription in Finney, I, 203—and W^2, W^1) and a copy by Charlotte Reynolds. Another Woodhouse transcript that Severn possessed in 1845 and a copy that J. F. Clarke sent Milnes in the same year (*KC*, II, 131, 139–140) have not survived.

The two authoritative states of text are, quite simply, those of the two extant holographs. George Keats gave the draft, which he had taken to America, to J. F. Clarke, and Clarke printed the poem in both the *Western Messenger* and the *Harbinger* from this MS (in the *Western Messenger,* but not in the *Harbinger,* changing the draft's "his" to "its" in 30). The later holograph differs from the draft in 6 ("Round" for the draft's "Of"), 11 ("-creeping" for "crawling"), 27 ("Earth" for "the Earth"), and 32 ("for a moment" for "like a Madman"). Neither holograph has a title, and neither numbers the stanzas.

Woodhouse initially transcribed the poem, as he indicates in W^2, "from a M.S. in Keats's writing." The differences between his long explanatory notes in W^3 and W^2 (clearly drafted in W^3 and revised in W^2) are good evidence that W^3 was the first copy made and that W^2 derives from W^3. Both W^3 and W^2 are headed "Ode to Apollo," and both (unlike W^1) have stanza numbers. In November 1818, seeing that J. H. Reynolds had entitled the poem in his copy "a fragment" (*KC*, I, 63), Woodhouse added a final sentence to his headnote in W^3, inserting these words just above the title of the poem: "He [Keats] produced shortly afterw^d the following fragment of an." W^1 (presumably from W^2, even though it lacks stanza numbers) is entitled "Fragment of an Ode to Apollo"; it is possible that Woodhouse originally headed this transcript "Ode to Apollo," and wrote in "Fragment of an" at a later time.

W^2 and Charlotte Reynolds' transcript are substantively identical except for Charlotte's erroneous "thy" for "thou" in 20, and they are very close in accidentals. The likenesses are such that either they were transcribed independently from the same source or else one derives from the other. Since Woodhouse specifies "a M.S. in Keats's writing" as his initial source and there is evidence that he copied W^2 from W^3, and since Charlotte did not transcribe *Unfelt, unheard, unseen* (on the same sheet with the Morgan holograph of *God of the golden bow*), which Woodhouse did transcribe but not in the W^2 book of transcripts, the most probable supposition is that she copied this poem from W^2 (see Section II.5). The three Woodhouse transcripts and Charlotte's copy are substantively the same as the Morgan holograph except for Charlotte's error noted above in 20 and W^2's, W^1's, and Charlotte's "its" for the holograph's and W^3's "his" in 30. If Charlotte did copy W^2, we are free to assume that Woodhouse took his first transcript, W^3, from the Morgan holograph, and then changed "his" to "its" (to agree with "its" in 29) in the course of recopying the poem in W^2 (see also the discussion of *Unfelt, unheard, unseen*).

Though J. F. Clarke had sent him a transcript of Keats's draft in 1845, Milnes apparently printed the poem from some other source now lost (there is no evidence that he had any of the MSS mentioned in the preceding paragraphs). The *1848* text is headed "Hymn to Apollo" but otherwise agrees substantively with that of the Morgan fair copy.

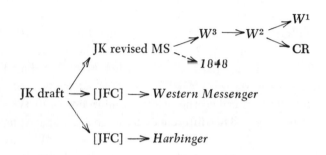

The Morgan fair copy is the proper basis for a standard text. Garrod follows *1848* except in title, where he substitutes Woodhouse's "Ode to Apollo," and in 6 and 11', where he chooses the draft readings "Of" and "crawling." His text, therefore, is a mixture of the two states, with draft readings in 6 and 11, fair copy readings in 27 and 32, and a title from Woodhouse. Allott bases her text on the Morgan MS, but gives a new title, "To Apollo," and (owing to Garrod's faulty apparatus) prints the draft's "Of" in 6.

This pleasant tale is like a little copse

Written in February 1817 (so dated in all six of the MSS). First published in the *Examiner,* 16 March 1817, p. 173, and then in C. C. Clarke's *The Riches of Chaucer* (1835), I, 53, and *1848*, II, 290. The text in the *Morning Chronicle,* 17 March 1817, is a reprint from the *Examiner,* and that in Robert Fletcher Housman's *A Collection of English Sonnets* (1835), p. 190, is a reprint from *The Riches of Chaucer.* Garrod, p. 459; Allott, pp. 103–104.

The extant holograph, written on two facing pages of Volume XII in C. C. Clarke's set of Chaucer's *Poetical Works* (14 vols., Edinburgh, 1782), is in the British Museum. There are transcripts by Woodhouse (two copies, W^2 and W^1), Isabella Towers (with the J. C. Stephens transcripts at Harvard—Garrod's "S" is an error for "St."), one of Woodhouse's clerks (Garrod's *T*), and Coventry Patmore.

C. C. Clarke in several places describes the untitled extant holograph as the original draft (see *KC*, II, 150, 170; Clarke's *The Riches of Chaucer*, I, 52–53; and *Recollections*, p. 139), but the MS is written out perfectly, without deletion or other sign of initial composition, and is more likely to be an early fair copy in spite of Clarke's reiterated account. Clarke's sister Isabella Towers transcribed this MS, including its peculiar "hath" in 9 and "for ever" in 11 (and also an emendation or copying error, "hath" for "has," in 10), under the heading "On Chaucer's 'Floure and the Leafe' written in my brother's Chaucer by the lamented young Poet." Clarke himself published the poem from this holograph in *The Riches of Chaucer*, with the title "Sonnet upon Reading the 'Flower and the Leaf' " and independent emendations or errors in 2 ("so" for "do"), 9 ("charm" for "Power"), and 10 ("hath" for "has"). David M. Main later printed a text from the same MS in *A Treasury of English Sonnets* (Manchester, 1880), p. 417.

Keats presumably provided copy—a slightly revised MS—for the *Examiner* version ("Written on a Blank Space at the End of Chaucer's Tale of 'The Floure and the Lefe' "). The *Examiner* text varies from the extant holograph in 9 ("has" for the MS's "hath") and 11 ("do ever" for "for ever" and also, uniquely, "a thirst" for "athirst"). Woodhouse, who took W^2 from "J.K's M.S." (probably a MS in the possession of Reynolds, who wrote an answering sonnet on 27 February 1817, and very likely the source from which the *Examiner*'s text derives), copied "has" (9) and "do ever" (11) in both W^2 and W^1, querying "?magic" for "power" (10) in the margin of W^2 (and also in the clerk's copy). The W^2 title is "Sonnet. Written on the blank space of a leaf at the end of Chaucer's tale of 'The flowre and the lefe,' " and that in W^1, transcribed from W^2, is "Sonnet Written on a blank space at the end of Chaucer's tale 'The flowre & the lefe.' " The clerk took his text from W^2, and Patmore copied the clerk's MS, changing "do" to "so" in 2. Patmore's transcript was printer's copy for *1848,* which incorporated the miscopied "so."

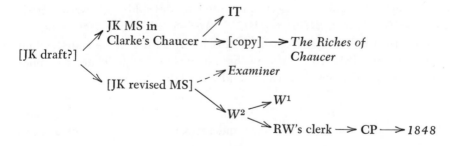

The *Examiner-W²* version, representing a later text than that of the holograph in Clarke's Chaucer, ought to be the basis for a standard text. Probably we should prefer *W²*'s "athirst" in 11, and head the poem by its first line rather than try to identify an authoritative title among the several different headings in the MSS and the *Examiner*. Garrod chooses the *W¹* heading, and for his text alters *1848*'s wording in 2, 9, and 11 (and also omits five of *1848*'s commas) so as to produce the wording of the extant holograph. Allott, similarly preferring *W¹*'s title but otherwise working more directly from the holograph, has the same substantive text as Garrod.

To Leigh Hunt, Esq.

Written in February 1817 (apparently extempore, when the final proof-sheets of *1817* were brought from the printer—see Clarke, *Recollections*, pp. 137–138; the Hunt sonnet of 1 December 1816 that Garrod refers to in his headnote is not an answer to this poem). First published (as the Dedication) in *1817*. Garrod, p. 2; Allott, pp. 102–103.

There are no extant MSS, and *1817* is our sole source of text. Garrod reproduces *1817* exactly, and Allott does not depart substantively. In his copy of *1817* Woodhouse inserted a comma after "voic'd" in 5 (Sperry, p. 162).

On Seeing the Elgin Marbles

Written on 1 or 2 March 1817 (*Letters*, I, 122; in the three earliest printings and the extant holograph—but not in the Woodhouse transcripts or in *1848*—this sonnet follows rather than precedes the next poem, but probably it was the earlier of the two to be written). First published in the *Champion*, 9 March 1817, p. 78, and the *Examiner*, 9 March 1817, p. 155, and then in *Annals of the Fine Arts*, 3 (April 1818), 172, and *1848*, I, 27. Garrod, p. 478; Allott, pp. 104–105.

In addition to the early printings, we have a holograph fair copy written in the copy of *1817* that Keats presented to Reynolds (Harvard—transcription in Rollins, *HLB*, 6 [1952], 165–166), three transcripts by Woodhouse (*W³*, *W²*, and a copy in his interleaved *1817*—transcription in Sperry, pp. 159–160), a copy by Thomasine Leigh in her commonplace book dated 1 January 1817, and a copy by Haydon.

There are no substantive differences among the texts except for the Woodhouse interleaved *1817*'s unique "pleasing" for "gentle" (6) and *1848*'s unique "indescribable" for "undescribable" (10). The extant MS in the presentation copy to Reynolds, a lost MS given to Hunt for the *Examiner* (see *KC,* II, 142), and a lost MS sent to Haydon (*Letters,* I, 122)—all three presumably from the same source, and written about the same time, early in March 1817—were the bases for the early printings in the *Champion,* the *Examiner,* and the *Annals,* respectively. Thomasine Leigh transcribed the poem from the *Champion* (which she followed almost exactly, and which is her source for the accompanying sonnet to Haydon and the first twenty lines of *To Charles Cowden Clarke* also in her commonplace book). Woodhouse took at least one of his texts "from the Examiner," as he notes in W^2; I should guess that W^3 was the first copy made, and that those in his interleaved *1817* and W^2 both derive from W^3 (I have no explanation for "pleasing" in the interleaved *1817*). Haydon made his copy, which he sent to Edward Moxon, Milnes's publisher, in 1845, from the *Annals* (*KC,* II, 141–142). The text in *1848* probably derives from Haydon's transcript.

The foregoing account and my diagram are partly based on the evidence of the relationships among the texts of the next poem, for which we have a similar set of MSS and circumstances but also some significant substantive variants to work with.

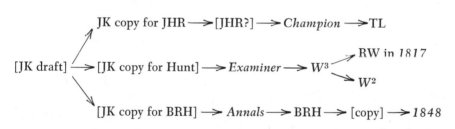

Any of the three earliest known versions—the Harvard MS, the *Examiner,* and the *Annals*—has a claim to be the basis for a standard text. In principle (since there are no substantive variants among them) perhaps the one version that we have in Keats's handwriting should be our choice. Both Garrod and Allott reproduce this text substantively. In accidentals Garrod is closer to the *Examiner* and the *Annals* versions than to any of the others.

To Haydon, with a Sonnet Written on Seeing the Elgin Marbles

Written on 1 or 2 March 1817 (dating the same as for *On Seeing the Elgin Marbles*). First published in the *Champion,* 9 March 1817, p. 78, and the *Examiner,* 9 March 1817, p. 155, and then in *Annals of the Fine*

Arts, 3 (April 1818), 171–172, and *1848,* I, 27–28. Garrod, pp. 478–479; Allott, pp. 105–106.

As for the preceding poem, we have, besides the early printings, a holograph fair copy in Keats's presentation copy of *1817* to Reynolds (Harvard —transcription in Rollins, *HLB,* 6 [1952], 165), three transcripts by Woodhouse (W^3, W^2, and a copy in his interleaved *1817*—transcription in Sperry, p. 160), a copy by Thomasine Leigh in her commonplace book dated 1 January 1817, and a copy by Haydon.

Though there are slight differences in titles, the significant substantive variants before *1848* occur in 1, where the Harvard holograph and the *Champion* have "Forgive me Haydon" (as opposed to "Haydon! forgive me" in the other texts); 7, where the Harvard MS, the *Champion*, and the *Annals* have "sleep" ("steep" in the others); 8, where W^3 and Woodhouse's interleaved *1817* have "might" ("strength" in the others— Woodhouse later penciled "Strength" in the margin of W^3); 11, where the *Champion* has "where" ("when" in the others); and 12, where the Harvard MS and the *Champion* have "o'erweening" ("o'erwise" in the others). Haydon's transcript and *1848* read "of" for "on" in 2, and *1848* shows further variants in 9 ("these" for "those") and 12 ("brainless" for "browless").

Keats made three fair copies early in March—the extant MS in the presentation copy to Reynolds, which was the basis for the *Champion* printing; a lost MS for Hunt, which was the source of the *Examiner* text; and a lost copy for Haydon, which the painter sent on to James Elmes for the *Annals* (*KC,* II, 141–142). The principal variants among them are those listed above for 1 and 12. Though the extant holograph shows, and the *Champion* printed, "sleep" in 7, the word was surely intended to be "steep" (uncrossed "t" misread as "l" is fairly common in Keats's MSS); the word must have looked the same in the lost MS sent to Haydon, for the *Annals* also printed "sleep." The *Champion's* "where" for Keats's "when" in 11 represents another common misreading of Keats's hand.

Thomasine Leigh copied the *Champion* text. Woodhouse transcribed this sonnet and the preceding poem "from the Examiner" (the W^2 note to the earlier applies to both poems). I think that he made W^3 first, with "might" in 8 a slip of the mind rather than of the pen, and then copied the poem into his interleaved *1817* (which also has "might") from W^3. He later realized his error, perhaps from a lost Reynolds copy that he saw in November 1818 (*KC,* I, 63), and penciled "Strength" in the margin of W^3. I take W^2, which reads "strength," to be the latest of the three Woodhouse transcripts. Haydon's copy, which he made from the *Annals* in 1845 for Milnes's publisher, Edward Moxon, was probably the basis for *1848*'s text. *1848*'s "of" in 2 also occurs in Haydon's transcript, and both "these" and "brainless" in 9 and 12 can be seen as misreadings of Haydon's very difficult handwriting. The diagram of relationships for this poem should be the same as that for the preceding.

As with *On Seeing the Elgin Marbles,* each of the three earliest versions —the Harvard holograph, the *Examiner,* and the *Annals*—has a claim to be the basis for a standard text. Here, however, substantive variants are at stake in 1 and 12. Since the second and third of these (*Examiner* and *Annals*) agree against the first, it might be best to follow numerical majority and print "Haydon! forgive me" and "o'erwise" in 1 and 12; if we choose the *Examiner* over the *Annals,* we can avoid having to emend the latter's "sleep" in 7. Garrod, though he takes his title from W^2, reproduces the *Examiner* text exactly except for adding a hyphen in 5. Allott, with a title closer to one of Keats's own, has the same substantive text as Garrod.

On a Leander Which Miss Reynolds, My Kind Friend, Gave Me

Written probably in March 1817 (the extant holograph has "March" at the end followed by a year that is best read as "1817," though the last digit is difficult to make out; Woodhouse took the date to be March 1816, but Keats did not meet the Reynoldses until later in that year). First published in *The Gem* (1829), p. 108, and then in Galignani (1829), p. 71 of the Keats section. Garrod, p. 535; Allott, p. 107.

The extant MSS are a holograph draft at Harvard, two transcripts by Woodhouse (W^2 and another Harvard copy that Garrod refers to as T), and a copy by J. C. Stephens. Woodhouse transcribed W^2 from the Harvard draft, which Keats signed, dated, and apparently gave to the Miss Reynolds of his title. (The poem is followed in W^2 by *Apollo to the Graces,* which Woodhouse took "From the orig¹ in Miss Reynolds's Possession.") W^2 has "sight" in 2, corrected marginally in pencil to "light," where Keats wrote "Light" in such a way that it can be read as "Sight," and Woodhouse's troubles with the beginning of 5—he first wrote and canceled "Gentle," began again with "Are ye so gentle," and finally deleted "Are ye," changed "so" to "So," and inserted another "are ye" after "gentle"— reflect the ambiguity of Keats's MS, which has as a final text "are ye so gentle" but with "so gentle" marked in pencil (either by Keats or by Woodhouse) to come before "are ye." Much later Woodhouse copied the *T* transcript from W^2.

The text in *The Gem* probably also derives from the extant holograph, since the editor of this volume was Thomas Hood, who had married one of the Misses Reynolds, Jane, in 1825. The *Gem* version ("On a Picture of Leander") varies substantively from the altered holograph and Woodhouse's transcripts only in 5 ("As if so gentle" for "So gentle are ye"). Both Stephens (who miscopied "you" for "ye" in 5) and Galignani took their texts from *The Gem*.

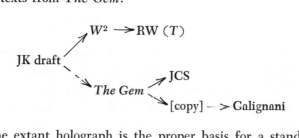

The extant holograph is the proper basis for a standard text, but the correct wording of 5 is still in question, since we cannot finally determine whether it was Keats or Woodhouse who changed "are ye so gentle" to read "so gentle are ye." Garrod takes his title from this MS (adding the word "Gem") but his substantive text and generally his accidentals from *The Gem* (and thus includes the almost certainly corrupt "As if so gentle" in 5). Allott bases her text on Keats's MS, printing "Are ye so gentle" in 5 (disregarding the transposition marked in the holograph—or perhaps unaware of it, since Garrod does not notice it in his apparatus) and punctuating 5–8 as a question. She departs substantively in 2: for the holograph's "Downlooking—aye and" she gives, following *The Gem*'s punctuation, "Down-looking ay, and"; since throughout her edition she makes a spelling distinction between "ay" meaning "ever" and "aye" meaning the affirmative, her text here reads, in effect, "Down-looking ever, and" where Keats intended "Downlooking—yes and."

On "The Story of Rimini"

Written in March 1817 (before the 25th—see *Letters*, I, 127). First published in *1848*, II, 292. Garrod, p. 461; Allott, pp. 106–107.

The extant MSS are a transcript by Brown and two transcripts by Hunt, the earlier written on a blank leaf at the end of a copy of Galignani (1829) and the later on a separate sheet, presumably the copy that Hunt sent Milnes in the 1840's (see *KC*, II, 156). Another Hunt copy, made for Alexander Ireland, has disappeared, but among Milnes's papers at Harvard is a clipping of part of a printed page headed "On Leigh Hunt's

Story of Rimini" and beginning, "We are indebted for the following beau-
tiful sonnet to a friend who possesses it in the handwriting of Leigh Hunt,
with a note at the foot, 'Copied from the manuscript of John Keats by his
ever grateful friend and _____'s humble servant and well wisher,
Leigh Hunt.' We believe that this little gem has not been published; at
all events, we have been unable to find it in any edition of the works of
Keats that we have examined." This is followed by the text of the sonnet,
substantively the same as that of the extant Hunt transcripts. Someone
has added a caret under the long printed dash and written "Alexander
Ireland's" in the margin. Though I have been unable to identify the book
from which this page was clipped, I do not think it predates *1848*.

According to Hunt's inscription at the end of his transcript in the
Galignani edition, the poem was "Written [i.e., either drafted or copied]
by Keats in a blank page of the 'presentation-copy' of his first volume of
poems." Presumably all of Hunt's transcripts derive from this lost MS.
Brown's transcript, which was printer's copy for *1848* (Milnes inserting
"Leigh Hunt's Poem" in the title on the MS), may have come from an
unknown Keats MS but more likely derives either from the holograph that
Hunt possessed or from another copy by Hunt (who was a close friend of
Brown's for many years in both England and Italy). In any event, there
are no substantive differences among the MSS, and one is free to follow
whichever transcript he wishes (in principle I think we should prefer one
of Hunt's to Brown's in this case, since Brown may have copied a Hunt
copy).

Except in restoring the transcripts' heading, Garrod reproduces *1848*
exactly, and Allott does not vary substantively.

On the Sea

Written probably on 17 April 1817 (the date on which Keats included
the poem in a letter to J. H. Reynolds; since the original MS of the letter
is lost, there is no sure basis for determining whether its text was a draft
or a fair copy, though Woodhouse's note that "O Sea" was "obliterated"
before the first line—see *Letters*, I, 132 and n.—may constitute some
slight evidence that the letter version was a draft). First published in the
Champion, 17 August 1817, p. 261, and then in *1848*, II, 291. Garrod,
p. 460; Allott, pp. 112–113.

Though lacking a holograph, we have eight transcripts of the poem—
four by Woodhouse (W^3, W^2, W^1, and a copy in his interleaved *1817*—
transcription in Sperry, pp. 158–159, and facsimile facing p. 129), two

by Woodhouse's clerks (one of them in a letterbook transcript of the letter to Reynolds—text in *Letters*, I, 132—the other Garrod's *T*), and one each by Charlotte Reynolds and Coventry Patmore. A fifth transcript by Woodhouse that Severn possessed in 1845 (*KC*, II, 131) has not survived. An unidentified transcript in Isabella Towers' copy of *1817*—in 1932 owned by Douglas Cleverdon, of Bristol, and since disappeared—almost surely derives from *1848* and can be ignored (see the second paragraph under *Blue! 'Tis the life of heaven*). The lost copy sent by Taylor to Hessey in 1853 (*KC,* II, 314–315) probably also derives from *1848*.

There are two basic texts—the earlier that of Keats's letter and the later that of the *Champion*—and Woodhouse's transcripts show a gradual progress of change from readings of the second to readings of the first. The *Champion* text differs from the letter (in the clerk's letterbook transcript) in 7 ("Be lightly moved, from where" for the letter's "Be moved for days from whence"), 9 ("Ye, that" for "O ye who"), 11 ("Or are your hearts disturb'd" for "O ye whose Ears are dinned"), and 14 (the *Champion* inadvertently omits "if"). Apparently Woodhouse first copied the poem from the *Champion* in his interleaved *1817,* and then transcribed W^3 from the interleaved *1817*. Both transcripts vary from the *Champion* in 9, where Woodhouse wrote "Oh ye" to fill out the meter; in 12, where he mistakenly wrote "with too much" for "too much with," later correcting both transcripts in pencil; and in 14, where he restored the missing "if." In 11 he wrote "clamour" for "uproar" in W^3, and it is on this unique variant in W^3 that the suggested priority of the interleaved *1817* transcript is based: Woodhouse could not have copied the correct "uproar" in his *1817* from the incorrect "clamour" in W^3. Subsequently Woodhouse saw another copy—either the lost transcript in "Reynolds's volume of Poetry" (see *KC*, I, 63), which Reynolds would have taken from Keats's letter, or else the letter itself, which Woodhouse at one time had and gave his clerk to finish transcribing in the letterbook—and he marked both the interleaved *1817* and W^3 with corrections and variants according to the letter text in 7, 11, and 12 (in the interleaved *1817,* however, leaving "hearts" uncorrected in 11, and in both transcripts leaving "where" and "that" unchanged in 7 and 9).

Woodhouse could have copied W^2 directly from the letter (or possibly from his clerk's letterbook transcript), but also could have taken W^2 from W^3, incorporating the variants marked there for 7, 11, and 12. W^2 agrees with the letter in "who" for the other texts' "that" in 9, but also agrees with the other texts' "where" against the letter transcript's "whence" in 7. Because W^2 has, like W^3, "Augt 1817. / Champion" at the end, and also because in W^2 Woodhouse first wrote "with too much," as originally in W^3, before correcting it currently to "too much with," I prefer to think that W^2 came from W^3. Charlotte Reynolds probably copied W^2 (her transcript and W^2 are strikingly close in minor details), and Woodhouse certainly took W^1 from W^2. Woodhouse's other clerk much later made a transcript from W^2, Patmore transcribed this clerk's copy, and Patmore's MS was printer's copy for *1848*. Though several removes from the earliest known version, *1848* varies substantively from Keats's letter text only in "where" for "whence" in 7.

$$
\begin{array}{l}
\text{Cham-} \rightarrow \text{RW in} \rightarrow W^3 \rightarrow W^2 \nearrow W^1 \\
\quad \nearrow \text{pion} \qquad 1817 \qquad\quad \searrow \text{CR} \\
\text{[JK} \longrightarrow \text{[JK let-} \qquad\qquad\qquad \text{RW's} \rightarrow \text{CP} \rightarrow 1848 \\
\text{draft?]} \quad \text{ter copy]} \qquad\qquad\qquad \text{clerk } (T) \\
\qquad\qquad\qquad \searrow \\
\qquad\qquad \text{RW's clerk (letterbook)}
\end{array}
$$

The main unsettled question in the text of this poem has to do with the source—and therefore the authoritativeness—of the *Champion*'s wording. If Keats supplied a revised MS for the periodical, then the *Champion*'s version should be the basis for a standard text. But if, as I have implied in the diagram above, the *Champion*'s readings in 7, 9 ("that"), and 11 are the result of Reynolds' revisions or editorial tinkering with the text that Keats sent him in the letter (I take the *Champion*'s omissions in 9 and 14 to be copying or printer's errors), then the letter (via the clerk's letterbook transcript) is the only wholly authoritative text. In the absence of better evidence I suggest that the letter version should be our choice. Garrod reproduces *1848* exactly, and Allott follows the same source substantively. Both therefore agree with the wording of the letter text except in "where" for "whence" in 7, the one reading of the *Champion* version that survived uncorrected in Woodhouse's succession of transcripts.

Unfelt, unheard, unseen

Written in 1817 (before 17 August, when Reynolds quoted part of a line in the *Champion*; the two transcripts are dated 1817). First published in *1848*, II, 258. Garrod, pp. 433–434; Allott, pp. 114–115.

We have two holograph MSS—the original draft in the British Museum (facsimile in *The Letters and Poems of John Keats*, ed. J. G. Speed, New

York, 1883, facing II, xxx) and a fair copy in the Morgan Library—and transcripts by Woodhouse (W^3) and C. C. Clarke.

After the first draft (which varies from the fair copy in 3 and 15), the MSS are substantively identical. Both Woodhouse and Clarke could have independently transcribed the Morgan MS, but we have no clear indications concerning their sources. Keats's fair copy of *God of the golden bow* follows on the last three pages of the Morgan MS containing this poem, and the W^3 transcripts of both of these have a peculiarity in common— Woodhouse underlined the stanza numbers that he added in each. In all of Woodhouse's transcripts, only one other text has lines under the stanza numbers (the W^3 copy of "Daisy's Song" in *Extracts from an Opera*). On this slight evidence one might suppose that he copied *Unfelt, unheard, unseen* and *God of the golden bow* at the same time, and, since they are together in the Morgan MS, from this single source. Clarke's transcript was printer's copy for *1848*. Milnes added the heading "Lines" at the top of Clarke's MS, and "nor" (12) was changed to "and" in the course of printing.

The Morgan fair copy is the proper basis for a standard text. Garrod reproduces *1848*, but restores Keats's "nor" in 12. Allott, following the Morgan MS, has the same substantive text as Garrod.

Hither, hither, love

Written perhaps in 1817 or 1818 (there is no external evidence for dating). First published in the *Ladies' Companion*, 7 (August 1837), 187. The text in the *Ladies' Pocket Magazine,* Part I (1838), pp. 229–230, is a reprint from the *Ladies' Companion*. Garrod, pp. 541–542; Allott, pp. 115–116.

The single extant MS is a generally unpunctuated holograph at Yale (facsimile in Anderson Galleries sale catalogue, 2–3 May 1934). In printing the poem in the *Ladies' Companion,* J. H. Payne described his source as "one of these unpremeditated effusions, in the handwriting of John Keats, just scribbled as if playing with his pen, in lines sometimes crooked, sometimes straight, and sometimes with a row of words blurred out with his finger, before the ink was dry. . . . His brother gave [the MS] to me as unpublished." Though the lines in the Yale holograph are "sometimes crooked, sometimes straight," there are no such blurrings as Payne comments on, and this fact led H. B. Forman (Hampstead Keats, IV, 37–38 n.) to the conclusion that Payne's MS was a now-lost first draft and the Yale MS a fair copy. Possibly Payne was exaggerating. In any event, his text and that of the extant MS are substantively identical throughout.

Garrod generally follows the punctuation of Payne's text, but prints "hath" in 22 for Payne's and the Yale MS's "has." Allott, who does not specify her source, has the same substantive text as Garrod.

You say you love, but with a voice

Written perhaps in 1817 or 1818 (there is no external evidence for dating). First published by Colvin in *TLS*, 16 April 1914, p. 181. Garrod, pp. 545–546; Allott, pp. 113–114.

The extant MSS are transcripts by Charlotte Reynolds, Woodhouse (W^2), and John Taylor (Garrod's W^3). Charlotte Reynolds' source is unknown, but was presumably either a lost holograph given to her or someone else in the Reynolds family or a copy of one. Woodhouse's transcript, which has two shorthand notations at the end, "from Miss Reynolds" in ink followed by "and Mrs. Jones" in pencil, is substantively identical with Charlotte's copy, and has, like hers, the heading "Stanzas." It is a fair assumption that he took his text from her album, although the preceding poem in W^2, *Apollo to the Graces,* is "From the orig^l in Miss Reynolds's Possession."

Taylor's untitled copy differs substantively from the other two in 3 ("Vesper" for Charlotte's and Woodhouse's "vespers"), 6 ("then you" for "with a"), 10 (the line is omitted), and 22 ("would" for "should"). Woodhouse saw this transcript, penciled its variants in 3, 6, and 22 into W^2 (he also recorded Taylor's dash after "statue's" in 18), and at the same time entered the W^2 readings for these same three lines in pencil on Taylor's transcript. His shorthand addition "and Mrs. Jones" obviously refers to Taylor's transcript, and may be taken to indicate that Taylor's copy derives from a MS in the possession of Isabella Jones, a close friend of Taylor's. My diagram is perhaps too speculative concerning Charlotte's and Taylor's sources, at least one of which could have been Keats's original draft, and is quite arbitrary concerning the chronological relationship between the two hypothesized Keats copies.

```
                        [JK copy for one ──➤ CR ──➤ W²
                      ↗ of the Reynoldses]
     [JK draft?] ⟨
                      ↘ [JK copy for Isa- ──➤ JT
                        bella Jones]
```

We do not know whether Charlotte Reynolds' or Taylor's source is the earlier, and theoretically either of their transcripts could be the basis for a standard text. Charlotte's MS, however, may represent the more accurate copying, whether by her or in her source (Taylor's omission of 10 is evidence of carelessness somewhere along the line). I think hers is the better choice. Colvin printed the poem from W^2, erring in "to" for "for" (the reading of all MSS) in 19. Garrod has Colvin's wording and accidentals apparently by way of one of H. B. Forman's editions. Allott's text, "from *Woodhouse* 3," by which she means Taylor's transcript, seemingly derives from Garrod's edition, since she also has "to" in 19 and, of Taylor's distinctive readings in 3, 6, and 22, includes in her text only that for 6, which happens to be the one variant from Taylor's MS that Garrod gives in his apparatus. Like Forman, both Garrod and Allott supply stanza numbers (there are none in the MSS or in Colvin's text).

Before he went to live with owls and bats

Written perhaps in 1817 ("circa 1817" in Brown's transcript; a more precise dating is not possible). First published in *Literary Anecdotes of the Nineteenth Century,* ed. W. Robertson Nicoll and Thomas J. Wise, II (1896), 277–278. Garrod, p. 533; Allott, pp. 288–290.

We have Keats's draft in the Huntington Library and transcripts by Brown and J. C. Stephens. Garrod's references to a W^3 transcript, from which he purports to give several readings but none differing from those that he records for Stephens' copy, appear to be a mistake (there is no transcript of the poem in the Morgan Library).

Brown's heading, "Sonnet (circa 1817)," suggests that this may be one of the poems that he "rummaged up" in April 1819 (see *Letters,* II, 104). His transcript, presumably from some lost revised MS, varies substantively from Keats's untitled draft in 1 ("live" for the draft's "feed"), 3 ("a Housewife's" for "an Husif's"), 6 ("did straightway" for "soon did"), 7 ("I do" for "he did"), 8 ("Your . . . your" for "His . . . his"), 10 ("valiant" for "worthy"), and 14 ("drawling" for "belching"). Possibly Keats made these extensive revisions at the time Brown transcribed the poem.

Stephens copied the extant draft (then in the possession of C. C. Clarke —see *KC,* II, 154); his two substantive variants, "pluck away" in 6 for the draft's "pluck" (with "way" in "straightway" left undeleted in the draft) and "Most" in 11 for "Of" (originally "Most" in the draft), are easily seen as misreadings of the Huntington holograph. Nicoll and Wise published the poem (including these variants) from Stephens' transcript, which at the time belonged to H. B. Forman.

```
                 ↗ [JK revision] —→ CB
JK draft ↙‾↖
                 ↘ JCS —→ [copy] —→ Nicoll and Wise
```

Brown's transcript, representing a revised version that has to be considered authoritative, is the proper basis for a standard text. Garrod's text, headed "Nebuchadnezzar's Dream" (a title that he mistakenly attributes to Brown), combines substantive readings from the draft in 1, 3, and 6 with readings from Brown's transcript in 7, 8, 10, and 14; there is an unusually high proportion of errors in his apparatus. Allott, taking her title from Garrod and her text supposedly from Keats's draft, actually produces even more of a hodgepodge, with readings not only from the draft but from Brown ("housewife's" in 3), from Stephens ("pluck away" in 6), and from Garrod's erroneous apparatus ("The" in 8, which is said to be in "*St.W³*" but apparently is simply a misreading of Stephens' "His," and "the" again in 13, another nonexistent reading).

The Gothic looks solemn

Written probably in September 1817 (either drafted or copied in a lost letter to Reynolds from Oxford, where Keats visited from about 3 September to 5 October). First published in Forman (1883), IV, 74 n. Garrod, pp. 554–555; Allott, pp. 284–285.

We have two transcripts by Woodhouse (*W²*, *W¹*—the *W²* version in *Letters,* I, 152) and the text of a lost copy sent by Brown to Henry Snook in March 1820 (the source of the first publication of the lines by Forman). Woodhouse's transcripts, headed "Lines— / Rhymed in a letter to J.H.R. from Oxford" (*W²*) and "Lines / Rhymed in a letter received (by J.H.R.) from Oxford" (*W¹*), have the same substantive text, and both quote a couple of introductory sentences from the lost letter. Woodhouse may have taken *W²* directly from the letter (and *W¹* from *W²*), but, since he did not include the letter itself among his letterbook transcripts, there is a good chance that he never actually saw it, and that he transcribed the poem and the introductory sentences instead from some other source, perhaps a lost copy made by Reynolds. Brown, who provides the title "On Oxford," transcribed some MS copy that he discovered among Keats's papers. His text differs substantively from Woodhouse's in 6 ("Stands" for Woodhouse's "Lives"), 8 ("faces" for "visages"), and 9 ("tassell'd . . . and" for "tassel . . . or").

$$[\text{JK in letter to JHR}]\underset{\searrow}{\overset{\nearrow}{}}\begin{array}{l}[\text{JHR?}]\longrightarrow W^2 \longrightarrow W^1 \\ [\text{JK revision}]\longrightarrow [\text{CB}]\longrightarrow [\text{copy}]\longrightarrow \text{Forman}\end{array}$$

Brown's text, presumably from a slightly revised holograph copy that Keats thought worth keeping, ought to be the basis for a standard text, though probably we should ignore his title, which does not sound authoritative. Garrod initially takes his text (and accidentals) from Forman, adds the title given in W^1, emends 8 and 9 according to W^2 and W^1, but retains the Brown-Forman "Stands" in 6 (he also omits the accent in "Vicè," 7). Allott, with a shortened version of the Woodhouse headings and "Text from K.'s letter," by which she means W^2 or W^1, actually has the same substantive text as Brown-Forman—that is, she chooses the better text, and merely errs in her statement of source.

O grant that like to Peter I

There is no evidence for dating. First published in *The Poems & Verses of John Keats,* ed. J. M. Murry (1930), II, 592. Garrod, pp. 568–569; Allott, p. 753.

Keats's MS at Harvard, our only source of text, consists of two quatrains, the second differing from the first in substituting "Old Jonah" for "This Peter" in 4. Pretty clearly the second quatrain is a revised version of the first (in the first Keats originally wrote "be" and "why" for "B" and "Y"). Murry and Garrod (the latter supplying punctuation) reproduce both quatrains, and Allott the second.

Think not of it, sweet one, so

Written about 11 November 1817 ("Ab^t 11 Novr 1817" in W^3, W^2, and W^1; "Nov 11. 1817" in Charlotte Reynolds' transcript). First published in *1848,* II, 257. Garrod, pp. 432–433; Allott, pp. 285–286.

Keats's original draft is in the Morgan Library (transcription in Finney, I, 229–230), and we have four transcripts by Woodhouse (W^3, W^2, W^1, and a copy in his interleaved *1818*), a transcript by Charlotte Reynolds, and one by C. C. Clarke (transcription at the beginning of Section I, above).

Of the two authoritative states of text among the MSS, the earlier is that represented by the extant draft, which Keats wrote on the last leaf of the original MS of *Endymion* (it was still with the *Endymion* MS when

Reynolds lent it to Milnes in 1847—see *KC,* II, 228), and the later is
that of a now-lost holograph copy "for a Lady" (see Clarke's note below),
probably one of the Reynolds sisters. The first three Woodhouse tran-
scripts and Charlotte Reynolds' copy—which do not vary substantively
among themselves except for the lack of a heading in W^3—all derive from
this lost holograph, and together represent the later state of text. Apart
from title (W^2, W^1, and Charlotte's transcript have "To _____" while the
draft is untitled), these transcripts differ from the draft in 3 ("but" for
the draft's "and"), 14 ("hill" for "rill"), and 19 ("Let" for "E'en let").
Woodhouse specifies his initial source for the poem in a note in W^2—
"from JK's M.S." Since W^3, W^2, and W^1 are virtually identical we cannot
be certain of the relationships among them, but Woodhouse's practices
elsewhere suggest that W^3 (the transcript lacking a title) is the copy made
directly from the lost holograph, that W^2 was taken from W^3, and W^1
from W^2. Charlotte Reynolds almost surely copied W^2 (see Section II.5).

At some later time, when he saw and noted variants from the MS of
Endymion in his interleaved *1818,* Woodhouse made at the end of his
book an exact copy of Keats's draft of the present poem, including all
canceled words and interlineations. He also entered a record of some of
these cancellations and variants—those for 3, 7, 8, 11, and 18—in W^2,
initially writing all but the first and last in shorthand and then rewriting
them in longhand. Still later he made a now-lost copy for C. C. Clarke,
with the main text in black ink and some canceled draft readings noted
in red ink. From this lost copy by Woodhouse, Clarke wrote out a tran-
script for Milnes, heading it "On . . . ." and dating it "Ap^l 1817"
(either Clarke's misreading of Woodhouse's "Ab^t . . . 1817" or else Wood-
house's own error—the position of the draft at the end of the *Endymion*
MS confirms the November dating).

Clarke included Woodhouse's canceled draft readings for 7, 8, 11, and
18 in parentheses at the right of his text, and he explains in a note at the
end of the transcript:

Woodhouse, who gave me the above, subjoined the following note:—"I rather
think the poem was originally written as altered: and in transcribing it *for a
Lady* (!) (from whom I had the copy, as given in black ink)—(W. made the
alterations in *red* ink) Keats probably altered it from its first form. The altera-
tion in the 3^d Stanza [i.e., the canceled first version of 11, "For each will I
invent a bliss"] is clearly either the original thought, or a very great improve-
ment. So in Stanza 2." C C C.

While Clarke's transcript has in marginal parentheses four of the five can-
celed draft readings that Woodhouse had entered in W^2, and the lost holo-

graph's and W^2's "Let" in 19, it also has "and" in its text in 3 and "rill" in 14, two distinctive draft readings that Woodhouse incorporated in his copy in the interleaved *1818*. The "and" in 3 could have come from Woodhouse's marginal variant in W^2, but not "rill," which does not appear in W^2 at all. One has to suppose that Woodhouse made his copy for Clarke from the interleaved *1818*, but that he may also have consulted W^2 at the same time.

Milnes used Clarke's transcript as printer's copy for *1848*. In preparing the MS he marked out the parenthetical canceled draft readings for 0 and 10 and the revised readings in Clarke's text for 7 and 11 (leaving the canceled draft readings to be printed); he also changed "tenderer" (16) to "more tender" on the MS. As printed from Clarke's MS thus marked, the *1848* text has canceled draft readings in 7 and 11, distinctive uncanceled draft readings in 3 and 14, a reading of the lost revised MS in 19, and Milnes's alteration in 16.

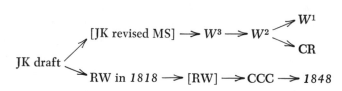

W^3, probably the only extant transcript made directly from the lost revised holograph, has the best claim to be the basis for a standard text. Garrod initially takes his wording and accidentals from *1848*, but incorporates the draft's and the transcripts' readings in 7, 11, and 16, and the draft's reading of 19, thus ending up with the substantive text of Keats's draft. In restoring the draft's and the transcripts' version of 7 (the MSS generally read "Shed one drop then—It is gone"), he punctuates in such a way as to change the syntax—"Shed one drop, then it is gone." Allott, presumably working more directly from the draft MS, has the same substantive text as Garrod, including his punctuation of 7. Garrod's procedure and Allott's choice of a base-text may both seem a little odd, since the two editors do not usually prefer an original draft to a known revised state of text.

Endymion: A Poetic Romance

Begun toward the end of April 1817 (*Letters,* I, 134, 139) and first completed in draft form on 28 November 1817 (the date at the end of the original MS, as recorded by Woodhouse in his interleaved *1818*); revised and recopied in January–March 1818 (see *Letters,* I, 196, 201–202, 206–207, 212, 226, 239, 246, 253). First published (toward the end of April) in *1818.* Garrod, pp. 63–188; Allott, pp. 116–284.

Keats's original draft, of which Books II–IV were still extant in 1847, when Reynolds lent the MS to Milnes (*KC,* II, 227), has not survived, but we have Woodhouse's elaborate notation of variants and cancellations in the draft of II–IV in his interleaved copy of *1818* now in the Berg Collection, New York Public Library. (The first draft of Book I apparently was disposed of earlier, separately from the rest, and there is no record of it.) Keats's revised fair copy for the printer of *1818* is in the Morgan Library.

In addition to these basic materials, we have four letters of late 1817 in which Keats copied passages from Book IV (from the draft MS, but with a few otherwise unknown substantive variants)—to Benjamin Bailey, 28 October, quoting 1–29 (MS at Harvard, text in *Letters,* I, 172–173), to Jane Reynolds, 31 October, quoting 146–181 (Yale, *Letters,* I, 176–177), to Bailey, 3 November, again quoting 146–181 (Harvard, *Letters,* I, 181–182), and to J. H. Reynolds, 22 November, quoting 581–590 (surviving in a letterbook transcript by one of Woodhouse's clerks, *Letters,* I, 189–190)—and three important letters of 1818 to John Taylor giving the revised text of I.777–781 (30 January, *Letters,* I, 218–219), discussing the proofs of Book I (27 February, *Letters,* I, 238–239), and commenting on an advance copy of the book and including a list of errata (24 April, *Letters,* I, 270–273—all three letter MSS are in the Morgan Library, and Woodhouse made transcripts of the three in his letterbook). There is a copy of *1818* with various corrections in an unidentified hand in the Tulane University Library (see Robert H. Swennes, *K-SJ,* 20 [1971], 14–17; Swennes, following H. B. Forman and Garrod, takes the corrections to be Keats's, and they closely correspond to the errata that Keats sent Taylor on 24 April 1818—but they are probably in Taylor's hand, and certainly are not in Keats's). Hunt's copy, with a number of corrections in another unidentified hand, is at Keats House, Hampstead (as is Dilke's copy, which, however, contains only corrections from the errata published in the second issue of the book). Charles Wells's copy, at Harvard, has alterations in still another unknown hand to I.348 ("waves" for "ways") and II.386 ("Crouch'd slumb'ring" for "a slumbering") as well as corrections from the published errata. Woodhouse, before he saw the draft MS in the possession of Reynolds, made several pages of notes at the end of W^2 giving cancellations and variant readings in Keats's fair copy (these notes of course are not of much importance since we have the fair copy MS itself), and he also transcribed Keats's rejected preface to the poem. The holograph MS of that original preface is in the Morgan Library.

There are several peculiarities about some of these additional materials that deserve mention in a paragraph simply as a help (or complication) for future study of the text. For one, Woodhouse does not generally distinguish, in the notes in his interleaved *1818,* between (1) canceled readings in Keats's lost draft, (2) uncanceled readings in the draft that vary from *1818,* (3) canceled readings in the extant fair copy MS, (4) uncanceled readings in the fair copy that vary from *1818,* and (5) notations that represent his own corrections or suggested revisions of *1818.* Because the fair copy MS is available we can identify those in categories (3) and (4), but the status of the others is not always certain, and Garrod's readings from Woodhouse (*D* [for "draft"] in his apparatus), which he took from H. B. Forman's notes, have to be considered with some caution. For another, there is the problem of the relationship between the markings in the Tulane *1818* and the errata that Keats sent Taylor on 24 April, which call for the same alterations in most instances and yet do not always match. Whatever their connection, it is perhaps curious that the Tulane *1818* shows only four of the five corrections that Taylor gave in the errata published in the second issue of the book (III.71 is unmarked in the Tulane copy). It is also curious that Taylor ignored one of Keats's substantive changes in the 24 April letter (that for II.748) when he made up the list of errata for that later issue. It is worth observing, perhaps as a measure of Keats's skill in proofreading, that there were at least a dozen other errors in *1818* (see below) that Keats seems never to have noticed. Finally, Hunt's copy of *1818* (according to Garrod, who cites it in forty-two places in his apparatus) has marginal readings and corrections that had to come either from both the draft and the fair copy MSS or else from Woodhouse's interleaved *1818.* This copy's notation of "surges" for *"savage"* at III.704, where Woodhouse had written "q surges?" in his own copy, suggests that Woodhouse indeed may have been the source. In any event, the *selection* of markings in Hunt's *1818* is difficult to explain.

The history of the text and the diagram representing it are simple. Keats drafted the poem, then wrote out a revised fair copy, and the poem was set in type from his revised fair copy.

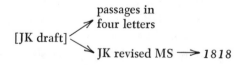

[JK draft] < passages in four letters / JK revised MS → *1818*

Reynolds seems to have had a hand in marking and making suggestions in the original draft—"You shall see the M.S of Endymion," he told Milnes at the end of 1846, "I had little to do in revising" (*KC*, II, 178) —but Woodhouse's record of cancellations and variants in the draft does not mention Reynolds or throw any light on his statement. At the other end of the production, we are similarly ignorant concerning another matter: early in March 1818 Keats asked his publishers to send the proofs of Book III to C. C. Clarke (*KC*, I, 12), and we do not know whether or not Clarke read the proofs, and, if so, what he contributed in the way of alterations to the poem. In the Morgan fair copy, however, we can see Taylor at work as editor—correcting Keats's slips of the pen, underlining and marking passages for revision or deletion, occasionally querying words, and sometimes suggesting alternate words and phrases. He apparently first went over the MS in pencil—none of the pencilings recorded in Garrod's apparatus is by Keats—and then sometimes he and sometimes Keats wrote over the pencilings in ink.

It is not possible, in the scope of the present study, to give a lengthy account of the interactions between author and editor in getting the work into final shape. Taylor's markings affect some 130 or 140 lines in Keats's MS, but he did not actually make (as opposed to suggest) changes in more than about two dozen lines. A typical example of his influence would be the change at I.368, where the fair copy reads "pretty" and Taylor underlined the word and wrote "pallid" and "waning" opposite the line on the verso of the preceding leaf of the MS. *1818* reads "pallid," but since Taylor did not *substitute* one of his words in the MS I think we are safe in concluding that Keats accepted the suggestion and made the change himself in proofs. In a similar instance, opposite "bob" in the MS at I.311 Taylor wrote "push" and "raise"; but *1818* reads "bob," and Woodhouse noted in W^2, "the words raise, push, were suggested to the Author: but he insisted on retaining *bob*." The overall spirit of the relationship is conveyed by the opening of Keats's letter to Taylor of 27 February 1818: "Your alteration strikes me as being a great improvement—the page looks much better. And now I will attend to the Punctuations you speak of. . . . I am extremely indebted to you for this attention and also for your after admonitions" (*Letters*, I, 238). Very likely the same relationship and tone were maintained through the publication of *1820*, where both Woodhouse and Taylor queried words and lines and suggested revisions but did not, so far as we know (except in *The Eve of St. Agnes*), actually enforce any changes against Keats's objections.

If we set aside the alterations marked in Taylor's hand in the MS,

1818's corrections of Keats's slips of the pen, and five lines that were corrected in the errata included in the second issue of *1818* (I.940, II.149 and 789, III.71, IV.739), there remain substantive differences between Keats's fair copy and *1818* in some eighty lines. Twenty-seven of these differences have to do with the expansion of Keats's contracted forms (the MS's "e'en" becomes "even" a dozen times, "o' " becomes "of" four times, " 't" becomes "it" seven times, and the other four differences are of a similar character); these seem worth mentioning mainly because they were important to Keats: in sending in corrections for II.782 and IV.151 he told Taylor, "Those abbreviations of *is 't* [for] *is it* and *done 't for done it* are of great consequence" (*Letters*, I, 273). Another five are *1818*'s corrections of Keats's verb forms (usually the change of a third-person form to a second-person, so as to agree with the second-person subject). Another thirteen are clearly *1818*'s errors, either in printing or in reading Keats's hand (these occur in I.283, 511, 550, 790; II.282, 524, 761, 793; III.286; IV.341, 443, 486, 548). The remaining thirty-eight may be seen in Garrod's apparatus for I.722 ("strange, and" is not in the MS), 756, 762, 849 (though the MS's "and" for "an" is perhaps just a slip of the pen); II.215, 302, 313, 319, 340 (possibly an error in *1818*, but more likely Keats's change in proofs), 353, 371, 402, 410, 474, 503, 538, 561, 607, 622, 723, 974 (perhaps *1818*'s error), 985 (perhaps just a slip of the pen in the MS), 990; III.342, 353, 358, 537 (perhaps a slip of the pen), 570, 588, 621, 655, 751, 752; IV.13, 429 (two lines condensed to one), 622, 649, 700/701 (the omission of two lines). My categories here are not very precise, but they will give some idea of the extent and kinds of difference between Keats's MS and the first printed text. Where *1818* is not clearly in error, the probability is that Keats himself was responsible for the changes in proofs.

1818 is of course the proper basis for a standard text, and both Garrod and Allott follow it, though not without emending in a number of places, usually on the basis of Keats's extant MS. Garrod departs from *1818* in some 130 lines (intentionally in about ninety of them). He corrects and emends *1818* substantively in I.182, 263, 283, 511 ("-head"), 550, 790; II.39, 282, 318, 340 (the MS does read "cold," but Keats may have changed the word to avoid repetition—cf. 338), 524, 748, 749 (the emendation here incorporates Taylor's alterations of the MS—*1818* followed or else restored the MS reading), 761, 782, 793, 973, 974; III.202, 286, 752 (Keats may have preferred "struck" and made the change in proofs), 811, 918 (the emendation here is probably Woodhouse's correction); IV.97 (the transposition for rhyme was marked by

Taylor, not by Keats), 151, 341, 443, 486, 548, 632. He alters punctuation, usually according to Keats's MS or the list of errata sent to Taylor, in I.14, 486, 733; II.272, 704–705, 837, 878 (in this and the preceding, though each emendation restores the MS punctuation, Garrod may be worsening what Keats intended to make better in proofs); III.201, 949, 950; IV.21, 537, 721, 845, 876. He emends spelling in I.515, 649; II.158, 793, 843, 856, 990, 1016; III.91, 156, 719; IV.23, 127, 423, 499, 558, 583, 626, 942; and capitalization in I.792, 958; II.448, 535, 697, 704–705, 729, 869; III.92; IV.845. He inserts quotation marks in I.293, 306, 944–959 (in this and other long passages according to Keats's specific request); II.680, 1017; III.430–443, 555, 571–600, 744, 745; and removes them in II.960, 961, 963, and IV.951 (but not in 952, thus retaining an extra opening mark). He adds a paragraph space (following Keats's request to Taylor) after IV.361.

Garrod errs substantively in I.511 ("dear-" for *1818*'s "deer-"), 520 ("has" for "hast"), 591 ("the opening" for "opening"); II.28 ("signing" for "sighing"), 461 ("imprison'd" for "prison'd"); III.279 ("the" for "thy"), 359 ("coming" for "come"), 486 ("round" for "around"), 652 ("mutterings" for "muttering"); IV.97 ("fell" for "feel"), 411 ("Phœbuts" for "Phœbus'"), 529 ("painful" for "plainful"). He inadvertently omits punctuation or gets it wrong in I.453, 664; II.559; III.43, 55, 122, 486, 547, 780, 787, 815, 880, 987; IV.20, 276, 794, 815, 909, 945, 988; and unintentionally changes spelling and capitalization in II.43; III.48, 241, 588, 738; IV.189, 687, 940. He omits the paragraph space after IV.29, and, to get down to extremely fine points, there is an inverted comma for an apostrophe in IV.429. (Twenty-two of these substantive and accidental errors also occur in H. Clement Notcutt's *Endymion . . . Type-facsimile of the First Edition,* 1927, which Garrod seems to have used instead of a genuine copy of *1818* as his base-text.) He does not emend "childrens'" (I.317), "cans't" (II.125), or "conchs" (II.921), and does not restore any of the MS's contracted forms except the two that Keats specifically mentions in his 24 April letter to Taylor.

Allott corrects and emends, in the same way as Garrod unless a different reading is indicated, in I.182 ("owlets'" for *1818*'s "owlets"—Garrod emends to "owlet's"), 263, 283, 317 (she corrects *1818* to "children's"), 511 (she gets "deer-head" right), 550, 661 (she follows the MS in "e'en"), 762 ("pleated," also in the MS), 790; II.39, 282, 318, 748, 761, 793, 973, 974; III.202, 286, 811, 918; IV.97, 341, 443, 486, 548, 632. She keeps *1818* readings in II.340 ("old"), 524 ("lighten'd"), 749 (the whole line), and III.752 ("struck"), all of which Garrod (rightly perhaps only in II.524) emends. She adds some of the same quotation marks that Garrod adds and, like him, makes a paragraph division after IV.361. In general her punctuation is much to be preferred to *1818*'s.

She appears to err substantively in I.33 ("always" for "alway," possibly an emendation), 39 ("valley" for "vallies"), 78 ("aye," which is her regular spelling for the affirmation—*1818* has "ay" meaning "ever"), 115 ("even" for "ev'n"), 120 ("valley" for "vallies"), 150 ("always" for "alway," again possibly an emendation); II.523 ("neck" for "necks"), 733 ("ere" for "in"), 958 ("thought" for "thoughts"), 985 ("Sometime" for "Sometimes," possibly an emendation to restore the MS text); III.785 ("his" for "its"); IV.234 (she omits the line), 663 ("silver" for "simple"). She does not make the changes (to "done't" and "is't") requested by Keats at II.782 and IV.151, and twice prints *1818*'s "on't" as "on it" (III.515, 663). She leaves out several spaces between paragraphs, and breaks I.196 and III.771 each into two half-lines.

In drear-nighted December

Written in December 1817 (so dated in W^2). First published in the *Literary Gazette,* 19 September 1829, p. 618, and then, in order, in *The Gem* (dated 1830 but issued in October 1829), p. 80, *NMM,* 26 (November 1829), 485, and Galignani (1829), p. 75 of the Keats section. Garrod, pp. 551–552; Allott, pp. 287–288.

We have a holograph fair copy in the University of Bristol Library (see Alvin Whitley, *HLB,* 5 [1951], 116–122—facsimile of the MS facing p. 120); three transcripts by Woodhouse (W^3, W^2, W^1); a transcript by Woodhouse's brother W. P. Woodhouse (see Colvin, *TLS,* 18 February 1915, p. 56); an unidentified transcript, perhaps made by someone in Leigh Hunt's family, that once belonged to Severn (Keats House, Hampstead); and a transcript by Isabella Towers (with the J. C. Stephens transcripts at Harvard).

Essentially there are two versions of the poem—one represented by the extant holograph, W^3, W^2, and W^1, and the other represented by the early printed texts. (A third version, incorporating Woodhouse's proposed revision of the entire final stanza—see *KC,* I, 64–65—and represented by W. P. Woodhouse's transcript, which, under the title "Pain of Memory," has the text of this rewritten final stanza, is clearly not authoritative. I have ignored this third version in the following discussion and omitted it from my diagram at the end.)

A now-lost holograph—possibly Keats's first draft—sold at Sotheby's to Charles Law on 13 June 1876 (see Hampstead Keats, IV, 61–62 n., for its readings), the extant Bristol fair copy, and W^3, W^2, and W^1 all agree in the distinctive readings "In drear" in 1 and 9 and "The feel of not to" in 21, while the *Literary Gazette, The Gem, NMM,* and Galignani (as well as the Hampstead copyist and Mrs. Towers) agree in "In a drear" in 1 and 9 and "To know the change and" in 21. The other substantive variants among the texts are, except for that in 20, of no significance: the Hampstead transcript has "great" for the other texts' "green" in 4; the Bristol fair copy has "of" for "at" in 20; both W^2 and W^1 underline "not" in 21; W^1 has "not"—a slip of the pen—for "none" in 22; the texts differ in "steel" vs. "steal" in 23, the Law and Bristol holographs, Galignani's text, and Mrs. Towers' copy all reading "steal"; and *The Gem* and *NMM* have "told" for "said" in 24. The Bristol fair copy is untitled, while W^3, W^2, and W^1 are headed "Song" and the early printed texts (except for that of *NMM,* which is untitled) are headed "Stanzas." Only in W^2 are the stanzas numbered.

Woodhouse's notations at the end of W^2, "from J: H: Reynolds" and "Decr 1817" followed (in shorthand) by "the date from Miss Reynolds' album," plus the variant that he entered opposite 20, *"of* in Miss R's Copy in Keats's hand writing," tell us that he got his text from Reynolds (almost certainly from a lost Reynolds copy in November 1818—see *KC,* I, 63–64), and that he saw both an otherwise unknown dated transcript in "Miss Reynolds' album" and the undated Bristol holograph ("Miss R's Copy in Keats's hand writing"). A penciled variant to 9 (but not to 1)— "a" followed by the initials "F.M.F. [?]" written above "In drear"—also appears in W^2, but seems not to be in Woodhouse's hand. The precise relationships among the Woodhouse transcripts are, as frequently, uncertain. W^1 was pretty clearly copied from W^2 (on the evidence of their agreement in underlining "not" in 21 and their agreement in accidentals generally), but there does not seem to be any basis for determining whether W^3 and W^2 are independent copies or one was made from the other.

The significant printings of the other version are those in the *Literary Gazette* and *The Gem*. Though the *Literary Gazette,* in reviewing *The Gem* on 24 October 1829 (p. 697), commented on the poem's reappearance in that annual and explained that "the proprietors [of the *Literary Gazette*] had previously printed their version from another copy," it seems fairly obvious that both texts ultimately derive from a single source. One may guess that Thomas Hood, who was editor of the preceding year's *Gem* but had quarreled with the publisher and withdrawn from the work (see Whitley's article cited above), had prepared a copy for the next year's volume and then, after resigning, offered the same poem (in "another copy") for publication to the *Literary Gazette*. Both Hood and Reynolds had published work of their own in the *Literary Gazette* in 1828 (Peter F. Morgan, *K-SJ*, 11 [1962], 88). The two printed texts could have been based on any of the three MSS—two lost transcripts and the Bristol holograph—that Woodhouse saw, all of which belonged to members of the Reynolds family, with which Hood was connected by his marriage in 1825. Both the Bristol MS and W^3 have part or all of the printed texts' 21—"To know the change and feel it"—written above or beside the original line, perhaps in the same hand in both MSS, and probably not by Woodhouse, even though he objected to the third stanza and, as I have mentioned parenthetically above, attempted elsewhere to rewrite it. It is not clear whether this reading was entered in the MSS before or after the printed texts appeared; it may have been (in the Bristol MS) the source of the line in the printed texts, but more likely was added to the MSS from one of the printed texts. In any event, it seems extremely unlikely that Keats was responsible for the printed texts' version of 21, and on the evidence we have I do not think we should consider it authoritative.

The Hampstead transcriber copied the *Literary Gazette* (Hunt has signed the transcript "John Keats" and added, "Lit: Gaz: 19 Sep^r / Said to be *'Unpublished'* "). Galignani reprinted the poem from the *Literary Gazette,* and Mrs. Towers took her text from Galignani. *NMM* quotes the poem from *The Gem* (in a review of it and several other annuals). My diagram is mainly intended to show general relationships among the texts. The exact details of the sources of W^3, W^2, and the earliest printed texts remain unknown.

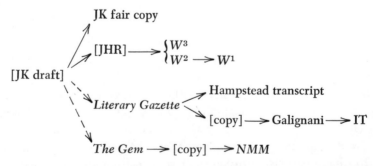

Since the authority of the printed texts' 1, 9, and 21 is uncertain, the Bristol MS is probably the best basis for a standard text, though one or the other of Woodhouse's first two transcripts also has a claim. The main question is whether to print "of" (Bristol MS) or "at" (the reading of Woodhouse's initial source and probably also of the lost transcript that he saw in "Miss Reynolds' album") in 20. I suggest that for critical reasons we arbitrarily consider "at" as authoritative, and prefer that to the reading of the extant holograph. Garrod follows one of H. B. Forman's texts based (in wording and most accidentals) on Galignani. Allott takes her text from the Bristol MS, though like Garrod and Forman (and also Woodhouse in W^2) she adds stanza numbers.

Apollo to the Graces

Written perhaps early in 1818 (Allott identifies "Don Giovanni" in Woodhouse's subtitle as a pantomime produced at Drury Lane in December 1817 and reviewed by Keats in the *Champion* on 4 January 1818). First published by Colvin in *TLS,* 16 April 1914, p. 181. Garrod, p. 545; Allott, p. 290.

We have Keats's draft (Harvard—facsimile in *Autograph Letters, Manuscripts and Documents: Selections from the Collection Formed by the Late Oliver R. Barrett,* Parke-Bernet sale catalogue, New York, 1950, p. 163) and a transcript by Woodhouse (W^2—transcriptions of both the draft and Woodhouse's copy in Rollins, *HLB,* 6 [1952], 172–174). The transcript, "From the orig[l] in Miss Reynolds's Possession," adds the subtitle "written to the Tune of the air [blank space] in Don Giovanni" and varies substantively from the draft in 3 ("at" for the draft's "on," which, however, was first written "at") and 14 ("Thro' " for "Though," a characteristic Keatsian slip of the pen). Rollins thinks that Woodhouse copied the draft, but it is also possible that he took his text instead from a lost fair copy.

Both the draft and W^2 have claims to be the basis for a standard text, our choice depending on whether we think the draft or a lost fair copy was Woodhouse's source for W^2. Colvin printed the poem from W^2, erring in 3 ("threshold" for "thresholds") and 6 ("Kingdom" for "Kingdoms"). Garrod follows the draft in "on" (3) and the transcript in "Thro' " (14), with a mixture of accidentals from both sources (plus some of his own devising). Allott, though she says "Text from *Woodhouse* 2," has errors deriving partly from Colvin by way of one of H. B. Forman's texts in 3 ("threshold of the" for "thresholds of") and 6 ("kingdom") and in the division of 8 into two lines.

To Mrs. Reynolds' Cat

Written on 16 January 1818 (so dated in all the MSS). First published in Thomas Hood's *The Comic Annual* (1830), p. 14. Garrod, p. 534; Allott, p. 292.

The three extant MSS—a fair copy by Keats ("To Mrs Reynolds's Cat") in the Buffalo and Erie County Public Library and two transcripts by Woodhouse (W^2, W^1)—vary substantively in title (both transcripts are headed "Sonnet / On Mrs Reynolds's Cat"), 9 ("dainty" in the holograph, "gentle" in W^2, "tender"—a copying error based on 8—in W^1), 12 ("has" in the holograph, "have" in the transcripts), and 14 ("bottled" in the holograph, "bottle" in the transcripts). Woodhouse presumably took his W^2 text from some holograph or copy in the Reynolds family, and W^1 from W^2. There is no way of knowing whether the W^2 readings, especially that in 9, are earlier or later than those in the extant holograph. The *Comic Annual* version, also probably deriving from a MS in the Reynolds family, reads "has" for "hast" in 1 and agrees with the holograph against the transcripts in 9, 12, and 14.

In the absence of any specific information about Woodhouse's and Hood's sources, the Buffalo fair copy should be the basis for a standard text. Both Garrod and Allott follow this MS, emending "has" to "have" in 12.

Lines on Seeing a Lock of Milton's Hair

Written on 21 January 1818 (so dated in seven of the MSS, all but the first draft). First published in *PDWJ*, 15 November 1838, and then in *1848*, I, 78–79. Garrod, pp. 479–481; Allott, pp. 292–294.

We have three extant holograph MSS—Keats's draft at Harvard (facsimile of 1–17 in *The Library of the Late H. Buxton Forman*, Anderson Galleries sale catalogue, New York, 1920, p. 87), his fair copy written in the 1808 facsimile of Shakespeare's First Folio at Keats House, Hampstead, and a fair copy included in a letter to Benjamin Bailey of 23 January 1818 (MS at Harvard, text in *Letters*, I, 211–212)—as well as transcripts by Brown, Dilke, Woodhouse (two copies, W^2 and W^1), and Charlotte Reynolds.

Keats originally drafted the poem at Hunt's, the first seventeen lines in a notebook belonging to Hunt and the rest on a separate sheet. Both extant holograph copies (in the Hampstead Shakespeare and the letter to Bailey) were made soon after the draft. The letter text differs from the Hampstead MS in title ("On seeing . . . Hair— / *Ode*" for the Hampstead

MS's "Lines on seeing . . . hair"), 26 ("Give" for "Leave"), 39 ("heard" for "caught"), and the arrangement of 37–38 (two lines in the letter, one line in the Hampstead MS). Because the Hampstead MS shows internal revisions from the draft text to that of the letter in 27 and 36, it seems clear that the letter text is the later of the two fair copies.

Brown ("Lines on seeing . . . hair") probably transcribed the Hampstead holograph, changing the verb endings from "-edst" to "-est" in 11 and 13, "thine" to "thy" in 20, and "at" to "of" in 32. He also miscopied Keats's "fashion" as "passion" in 23, subsequently correcting the error after someone—I should suppose Woodhouse—queried the word in the margin of the MS. Still later he copied over in ink a penciled "I swear" apparently added by Woodhouse after 21 (see below), and changed 37–38 from a single line (as he had originally written it) to two lines, again going over a penciled alteration in ink. Dilke copied Brown's transcript in its earlier state, before "passion" was corrected to "fashion" and before "I swear" was written in and 37–38 were made into two lines; he otherwise varies from Brown only in "offering" for "offerings" (33) and in six differences of punctuation, spelling, and capitalization, and he has the "CB" flourish at the end.

Though we cannot be certain about Woodhouse's source for W^2, his note to 37–38 gives us a clue: "In the copy from which I took this, these 2 lines were written in one: I have separated them on account of the rhyme to 'unaware.' " Among extant MSS, the only ones having 37–38 as a single line are the Hampstead holograph, Brown's transcript (before the lines were divided there), and Dilke's copy. Woodhouse took at least his date from Brown ("21 Jany 1818. C.B."), and I think he took his text as well, for in its first completed state W^2 had the same title and the same substantive text (including Brown's "-est" endings in 11 and 13, "thy" in 20—Woodhouse first wrote "thine" but corrected it to "thy" before going on to the next word—and "of" in 32). In the margin of W^2 beside "fashion" (23) Woodhouse notes in pencil, again obviously from Brown's transcript, "originally passion." W^1 has the same text as W^2 in the state just described (except for "thine" in 20, no doubt from the same impulse that made Woodhouse first write "thine" in W^2), and was almost surely copied from W^2.

Upon seeing Keats's letter to Bailey, sometime in 1821, Woodhouse made a number of changes in W^2. He deleted "Lines" from the title and inserted "Ode" beneath it, erased and changed the verb endings to "-edst" in 11 and 13, deleted "of" and wrote in "at" in 32 (noting "B.B." as his source), and recorded the letter's unique variant in 26 and the fact that 37–38 "are written separate in B.B's copy" (by which he means the holograph letter, not a transcript by Bailey). Charlotte Reynolds' transcript is substantively identical with W^2 in this altered state (though she has "-est" in 11 and 13) and probably was copied from it.

The most curious feature of several of the MSS has to do with a penciled "I swear" appearing after 21 in W^2, W^1, Brown's transcript (where the penciled words were subsequently inked over by Brown), and the letter to Bailey. When he first copied the poem Woodhouse noted in W^2, opposite 21, which came at the bottom of a page, "Should there not be a short line to rhyme with 'ear' at the end of this page, such as—'I swear'?" It seems that Woodhouse later followed his own suggestion, inserting "I swear" not only in W^2 but in the other three MSS as well, for all four pencilings are in the same hand and the hand is almost certainly Woodhouse's.

Woodhouse's "I swear" appears in both of the earliest printings of the poem. The *PDWJ* version derives from Brown's transcript (with which it agrees substantively except for the omission of the sixth line, a mistake rectified in an erratum published two weeks later, on 29 November 1838). Milnes printed the poem as part of the letter to Bailey, which he took from a letterbook transcript by one of Woodhouse's clerks. His text of the poem itself, however, for which the clerk includes only a title and the first line in his transcript of the letter, almost certainly came from Brown's copy, the only source known to have been available to him. The *1848* version is headed "On Seeing . . . Hair" (the clerk's title), but otherwise varies from Brown's copy only in 32 ("wed" for "mad," a copying or printing error) and 42 ("I thought" for "Methought," presumably a change by Milnes). Since Brown's MS shows no signs of having been handled by a printer, probably *1848* was set from a lost copy of it.

JK letter to Bailey

CWD

JK draft ⟶ JK copy (Hampstead)

W^1

W^2

CB

CR

[CB] ⟶ *PDWJ*

[copy] ⟶ *1848*

The textual history of this poem is especially complicated, and two difficult editorial problems emerge from the above details: the choice of base-text and the question of the authoritativeness of certain readings that appear only in the transcripts. Each of three MSS—the Hampstead holograph (which, though it is early, seems to be a seriously considered version), the letter to Bailey (copied from the preceding), and Brown's transcript (possibly Keats's approved form of the poem)—has a claim to be the basis for a standard text. The principal readings at stake, in addition to the title, are those discussed above for 20 ("thine" in the two extant holograph copies, "thy" in Brown), 22 ("I swear" in Brown, omitted in the other MSS), 26 ("Give" in the letter, "Leave" in the others), 32 ("of" in Brown, "at" in the others), 39 ("heard" in the letter, "caught" in the others), and the treatment of 37–38 (one line in the Hampstead MS, two lines in the others). It may be that in this one instance an eclectic text—which most editors have in effect adopted, whether or not they were aware of doing so—would be the best solution. I should prefer, however, since there are many evidences that Keats regularly reviewed and sometimes marked Brown's transcripts, to consider Brown's the authorially approved final text. In each reading at issue (even the "I swear" that apparently originated with Woodhouse) there is no evidence that a Brown variant or alteration was made without Keats's knowledge (if not at his request), and there is a general probability, based on Keats's and Brown's relationship as author and copyist, that Keats did see and approve Brown's text. Concerning "I swear" in particular, it may well be that Brown's copying over the penciled words in ink signifies Keats's acceptance of Woodhouse's suggestion. With nothing else to go on, I think we should arbitrarily decide that it does.

Garrod takes his text from one of H. B. Forman's, which in turn is based on *1848* but has the title of the Hampstead MS, "thine" in 20, and indentions and a great many accidentals common to both holograph copies (plus some of Forman's own devising). Garrod includes "I swear" (22) in angle brackets. The weakest feature of his (and Forman's) text is the retention of *1848*'s "I thought" (42); Garrod records the readings of the three holographs and Dilke's transcript for this line, but the fact is that all seven of the MSS after the draft have "Methought" (the draft has "It seem'd"). Allott follows Keats's letter copy, but introduces "I swear" in square brackets, has "offering" for "offerings" in 33 (an error also deriving from Forman), and substitutes "caught" for the letter's "heard" in 39.

On Sitting Down to Read "King Lear" Once Again

Written on 22 January 1818 (*Letters,* I, 214—also the date in the Hampstead holograph and in all the transcripts except W^1 and Jeffrey's).

First published in *PDWJ*, 8 November 1838, and then in *1848*, I, 96–97. Garrod, p. 483; Allott, pp. 295–296.

Two holographs are extant—Keats's original draft in the National Library of Scotland and his fair copy written in the 1808 facsimile of Shakespeare's First Folio at Keats House, Hampstead (facsimiles in Caroline F. E. Spurgeon, *Keats's Shakespeare*, 1928, facing p. 50, and Dorothy Hewlett, *A Life of John Keats*, 3rd ed., 1970, p. 132)—and we have transcripts by Brown, Dilke, Woodhouse (two copies, W^2 and W^1), Charlotte Reynolds, and John Jeffrey (in a copy of Keats's letter to George and Tom Keats of 23, 24 January 1818   text of the poem in *Letters*, I, 214–215).

Of the four recoverable states of text, the earliest is that of Keats's draft, which reads "Pages" in 4, "Damnation" in 6, "this" in 10, "through the old o[a]k forest I am" in 11, "in" in 13, and "to" in 14. A second state is that of the Hampstead fair copy, which initially had the same substantive text as the draft, but shows "this" altered to "our" (10) and "to" altered to "at" (14). Brown transcribed this MS, and both Dilke's copy (virtually identical with Brown's in accidentals as well as wording) and the *PDWJ* text derive from Brown.

Still another state is represented by Woodhouse's and Charlotte Reynolds' transcripts, which are substantively identical with the draft except that they have "Hell-torment" in 6. Woodhouse's notations at the end of W^2—"J.H.R." followed by "22 Jany 1818. C.B."—indicate that he got his text from Reynolds (most probably a lost Reynolds copy from some unknown source, ultimately the draft) and the date from Brown (from whose transcript Woodhouse also recorded variants to 6, 10, and 14 in W^2 and the variant to 14 in W^1). W^1 was probably transcribed from W^2, and Charlotte Reynolds also seems to have copied W^2 (her transcript omits commas in 5 and 13 but otherwise is very close to W^2).

A fourth version is that of the letter to George and Tom, in which Keats copied the sonnet on the day after he drafted it. The letter text, surviving only in Jeffrey's transcript, has "volume" for "Pages" in 4, "Hell torment" in 6, "our" in 10, a transposition of "I am" in 11 ("I am through the old oak forest"), "with" for "in" in 13, and "at" in 14. It also shows two variants that are probably Jeffrey's errors rather than Keats's—"if" for "of" in 2 and the omission of "humbly" in 7. Milnes printed the poem in *1848* as part of the letter from an amanuensis' copy of Jeffrey's transcript.

Unfortunately the order of the three versions subsequent to the draft is not at all clear. The Hampstead MS's alterations in 10 and 14 may have been made in the process of copying, and it is possible that Keats wrote out this MS on the same day on which he drafted the poem, and then copied the poem again, incorporating the revised 10 and 14, in the letter a day later (the date of the Hampstead MS, however, because it is the known date of composition, cannot be used to date the MS itself). The rest of the letter text's variants are unique except in 6, where "Hell torment" agrees with the reading of Woodhouse's transcripts. Since Jeffrey is generally unreliable as a copyist, and since he did not include any indications of deletions and revisions in his transcript (which, if we had them, might clarify the relationship of the letter text to the other known states), it is probably best to consider the letter, the Hampstead MS, and Woodhouse's text as all deriving independently from the draft, and to leave the chronological order among the states unsettled.

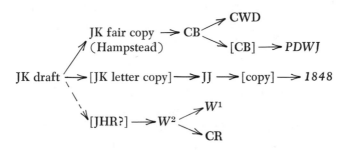

Again because of Jeffrey's general unreliability, the proper (in this case the safest) basis for a standard text is the Hampstead holograph. Both Garrod and Allott reproduce this MS substantively (though in accidentals Garrod, following one of H. B. Forman's texts, is closer to Brown's transcript than to any other MS source).

When I have fears that I may cease to be

Written in January 1818 (Keats calls it "my last Sonnet" in copying it out for Reynolds on 31 January; what is apparently his next-to-last, *On Sitting Down to Read "King Lear" Once Again,* was composed nine days earlier, on the 22nd—*Letters,* I, 222, 214). First published in *1848,* II, 293. Garrod, p. 462; Allott, pp. 296–298.

Though lacking a holograph MS, we have six transcripts—by Charlotte Reynolds, one of Woodhouse's clerks (in a letterbook copy of Keats's lost letter to Reynolds of 31 January 1818—text of the poem in *Letters,* I, 222), Woodhouse (two copies, W^2 and W^1), Brown, and Dilke. The transcripts differ substantively among themselves only in 4, where Charlotte Reynolds, W^1, Brown, and Dilke have "rich garners" and Woodhouse's clerk and W^2 have "full garners," and in 7, where Charlotte, the clerk, W^2, and W^1 have "feel" and Brown and Dilke have "think." On this slight evidence (together with knowledge of general practices elsewhere) we may construct the following.

Charlotte Reynolds' copy, with "rich garners" and "feel," probably came, as she says it did, "From J. Keats' letter to J H R 31 Jan 1818." So, of course, did the transcript of the letter by Woodhouse's clerk, who wrote "full garners" (an error based on "full" later in the same line) and "feel." Woodhouse seems to have copied W^2 from the clerk's transcript, incorporating the clerk's "full garners" and "feel" and initially dating the poem "From JK's letter to W.H.R. [*sic*] Feby 1818." Subsequently Woodhouse saw Brown's transcript and recorded "rich C.B." in W^2 opposite 4 (but overlooked Brown's other variant in 7), and still later he corrected his date to 31 January, perhaps on the basis of Charlotte Reynolds' transcript (he also, probably at the same time, added the 31 January date to the clerk's letter transcript). He made W^1 from W^2 after he entered the Brown variant to 4 (W^1 has "rich garners" and "feel") but before he changed the date (W^1 is dated February 1818). Brown copied a holograph with "rich garners" and "think," possibly in April 1819, when he was "rummaging up some of [Keats's] old sins—that is to say sonnets" (*Letters*, II, 104); it is not known whether his source was the same MS from which Keats made the letter copy for Reynolds (in which case Keats would have altered "think" to "feel" in the process of copying the poem) or a slightly revised MS. Brown's transcript was the source of Dilke's copy (Dilke follows it perfectly in every detail), and was printer's copy for *1848*.

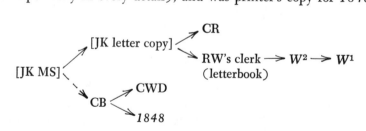

Since there is no good evidence that Keats's letter copy represents a later version than Brown's, I think we should prefer Brown's transcript as the basis for a standard text. Garrod reproduces *1848* exactly except for adding a hyphen in 3 and lowercasing the first two nouns in 14. Allott also follows *1848*, in effect, like Garrod, producing the same substantive text as Brown's.

O blush not so! O blush not so

Written probably on 31 January 1818 (it is not absolutely certain that Keats's letter version of that date represents the original draft, and the holograph of the letter has been lost). First published in Forman (1883), II, 279–280. Garrod, p. 544; Allott, pp. 298–299.

Though no MS in Keats's hand has survived (Garrod's *"H"* is a mistake), we have transcripts by Woodhouse (W^3), Brown, and one of Woodhouse's clerks (in a letterbook copy of Keats's letter to Reynolds of 31 January 1818—text of the poem in *Letters,* I, 219–220). The substantive variants among the MSS make fairly clear that each transcriber worked from a different immediate source. Woodhouse's clerk, copying the lost letter, has "ye" in 2, 3, and 13, "want" (altered from "wont") in 5, "naught" in 7, "sigh . . . sigh" in 9, "of the" in 15, and "yes . . . no" in 17. Woodhouse, who heads the poem "Song," has these same readings except for "nought" in 7, "say . . . say" in 9, "of our" in 15, and "aye . . . nay" in 17. At some later time Woodhouse penciled "sigh" over each "say" in 9 (probably from the clerk's transcript) and apparently tried his hand at two revisions, penciling "and blush all the while" in shorthand over "the blushing while" in 3 and "lips" over "hips" (the reading of all MSS) in 11. Brown (also with "Song") copied "you" in 2, 3, and 13, "won't" in 5, "nought" in 7, "sigh . . . sigh" in 9 (he also wrote "no," a slip of the pen, for the first "not" in this line), "of the" in 15, and "yes . . . no" in 17. He must have taken his text from a lost revised copy by Keats; possibly this is one of the poems in his transcripts that he described to Milnes as being "of an exceptionable kind . . . written and copied for the purpose of preventing the young blue-stocking ladies from asking for the loan of [Keats's] MS Poems" (*KC*, II, 103). I should guess that Woodhouse got the poem from a copy by Reynolds (cf. the sources proposed for Woodhouse's transcripts of the preceding and following pieces, however).

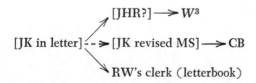

On general principles (mainly Brown's consistently direct connection with holograph MSS) I think we should take Brown's version as the basis for a standard text. Forman printed the poem from some now-lost MS

deriving either from Brown or from the MS that Brown copied (Forman
in a note mentions the poem's having "been handed about in manuscript
and more than once copied," and Brown's MSS were not available to him
at the time). His text has all of Brown's distinctive readings, and varies
from it only in title (Forman's heading is "Sharing Eve's Apple") and in
11 ("these" for the extant MSS' "those" and "lips" for "hips"). Garrod
combines Woodhouse's and the clerk's "ye" in 2, Brown's "you" in 3 and
13, Woodhouse's "say . . . say" in 9, Forman's "these" in 11, and Wood-
house's "of our" and "aye . . . nay" in 15 and 17. Allott follows the clerk's
transcript, but has Brown's "won't" in 5 and "you" in 13.

Hence burgundy, claret, and port

Written on 31 January 1818 (drafted in a letter to Reynolds so dated
by Woodhouse; Charlotte Reynolds' transcript of this and the next poem
is dated the following Saturday, "Feb 7 1818," but this may be a misread-
ing of Woodhouse's "Feby 1818" in W^2, and her "From J. Keats' letter to
J H R 31 Jan 1818" at the end of *When I have fears,* the one poem she
seems to have copied directly from Keats's letter, is probably the more
reliable date for the letter). On the relationship of this to *God of the
meridian* see the discussion of the next poem. First published in *1848,* I,
81–82. Garrod, p. 481; Allott, pp. 299–300.

No holograph is extant, but there are transcripts by Woodhouse (W^2),
one of his clerks (in a letterbook copy of the lost letter to Reynolds—text
of the poem in *Letters,* I, 220–221), Charlotte Reynolds, Brown, and
George Keats. The only substantive differences among the MSS occur in
the title (Brown and George Keats head the poem "Song. 1818," while the
other transcripts are untitled) and in 3 (where W^2 and Charlotte Reyn-
olds have "courtly," the clerk "couthly," which Woodhouse verified with
"so" in the margin, and Brown and George Keats "earthly") and 8 (where
Charlotte has a unique "the" for "my").

From Keats's introduction to it—"I cannot write in prose, It is a sun-
shiny day and I cannot so here goes"—the text in the letter to Reynolds
would appear to be the original version. Though Woodhouse seems to
have taken *When I have fears,* another poem that Keats included in the
same letter, from his clerk's letterbook transcript, here it is more likely
that both he and his clerk transcribed the letter independently (see the
next poem). Charlotte Reynolds probably took her text from W^2. Brown
transcribed a slightly revised lost copy having "earthly" in 3, and George
Keats followed Brown's text almost exactly (he varies only in a capitaliza-

tion and the omission of two commas). Milnes printed the poem in *1848*
as part of the letter from an amanuensis' copy of Woodhouse's clerk's
transcript, emending the clerk's "couthly" to "earthly" perhaps on the basis
of Brown's transcript.

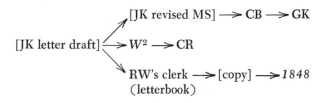

Brown's transcript, with "earthly," would appear to be the proper basis
for a standard text. Garrod reproduces *1848* exactly (except in his in-
dentions). Allott follows the clerk's letter transcript, printing "couthly"
in 3.

God of the meridian

Written on 31 January 1818 (dating and circumstances of composi-
tion the same as for the preceding poem). This poem has frequently been
printed as the final twenty-five lines of *Hence burgundy, claret, and port,*
but the textual evidence (a significant amount of space between these lines
and *Hence burgundy* in the transcripts deriving from Keats's lost letter to
Reynolds, and the absence of these lines in Brown's transcript of *Hence
burgundy*) as well as differences in tone and meter (*Hence burgundy* is
in anapests, while the more serious *God of the meridian* is in iambs)
favor treating them as separate pieces. First published in *1848*, I, 82–83.
Garrod, p. 482; Allott, pp. 300–301 (as part of the preceding poem).
We have two transcripts by Woodhouse (*W²* and *W¹*, the latter con-
taining 13–25 only, with the preceding leaf missing), a transcript by one
of Woodhouse's clerks (in a letterbook copy of Keats's letter to Reynolds,
31 January 1818—text of the poem in *Letters*, I, 221), and a transcript
by Charlotte Reynolds. There are no substantive differences among the
MSS. Apparently Woodhouse and his clerk took their texts independently
from Keats's lost letter. Woodhouse's note in *W²* opposite the beginning
of *Hence burgundy*—"The lines . . . are extracted from a letter to J.H.R."
—applies to both that poem and *God of the meridian,* and his indepen-
dence of the clerk's transcript might be evidenced by the fact that he has
a long dash and some x's after "unalarmed" in the final line, indications
of fragmentariness that probably were in the original MS but do not appear

in the clerk's transcript. Presumably he made W^1 from W^2, and Charlotte Reynolds (who similarly includes dashes and x's at the end) probably also copied W^2. *1848*'s text, with "bare" for "bear" in 19, was printed as part of the letter from an amanuensis' copy of the clerk's transcript.

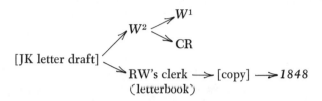

Since they do not differ substantively, either W^2 or the clerk's transcript can be the basis for a standard text. Garrod follows *1848*, altering punctuation and spelling in 4, 8, and 24, and correcting "bare" to "bear" in 19. Allott takes her text from the clerk's transcript, combining it with *Hence burgundy* as a single poem. It is possible that Keats intended "Too" rather than "To" in 10, since "to" for "too" is a fairly common slip of the pen in his MSS elsewhere.

Robin Hood

Written at the beginning of February 1818 (copied out in a letter to Reynolds of 3 February). First published in *1820*. Garrod, pp. 270–272; Allott, pp. 301–304.

The extant MSS are all transcripts—two by Woodhouse (W^2, W^1) and one each by Brown, Dilke, and George Keats. Though no holograph has survived, at least three are known to have existed: (1) a MS once in the possession of S. R. Townshend Mayer and examined by H. B. Forman (see Hampstead Keats, III, 176–180 nn., for description and a record of variants and canceled readings); (2) Keats's copy of the poem in his 3 February 1818 letter to Reynolds (the original MS has disappeared, and the letter is known only through a letterbook copy by Woodhouse, who includes a heading and the first line of the poem and refers to his W^2 transcript for the rest—see *Letters*, I, 225); and (3) a lost revised MS copied by Brown and probably also by George Keats.

The Townshend Mayer MS, which Keats either gave to Hunt or left at Hunt's house, and which has Shelley's draft of *To the Nile* on the same paper (a product of the sonnet-writing contest that took place at Hunt's on 4 February), is described by Forman as the original draft, showing many deletions and corrections and varying substantively from the *1820* text in 10 ("paid no Rent and Leases"), 18 ("Jests"), 37 ("and all is past"), 39 ("tufted"), 44 ("Woodma[n] 's"), and 62 ("You and I a stave will try"), with alternate readings left uncanceled in 18, 19, 31, and 32. Woodhouse took his W^2 text either from the lost letter to Reynolds or, perhaps more probably, from a copy of that text made by Reynolds (in either case, Woodhouse added the letter date and a short extract from the letter at the end of his transcript). W^2 has the draft reading of 10 but none of the others noticed just above; it varies substantively from *1820* in 25 ("Never any of") and 32 ("Messenger to"), underlines "should be" in 38 and "should" in 40, and encloses "Strange . . . money" (47–48) in quotation marks. Subsequently in W^2 Woodhouse recorded variants from Brown's transcript to 10 ("knew nor . . . nor"), 25 ("one of all"), and 47–48 (Brown's omission of quotation marks). W^1 was probably taken from W^2, and before Woodhouse entered these variants in W^2.

Brown's transcript derives from some now-lost revised copy by Keats. It differs substantively from *1820* only in 32 ("Messenger to"), but underlines "should be" and "should have" in 38 and 40. Dilke's transcript, while it varies from Brown's in seventeen minor details (mostly of capitalization), was nevertheless clearly taken from Brown's (they have the same distinctive title and many accidental details in common, and Dilke added the "CB" flourish at the end). George Keats's transcript, on the other hand, was not made from Brown's in this case (there is but a single substantive difference between them—George's unique "his" in 46, a copying error—but George has a variant heading and several dozen variants in accidentals); very likely George copied the same holograph that Brown worked from.

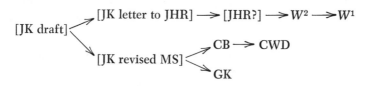

1820, set from a lost copy by Keats or Brown (it is very close in minor details to Brown's extant transcript, though varying substantively in 32), is the proper basis for a standard text. Garrod reproduces *1820* exactly, and Allott does not depart substantively.

Lines on the Mermaid Tavern

Written at the beginning of February 1818 (dating the same as for the preceding poem). First published in *1820*. Garrod, pp. 269–270; Allott, pp. 304–306.

In addition to the *1820* text, we have two holograph copies—the earlier at Harvard and the later in George Keats's notebook in the British Museum (Garrod's *E*, which he should have listed as an autograph rather than as a transcript)—and a transcript by Dilke, a transcript by Brown, and three by Woodhouse (W^2 and two W^1 copies). The original of Keats's letter to Reynolds of 3 February 1818, in which he copied the poem, has disappeared, and Woodhouse's letterbook transcript of the letter includes only the first line, referring to W^2 for the rest of the poem (see *Letters*, I, 225). The MS that Dilke sent Milnes in the 1840's (*KC*, II, 161) is almost surely the Harvard holograph.

Keats's draft has not survived. The Harvard MS appears to be an early fair copy, written probably about the same time as the copy in the lost letter to Reynolds. Dilke clearly took his text from the Harvard MS (with a few changes in punctuation and capitalization, but enough peculiar likenesses as to leave no doubt about his source). Brown may also have copied this MS, but since he has "O" for "Old" in 9 it is probably safer to hypothesize a lost holograph, perhaps the original draft, as the basis for his transcript. At some later time, possibly when he made the extant fair copy, Keats read over Brown's transcript and changed "Fairer" to "Choicer" in 4. Woodhouse took his W^2 text, just as he did that of *Robin Hood*, either from the lost letter to Reynolds or from a copy made by Reynolds (and then, if he followed what seems to have been his usual practice elsewhere, took the W^1 copies from W^2). Woodhouse also has "O" for "Old" in 9, and either he or his source misread Keats's "Sipping" in 20 as "Lipping" (an easily understood mistake, since Keats's "S" and "L" are sometimes indistinguishable; the second W^1 transcript shows "Sipping" altered to "Lipping," but here I think Woodhouse simply miscopied his own word and then changed it to agree with his other transcripts). Subsequently Woodhouse saw Brown's transcript, and noted variants from it in W^2 ("Choicer" in 4, "bouze" for "booze" in 12, "Sipping" in 20).

If we set aside Keats's alteration in line 4 of Brown's transcript, all of the versions just mentioned represent a single early state of text, with "Fairer" in 4, "Sweeter" in 8, "Old [*or* O] generous" in 9, and 24–26 as given in Garrod's apparatus. They differ substantively among themselves only in 9 ("Old" in the Harvard MS and Dilke's copy, "O" in the transcripts by Brown and Woodhouse) and 20 ("Sipping" in the Harvard MS, Dilke, and Brown, "Lipping" in Woodhouse). They also differ in their spelling of "bowse" in 12 ("bouze" in the Harvard MS, Dilke, and Brown, "booze" in the Woodhouse transcripts) and in their hyphenation of the last three words of 19 ("new-old sign" in the Harvard MS and Dilke, "new old-sign" in Brown, and "new old sign" in the Woodhouse transcripts).

The next state of text is represented by Keats's revised MS in the British Museum notebook, which has "Choicer" in 4, "Richer" in 8, "delicious" in 9, and the *1820* text of 24–26. Keats made this copy in or before January 1820, when George Keats wrote his transcripts in the same notebook to take back to America, and there is a good chance (though it cannot be proved) that Keats worked from Brown's transcript rather than from any MS of his own, revising 4, 8, 9, and 24–26 in the process of copying. But this is guesswork, and my diagram is very speculative concerning the sources of Brown's transcript and the revised holograph fair copy.

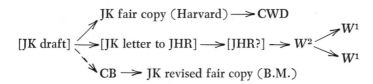

The latest text, that of *1820,* printed from a lost MS by Keats or Brown, combines readings from the two earlier states, keeping 4 and 24–26 of Keats's revised fair copy but reverting to "Sweeter" in 8 and "O generous" in 9; there is a single unique substantive reading in *1820,* "Said" for "Says" in 18. *1820* is as usual the proper basis for a standard text, and requires emending only in 19, "new old-sign" (the reading of Brown's transcript). Garrod emends to "new-old sign" (as in the Harvard MS and Dilke's copy), and otherwise reproduces *1820* exactly. Allott does not depart substantively from *1820.*

Welcome joy and welcome sorrow

Written in *1818* (so dated in all seven of the MSS; a more precise dating is not possible). First published in *1848,* I, 285–286. Garrod, pp. 502–503; Allott, pp. 386–388.

The extant MSS are an unidentified fair copy, possibly a holograph, in the possession of Dorothy Withey, of Stratford-upon-Avon, and transcripts by Brown, Woodhouse (two copies, W^2 and W^1), George Keats, J. C. Stephens, and C. C. Clarke.

The MSS, all headed "Fragment" and with the epigraph based on *Paradise Lost* II.899–901, differ significantly only in 13, where Miss Withey's

MS, Stephens, and Clarke read "shipwreck'd" and Brown, Woodhouse, and George Keats have "storm-wreck'd." Stephens mistakenly wrote "fine" instead of "fair" in 5; Clarke wrote "are" for "burn" in 8; both Stephens and Clarke have "aspic" for "aspics" in 17; and George Keats's copy transposes 14 and 15.

Miss Withey's MS (which one might take to be in Woodhouse's hand were it not that W^2 and W^1 have different readings and obviously came from a different source) is pretty clearly the MS that Clarke transcribed, or else a copy of it; in both Miss Withey's MS and Clarke's transcript, 9 is first written and then canceled after 7, and Clarke notes "struck out here" beside the deleted line in his transcript. Stephens' copy probably also derives from the same source (he could not have got "burn" in 8 from Clarke, who in any case made his transcript for Milnes—many years after Stephens made his), and I take Stephens' and Clarke's variants in 5, 8, and 17 to be independent copying errors. Clarke's transcript was printer's copy for *1848*, which reproduced his "are" in 8, "ship-wreck'd" in 13, "aspic" in 17, and practically all of his accidentals.

Brown probably copied a lost holograph containing "storm-wreck'd" in 13. George Keats's transcript follows not only Brown's wording and a preponderance of his accidentals but also a peculiarity of his epigraph: Brown first wrote "Under the flag of each his faction" as a single line, then deleted the last four words, rewriting them on a second line, and George copied "Under the flag" at the left margin just where Brown's remaining three words begin. Brown was unquestionably George's source. Woodhouse copied either Brown (from whom he took his date in W^2) or else, what is perhaps more likely, the same lost MS that Brown worked from; he presumably transcribed W^1 from W^2 (correcting "embryo" to "embryon" in W^1, following a penciled notation that he had made in W^2).

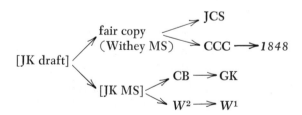

We do not actually know whether Miss Withey's MS (with "ship-wreck'd") or the consensus of Brown's and Woodhouse's transcripts (with "storm-wreck'd") represents the later state of text. Since MSS once in

Clarke's possession tend to be early versions, perhaps we should prefer Brown's or Woodhouse's transcript as the basis for a standard text. Garrod takes his text from *1848,* but corrects "embryo" to Milton's "embryon" in the epigraph, "are" to "burn" in 8, and "shipwreck'd" to "stormwreck'd" in 13, and alters spelling and punctuation in five places. He errs in retaining Clarke's and *1848's* "aspic" in 17 and in omitting the period at the end of the last line. Allott also follows *1848,* emending "embryo" to "embryon" in the epigraph and "are" to "burn" in 8, but retaining *1848's* "shipwreck'd" in 13 and "aspic" in 17. She accidentally transposes 22–23 and 24–25.

Time's sea hath been five years at its slow ebb

Written on 4 February 1818 (the date in Woodhouse's and Charlotte Reynolds' transcripts). First published in *Hood's Magazine,* 2 (September 1844), 240, and then in *1848,* II, 297. Garrod, p. 466; Allott, pp. 306–307.

The extant MSS are transcripts by Woodhouse (two copies, W^2 and W^1), Charlotte Reynolds, one of Woodhouse's clerks (Garrod's *T*), and Coventry Patmore. Another copy by Woodhouse that Severn possessed in 1845 (*KC,* II, 131) has not survived.

The transcripts do not differ substantively except that W^1 is untitled (the others are headed "To _____") and has a unique "has" for "hath" in 1, and Patmore changed "thy" to "thine" in 4. Woodhouse's source for W^2 is not known (it was probably, from the position of the poem in the W^2 book of transcripts, a holograph MS or a copy by J. H. Reynolds). The rest of the MSS derive from W^2—the W^1 transcript, Charlotte Reynolds' copy, and the clerk's copy all directly, and Patmore's from the clerk's transcript (Patmore includes a version of the note—"the Lady whom he saw for some few moments at Vauxhall"—that Woodhouse added with an asterisk after the heading in the clerk's MS). Patmore's transcript was printer's copy for *1848,* which followed it in the mistaken "thine" in 4.

The *Hood's* text is a quite different version, with unique substantive variants in 1, 7, and 13–14. Although Hood explained to W. F. Watson, in a letter of 8 October 1844 (forthcoming in Peter F. Morgan's edition of Hood's letters), that the sonnet "was sent me, *copied,* from [Keats's] M.S.," nothing further is known of his source. The variants may represent an intervening revision by Reynolds or some other copyist, editorial tinkering by Hood, or a combination of these.

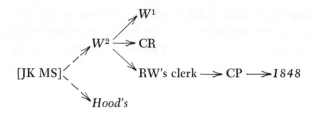

While the relative authoritativeness of W^2's and *Hood's* readings is uncertain, I think W^2 is probably the better basis for a standard text. Both Garrod and Allott follow *1818* (Garrod exactly), and thus both incorporate Patmore's change of "thy" to "thine" in 4.

To the Nile

Written on 4 February 1818 (*Letters*, I, 227–228). First published in *PDWJ*, 19 July 1838, and then in *1848*, I, 99–100. Garrod, p. 484; Allott, pp. 307–308.

Though we lack both the original draft produced in the sonnet-writing contest with Hunt and Shelley on 4 February (probably the MS that Clarke thought Hunt had in 1846—*KC*, II, 155) and a holograph copy dated 6 February (see below), we do have three transcripts by Woodhouse (W^2, W^1, and one in his interleaved *1817*—transcription in Sperry, pp. 160–161) and copies by Charlotte Reynolds, Brown, and Dilke. The lost transcript sent by Taylor to Hessey in 1853 (*KC*, II, 314) probably was made from *1848*.

The earlier of the two recoverable states of text, represented by Woodhouse's and Charlotte Reynolds' transcripts, has "Stream" in 2, "Art thou so beautiful, or a wan smile, / Pleasant but to those Men who, sick" in 6–7, "them" in 8, and "And ignorance doth make" in 10. In place of these readings, the later state, represented by Brown's copy with three lines in Keats's hand, has "Chief" (2), "Art thou so fruitful? or dost thou beguile / Such Men to honor thee, who, worn" (6–7), "for" (8), and "Tis ignorance that makes" (10).

W^2 ("from J.K.'s M.S."), the two other Woodhouse transcripts, and Charlotte Reynolds' copy are all dated 6 February, and pretty clearly derive from a lost holograph that probably had that date on it (perhaps a MS in the possession of J. H. Reynolds, since Reynolds included the sonnet in his "volume of Poetry" that Woodhouse saw in November 1818— see *KC*, I, 63). I should guess that Woodhouse took W^2 from this lost holograph, and copied both W^1 and the version in his interleaved *1817* from W^2. He later in W^2 entered in shorthand the variant readings to 2, 6–8, and 10 from Brown's transcript (which he cites as his source specifically for the variant in 10). Charlotte Reynolds, though she has unique variants in 11 ("bestow" for "bedew"), 12 ("doth" for "dost"), and 14 ("doth" again), probably also copied W^2.

Brown's transcript is the real oddity among the MSS. He omitted 6–8 as he copied, and Keats wrote in the revised lines in the space that Brown left for them. In the scholarly manner of Woodhouse (and *not* in the unscholarly manner of Brown, who was a fairly accurate copyist but does not cite variants in any other of his transcripts), Brown records in two notes the earlier readings of 2 and 6–7 (with "Pleasing . . . after" for Woodhouse's "Pleasant . . . sick with"). And there is a penciled "them" written above "for" (8) in a hand that appears to be neither Keats's nor Brown's. The best explanation for the first of these peculiarities, Brown's leaving space for Keats's 6–8, is that Brown made his copy while Keats was trying to reconstruct or revise his original text. I think "them" (which was entered while Brown still possessed his copy, since the word appears in the *PDWJ* version) was penciled in by Woodhouse at the time that he took the variant readings from Brown's transcript. Dilke's transcript is an exact copy of Brown's in all particulars (save that he omits Brown's notes and saw the MS before "them" was inserted above the line in 8).

Brown's transcript was the basis for the *PDWJ* text and the source of printer's copy for *1848*. Both early printings made choices among the readings presented in the transcript. *PDWJ* has the revised text except for "Stream" in 2 and "them" in 8; *1848* printed both of these variants plus "Those" for "Such" in 7 (Keats first wrote "Those," then deleted it and substituted "Such" in his revised lines in Brown's transcript).

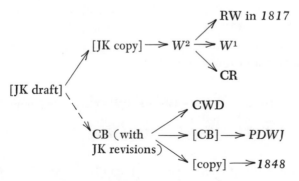

Brown's transcript with Keats's revised lines should be the basis for a standard text, and I think we should print "for" rather than "them" in 8

(since the latter word appears to be a mistaken correction based on the earlier version). Garrod follows *1848,* altering punctuation and capitalization in 3, 4, and 9, and changing "Those" to "Such" in 7. He does not emend "Stream" or "them" in 2 and 8. Allott takes her text "from *1848,* which follows Brown's transcript corrected in K.'s hand," but prints "Chief" in 2, "Such" in 7, and "for" in 8. She has, that is, all the right readings, and merely a misleading explanation of her source.

Sponsor, a jealous honorer of thine

Written on 5 February 1818 (the date in all five of the MSS). First published in *1848,* I, 11. Garrod, p. 476; Allott, pp. 308–309.

We have two holograph MSS—the original draft in Harvard's Dumbarton Oaks Research Library, Washington, D.C. (see Ethel B. Clark, *HLB,* 1 [1947], 90–100—facsimile of the MS facing p. 90), and a fair copy in the Morgan Library (facsimile in the *Bookman,* 31 [1906], 16)—and transcripts by Woodhouse (W^2), one of his clerks (Garrod's *T*), and W. A. Longmore (facsimile in the Clark article, facing p. 91).

There are no substantive differences among the MSS (except that Longmore's late transcript has "quill" for "quell" in 7). Keats's fair copy in the Morgan contains the final text of the Dumbarton Oaks draft; W^2 ("f^m JK's M.S.") is a copy of the Morgan MS; and Woodhouse's clerk transcribed W^2. Milnes printed the poem in *1848* probably from an amanuensis' copy of the clerk's transcript, the only source known to have been available to him. The *1848* text has "quill" for Keats's, Woodhouse's, and the clerk's "quell" in 7, and " 'scape" for the MSS' "escape" in 9. At the end of 1870 W. A. Longmore, son of Eliza Reynolds, sent Milnes a fairly accurate copy of the Dumbarton Oaks draft, and in 1875 lent him the MS itself (*KC,* II, 331–332, 334, 340); Milnes included in a note to the poem in *1876* a text representing most of the punctuation and spelling peculiarities of Longmore's transcript.

$$\text{JK draft} \begin{cases} \text{JK fair copy} \longrightarrow W^2 \longrightarrow \text{RW's clerk} \longrightarrow \text{[copy]} \longrightarrow 1848 \\ \text{WAL} \longrightarrow \text{[copy]} \longrightarrow 1876 \text{ note} \end{cases}$$

Keats's fair copy is the proper basis for a standard text. Both Garrod and Allott follow this MS, modernizing the punctuation.

Blue! 'Tis the life of heaven—the domain

Written on 8 February 1818 (the date in all five of the extant transcripts). First published in *1848,* II, 295. Garrod, p. 464; Allott, pp. 309–310.

Keats's original draft, formerly in the possession of one of George Keats's daughters in Louisville, who gave it to Oscar Wilde, has disappeared, but a facsimile is included in Wilde's article about it in *Century Guild Hobby Horse,* 1 (1886), 81–86. The extant MSS are all transcripts—by Woodhouse (two copies, W^2 and W^1), Charlotte Reynolds, one of Woodhouse's clerks (Garrod's *T*), and Coventry Patmore. A version written by Reynolds in a copy of his *The Garden of Florence* (1821), now apparently lost, is reported and transcribed by A. J. Horwood, *Athenaeum,* 3 June 1876, p. 764. The unidentified transcript in Isabella Towers' copy of *1817* (in 1932 owned by Douglas Cleverdon, of Bristol) was clearly taken from *1848* (it repeats *1848*'s misreading, "made" for "mock," in the epigraph), and can be ignored. Another copy by Woodhouse that Severn possessed in 1845 (*KC,* II, 131) has also not survived.

Apparently all texts after the original draft derive from a single lost holograph written, as Woodhouse notes in W^2, "in a M.S. collection of the Poetry of [Reynolds,] Keats & others." The poem is an answer to the last two lines of Reynolds' sonnet *Sweet poets of the gentle antique line,* later published in *The Garden of Florence,* and both Woodhouse in W^2 and Charlotte Reynolds copied Reynolds' sonnet and then Keats's, heading the latter "Answer. J. Keats." Woodhouse took W^2 "from K's M.S.," and presumably made W^1 (with a more elaborate heading, "Lines Written upon reading a Sonnet by J. H. Reynolds, which will be found p: 17," referring to the W^1 copy of Reynolds' poem) from W^2. Charlotte Reynolds' transcript probably also came from W^2, as did the clerk's late transcript ("Answer—by J Keats," to which Woodhouse added "to a Sonnet ending thus" and a quotation of the last line and a half of Reynolds' sonnet). Patmore followed the clerk's MS (omitting "by J Keats" in the clerk-Woodhouse heading), and his transcript was printer's copy for *1848.*

Reynolds' transcript in *The Garden of Florence* has variants from the extant MSS in 1 ("hue" for the MSS' "life"), 2 ("bright" for "wide"), and 6 ("With all his tributary" for "And all its vassal"). Because it is virtually certain that he worked from the same MS that Woodhouse copied, the variants have to be considered his own alterations, whether intentional revisions, careless errors, or the results of copying from memory (see Woodhouse's remark concerning Reynolds' transcripts of some other sonnets—"Perhaps he wrote them from Memory"—in *KC*, I, 63). In any case the differences are illuminating, since a number of transcripts that we have of other poems derive from lost copies made—perhaps in the same casual manner—by Reynolds.

Among extant MSS there are no substantive variants until we get to Patmore's transcript, where "orbs" in the second line used as epigraph is changed to "those" (the other transcripts and Reynolds' published text have "orbs") and "to" in 9 is miscopied or changed to read "of." *1848* printed Patmore's slightly altered heading, "those" in the epigraph, and "of" in 9, and understandably misread his "mock" in the epigraph as "made" (an error corrected, however, in the *1848* errata).

W¹
W² → CR
[JK draft ⟶ [JK revised RW's clerk ⟶ CP ⟶ *1848*
—Wilde MS]   MS]

[JHR in *The Garden of Florence*]

Two things ought to be clear from the above—that the use of Reynolds' lines as epigraph first appears in Woodhouse's addition to the transcript by his clerk (though of course Woodhouse and Charlotte Reynolds both had copies of Reynolds' sonnet to refer to), and that "those" in the epigraph and "of" in 9 are corruptions beginning with Patmore. Obviously W² is the proper basis for a standard text, and probably we should head the poem by its first line and remove the quotation from Reynolds' sonnet to an explanatory note. Both Garrod and Allott reproduce *1848* (Garrod exactly except for adding a comma in 10), and thus both have the Patmore-*1848* heading and Patmore's errors of wording in the epigraph and 9.

O thou whose face hath felt the winter's wind

Written on 19 February 1818 (drafted or else immediately copied—it is not known which—in a letter to Reynolds of that date). First published in *1848*, I, 90. Garrod, pp. 482–483; Allott, pp. 310–311.

The holograph of Keats's letter to Reynolds is in the Robert H. Taylor

Collection, Princeton University Library (text of the poem in *Letters*, I, 233). The single extant transcript is by Woodhouse (copying the letter in his letterbook), who changed Keats's "has" to "hath" in 2 and 5. Milnes printed the poem as part of the letter from an amanuensis' copy of Woodhouse's transcript, altering " 'mong" to "among" in 3 and "shall" to "will" in 8.

$$\text{JK letter} \longrightarrow \text{RW (letterbook)} \longrightarrow \text{[copy]} \longrightarrow \textit{1848}$$

The holograph letter is of course the proper basis for a standard text. Both Garrod and Allott follow the letter (Garrod with an intermixture of *1848* accidentals but not any of Woodhouse's or *1848*'s substantive changes).

Extracts from an Opera

Written in 1818 (so dated in the various transcripts; several writers place the six lyrics among the "many songs & Sonnets" that Keats mentions in February 1818—*Letters*, I, 228—but this more specific dating is highly conjectural). First published in *1848*, II, 264–267. Garrod, pp. 438–440; Allott, pp. 313–316.

We have no extant holograph of any of the lyrics. The surviving MSS are transcripts of all six known songs by Brown and Woodhouse in W^2, and partial transcripts by Woodhouse in W^3 (the second and fifth songs only) and Charlotte Reynolds (the first, fifth, and sixth songs). There are no significant differences among the MSS (Brown has "ought" in the fourth line of the fourth lyric where W^2 has "aught," and Charlotte Reynolds omits "up" in the sixth line of the final lyric). One may suppose that Brown transcribed a lost holograph (or holographs). Woodhouse's source is unknown; he took at least his W^2 date from Brown, and could have taken his texts as well, since they are very close to Brown's in minor details. Charlotte Reynolds probably copied W^2. There seems to be no ready explanation for her selection of lyrics from the group, or for Woodhouse's in the W^3 scrapbook. Brown's transcript was printer's copy for *1848*.

In principle (and in the face of ignorance) I think Brown's MS should be the basis for a standard text. Garrod reproduces *1848* exactly except in the second poem, where he omits the first stanza number and emends the punctuation of 3, and in the third poem, where he accidentally transposes "-roasted" and "-toasted" in 13 and 15. (His headnotes concerning dating are misleading, since Brown's transcript and W^2 do not date the poems separately but give a single date, "1818" and "C.B. 1818" respectively, for the whole.) Allott does not depart substantively from the Brown-*1848* text.

Four seasons fill the measure of the year

Written in the second week of March 1818 (after Keats's arrival at Teignmouth on the 6th or 7th and before he copied the poem in a letter to Benjamin Bailey on the 13th). First published in Leigh Hunt's *Literary Pocket-Book* for 1819 (1818), p. 225, and then in Galignani (1829), p. 71 of the Keats section. Garrod, p. 536; Allott, pp. 312–313.

We have a holograph copy in the 13 March letter to Bailey (MS at Harvard, text in *Letters*, I, 243), two transcripts by Woodhouse (W^2 and that in a letterbook copy of the letter to Bailey), and a transcript each by J. C. Stephens, one of Woodhouse's clerks (Garrod's *T*), and Coventry Patmore. The copy that C. C. Clarke sent Milnes via Severn in 1846 (*KC*, II, 155) has not survived.

Of the two known states of text, the earlier is represented by Keats's untitled version in the letter, which Woodhouse twice copied from the letter MS ("transcribed from K's letter to B.B." in W^2), his clerk copied from W^2 (with "came" for "come" in 7), and Patmore transcribed from the clerk's MS (restoring "come"). The other state is that of Hunt's *Pocket-Book,* which adds a title, "The Human Seasons," and varies substantively from the first state in 2, 3, 5, 6–10, 13, and 14. Both Stephens and Galignani took their texts from the *Pocket-Book*—Stephens with independent substantive variants in 4 ("at" for "with"), 9 ("its" for "his"), and 14 ("forget," coincidentally the reading of Keats's letter, for "forego"), and Galignani emending "His" to "Is" in 8.

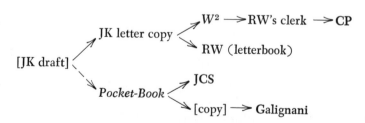

The considerable problem presented by the texts of this poem is whether or not Keats was responsible for the extensive changes between the earlier version (the letter copy) and that of the *Pocket-Book*. One assumes that the *Pocket-Book* text derives from a holograph, but the variants—transpositions in 2, single word changes in 3, 5, 13, and 14, and the complete revision of 6–10—amount almost to a rewriting of the poem. If Keats did in fact provide the *Pocket-Book* version, then it of course should be the basis for a standard text. If Hunt was responsible, however—and the frequency with which unique readings appear elsewhere in Keats's texts published by Hunt and other periodical and annual editors makes this a definite possibility (see Section III.2)—then we should base our texts on the letter version. There is very little evidence for deciding, but I think the earlier text is the more reliably authoritative.

Both Garrod and Allott print the *Pocket-Book* version, though neither includes the *Pocket-Book*'s title. If Keats was responsible for this later text, his MS very likely did have "nigh / His" in 7–8; but extant holographs of other poems often show "n" for "h" and added initial "h," and "high / Is" (Milnes's emendation in *1876*) makes much better sense than either the *Pocket-Book* wording or Galignani's emendation.

For there's Bishop's teign

Written on 21 March 1818 (in a letter to Haydon of that date). First published in Tom Taylor's *Life of Benjamin Robert Haydon, Historical Painter, from His Autobiography and Journals* (1853), I, 362–363. Garrod, pp. 555–556; Allott, pp. 316–318.

The holograph draft in Keats's letter to Haydon (MS at Harvard, text in *Letters,* I, 249–251) is our sole source of text. Taylor's version (as part of the letter) includes some of Keats's introductory prose as the first line of the poem ("Here all the summer could I stay"), and has substantive errors in 3, 13, 19, 24, 25, 34, 35, 36, 39, and 42. Most of these —all but the spurious first line and "violets . . . Sit" for Keats's "violet . . . Sits" in 34–35—were corrected by H. B. Forman when he made a fresh text in 1883. Garrod takes his wording and accidentals from Forman, but banishes the added first line and corrects 34–35 to produce the same substantive text as Keats's letter draft. Allott follows the letter MS, but has Taylor's and Forman's "violets . . . Sit" in 34–35.

Where be ye going, you Devon maid

Written on 21 March 1818 (in a letter to Haydon of that date). First published in Tom Taylor's *Life of Benjamin Robert Haydon* (1853), I, 363–364. Garrod, pp. 546–547; Allott, pp. 318–319.

As for the preceding poem, the holograph draft in Keats's letter to

Haydon (MS at Harvard, text in *Letters,* I, 251) is our sole source of text. Taylor's version (as part of the letter) has substantive errors in 1, 2, 5, 7, 8, and 14. Forman's 1883 text corrected most of these, but still varies from the letter in 2 ("in the" for Keats's "ithe") and 14 ("Your . . . the" for "And your . . . *this*"). Garrod reproduces Forman exactly except for adding a hyphen in the last line. Allott's text is closer to the holograph, but nevertheless omits "And" in 14. None of the editors follows Keats's underlining to emphasize sexual puns in 13 (*"nook"*) and 14 (*"on this willow"*).

Over the hill and over the dale

Written on 23 or 24 March 1818 (Dawlish Fair was on the 23rd; Keats either drafted or copied the poem in a letter to James Rice on the 24th). Lines 1–4 first published in *1848,* I, 119, and the complete poem first in Lowell, I, 610–611. Garrod, pp. 487–488; Allott, p. 319.

We have a holograph version in the letter to Rice of 24 March (MS at Harvard, text in *Letters,* I, 256–257), a transcript of the poem by Woodhouse (W^3), and a copy of 1–4, with an incomplete reference to W^3 for the rest, in Woodhouse's letterbook transcript of the letter. W^3 ("From a letter sent by Keats to Rice") unaccountably varies from the holograph text in 2 ("water" for "bourn") and 11 ("or" for "and"), and has "O (who) would not" for the letter's "O would not" in 19. Milnes printed 1–4 as part of the letter from an amanuensis' copy of Woodhouse's transcript in the letterbook. Lowell gives the poem from the letter (but with "lay" for "sat" in 8, Woodhouse's "or" in 11, and "O [who] wouldn't" for Keats's "O would not" in 19).

The holograph letter is of course the proper basis for a standard text, and both Garrod and Allott follow this MS (Garrod with only a few changes in punctuation and with roman for Keats's underlined "there" in 13). There is a chance that Keats intended "Or would not" rather than "O who would not" in 19; Garrod follows Woodhouse and Lowell in giving "O <who> . . ." and Allott prints "Oh, who . . . ."

Dear Reynolds, as last night I lay in bed

Written on 25 March 1818 (Woodhouse's date for the letter to Reynolds in both W^2 and his letterbook). First published in *1848,* I, 113–116. Garrod, pp. 484–487; Allott, pp. 320–326.

The single extant MS is Woodhouse's W^2 transcript, from Keats's lost letter, headed "To J. H. Reynolds Esqr" (text in *Letters,* I, 259–263); in the letterbook one of Woodhouse's clerks transcribed the prose that followed these lines in the lost holograph, but he includes only the first line and a half of poetry, and Woodhouse has added a note referring to W^2 for the rest. Though in *1848* Milnes took the prose from the letterbook, his source for the lines themselves is unknown, since it is fairly clear that the W^2 book of transcripts was not available to him. The *1848* text differs substantively from W^2 in 38, 61, 73, 75, 90, 94, and 109, and omits the final four lines. Milnes corrected 73, 90, and 94 in his one-volume revised *Life* of 1867.

Since Milnes's source is unknown, W^2 is obviously the proper basis for a standard text, though I think we should not regard Woodhouse's title there as authoritative. Garrod follows W^2 almost exactly in every detail ("pontiff" for Woodhouse's "pontif" in 20 is the only clear difference between his text and W^2, though he might have noted the original reading "Gloams" in 21, which Woodhouse verified with *"so"* in the margin and then seems to have corrected to "Gleams"). Allott also takes her text from W^2, emending "patent" to "patient" in 14 (accepting S. R. Swaminathan's suggestion in *N&Q,* August 1967, pp. 306–307) and dividing 82 into two half-lines.

To J. R.

Written perhaps in April 1818 (Lowell, I, 615–618, and others, on the basis of the inscription in a copy of *Guzman d'Alfarache* now at Harvard, have conjectured that "J. R."—James Rice—visited Keats at Teignmouth on 18–20 April; but the poem may of course refer to some other occasion that we know nothing about). First published in *1848,* II, 296. Garrod, p. 465; Allott, pp. 351–352.

We have a holograph MS at Harvard and transcripts by Woodhouse (W^2), one of his clerks (Garrod's T), and Coventry Patmore. All four MSS are headed "To J. R.," and there are no substantive differences among them. The extant holograph may be Keats's original draft, though there are signs of composition (as opposed to copying) only toward the end, where "keep" in 12 appears to have been written over another word, perhaps "wrap," and there are a canceled line and a half between 12 and 13. Woodhouse certainly transcribed this MS (like the holograph, W^2 has very little punctuation, but agrees with Keats's marks at the end of 8, 10, and 12; and Woodhouse left a blank space, in which he later penciled "keep," where he could not initially make out Keats's word in 12). The clerk followed W^2, Patmore copied the clerk's MS, and Patmore's transcript was printer's copy for *1848*. Milnes mistakenly altered the title to "To J. H. Reynolds" (the *1848* heading) on Patmore's MS.

$$\text{JK MS} \longrightarrow W^2 \longrightarrow \text{RW's clerk} \longrightarrow \text{CP} \longrightarrow 1848$$

Clearly the extant holograph is the proper basis for a standard text. Both Garrod and Allott correct Milnes's title but otherwise follow *1848* (Garrod exactly except for omitting a hyphen in 13).

Isabella; or, The Pot of Basil

Written in February–April 1818 ("the first few stanzas" before Keats departed for Teignmouth on 4 March, and the rest probably late in March, after finishing work on *Endymion,* and in April; completed by 27 April— *Letters,* I, 274). First published in *1820.* Garrod, pp. 215–235; Allott, pp. 326–351.

The ample materials for this poem begin with Keats's original draft, which was once in the possession of Severn and was given away by him in fragments of a stanza or two apiece. We have or know something about roughly two-thirds of the MS, as follows (the details partly from Garrod's headnote):

1–48	Texas Christian University ("the first few stanzas" referred to in *Letters,* I, 274—facsimiles of 1–48 in Lyle H. Kendall, Jr., *A Descriptive Catalogue of the W. L. Lewis Collection,* Part One, Fort Worth, 1970, following p. 114; facsimile of 1–24 in Sotheby sale catalogue, 13 August 1941)
49–56	Harvard (facsimile in Sotheby sale catalogue, 28 July 1930)
57–64	Historical Society of Pennsylvania
65–72	Harvard (facsimiles in Sotheby sale catalogue, 28 July 1930, and *Historical & Literary Autographs: The Collection of the Late Alfred C. Meyer,* Anderson Galleries sale catalogue, New York, 1938, Part One, p. 34)
81–88	Historical Society of Pennsylvania
89–96	Harvard (facsimiles and transcriptions of this and the next item in *The Renowned Library of the Late John A. Spoor,* Parke-Bernet sale catalogue, New York, 1939, Part I, pp. 150–152)
113–120	Harvard

193–200   Welbeck Abbey (transcription in the *Athenaeum,* 6 April
          1912, pp. 389–390)
216–224   Welbeck Abbey (details in the *Athenaeum,* as for the pre-
          ceding)
225–232   Cornell (details in *TLS,* 27 June 1942, p. 319)
233–248   Harvard (facsimile in *The Library of Jerome Kern,* Ander-
          son Galleries sale catalogue, New York, 1929, p. 252)
249–256   Cornell (details in *TLS,* as for 225–232)
257–326   Harvard (facsimiles of 321–326 and 345–352 in Christie
          sale catalogue, 1 July 1970)
337–339   University of Texas
340–342   The Carl H. Pforzheimer Library (transcriptions of this
          and the third item below in *Shelley and His Circle,*
          Vol. VI, ed. Donald H. Reiman, Cambridge, Mass.,
          1973, p. 798)
345–352   Harvard
361–364   University of Texas
365–366   The Carl H. Pforzheimer Library
385–392   National Library of Scotland
411–416   National Library of Scotland
417–424   Harvard
425–432   University of Texas
433–472   Harvard
473–480   Formerly owned by Owen D. Young (facsimile of this and
          497–503 in *The Library of Jerome Kern,* p. 253)
481–488   "Given by Severn to Miss Kennaway" with an earlier stanza
          not identifiable (Garrod, p. 215)
489–496   University of Texas (facsimiles in Maggs Bros. sale cata-
          logue, August 1915, and American Art Association sale
          catalogue, 15 February 1927)
497–503   Formerly owned by Owen D. Young

Keats's fair copy, in the notebook that George Keats later filled with
transcripts to take back to America, is in the British Museum (facsimiles
of a page each in Colvin, facing p. 394, and Hampstead Keats, facing
III, 54; transcription of the whole with interspersed commentary in Rid-
ley, pp. 24–53), and we have a shorthand transcript by Woodhouse (W^3
—facsimile of the first page of text in Finney, facing I, 372) and also
two longhand transcripts by Woodhouse (W^2, W^1), one of which was
printer's copy for *1820.* A fourth Woodhouse transcript (*KC,* I, 79)—
though not necessarily the last of the four—has not survived. Keats quotes
319–320 in a late letter to Fanny Brawne (*Letters,* II, 256); his letter
to Reynolds of 27 April 1818 contained the draft text of 89–104 and

233–240, but the holograph of the letter has been lost, and Woodhouse's clerk included only the opening lines of the three stanzas in his letterbook transcript, to which Woodhouse added the draft reading of 237 (*Letters,* I, 275).

I think it safe to assume that the draft and the fair copy, which Keats made soon after completing the draft, are the only versions that ever existed in the poet's own hand (see *Letters,* I, 274, 283; I take both passages as references to the writing of the extant fair copy, which Keats subsequently lent rather than gave to Reynolds). Woodhouse's shorthand transcript was clearly based on the latter MS (it records peculiarities of the fair copy in such readings as "seath" in 117, "peal" altered to "peel" in 120, the incomplete 200, "drank" with "a" underlined in 267, "though" with "o" underlined in 287, and "Campaign" altered to "Champaign" in 347, all of which Woodhouse wrote in longhand in the transcript). The difficult problem is to determine the sources of W^2 and W^1, which have virtually identical texts and in each case theoretically could have come (1) from Keats's fair copy, (2) from Woodhouse's shorthand transcript, (3) from a lost intervening Woodhouse transcript, or (4) one from the other (i.e., W^2 from W^1 or W^1 from W^2—in any event, contrary to Garrod, p. xxxvii, they were not taken from Keats's *draft*). There are too many differences between W^2W^1 and Keats's fair copy to suppose that either transcript was made directly from the fair copy. But for the other possibilities the evidence is inconclusive. I should guess either that W^2 and W^1 independently derive from the shorthand transcript, or that W^2 was made from the shorthand transcript and W^1 from W^2. As originally written, W^1 has readings in 30, 63, 267, and 350 that agree with the shorthand against W^2, and also readings in fourteen other lines that agree with W^2 against the shorthand. Probably the best explanation for these circumstances is that Woodhouse copied W^1 from W^2 but may also have consulted his shorthand at the same time.

What is most interesting is the number of changes that Woodhouse made in the course of his copying. *1820*'s "pray thee" (187), "I'll" (207), "And" (287), "hast" (334), "champaign" (347), "Through" (412), and "and sun" (417) all first appear in the shorthand transcript, and so probably does "pale" (281), though the shorthand reading is questionable, since the symbols for "poor" and "pale" are almost identical (Keats's fair copy has "poor," while W^2 and W^1 read "pale"). *1820*'s "lips" (30), "least" (40), "Thy" (62), "Thine" (63), "Sang" (78), "the" (144), "footstep" (196), "weeps" (233), "Time after time" (261), "drunk" (267), "which" (276), "one" (303), "it" (304, based on a marginal "q[uery]. *it*" in the shorthand transcript), "And" (309), "should'st" (350), "this" (359), "fringed" (405), "From" (453), "her Basil" (472), "on" (489), and "In" (500) all first appear in W^2 and W^1. It is no wonder that Woodhouse admired the poem as much as he did, since he seems to have contributed to its wording in nearly thirty lines in his successive transcripts and probably effected or influenced other changes in the proofs.

Keats read over W^1 and made changes and corrections, sometimes in response to queries on the MS by Taylor and Woodhouse, in 145, 151–152, 159, 199–200, 287, 315, 373, 382, 393, 394, and possibly other lines (Taylor seems to have changed "speak" to "breathe" in 30 and to have written in the *1820* text of 55–56, 159, and 373–374, and an intermediate version of 398; I cannot identify the hand that corrected "seathe" or "scathe" to "seeth" in 117). Keats also added some instructions—"Stop this as you please" opposite 46, "Please point this as you like" opposite 246–247—and gave Woodhouse or the publishers a choice of readings in 200. From this W^1 transcript, where the main title "Isabella" shows up for the first time (probably it was a later addition), the *1820* text was set in type. The correcting of stanza indentions, the deletion of extraneous material (Woodhouse's "Written at Teignmouth in the Spring of 1818 at the suggestion of J.H.R." at the end of the transcript), and the appearance of "Stet" in two places all support Garrod's conclusion (p. xxxvi), based on remnants of sealing wax supposedly used to close up other parts of the MS and leave the *Isabella* pages free for the compositor, that W^1 was used as printer's copy. The further new readings that appear for the first time in *1820*—"the" (6), "more" (75), "this" (102, though "is" is penciled over the last letter of "the" in W^2, and "this" is altered to "the" in W^1), "courteously" (189), "comfort me within" (304), "Love impersonate was ever" (398), and "your" (485, the reading of Keats's draft, however; a penciled "q[uery] your" appears opposite the line in W^2)—may have originated with Keats, Woodhouse, Taylor, or all of them working together.

JK draft →JK fair copy →RW shorthand →W^2→W^1→*1820*

Since, as far as we know, Keats all along approved the changes made in the poem, we must continue to regard *1820* as the proper basis for a standard text. Garrod follows *1820,* adding a comma in 249, lowercasing "Basil" in 416, 423, 428, 458, 472, 473, 488, 490, 494, 496, 498, and 504, and changing "your" to "you" in 485 (following the fair copy and the transcripts). He errs in omitting a dash at the end of 102, a semicolon at the end of 132, a colon at the end of 202, a comma at the end of 253, and the apostrophe in " 'Twas" in 495. Allott does not depart substantively from *1820*.

Mother of Hermes! and still youthful Maia

Written on 1 May 1818 (the date that Keats gives, along with a copy of the lines, in a letter to Reynolds of 3 May 1818). First published in *1848*, I, 135. Garrod, p. 488; Allott, pp. 353–354.

The extant MSS are a letterbook transcript by one of Woodhouse's clerks (copying the letter to Reynolds—text of the poem in *Letters*, I, 278), a transcript by Woodhouse (W^2), and a late copy by another of Woodhouse's clerks (Garrod's T).

The MSS do not differ substantively. The first clerk, working from the lost holograph of the letter, copied 11 ff. as three lines:

> Of Heaven, and few ears rounded by thee
> My song should die away content as theirs
> Rich in the simple worship of a day.—

In going over his clerk's transcript Woodhouse inserted double virgules in red ink after "span" in 10, "ears" in the next line, "away" and "theirs" in the next line, and "day" at the end, and noted beside the text, "Perhaps the lines sho^d be divided as shewn in red Ink. R.W." In W^2, where he added the title "Ode to May—Fragment" (Keats in his letter speaks of intending "to finish the ode all in good time"), Woodhouse divided the lines according to his own suggestion in the letterbook transcript:

> Of heaven, and few ears,
> Rounded by thee my song should die away,
> Content as theirs,
> Rich in the simple worship of a day.

Because Woodhouse wrote "Perhaps . . ." in his note in the letterbook, and did not comment on the lines in W^2, it seems very likely that W^2 was made from the clerk's transcript rather than independently from Keats's letter. The later clerk transcribed W^2. Milnes printed the poem as part of the letter from an amanuensis' copy of the first clerk's letterbook transcript, dividing the final lines according to Woodhouse's markings there. *1848* introduced a single substantive change, "on" for the transcripts' "in" in 7.

$$[\text{JK draft}] \longrightarrow [\text{JK letter copy}] \longrightarrow \text{RW's clerk} \nearrow^{W^2 \longrightarrow \text{RW's clerk } (T)}_{(\text{letterbook}) \searrow [\text{copy}] \longrightarrow 1848}$$

The first clerk's letterbook transcript appears to be the proper basis for a standard text. Garrod reproduces *1848* exactly, retaining the erroneous "on" in 7. Allott follows the letterbook transcript, dividing the last lines as Woodhouse had marked them. It seems reasonable to accept Woodhouse's suggestion as long as it is understood that the rearrangement of lines is an emendation rather than a restoration of any known Keats text. Garrod has no note on the final lines (nor does he record the transcripts' reading for 7).

To Homer

Written in 1818 (so dated in all four of the transcripts; a more precise dating is not possible). First published in *1848,* II, 294. Garrod, p. 463; Allott, pp. 352–353.

We have a transcript each by Brown and Dilke and two by Woodhouse (W^2, W^1). The only substantive differences among the MSS occur in 3 and 6. Brown copied a lost holograph having "As one who strives against a level glance" in 3 and "For Jove" in 6. Subsequently Keats read over this transcript and deleted the last five words of 3, adding "sits ashore and longs perchance" above the canceled text. Dilke copied Brown's transcript in this revised state (he later, after seeing *1848,* marked "wast thou" in 5 to read "thou wast" and changed "spumy" in 7 to "spermy"). We do not know Woodhouse's source for W^2, which has the revised text of 3 (with the original reading in the margin in shorthand, no doubt from Brown's transcript, from which he also took the date) and "And Jove" in 6, which may be either an authoritative reading or a copying error. Possibly he took his text from Brown, altering 6 in the process of copying. W^1 is substantively the same as W^2, from which it presumably was made.

Brown's transcript was not in this case printer's copy for *1848,* but was almost surely the source from which printer's copy was taken. *1848* varies twice from Brown's text—"thou wast" for "wast thou" in 5 (either Milnes's intentional alteration or a copying or printing error) and "spermy" for "spumy" in 7 (a copying or printing error). My diagram is quite speculative concerning the source of W^2.

$$[\text{JK MS}] \longrightarrow \text{CB} \overset{\nearrow \text{CWD}}{\underset{\searrow [\text{copy}] \longrightarrow 1848}{\longrightarrow \text{W}^2 \longrightarrow \text{W}^1}}$$

Since Woodhouse's source and the authoritativeness of his "And Jove" in 6 are uncertain, Brown's transcript with Keats's revision should be the basis for a standard text. Garrod follows *1848*, omitting a comma at the end of 13 and changing "spermy" back to "spumy" in 7, but failing to correct *1848*'s "thou wast" in 5. Allott does not depart substantively from her source, Brown's transcript.

Give me your patience, Sister, while I frame

Written on 27 June 1818 (in a letter to George and Georgiana Keats under that date). First published in the New York *World*, 25 June 1877, p. 2. Garrod, pp. 567–568; Allott, pp. 354–356.

There are two holograph versions, Keats's original draft in the letter of 27, 28 June 1818 (MS at Harvard, text in *Letters*, I, 303–304) and a revised copy, made after the first letter was returned to him, in the 18 September section of his letter to George and Georgiana of 17–27 September 1819 (MS in the Morgan Library, text in *Letters*, II, 195). I have not identified the "MS. owned by J. G. Speed"—obviously a copy from the second letter, if not the holograph letter itself—that Garrod refers to in his headnote.

In recopying the poem in the later letter Keats altered his text substantively in 2, 4, 14, 16, 18, and 19. These changes all seem considered revisions, and I would suggest that the later letter (which was the source of the first publication of the lines in 1877) is in this instance the better basis for a standard text. Both Garrod and Allott take their texts from this letter, Garrod with the title "Acrostic of My Sister's Name" (from Keats's prose in the letter) and Allott with the shorter heading "Acrostic." Garrod follows M. B. Forman's 1931 Oxford edition of Keats's letters in emending "Glow" in 12 to "Glowed"—an unnecessary change, as Allott points out.

Sweet, sweet is the greeting of eyes

Written on 28 June 1818 (in a letter to George and Georgiana Keats under that date). First published by Lowell, II, 28. Garrod, p. 547; Allott, p. 356.

The holograph draft in Keats's letter to George and Georgiana of 27, 28 June 1818 (MS at Harvard, text in *Letters,* I, 304) is our sole source of text. Lowell (in printing the letter), Garrod, and Allott all follow the MS accurately.

On Visiting the Tomb of Burns

Written on 1 July 1818 (the day on which Keats visited Burns's tomb and afterward either drafted or copied the sonnet in a letter to Tom Keats). First published in *1848,* I, 156–157. Garrod, p. 489; Allott, pp. 357–358.

The single extant MS is a transcript by John Jeffrey (in a copy of the letter to Tom of 29 June, 1, 2 July 1818—transcriptions in J. C. Maxwell's article, *K-SJ,* 4 [1955], 77, and in *Letters,* I, 308–309). Milnes printed the poem as part of the letter from an amanuensis' copy of Jeffrey's transcript. The *1848* text has "Though" for Jeffrey's "Through" in 7, "Sickly" for "Fickly" in 11, and "oft have" for "have oft" in 13. In 12, where Jeffrey had omitted the initial word, noting that "An illegible word occurs here," Milnes supplied the verb "Cast."

Jeffrey's transcript, our only MS version, should be the basis for a standard text. Garrod reproduces *1848,* changing only capitalization, spelling, and punctuation in 1, 5, 10, and 12, and thus retaining *1848's* substantive changes and "Cast" in 7, 11, 12, and 13 (he also keeps *1848's* colon at the end of 8, where there is no punctuation in Jeffrey's MS). Allott follows Jeffrey's transcript substantively except for incorporating *1848's* "Sickly" and "Cast" in 11 and 12; she does not add punctuation at the end of 8. Probably we should stick with Jeffrey's "Fickly" in 11, even though Keats's "S" is sometimes misread as "T," and therefore might also be misread as "F." For the missing verb in 12 we are free to choose another word if we can think of a better one than Milnes's "Cast."

Old Meg she was a gipsy

Written on 3 July 1818 (drafted in the morning in a letter to Fanny Keats, and copied almost immediately by both Brown in his journal and Keats in a second letter—see *Letters,* I, 311, 317, 438, and *KC,* II, 61–62; Rollins' note on the date in *Letters,* I, 312, is misleading, since the change from 2 to 3 July occurs on the preceding page a few lines before the text of the poem). First published in *PDWJ,* 22 November 1838, and then again in *PDWJ,* 22 October 1840, *Hood's Magazine,* 1 (June

1844), 562, and *1848,* I, 160–161. Garrod, p. 490; Allott, pp. 358–359.

We have both Keats's draft in the letter to Fanny Keats (MS in the Morgan Library, text in *Letters,* I, 311–312) and the copy that he made shortly afterward in a letter to Tom Keats (MS at Harvard, text in *Letters,* I, 317–318). The two letter texts differ very little from one another—the first reads "has" in 13 (corrected to "had" in the second letter), and the second reads "And" in 27 (a slip of the pen for "An" in the first). The first letter has the poem in quatrains, except for a final six-line stanza, while the second has no stanza divisions.

Though there are no extant transcripts, a lost copy that Brown took from the draft at the time Keats wrote the poem is of considerable importance as the basis for all of the early printings (Brown also intended to include the poem in his "Life" of Keats—see *KC,* II, 62). Brown's transcript, which we can reconstruct from the early printings, corrected Keats's draft version to "had" in 13, changed "o' " of both letter texts to "of" in 7 and 22, and arranged the first twenty-four lines into three eight-line stanzas. This is the form that the poem has in both of the *PDWJ* printings (the second in Chapter IV of Brown's "Walks in the North"— the text is reprinted in *Letters,* I, 438–439), in *Hood's* (printed probably from a copy sent in by Milnes, who was a frequent contributor to the magazine, though he would have known better than to head the poem, as it is in *Hood's,* "Now First Published"), and in *1848* (where "chip hat" in 28 was changed by mistaken emendation or printer's error to "ship-hat"). Milnes printed the letter to Tom in *1848* from an amanuensis' copy of a Jeffrey transcript, but for the poem itself, which Jeffrey omitted, I assume that he used Brown's transcript as printer's copy (see the third paragraph under *To Ailsa Rock*).

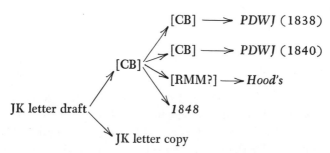

The consensus of the two holograph letters (with "had" in 13 and "An" in 27) should be the basis for a standard text, and an editor may choose whichever of the stanza/line arrangements better pleases him.

None of the early printed titles—"Meg Merrilies. A Ballad, written for the amusement of his young sister" in *PDWJ* (1838), "Meg Merrilies" in *PDWJ* (1840), and "Old Meg" in *Hood's*—is authoritative. Garrod follows the earlier letter in wording (except that he prints Brown's "of" in 7 and corrects "has" to "had" in 13), spelling, capitalization, and stanza division, but accepts *1848*'s punctuation and takes his title from *Hood's*. Allott has the same substantive text as Garrod (including "of" in 7) and the same arrangement of stanzas, but more properly heads the poem by its first line.

There was a naughty boy

Written on 3 July 1818 (in a letter to Fanny Keats on that day). First published in Forman (1883), II, 290–294. Garrod, pp. 557–559; Allott, pp. 359–363.

The holograph draft in Keats's letter to Fanny Keats (MS in the Morgan Library, text in *Letters,* I, 312–315) is our sole source of text. In first publishing the lines (under the title "A Song about Myself") Forman added section numbers (1 through 4), misread Keats's "finger" as "fingers" in 85 and "There" as "Then" in 96, divided 58 and 89 each into two lines, and printed the last six lines as five:

> So he stood in his shoes
>   And he wonder'd,
>   He wonder'd,
> He stood in his shoes
>   And he wonder'd.

Garrod follows Forman's punctuation, capitalization, and spelling, omits the title and section numbers, corrects the wording of 85 and 96, gives 58 and 89 as single lines, but also prints the last six lines as five, though in a different arrangement from Forman's:

> So he stood in
>   His shoes and he wonder'd,
>   He wonder'd,
> He stood in his
>   Shoes and he wonder'd.

(Rollins' text in *Letters* divides the second of these lines into two—"His shoes / And he wonderd.") Garrod's period at the end of 35 is a mistake. Allott ("Text from K.'s letter") has Forman's title and section numbers, his "Then" in 96 (but "finger" correct in 85), his arrangement of the various lines commented on above, and Garrod's period in 35.

Ah, ken ye what I met the day

Written on 9 or 10 July 1818 (Keats got the subject on the 9th and either drafted or copied the poem in a letter to Tom Keats on the 10th). First published in Forman (1883), III, 180–181. Garrod, pp. 552–553; Allott, pp. 363–364.

The holograph version in Keats's letter to Tom (MS in the British Museum, text in *Letters,* I, 327–328) is our sole source of text. Forman printed the poem as part of the letter, emending Keats's "craggis" in 3 to "craggi[e]s" and "A" in 5 to "A[h]," and misreading "thence" in 30 as "there." Garrod reproduces Forman's text, omitting the brackets in 3 and 5 and Forman's apostrophes in "An' " in 39 and 40, but retaining "there" in 30. Allott follows the letter text accurately except for introducing a line space between 24 and 25.

To Ailsa Rock

Written on 10 July 1818 (*KC,* II, 62; *Letters,* I, 329). First published in Hunt's *Literary Pocket-Book* for 1819 (1818), p. 225, and then in Alaric A. Watts's *The Poetical Album: or Register of Modern Fugitive Poetry* (1828), p. 167, Galignani (1829), pp. 71–72 of the Keats section, *PDWJ,* 13 September 1838, and *1848,* I, 167. Garrod, p. 491; Allott, pp. 364–365.

We have a holograph version in Keats's letter to Tom of 10–14 July (MS in the British Museum, text in *Letters,* I, 329–330) and transcripts by C. C. Clarke (Garrod's W^3) and J. C. Stephens. Clarke's surviving transcript is the one that Woodhouse expected "C. C. C. was to lend me" in August 1823 and may have received at the end of that year (*KC,* I, 275); the copy that Clarke sent Milnes via Severn in 1846 (*KC,* II, 155) is not now known.

The two principal texts of this sonnet differ substantively only in 2, where the holograph letter, *PDWJ,* and *1848* read "by" and the *Literary Pocket-Book,* Clarke, Watts, Stephens, and Galignani have "from." Keats's comment following the poem in the letter—"This is the only Sonnet of any worth I have of late written"—suggests that the letter version is a copy rather than the original draft. Brown made a copy at the time (probably in his journal) and intended to include the sonnet in his "Life" of Keats

(*KC*, II, 62). His lost transcript served as the basis for the *PDWJ* print-
ing (where the poem is headed "Ailsa Rock: in height 940 feet from the
sea, near the Ayrshire Coast," and "steep" in 13 is misprinted "sleep")
and was almost surely printer's copy for *1848*. (As with the five other
poems that Brown would have given in his "Life," all of which Milnes
incorporated into letter texts or his narrative in Volume I, the disappear-
ance of the transcript along with almost all of Milnes's MS for Volume I
may be taken as evidence that the transcript was printer's copy.)

Presumably the version in the *Literary Pocket-Book* came from a MS
supplied by Keats. All the remaining texts derive from this earliest print-
ing—Clarke's transcript directly (he notes "Literary Pocket Book for
1819" at the end), Stephens' transcript perhaps also directly (he similarly
has "Lit Pocket Book" at the end but miscopied "fowls' " as "fatal" in 2,
"or" as "&" in 7, and "Drown'd" as "Crowned" in 13), Galignani's text
probably by way of a single intervening copy made for the printer, and
Watts's version by way of some lost MS copy perhaps several removes from
the *Pocket-Book* text (Watts says in his Preface that "every poem is scru-
pulously referred to the work from which it has been derived," but Keats's
sonnet, unlike most of the other pieces in the volume, is not accompanied
by a reference to some "work" or periodical as the source, and one may
suppose therefore that Watts had the poem in MS; his text contains several
errors—"thunders" for "shoulders" in 3, "on" for "in" in 7, "dread" for
"dead" in 10, and "bow" for "wake" in 14).

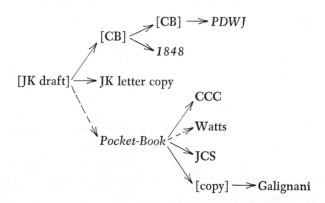

The choice of base-text for a standard edition—either Keats's letter
copy or the *Pocket-Book* version—depends on whether the *Pocket-Book*'s
"from" in 2 is considered authoritative or the result of Hunt's editing. The
frequency of unique variants in Hunt's texts of other Keats poems sug-
gests that we ought to follow the letter in this instance. Garrod takes his

text from the *Pocket-Book*. Allott, with "Text from K.'s letter," nevertheless has the *Pocket-Book*'s "from" in 2 and "is it" for Keats's "ist" in 5.

This mortal body of a thousand days

Written on 11 July 1818 (*Letters*, I, 322, 324, 332). First published in *1848*, I, 159. Garrod, p. 489; Allott, pp. 365–366.

There are no extant MSS, and *1848*—printed from a lost transcript by Brown, who quoted 3–4 in an article in the *Liberal*, 1 (1822), 328, and at one time intended to include the poem in his "Life" of Keats (*KC*, II, 63)—is our sole source of text. Garrod reproduces *1848* exactly, and Allott follows it substantively except in 5, where she has "own" for "old." This variant in 5 first appeared in Milnes's one-volume *Life* of 1867, and subsequently in *1876*; since we do not know the basis on which Milnes (or his printer) changed the text, probably we should retain "old."

All gentle folks who owe a grudge

Written on 17 July 1818 (the letter text of that date is probably the original draft, even though there are no deletions or other signs of fresh composition). First published in Forman (1883), II, 303–306. Garrod, pp. 560–561; Allott, pp. 366–368.

The holograph version in the first section of Keats's letter to Tom of 17–21 July 1818 (MS at Keats House, Hampstead—facsimile in Williamson, plate XIII, and text in *Letters*, I, 334–336) is our only authoritative text. An unidentified transcript at Harvard (a copy of the letter that Severn had made for Milnes—see *Letters*, I, 333 n.), the first printing of the poem by Forman, and Garrod's and Allott's texts all derive from this source. Forman added a title ("The Gadfly"), numbered the stanzas, omitted the last three words of 26 (printing "His seat * * *"), and mistakenly emended "Wert" (44) to "wort." Garrod generally follows Forman in accidentals (but not in title or stanza numbers), gives the full text of 26, prints "wort" in 44, and misprints "folks" (1) as "folk." Allott reproduces the letter text more directly (and more accurately) but like Forman adds stanza numbers.

Of late two dainties were before me plac'd

Written on 17 or 18 July 1818 (Keats saw Kotzebue's *The Stranger* on the evening of the 17th and wrote this sonnet about the performance either that night or the next day; probably the letter text of the 18th is the original draft). First published in the *Athenaeum*, 7 June 1873, p. 725. Garrod, p. 537; Allott, p. 369.

As for the preceding poem, the holograph version in Keats's letter to Tom of 17–21 July 1818 (MS at Keats House, Hampstead—facsimile in Williamson, plate XIV, and text in *Letters*, I, 337) is our only authoritative text. An unidentified transcript of the letter at Harvard, the first printing of the poem in the *Athenaeum*, and Garrod's and Allott's texts all come directly from this source.

There is a joy in footing slow across a silent plain

Written in July 1818 (on or before the 22nd, when Keats copied the lines into a letter to Bailey). Lines 1–6, 25–26, and 41–48 first published in *NMM*, 4 (March 1822), 252, and a complete text first in the *Examiner*, 14 July 1822, p. 445, and then in *1848*, I, 180–181. Garrod, pp. 491–493; Allott, pp. 370–372.

There are two holographs at Harvard—an earlier version that may be Keats's original draft and a revised copy in his letter to Bailey of 18, 22 July 1818 (text in *Letters*, I, 344–345)—and we have a transcript by Dilke, two transcripts by Woodhouse (W^3, W^2), and an unidentified transcript inserted in George Keats's notebook in the British Museum (Garrod's *E*). The MS that Dilke sent Milnes in the 1840's (*KC*, II, 161) is pretty surely the earlier Harvard holograph.

The earlier holograph has a title at the end of the text, "Lines written in the highlands after a visit to Burns's Country." The untitled letter copy, made soon after this (perhaps only a few days later, or even on the same day), shows substantive revisions in 1 ("joy" for the earlier holograph's "charm"), 6 ("the tale" for "each tale"), 8 ("the tongue," correcting the earlier MS's omission of "the"), 21 ("wedded" for "lidded"), 27 ("Man" for "one"), 36 ("fill" for "pain"), 45 ("the" for "his"), and 46 ("bleak" for "black"). All subsequent texts derive from one or the other of these holographs.

Brown took a copy of the earlier holograph, probably in his journal at the time Keats wrote the lines, and intended to include a text in his "Life" of Keats (*KC*, II, 64). His lost transcript was the source of the partial text printed at the end of his article on "Mountain Scenery" in *NMM* (where the seven-foot lines are divided into alternating tetrameters and trimeters) and was again the source of the *Examiner* text (where a headnote complains of the "mutilated" version in *NMM* and the lines are given as heptameters under the title "Lines Written in the Scotch Highlands"). Milnes printed the letter to Bailey in *1848* from an amanuensis' copy of

Woodhouse's letterbook transcript, but for the lines themselves, which Woodhouse omitted, he almost certainly used Brown's transcript as printer's copy (see the discussion of *To Ailsa Rock*). The *NMM, Examiner,* and *1848* texts have in common three substantive variants from the earlier holograph—"where" for "when" in 2, "in days" for "by times" in 5 (*1848* has "in times," a combination that Milnes may have invented after consulting the holograph), and "lose" for "loose" in 46 (correcting Keats's misspelling in both holographs); the *Examiner* and *1848* texts have "the tongue" in 8 (a line not included in *NMM*'s partial text) and paragraph spacings after 12, 22, 28, and 38. In addition, *1848* shows unique variants in 2 ("had been" for "has been"), 4 ("nettled" for "nettles"), 10 ("surf" for "scurf"), and 46 ("in" for "on"), all of which may be attributed to Milnes or his printer.

Dilke's transcript is also a copy of the earlier holograph; it has two substantive variants—"the tongue" in 8 and "world's" for the holograph's "Soul's" in 23—but is extremely close to the holograph's accidentals and does not have the "CB" flourish at the end. The unidentified transcript in George Keats's notebook was taken from the *Examiner*; like *NMM*, this transcript divides the lines into alternating tetrameters and trimeters, but it has the *Examiner*'s distinctive title and accidentals, and also the *Examiner*'s footnote ("Burns") to 28.

Woodhouse twice copied the lines from the letter to Bailey sometime in 1821. "K's own punctuation is adhered to," he notes in W^3 (a transcript that he made for Taylor), and "Copied from K's letter.—I have adhered to his own punctuation throughout" in W^2. Though he lowercased a number of capitalized words (especially in W^3, where he also wrote "has" for "hath" in 22), Woodhouse did a good job of preserving Keats's punctuation, varying in only six places in W^3 and five in W^2. Since three of the six W^3 punctuation variants do not appear in W^2, I suppose that he took both copies directly from the letter.

Both the earlier and the revised versions have claims to be the basis for a standard text. The choice depends primarily on how seriously we think Keats was working when he altered 1, 6, 21, 27, 36, 45, and 46 in the letter copy. Should we decide in favor of the earlier version, there is the further problem of whether Brown's variants in 2 ("where") and 5 ("in days") are authoritative. In this instance, however, mainly because Keats's changes do have the character of considered revisions, I suggest that we follow the letter copy and ignore Brown's variants.

Garrod reproduces the earlier holograph substantively (correcting the omission of "the" in 8 and the misspelling of "lose" in 46), with a mixture of accidentals from the earlier holograph, the letter, and *1848*; he errs only in omitting a period at the end of 22. Allott follows the letter copy, also correcting "loose" to "lose" in 46, but prints Brown's and *1848*'s "where" in 2.

Not Aladdin magian

Written between 24 and 26 July 1818 (Keats visited Staffa on 24 July, and either drafted or, more probably, copied the poem in a letter to Tom Keats on 26 July). First published in the *Western Messenger*, 1 (July 1836), 822–823, and then in *PDWJ*, 20 September 1838, and *1848*, I, 186–187. Garrod, pp. 493–495; Allott, pp. 372–375.

We have two holograph versions—the earlier in Keats's letter to Tom of 23, 26 July 1818 (MS at Harvard, text in *Letters*, I, 349–351) and the later in the 18 September section of the letter to George and Georgiana of 17–27 September 1819 (MS in the Morgan Library, text in *Letters*, II, 199–200)—and two transcripts by Woodhouse (W^2, W^1), a copy by Charlotte Reynolds, and a copy by Brown (transcription in Sharp, pp. 35–36 n.). The extant Brown transcript is the one that Severn mentions having in 1845 (*KC*, II, 131) and is not the same as another transcript, now lost, from which Brown would have given the poem in his "Life" of Keats (*KC*, II, 63). This latter version can be reconstructed from the *PDWJ* and *1848* texts.

The details for this poem are almost as complicated and puzzling as those for *Hush, hush! tread softly*. There are unique substantive variants, some of them involving entire lines, in Keats's first letter (4), in his second letter (19, 35, 36, 37, 43), in W^1 ("each" for "every" in 49f), in *PDWJ* ("these" for "the" in 40), and in Brown's extant transcript (31, 41, 46). Keats's first letter, W^2, W^1, and Charlotte Reynolds' transcript have all of the fifty-seven lines printed by Garrod (though in W^1 Woodhouse wrote the final eight lines in pencil); Keats's second letter omits 7–8 and breaks off after 44; *PDWJ* and *1848* omit 49*a–f*; and Brown's extant transcript omits 39–40 and ends with 49 (another hand has added 50–51 in pencil). The various titles are "Lines / On Visiting 'Staffa'— the Giant's Causeway in Ireland" (W^2, with a deleted word, possibly "Lycidas's," before "Lines," and the last five words lightly marked out in pencil), "Lines / On Visiting Staffa" (W^1), "Lines / On Visiting 'Staffa' " (Charlotte Reynolds), "Fingal's Cave in Staffa.—Fragment" (*PDWJ*), and "On Fingal's Cave. A Fragment" (Brown's extant transcript); the texts in Keats's letters and *1848* are untitled. If we set aside the titles and the unique variants, the principal substantive differences among the texts appear in 9, 27, 45, 46, and 49*a–f*.

Two early versions are represented by Keats's first letter and Woodhouse's and Charlotte Reynolds' transcripts, which agree in "at" (9), "architected" (27), "stupid" (45), and the inclusion of 49*a–f*, and differ only in 4 (where Keats's letter omits "a") and 46 (where the letter reads "Hath" for the other MSS' "Has"). Woodhouse's source is unknown, but the W^2 version is among poems taken from one or another Reynolds source, and I should guess that his text derives—probably by way of a lost Reynolds copy—from some unknown letter to Reynolds or one of his sisters written about the same time as the extant letter to Tom Keats. Very likely both W^1 and Charlotte Reynolds' transcript were made from W^2. George Keats lent James Freeman Clarke the holograph of the letter to Tom, and Clarke published the poem in the *Western Messenger* from this MS (*KC*, II, 140).

A later version is represented by the September 1819 letter to George and Georgiana, in which Keats recopied the poem from the letter to Tom, omitting several lines and making substantive changes in a number of others, including "on" for "at" in 9. Since there are signs that Keats was working casually in making this copy, its variants and omissions probably should not be taken too seriously (see Section II.1).

The main difficulties arise when we consider Brown's copies of the poem. *PDWJ* and *1848,* representing Brown's lost transcript, omit 49*a–f* and read "at" in 9, "architectur'd" in 27, "dulled" in 45, and "Hath" in 46. Brown's extant transcript also omits 49*a–f* and has the same readings for 27 and 45, but shows "on" in 9 and "Has" in 46, and contains the unique variants recorded by Garrod for 31, 39–40, 41, and 46. These details do not fit any pattern. One might surmise that, as with some other poems from the Scottish tour, Brown's lost transcript came from an early holograph version, possibly one earlier than those of the letter to Tom and the Woodhouse–Charlotte Reynolds transcripts, but we are in complete ignorance on the point, and the variants in the extant copy that Brown gave Severn are simply unexplainable. Milnes printed the letter to Tom from an amanuensis' copy of a Jeffrey transcript, but for the poem itself, which Jeffrey omitted, he almost certainly used Brown's lost transcript as printer's copy (as we can infer from the similarities between the *PDWJ* and *1848* texts and the fact that Brown's MS has disappeared—see *To Ailsa Rock*). The middle line of my diagram is fairly secure, but the upper and lower branches are largely conjecture.

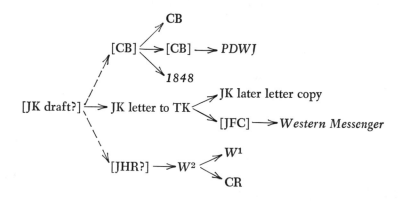

At least four texts have claims to be our basis for the standard—those of the two extant letters, Brown's lost transcript (as represented by *PDWJ* and *1848*), and *W²*. Since Brown's and Woodhouse's sources are so uncertain, and Keats's later letter varies so peculiarly from the others, I would propose that the earlier letter is our safest choice. Garrod's text is based substantively on this earlier letter, with a title from the Woodhouse transcripts ("On Visiting Staffa") and accidentals from one of H. B. Forman's editions. He corrects Keats's omission of "a" in 4, but errs in including *W¹*'s "each" in 49f (which is either a copying mistake or a correction of the meter by Woodhouse, but in any case is not authoritative), and also in his period at the end of 12 and his closing quotation mark in 49 (which belongs at the end of 49f). Allott takes her text from Keats's later letter as far as it goes, and then adds the final thirteen lines from the earlier letter—an odd procedure, but probably one that is defensible in the face of so many strange and incomprehensible circumstances connected with the texts of this poem.

Read me a lesson, Muse, and speak it loud

Written on 2 August 1818 (*Letters,* I, 352, 357; *KC,* II, 63). First published in *PDWJ,* 6 September 1838, and then in *1848,* I, 189. Garrod, p. 495; Allott, pp. 375–376.

The single extant MS—an untitled holograph copy in the letter to Tom Keats of 3, 6 August 1818 (MS at Harvard, text in *Letters,* I, 357–358) —does not vary substantively from the two earliest printed versions (there are no extant transcripts). Brown copied the poem, probably in his journal at the time Keats wrote it, and intended to include it in his "Life" of Keats (*KC,* II, 63). His lost transcript was the source of the *PDWJ* version ("Sonnet, Written on the Summit of Ben Nivis") and was almost certainly printer's copy for *1848* (see *To Ailsa Rock*).

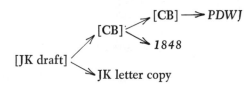

In principle (since there are no substantive variants) either Keats's letter copy or Brown's lost transcript as reconstructed from *PDWJ* and *1848* can be the basis for a standard text. Garrod reproduces *1848* exactly (except for a spelling change in 4), and Allott, following the letter copy, has the same substantive text as Garrod.

Upon my life, Sir Nevis, I am piqu'd

Written on 3 August 1818 (in a letter to Tom Keats under that date). First published in Forman (1883), III, 207–209. Garrod, pp. 561–563; Allott, pp. 376–379.

Keats's draft in his letter to Tom of 3, 6 August 1818 (MS at Harvard, text in *Letters,* I, 354–357—facsimile of 1–41 in Sotheby sale catalogue, 6 May 1936) is our sole source of text. Forman printed the lines as part of the letter, reading "when" for Keats's "where" in 58. Garrod, though he has some of Forman's punctuation and capitalization, corrects 58 to "where," and may be said to have done an independent editing job generally in this instance. Allott, also following the letter MS, emends Keats's "Gentleman" to "gentlemen" in 9, and has three errors—the misprint "shal" for "shall!" in 43, the omission of Keats's second footnote (to "Block-head" in 53), and Forman's "when" in 58.

On Some Skulls in Beàuley Abbey, near Inverness

Written by Keats and Brown early in August 1818 (they arrived at Inverness on the 6th, and Keats sailed for London on the 8th), or possibly some weeks or even months later. First published in *NMM,* 4 (January 1822), 47–48. Garrod, pp. 547–550; Allott, pp. 379–382.

We have three sources for this poem—a MS fair copy by Brown among Woodhouse's papers in the Morgan Library (Garrod's W^3), the text published by Brown in *NMM,* and a version from a lost Woodhouse transcript printed by Colvin, pp. 553–556 (Garrod confusingly calls this "Brown's copy," and Allott "Brown's transcript"). Colvin is our only source for Woodhouse's record of the lines contributed by Keats (1, 2, 7–12, 43–48, and 55–60).

The *NMM* version differs substantively from Brown's MS in title ("Stanzas on Some . . ." for Brown's "On Some . . .") and in 3 ("sever'd" for "shafted"), 14 ("For" for "Since"), 47 ("idler," probably a misprint, for "idle"), and 91 ("farther" for "further"). The Woodhouse text as given by Colvin agrees with Brown's MS in all of these lines, but has substantive variants in 41 ("Scot" for Brown's "Sect"), 64 ("badness" for "sadness"), 65 ("this" for "their"), 71 ("how" for "here"), and 80 ("mask" for "mark"), each of which pretty surely represents Woodhouse's misreading of Brown's hand or Colvin's miscopying of Woodhouse, since some Brown version, very likely the extant MS, must have been Woodhouse's source.

While accepting Colvin as our authority for which lines Keats wrote, we must choose between Brown's MS and *NMM* (and their variants in 3 and 14) as the basis for a standard text. Since we know nothing of the chronological relationship of the two texts, or of *NMM*'s editorial handling of the poem, I think we should prefer Brown's MS as the standard. Garrod generally reproduces this MS, misreading it substantively in 29 ("his" for Brown's "her"), 30 ("first" for "fresh"), and 85 ("ring" for "sing"), and incorporating Woodhouse's or Colvin's errors in 65 ("this" for "their") and 80 ("mask" for "mark"). Allott, also taking her text "from *Woodhouse* 3," by which she means Brown's MS, has the same five substantive errors as Garrod. Both Garrod and Allott adopt Colvin's practice of italicizing the passages written by Keats, but they mistakenly, following an error in one of H. B. Forman's texts, print 7–12 (which Colvin italicizes) in roman.

Nature withheld Cassandra in the skies

Translated from Ronsard's *Nature ornant Cassandre qui devoit* on or shortly before 21 September 1818 (*Letters*, I, 369, 371). First published in *1848*, I, 241. Garrod, p. 497; Allott, pp. 383–384.

We have a holograph version (written in pencil and gone over in ink by Woodhouse) on a blank page of the 1806 *Poetical Works of William Shakespeare* at Keats House, Hampstead (transcription in Hampstead Keats, IV, 164 n.), and transcripts by Woodhouse (two copies, W^3 and W^2) and Charlotte Reynolds.

The extant holograph varies substantively from the transcripts in 2 ("meet" for the transcripts' "more"), 5 ("Love meanwhile held" for "Meanwhile Love kept"), 6 ("charm'd" for "filled"), 7 ("To" for "With"), 9 ("I beheld her on the Earth" for "from the heavens I saw her first"), 10 ("began to burn—and only" for "took fire—and only burning"), and 11 ("sad Lifes" for "life's sad"). The transcripts do not differ substantively among themselves (the holograph's and Charlotte Reynolds' "dies" in 3, where Woodhouse has "dyes," is a spelling variant).

Keats copied the lines into a letter to Reynolds of late September 1818 (*Letters*, I, 371), but the original letter has not survived, and Woodhouse in transcribing it in his letterbook gives only the first line, referring to W^2 for the rest. I should guess that Woodhouse made his W^3 text of the lines first, probably from Keats's letter though possibly from a lost transcript by J. H. Reynolds, and then copied W^2 from W^3 (subsequently adding in W^2 some brief extracts from the letter, probably from his letterbook transcript). Charlotte Reynolds' transcript, though it is quite close to W^2 in accidentals, perhaps in this instance came from the same MS that Woodhouse copied rather than from W^2, since she adds a heading not in W^2 ("Sonnet translated from Ronsard") and gives only "1818" where W^2 dates the lines alternatively September and December 1818; she also, however, has four spaced x's at the end, just as in W^2, where the original letter (according to Woodhouse's note in the letterbook transcript) had "2 strokes . . . drawn for the last lines."

Milnes printed the translation as part of the letter to Reynolds, introducing into a copy of the letterbook transcript a text taken from some unknown source (since, so far as we can determine, none of the extant transcripts was available to him, and he clearly did not use the extant holograph). The *1848* text is the same as that of the transcripts except for a unique "Beauty's fairest dies" for the MSS' various forms of "beauty —fairest dyes" in 3. Milnes supplied in brackets his own translation of the last two lines of Ronsard's sonnet, which Keats omitted.

The chief problem here is the uncertainty of the status of the holograph. One might take it to be an original draft, were it not for the fact that the Shakespeare volume in which it is written bears the inscription "John Hamilton Reynolds to John Keats 1819." It is possible that Keats drafted the lines in it earlier, in September 1818, while he had the book on loan from Reynolds (and before Reynolds formally gave it to him), but it is perhaps more likely that the holograph is a later version, penciled in the book some months or more after Keats wrote the text represented by the transcripts. Milnes's source and the authoritativeness of his 3 are also in question. I think we should choose either the holograph or W^3 as the basis for a standard text, though Charlotte Reynolds' transcript also has a claim to consideration.

Garrod reproduces *1848,* changing "dies" to "dyes" in 3 and "-ed" verb endings to "-'d" in 4, 6, 8, and 12. Allott takes her text from W^3, but has, like Garrod and probably owing to Garrod's faulty apparatus, *1848's* "Beauty's fairest" rather than Keats's and the transcripts' "beauty—fairest." Both editors adopt a shortened form of Charlotte Reynolds' heading ("Translated from Ronsard").

Fragment of Castle-builder

Written in 1818 (so dated by Woodhouse from a lost transcript by Brown). Lines 24–71 first published in *1848,* I, 283–285, and 1–23 first by Colvin in *TLS,* 16 April 1914, p. 181. Garrod, pp. 500–502; Allott, pp. 390–393.

The single extant MS is a transcript by Woodhouse (W^2) headed "Fragment, of Castle-builder" and dated "CB. 1818." It is possible that both W^2 and *1848* derive from the same lost Brown transcript, but we have no way of knowing for sure. *1848* adds "the" to the title and varies from W^2 in 29 ("gold-fish vases" for W^2's "golden fishes") and 65 ("sofas" for "sofa," which, however, Woodhouse first wrote as "sofas"). Without more information, I think we must regard the *1848* readings as less certainly authoritative than Woodhouse's, and prefer W^2 as the basis for a standard text. Colvin printed 1–23 from W^2 upon the rediscovery of the transcript in the twentieth century.

Garrods' text is a curious mixture—his title from *1848,* 1–23 from

W^2 (with the addition of the first speaker-heading and five changes in accidentals), and 24–71 from *1848* (with nine changes in accidentals and the correction of "sofas" to "sofa" in 65). His "golden vases" (29) is a combination of Woodhouse's "golden fishes" and *1848*'s "gold-fish vases." Allott follows W^2, but nevertheless also has *1848*'s title and Garrod's "golden vases" in 29. For Woodhouse's "A viol, bow strings torn" in 40 she prints (accepting an emendation by H. B. Forman) "A viol-bow, strings torn."

And what is love? It is a doll dress'd up

Written in 1818 (so dated by Woodhouse from a lost Brown transcript; a more precise dating is not possible). First published in *1848*, I, 283. Garrod, pp. 499–500; Allott, pp. 393–394.

The single extant MS is an untitled transcript by Woodhouse (W^2). Woodhouse's source is not known, though he records the date "C.B. 1818" (the last digit apparently written over an original "9"). The *1848* text, possibly printed from the lost Brown transcript, adds a title ("Modern Love"), and has "Then" for Woodhouse's "Till" in 9 and "deep" for Woodhouse's "high" in 12. As with the preceding poem, I think we must regard the *1848* readings as less certainly authoritative than Woodhouse's, and consider W^2 the better basis for a standard text.

Garrod reproduces *1848* exactly except for changing "Then" to "Till" in 9 and "Anthony" to "Antony" in 10. Allott, taking her text from W^2, nevertheless has *1848*'s "Then" in 9. Thus neither editor prints both W^2 or both *1848* readings in 9 and 12.

'Tis the "witching time of night"

Written on 14 October 1818 (drafted in a letter to George and Georgiana Keats on that day). First published in the *Ladies' Companion,* 7 (August 1837), 187, and then in *1848*, I, 233–234. The text in the *Ladies' Pocket Magazine,* Part I (1838), pp. 231–232, is a reprint from the *Ladies' Companion.* Garrod, pp. 495–497; Allott, pp. 384–386.

We have a single extant holograph—the draft in Keats's 14–31 October 1818 journal letter (MS at Harvard, text in *Letters,* I, 398–399)—and a transcript by John Howard Payne. The transcript, which Payne sent Milnes in 1847, was taken from a lost copy of the lines made by George Keats from the letter (*KC,* II, 224–225). It varies from the letter only in "starlight" for Keats's "Stars light" in 24. The same lost

George Keats copy was also Payne's source for the text included in his article in the *Ladies' Companion*. In *1848* Milnes printed Keats's journal letter from an amanuensis' copy of a Jeffrey transcript, but for the poem itself, which Jeffrey omitted, he apparently inserted a copy taken from Payne's transcript, the only source known to have been available to him. *1848*'s two further substantive changes, the alteration of "time" to "hour" in 1 and the omission of "then" in 20, were made either in the lost printer's copy or in proofs.

$$\text{JK letter draft} \longrightarrow \text{[GK]} \begin{cases} \text{[JHP]} \longrightarrow \textit{Ladies' Companion} \\ \text{JHP} \longrightarrow \text{[copy]} \longrightarrow 1848 \end{cases}$$

Keats's letter is of course the proper basis for a standard text, and probably one or the other emendation—to "starlight" or "stars' light"—is in order for the holograph's "Stars light" in 24. Garrod takes his text from *1848*, altering punctuation in 13 and spelling in 45 and capitalizing "poet" in 32, 53, and 56—all according to the holograph letter. He retains Payne's and *1848*'s "starlight" in 24, but does not correct *1848*'s substantive corruptions in 1 and 20. Allott follows the letter text accurately, emending only "Stars light" to "stars' light" in 24.

Where's the poet? Show him! show him

Written in 1818 (so dated in Brown's transcript and the other MSS deriving from it; most writers connect the poem with Keats's "camelion Poet" letter to Woodhouse of 27 October 1818—*Letters*, I, 386–388). First published in *1848*, I, 282–283. Garrod, p. 499; Allott, pp. 389–390.

The three extant MSS, all of which are transcripts—by Brown, George Keats, and Woodhouse (W^2)—do not differ substantively except that Woodhouse has "mine" (a copying error) for "nine" in 2. Brown's transcript, from a lost holograph and headed simply "Fragment. 1818," was copied by both George Keats (who has the same heading as Brown and generally the same accidentals) and Woodhouse (who notes "from CB." at the end). The *1848* text almost surely also derives from Brown's transcript, the only source known to have been available to Milnes. Because Brown's MS shows no signs of having been used as printer's copy, and because it has an "x" by the title and a light line drawn vertically through the text (possible indications that Milnes had the MS copied by an amanuensis), I think it probable that *1848* was set from a copy of Brown's transcript rather than from the MS itself.

$$[\text{JK MS}] \longrightarrow \text{CB} \nearrow \text{GK} \\ \searrow \text{W}^2 \\ \searrow [\text{copy}] \longrightarrow 1848$$

Brown's transcript is the proper basis for a standard text. Both Garrod and Allott follow *1848* (Garrod exactly except in indentions and four marks of punctuation), and thus have the same wording as Brown's MS.

Fancy

Written toward the end of 1818 (it is probably one of the poems that Keats promised his brother and sister-in-law on 18 December; he copied it out for them on the following 2 January—*Letters,* II, 12, 21–24). First published in *1820*. Garrod, pp. 264–267; Allott, pp. 441–446.

We have, besides the *1820* text, a holograph copy in the letter to George and Georgiana of 16 December 1818–4 January 1819 (MS at Harvard, text in *Letters,* II, 21–24) and transcripts by Dilke, Brown, and Woodhouse (W^2). Basically there are three states of text—represented by the letter copy, the three transcripts, and *1820*—though the order of the first two states is not certain, and there are small differences among the transcripts. The letter text, while it contains the same number of lines as the transcripts, has unique substantive readings in 18, 24, 25, 30, 33, 34, 55, 59, and 62. These may derive from a lost original or early draft, or may be the result of the same kind of casual tinkering-while-copying that we see in some of Keats's other letter copies (e.g., the later holograph of *Not Aladdin magian*).

Dilke's untitled transcript, which in this instance does not derive from Brown (as the occasional substantive and many accidental differences show, plus Dilke's omission of the "CB" flourish), was almost certainly made from a lost holograph, though whether before or after the date of Keats's letter copy (2 January 1819) is not known. Since Dilke is usually accurate in minor details, his copy is very likely the closest we can get to Keats's text in the state represented by the three transcripts. Brown's copy ("Ode to Fancy") also was taken from a lost holograph. If we consider Brown's "show" (20) and Dilke's "When" (63) and "Quick" (91) as simple copying errors, then Brown's transcript varies significantly from

Dilke's only in 12 ("doth" for Dilke's "does"), 29 ("bring, in" for "bring thee"), 50 ("Hedge-grown" for "Hedgerow"), and 54 ("self-same" for "same soft")—Brown agreeing with the letter text in 12, and Dilke with the letter text in 29, 50, and 54. Both may have transcribed the same holograph, but if so one has to suppose that Keats made slight revisions in the MS between the two copyings, whichever was the earlier. Woodhouse took his text "from C.B.," and except for correcting Brown's error in 20 his transcript shows no substantive differences from its source. (The two lines after 66 are lightly marked out in Brown's copy; Woodhouse, unsure whether or not to include them, wrote them in pencil in his transcript.)

1820 varies from all earlier texts in the details given in Garrod's apparatus for 6, 15, 28, 34, 44, 45, 57–58, 66/67, 68, 68/69, 76, 89, 90/91 (but not in 16 and 54, for which Garrod has misrepresented TW^2). That is, it omits eighteen lines and shows changes in eleven others. Though the publishers may have been responsible for the deletion of the couplet following 68 and some of the lines following 89, the alterations in general are so extensive that they must be attributed to the poet. Keats did considerable revising either in another MS or (much less likely) in proofs. Either Keats or Brown made the lost printer's copy for *1820*.

1820 is of course the proper basis for a standard text. Garrod reproduces *1820* exactly except for the omission of a semicolon at the end of 34 (he also errs in his headnote—the note that he quotes does not appear in W^2). Allott divides 89 into two half-lines and repunctuates 27 in an interesting way (though neither change is warranted by the extant texts, and in the latter instance all of them have heavier punctuation after "commission'd" than after "Fancy").

Bards of passion and of mirth

Written toward the end of 1818 (dating the same as for the preceding poem; both Ward, p. 232, and Gittings, *John Keats*, p. 269, think Keats drafted the poem on 17 December, after Bentley brought over "a cloathes' basket of Books" that undoubtedly included the set of Beaumont and Fletcher—*Letters*, II, 11–12—but he could have written it earlier or later). First published in *1820* (under the title "Ode"). Garrod, pp. 268–269; Allott, pp. 446–447.

In addition to *1820*, we have a holograph version written in Volume III of the 1811 *Dramatic Works of Beaumont and Fletcher* at Keats House, Hampstead (facsimile in Williamson, plate IV), a holograph copy in the 2 January section of Keats's letter to George and Georgiana of 16 December 1818–4 January 1819 (MS at Harvard, text in *Letters,* II, 25–26), a transcript by Brown, and two copies by Woodhouse (W^2, W^1).

Keats's untitled MS in the Beaumont and Fletcher has deletions and revisions after 4 and in 5, 13, 21, 25, and 29, but otherwise is straightforwardly written out. It is probably a very clean draft rather than a revised version. Keats copied this text in his letter to George and Georgiana, making slight changes in 16 and 23. Brown's transcript, headed "Ode. 1818," also apparently derives from the Beaumont-Fletcher holograph; it does not vary substantively, follows the holograph's "another's" in 10, and has "dasies" in 14 where Keats had written "daises." W^2 ("Ode") has the same text as the Beaumont-Fletcher MS and Brown's transcript, including the unrhymed line following 30, after which Woodhouse left a line space and noted, "a line is omitted here in the Copy from which I took this." Woodhouse underlined "have" in 39, and at some later time altered 19–20 in pencil so as to produce "But divine melodious truth, / sophic numbers fine & sooth." I take the note at the end of W^2, "from J.H.R. 26 Mar 1819," to refer to a Reynolds copy and probably the date that Reynolds put on his MS when he copied the poem rather than the date on which Woodhouse made his transcript. Because W^2 shows "another's" in 10, a deleted word—perhaps the Beaumont-Fletcher MS's "daises" or another misspelling—before "daisies" in 14, and "sprights" with the "r" deleted in 32 (the Beaumont-Fletcher MS has "spights"), I should guess that Woodhouse's source, the lost Reynolds copy, came from the Beaumont-Fletcher MS. The untitled W^1 pretty clearly derives from W^2. Here Woodhouse left a space after 30, into which he later penciled the unrhymed line, and he again underlined "have" in 39; W^1's single substantive variant, in 20 ("In Philosophic"), is of no significance.

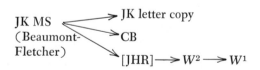

The *1820* version, from a lost copy by Keats or Brown, has new readings in 19–20 (though the *1820* transposition in 19 is marked in pencil in W^2) and 30, and omits the unrhymed line after 30. It is the proper basis for a standard text. Garrod follows it exactly except for omitting a semicolon at the end of 12, and Allott does not depart substantively.

Spirit here that reignest

Written perhaps in 1818 (the only clue to dating is the fact that Keats drafted or copied the poem in the same volume of Beaumont and Fletcher in which he wrote the preceding poem toward the end of 1818). First published in *1848,* II, 262. Garrod, pp. 436–437; Allott, pp. 388–389.

The two extant MSS are an untitled holograph, probably the original draft, written on a blank page in Volume III of the 1811 *Dramatic Works of Beaumont and Fletcher* at Keats House, Hampstead (Garrod does not mention this MS), and a transcript by Brown. Brown ("Song") has the same text as the holograph—including "burneth," "mourneth," "danceth," and "pranceth" where the second-person verb ending seems called for in 3, 4, 13, and 14—except for "While nudging" in 17 (the holograph reads "A nudging"). His transcript served as printer's copy for *1848,* which emended the verbs in 3, 4, 13, and 14 to "-est" but otherwise reproduced his words. Brown either copied the extant holograph, perhaps changing 17 at Keats's request, or followed a slightly revised lost MS.

JK draft - ->CB——>*1848*

In the absence of any evidence in the matter, I think we should consider Brown's transcript the better basis for a standard text. Garrod takes his text from *1848,* emending 17 according to the wording of Keats's MS and omitting commas at the end of 8, 9, and 19. Allott follows the holograph, changing the verb endings in 3, 4, 13, and 14.

I had a dove and the sweet dove died

Written at the end of December 1818 or the beginning of January 1819 (Woodhouse dates the poem 1818 on the basis of a lost Brown transcript; Keats copied it in a journal letter to George and Georgiana Keats on 2 January 1819, introducing it with the remark, "In my journal I intend to copy the poems I write the days they are written"—*Letters,* II, 26–27). First published in *1848,* II, 260. Garrod, p. 435; Allott, p. 448.

In addition to the holograph copy in the letter to George and Georgiana (MS at Harvard, text in *Letters,* II, 27), there are transcripts by Woodhouse (W^2) and Milnes. The Brown transcript that Woodhouse refers to as his source of text has not survived.

Keats's letter copy, representing one of the two authoritative states of text that are known for this poem, reads "mourn . . . it was" in 3, "did" in 5, "dove" in 6, and "I gave" in 9. Woodhouse's transcript, "from C.B." and ultimately deriving from some lost holograph, represents the other state, with "grieve . . . Its feet were" in 3, "would" in 5, "bird" in 6, and "gave" in 9. Milnes's transcript, which was printer's copy for *1848*, agrees substantively with W^2 except in 5 ("should" for "would"), 7 ("in" for "on"), 8 ("would" for "could"), and 10 ("lie" for "live," apparently just a slip of the pen). I think we may assume that Milnes took his text from the lost Brown transcript (his heading is in Brown's characteristic form, "Song. 1818"), and that his variants in 5, 7, and 8, like his error in 10, are not authoritative. *1848* has the text of Milnes's transcript except for the correction of "lie" to "live" in 10. Unfortunately there is no way of knowing whether the W^2 version is earlier or later than that of the letter copy. My diagram arbitrarily shows W^2 as the later text.

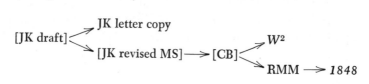

The modern editing of this short poem has been rather casual, to say the least. Since the chronological relationship of the two authoritative versions is uncertain, editors have a choice between the letter copy and W^2 as the basis for a standard text. Both Garrod and Allott combine readings of the two states. Garrod takes his accidentals (but not any substantive peculiarities) from *1848*, prints readings from the letter copy in 3 ("it was"), 5, and 6, but includes the W^2-Milnes-*1848* "grieve" in 3 and "gave" in 9. Allott bases her text on the letter copy, but prefers the W^2-Milnes-*1848* "Its feet were" in 3 and inadvertently takes over Milnes's and *1848*'s "should" in 5. Garrod omits four substantive variants and has errors in his apparatus to 5 and 6; four of Allott's five textual notes give wrong readings for W^2.

Hush, hush! tread softly! hush, hush, my dear

Written in 1818 (so dated in Brown's transcript; a more precise dating is not possible, regardless of whether Keats was providing words for Charlotte Reynolds' music, was dramatizing an event concerning Isabella Jones, or was doing both of these at once—see Bate, p. 382 n.). First published in *Hood's Magazine*, 3 (April 1845), 339, and then in *1848*, II, 259–260. Garrod, pp. 434–435; Allott, pp. 448–450.

A holograph version, probably Keats's original draft, is extant at Harvard, and we have transcripts by Brown, Dilke, Woodhouse (two copies, W^3 and W^2), and Fanny Brawne (this last written in a copy of Hunt's *Literary Pocket-Book* for 1819 [1818] at Keats House, Hampstead—facsimiles in Williamson, plate IX, and Gittings, *John Keats: The Living Year,* Cambridge, Mass., 1954, facing pp. 58 and 86).

Textually this is the strangest poem in the Keats canon. The holograph has a line left unfinished (23); Brown's transcript, ending at the bottom of a page with 20, lacks the last four lines, which were supplied on the verso of his MS by Milnes; Dilke stopped copying after "morning's" in 22; Woodhouse's W^3 transcript is a slapdash affair, with a number of corrections in pencil and a line left blank (20) and later filled in in pencil; Woodhouse's W^2, "from C.B.," has (uncharacteristically) four substantive variants from the stated source; three of the texts (W^3, W^2, and *Hood's*) have a total of ten unique variants; no two versions are substantively identical (though, apart from title, the holograph has the same readings as Brown's copy through 20 and Dilke's through 22); and there are very few patterns of resemblance among the texts.

The unique variants—in 1, 2, 9, 10 (two variants), and 15 of W^3; 14 of W^2; and 3, 11, and 17 of *Hood's*—have to be set aside. The texts are all headed "Song" except for the holograph and W^3, neither of which has a title. W^3 and W^2 agree in "my" for the other texts' "O" (4, though there is a penciled "O" in the margin of W^2) and "cyc . . . lip" for "eyes . . . lips" (16—Woodhouse subsequently altered the words to "eyes . . . lips" in pencil in W^3). Fanny Brawne and *Hood's* agree in "tread softly" for the other texts' "soft tiptoe" (7), "darkness" for "dusk" (15—W^3 has "dusk" with a penciled "dark" beside it), "chink" for "clink" (18), "dream" for "sleep" (20), and "may" for "shall" (21). W^3 and *Hood's* agree in "That" for the other texts' "Who" (6). W^3, Fanny Brawne, and *Hood's* all have "Hath" where the other texts read "Has" (14). Fanny Brawne, *Hood's,* and Milnes's completion of Brown's transcript have "morning" for the other texts' "morning's" (22—actually Keats wrote "mornings"). In 23 the holograph reads "The Stock dove shall hatch her soft brace and above our heads coo," with "hatch her," "soft brace," and "above our heads" all separately marked out in pencil and nothing written in to replace the deleted text; Fanny Brawne and *Hood's* have "The stock dove shall hatch her soft brace and shall coo"; and the other texts have "The stock-dove shall hatch her soft twin-eggs and coo" (except that Milnes copied "his" for "her" in his completion of Brown's transcript, and W^3 has penciled interlineations that produce the same text as Fanny Brawne and *Hood's*).

With so many odd circumstances and mixed-up relationships among the texts, one can only speculate very tentatively on some of their sources. Brown's transcript (as far as it goes) appears to be a copy of the extant holograph, and Dilke's transcript (as far as it goes) is certainly a copy made from Brown's (there are only two slight differences between the two). Perhaps the incompleteness of these transcripts has to do with the state of Keats's MS in 23: Keats did not settle on a final version of the line, Brown may have left both 23 and 24 incomplete, and Dilke may have copied as far as Brown's transcript went at the time. Milnes's source for the four lines that he added to Brown's MS is unknown; his "his" for "her" in 23 could be a misreading of Brown's hand (Brown's "s" and "r" in other MSS have been misread and interchanged by copyists and printers), but it is also possible that he took the lines partly or entirely from some other source. We have the additional problem that Woodhouse's transcripts (the W^2 text is "from C.B.") differ in 23 from the holograph, proposed just above as Brown's source. Possibly Brown's MS did have the text of 23 that Milnes and Woodhouse agree in (apart from Milnes's "his"), perhaps even in Keats's hand as he attempted on the missing part of Brown's transcript to revise the line that he left unfinished in the extant holograph. Brown's MS as completed by Milnes was printer's copy for *1848*. As a result, *1848* has the substantive text of the holograph through 21, with Milnes's "morning" in 22 and "his soft twin-eggs and coo" in 23.

Fanny Brawne's and *Hood's* texts, agreeing against other texts in 7, 14, 15, 18, 20, 21, 22, and 23, derive from a revised holograph, or possibly from two copies representing more or less the same revised state of text. Their variants in 18 ("chink"), 20 ("dream"), and 21 ("may") look like copying errors, and it is probable that at some point along the line they had a source in common. *Hood's* unique variants very likely represent alterations in an intervening copy (perhaps by someone in the Reynolds family), editorial changes, printer's errors, or some combination of these three.

Woodhouse's transcripts are a special problem. I think that Woodhouse did take W^2, as he says, "from C.B.," and have no explanation for the substantive differences from Brown in 4 ("my" for Brown's "O"), 14 ("the" for "her"), and 16 ("eye . . . lip" for "eyes . . . lips"), or for his text in 23 (see above). Subsequently he seems to have tried his hand at some penciled revisions in W^2, changing the exclamation to a question mark at the end of 1 and tentatively deleting "All" and "That" in 2 and 3. W^3, with six unique variants and also readings in common with both the earlier text of the extant holograph and the revised text represented by Fanny Brawne and *Hood's,* bears no understandable relation to W^2 or to any other known text. I should guess, because of its unusual appearance, that W^3 was written from dictation, from shorthand taken from dictation, or from memory. I have omitted it from the diagram quite simply because I do not know where to put it.

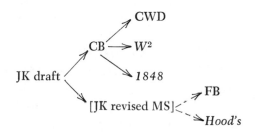

For a standard text I think we should ignore all unique variants and also the W^3 and W^2 peculiarities (because W^3's source is unknown and W^2 in this instance does not appear reliable). Probably Fanny Brawne's transcript best represents the revised state of text. Her copy varies from the extant holograph in 7 ("tread softly" for "soft tiptoe"), 14 ("Hath" for "Has"), 15 ("darkness" for "dusk"), 18 ("chink" for "clink"), 20 ("dream" for "sleep"), 21 ("may" for "shall"), 22 ("morning" for "mornings"), and 23 ("soft brace and shall coo," which except for "shall" is a shortened version of the words that Keats deleted in the holograph). The variants in 18, 20, and 21—possibly also that in 22—may represent corruptions, and can be emended according to the holograph in agreement with other texts.

Garrod reproduces *1848* exactly except in 22–23, where he prints "morning's" and the Fanny Brawne–*Hood's* "her soft brace and shall coo." In effect his text is the same as the extant holograph's with an emendation in 23. Allott has the same wording as Garrod throughout.

Ah, woe is me! poor Silver-wing

Written in 1818 or 1819 (a more precise dating is not possible). First published in *PDWJ,* 25 October 1838, and then in *1848,* II, 263. Garrod, pp. 437–438; Allott, pp. 490–491.

The single extant MS, a transcript by Brown headed "Faery Song," was the basis for *PDWJ's* text (there titled "Faery Dirge") and was printer's copy for *1848.* Garrod reproduces *1848* exactly except for capitalizing "silver-" and "page" in 1, 5, 8, and 12 (Brown capitalizes these and also "lady" in 2 and 7). Allott, following Brown's transcript, has the same substantive text as Garrod.

The Eve of St. Agnes

Written during the last two weeks of January and perhaps also the first few days of February 1819 (*Letters,* II, 58; for the date of Keats's return from Chichester, after he finished the draft, see Rollins, *HLB,* 8 [1954], 244–245); revised in September 1819 (*Letters,* II, 157, 162 164). First published in *1820.* Garrod, pp. 236–256; Allott, pp. 450–480.

Keats's original draft is at Harvard, complete except for the missing first sheet containing 1–63 (facsimiles of 206–225 plus some canceled lines in Lowell, facing II, 168, and Bate, facing p. 444; of 216–240 in Finney, facing II, 554; and of 259–297 in Ridley, after p. 162), and we have two transcripts by Woodhouse (W^2, W^1) and a transcript by George Keats (transcription in Ridley, pp. 180–190; the MS referred to by R. H. Stoddard in a letter to Milnes of 1877—*KC,* II, 364—is probably, if it actually existed, this same transcript). A letter from Keats to John Taylor of June 1820 requests two alterations in the proofs (MS at Harvard, text in *Letters,* II, 294–295; there is also a transcript by Woodhouse in his letter-book).

In broad outline, the history of the text is simple (see my article in *SB,* 16 [1963], 207–212, reprinted in *Hoodwinking,* pp. 158–166). Keats drafted the poem early in 1819; Woodhouse transcribed the draft in April 1819; Keats revised the poem in September and had it "copied fair" (see below); Woodhouse read the fair copy sometime between September and the following January and entered corrections and new readings between the lines and opposite the original text in W^2; George Keats transcribed the fair copy in January 1820; and this same fair copy, after further revision by Keats and editing by his publishers, was probably printer's copy for *1820.* There is, however, a degree of fluidity among the texts that we do not encounter in Keats's other poems. It is clear, for example, that Keats further revised his original draft after Woodhouse copied it, and also further revised the fair copy after first Woodhouse and then George Keats saw and used it; it is also clear that Woodhouse filled in blank spaces and altered the texts of both W^2 and W^1 at various times after he took his initial transcript. We lack the all-important fair copy containing Keats's revised text, but there are plenty of complications among the MSS that we have.

Keats's original MS, on the same "thin paper" on which he wrote the 16 December 1818–4 January 1819 journal letter to George and Georgiana (*Letters*, II, 58 and n.), is one of his roughest and most heavily worked-over drafts, and it is a minor miracle that Woodhouse in copying it got so many of the words right. The W^2 transcript has a note opposite the beginning of the poem, "This Copy was taken from K.'s original M.S. . . . ," and another at the end, "Copied from J.K's rough M.S. 20 Ap^l 1819 / written about the latter end of 1818 or beginning of 1819," but these do not necessarily mean that W^2 was made directly from the draft. Woodhouse also copied *Hyperion* on the same 20 April, and there is abundant evidence that the W^2 transcript of that poem *was* made directly from Keats's MS; it seems unlikely that Woodhouse would have written out both poems in longhand on the same day. Blank spaces in W^2, later filled in by Woodhouse, where Keats's draft is perfectly clear and readable (e.g., in 159–162), and a number of initial misreadings by Woodhouse—"Awaking" for Keats's "Awakening" (289), "in passioned fear" for "Impassion'd far" (316), "windows—dark St Agnes' moon" for "windows dark. St Agnes moon" (324), "tempests" for "tempest's" (342), "footway" for "footworn" (368), all of which could have come from the ambiguities of shorthand notation—support the hypothesis that Woodhouse copied W^2 "from J.K's rough M.S." via an intervening shorthand transcript, in the same way that he did *Isabella* and *The Eve of St. Mark*.

W^2 readings like "report" (67, later altered to "resort") where Keats had written "ressort" with a long first "s" (so that the word looks like "report") and "care quick" (255) where Keats had written "an guish" in such a way that it can be read as "cre quick" or "are quick," as well as several blank spaces (later filled in) where Keats's draft text is virtually unreadable, are unmistakable signs that Woodhouse made his first transcript from the draft we have. On the other hand, there are a few readings in W^2 (particularly in 123 and 223), and W^2's initial substitution of "Lionel" throughout for the draft's "Porphyro," that could not have come directly from the draft; and we have to assume that Keats provided some instructions (concerning the name of the hero) before Woodhouse made his first copy, and perhaps also some help as he copied.

Substantive differences between W^2 and W^1 (not counting those where Woodhouse later corrected or altered W^2 according to the revised text of the poem but did not change W^1) occur in 4, 14 (W^1 has "seem'd"), 91 (W^1 has "that" for "the"), 129 (W^1 has "Like"), 135, 167 (W^1 has "that night perhaps"), 342, 349 (W^1 has "or" for "and"), 368, and 374 (W^1 has "coffin'd"). The probability in every instance is that the W^1

reading is an alteration or error made by Woodhouse in the process of recopying the poem from W^2. There are enough peculiar likenesses in wording and accidentals to suggest that one of the extant Woodhouse transcripts had to have come from the other (rather than independently from either Keats's draft or the hypothesized shorthand transcript), and there are signs of the priority of W^2 (e.g., in 358–359, where Woodhouse deleted and rewrote some words and squeezed in his punctuation in W^2 but copied the lines more straightforwardly in W^1). Taken together, the available evidence points to Woodhouse's having first made a shorthand copy, then written out W^2 from the shorthand, and later copied W^1 from W^2. (I was wrong, in the *SB* article reprinted in *Hoodwinking*, to propose that W^2 and W^1 were independent copies of Keats's draft and that W^1 "would seem to be the earlier.")

In September 1819 Keats revised the poem and, as Woodhouse says in an important letter to Taylor of 19, 20 September, "had [it] . . . copied fair" (*Letters*, II, 162). This lost fair copy—Woodhouse's wording suggests that it may have been made by someone other than Keats, and, if so, Brown is of course the likeliest candidate—was the source of Woodhouse's corrections and variant readings in W^2 (Woodhouse continues his note opposite the beginning of the W^2 transcript, "[Keats] afterwards altered it for publication, & added some stanzas & omitted others.—His alterations are noticed here"). It was also the source of George Keats's transcript made to take back to America in January 1820. The agreement of George Keats's transcript and *1820* against Woodhouse's text with the W^2 "alterations" in 7, 113, 116 (George has "secret"), 213, 226, 255, 260 (W^2 and W^1 have "faintest" for "dying"), 272, 274 (W^2 and W^1 have "Amid the quiet of St Agnes' night," and the *1820* reading penciled opposite the text of W^2 may not be in Woodhouse's hand), 286 (W^2 and W^1 have "seems"), 289, and 311 (W^2 and W^1 have "art thou") makes reasonably certain that Woodhouse saw the fair copy before Keats entered further revisions that George incorporated in his transcript. (On the basis of Woodhouse's note in W^2 after the revised text of 375–378—"Altered 1820," with "before March" added in shorthand—Gittings, *John Keats*, p. 386 n., seems to suggest that Keats made all his revisions before March 1820. But Woodhouse's dating here has to apply specifically to 375–378, and it means that Keats restored the original version of these lines before he turned his MS over to the publishers. The "alterations" that Woodhouse records in W^2 were made before January 1820, when George Keats took his copy. At least this appears to be the best explanation for the agreement in the lines cited above between George's transcript and *1820* against Woodhouse; the new readings represent changes made by Keats after Woodhouse noted the variants from the fair copy.) Garrod designates the W^2 "alterations" as w and George Keats's transcript as E, and rightly says in his Introduction (p. xli) that the "agreement . . . of E and w represents Keats' fair copy"—to which might be added that, where E and w disagree (not counting George's copying errors, which are fairly numerous), E represents a slightly later stage of revision.

The lost revised MS—the fair copy by Keats or Brown—was probably printer's copy for *1820,* but the MS was edited by Taylor (and surely also by Woodhouse) before it was set in type. As Woodhouse says in the rest of his note opposite the beginning of the W^2 transcript, "The Published Copy [*1820*] differs from both [the original draft and Keats's revisions] in a few particulars. K. left it to his Publishers to adopt which they pleased, & to revise the Whole." *1820* varies substantively from the fair copy text as represented by George Keats's MS and Woodhouse's "alterations" (and from George's MS alone where Keats further revised after Woodhouse saw the fair copy) in title (all MSS have "Saint Agnes' [*or* Agnes] Eve" except the draft, where the first leaf is missing) and in 9, 32, 38, 54/55 (the omission of a stanza that Keats added in revision—see *Hoodwinking,* p. 161, for Woodhouse's text and Garrod, p. 238 n., for George's; Garrod's "pleasure" in the seventh line of the stanza is a misprint for "pleasures"), 64, 68, 70 (the revised "a la mort" appears to be Keats's error), 75, 98, 115, 122, 123, 132, 134, 135, 136, 137, 143, 145, 146, 147, 154, 167, 179, 182, 193, 194, 197, 199, 225, 264, 281, 297 (two variants), 309 (two variants, in the first of which George's MS and Woodhouse's "alteration" read "And tun'd, devout"), 311, 314–322 (see *Hoodwinking,* p. 162, for Woodhouse's text and Garrod, p. 252 nn., for George's), 325, 364, 368, and 375–378. In 64, 75, 115, 136, 137, 143, 145, 147, 167, 197, 225, 297 ("sank"), 325, 364, and 368 the *1820* text has readings not occurring earlier in any MS; in 123 and 281 *1820* has readings that first appear in W^2; in 135 *1820* agrees with a change made by Woodhouse in copying W^1; in 98, 146, 182, and partially in 145 and 147, *1820* incorporates revisions penciled in the margin and opposite the text of W^1 (Woodhouse's other proposed revisions there—for 4, 143, 189, 312, and 378—were ignored); in the rest of these variants the *1820* text represents a return to readings of Keats's draft, which the publishers had in one of Woodhouse's transcripts (probably W^1—Woodhouse says "turn to it" in the letter to Taylor quoted below).

My diagram does not include Woodhouse's "alterations" noted in W^2 from the lost fair copy, nor does it represent editorial changes made in the fair copy before it was set in type.

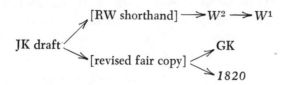

For most of the forty or so substantive differences between the lost fair copy and *1820* we can say that Keats was responsible, or that he approved the changes if he did not actually initiate them. We know that he read proofs of the poem and in at least two instances requested that his MS readings be restored (*Letters*, II, 294–295). But a few of the changes were clearly enforced by the publishers *against* his wishes. The rewriting of 314–322 in particular shocked Woodhouse and aroused a very strong reaction in Taylor. Woodhouse's account in his 19, 20 September letter to Taylor deserves quoting at length:

There was another alteration, which I abused for "a full hour by the *Temple* clock." You know if a thing has a decent side, I generally look no further— As the Poem was orig[y] written, *we* innocent ones (ladies & myself) might very well have supposed that Porphyro, when acquainted with Madeline's love for him, & when "he arose, Etherial flush[d] &c &c (turn to it) set himself at once to persuade her to go off with him, & succeeded & went over the "Dartmoor black" (now changed for some other place) to be married, in right honest chaste & sober wise. But, as it is now altered, as soon as M. has confessed her love, P. winds by degrees his arm round her, presses breast to breast, and acts all the acts of a bonâ fide husband, while she fancies she is only playing the part of a Wife in a dream. This alteration is of about 3 stanzas; and tho' there are no improper expressions but all is left to inference, and tho' profanely speaking, the Interest on the reader's imagination is greatly heightened, yet I do apprehend it will render the poem unfit for ladies, & indeed scarcely to be mentioned to them among the "things that are."—He says he does not want ladies to read his poetry: that he writes for men—& that if in the former poem there was an opening for doubt what took place, it was his fault for not writing clearly & comprehensibly—that he sh[d] despise a man who would be such an eunuch in sentiment as to leave a maid, with that Character about her, in such a situation: & sho[d] despise himself to write about it &c &c &c—and all this sort of Keats-like rhodomontade. (*Letters*, II, 163)

Taylor wrote back to Woodhouse on 25 September:

This Folly of Keats is the most stupid piece of Folly I can conceive. . . . I don't know how the Meaning of the new Stanzas is wrapped up, but I will not be accessary (I can answer also for H[essey]. I think) towards publishing any thing which can only be read by Men. . . . As it is, the flying in the Face of all Decency & Discretion is doubly offensive from its being accompanied with so preposterous a Conceit on his part of being able to overcome the best founded Habits of our Nature.—Had he known truly what the Society and what the Suffrages of Women are worth, he would never have thought of depriving himself of them.—So far as he is unconsciously silly in this Proceeding I am sorry for him, but for the rest I cannot but confess to you that it excites in me the Strongest Sentiments of Disapprobation—Therefore my dear Richᵈ if he will not so far concede to my Wishes as to leave the passage as it originally stood, I must be content to admire his Poems with some other Imprint, & in so doing I can reap as much Delight from the Perusal of them as if they were our own property, without having the disquieting Consideration attached to them of our approving, by the "Imprimatur," those Parts which are unfit for publication. (*Letters,* II, 182–183)

The final comment on the matter is Woodhouse's cryptic sentence in his note in W^2: "K. left it to his Publishers to adopt which [readings] they pleased, & to revise the Whole."

1820 should continue to be the basis for a standard text, but in this one instance among *1820* poems some major emendations may be desirable. It is obvious that the publishers forced the restoration of the original 314–322, and almost as certain that they insisted on the omission of the additional stanza between 54 and 55 and also on the rewriting, partly by Woodhouse, of 98, 143, and 145–147 (passages of the same objectionable tendency, from the point of view of the letters just quoted). In 1963 (in the *SB* article reprinted in *Hoodwinking*) I urged the reincorporation of Keats's fair copy text of these passages. Neither Gittings' implied answer to my suggestion—"It is sometimes forgotten by those who wish to restore Keats's second version . . . that Keats gave his publishers the authority quoted above [in Woodhouse's W^2 note], saw what they had done in proof, and made no protest" (*John Keats,* p. 395 n.)—nor Allott's remark that "a final if reluctant approval of the *1820* text seems to be implied in [Keats's] insistence when overseeing the proofs of the poem on the restoration of a number of his MS readings" (p. 452) really counters the force of Taylor's reaction in the letter to Woodhouse. Taylor says flatly that Keats must return to the earlier text of the passage in question or find another publisher. I shall stick with my original contention that the *1820* text does not, even theoretically, represent Keats's final intentions in the poem.

Garrod reproduces *1820,* adding a closing quotation mark in 144, erring substantively in 82 ("not" for "no"), and inadvertently omitting punctuation at the end of 134, 265, 319, and 331. He does not supply punctuation at the end of 301 (where at least a comma is called for) and does not correct 342 (where *1820*'s closing quotation mark should have been left off). There is an especially high proportion of errors in his apparatus, and some twenty substantive variants among the MSS are not recorded. Allott follows *1820* substantively, repairs the punctuation of 301 and 342, and emends punctuation interestingly in 238 (on the basis of W^2 and W^1, which do not, however, represent the punctuation in Keats's draft). There are several substantive errors in the important passages that she quotes in her notes on pp. 457 and 474.

The Eve of St. Mark

Written between 13 and 17 February 1819 ("13/17 Feby 1819" in W^2). First published in *1848*, II, 279–283. Garrod, pp. 449–453; Allott, pp. 480–487.

We have two complete or nearly complete holograph MSS—a draft in the notebook in which George Keats later made copies of Keats's poems to take back to America (British Museum) and a fair copy in the 20 September section of the 17–27 September 1819 journal letter to George and Georgiana (MS in the Morgan Library, text in *Letters*, II, 201–204)— as well as a leaf containing a separate draft of 99–114 and, on the reverse side, another sixteen-line pseudo-Chaucerian fragment that is usually associated with the poem (Garrod's 98*a*–*p*, also in the Morgan—facsimiles of both sides of the leaf in H. B. Forman's *Poetical Works,* Oxford, 1906, after p. 342, and of the sixteen-line extra fragment in the *Bookman,* 31 [1906], 16). There are also transcripts by Brown and Woodhouse (W^2). I have been unable to locate Woodhouse's shorthand transcript once owned by A. Edward Newton (facsimile of the first page, containing 1–50, in Newton's *A Magnificent Farce and Other Diversions of a Book-Collector,* Boston, 1921, p. 121).

The British Museum holograph is the earliest version we have, and, except for the prior draft of 99–114 in the Morgan leaf, is very likely the original draft, even though many lines in it are written out in final form without alteration. Brown transcribed this MS, as his text evidences in 12 (where he first copied Keats's "dasies" and then inserted an "i"), 33 (where he copied "Moses'"—Keats's "Aron's" is written in such a way that both "Moses'" and Woodhouse's "Aaron's" could come from it), 45 (where Keats deleted but did not replace his text, and Brown originally omitted the line), and 101 (where Keats's "hir" looks like "his" and Brown originally wrote "his"). The transcript varies substantively from the British Museum holograph in 22 ("organ" for "organs"), 33 ("Moses' "), **53** ("plaited" for "pleated"), **59** ("homewards" for "townwards," unnoted by Garrod), and 66 ("and" for "of"). Brown's MS was printer's copy for *1848,* which incorporated these five variants into its text and misread "mid" as "and" in 32 (*1848*'s "unfinished" in parentheses after the title was written into the MS by Milnes).

W^2, "Copied from J.K's M.S.," also came from the British Museum holograph, but I think not directly. W^2 differs substantively from the holograph in 12 ("Of" for Keats's "And"), 22 ("organs" altered to "organ," but probably after Woodhouse saw Brown's copy), 40 (the omission of "old," later added in the margin from "CB"), 49 ("to" later altered to " 'gainst" from "C.B."), 62 ("About"), 65 ("fell"), 68 ("lonely"), 74 ("giant's"), 82 ("Angola"), 88 ("their," with "her" later inserted above the line from "C.B."), 92 ("in," with "for" later penciled in the margin from "CB"), 100 ("waken"—the "n" added afterward, probably from the text in the Morgan leaf), and 115 ("eye had," with "eyelids CB." penciled in the margin). The transcript shows 45–46 and some words in 81 and 84 first written in pencil and later in ink; W^2 also has, uncanceled, the two lines between 68 and 69 that Keats wrote and then deleted in his MS, and at the end of the transcript, after a space and without any explanatory comment, the text of the sixteen-line Morgan fragment beginning "Gif yc wol stonden hardie wight." Woodhouse's blank spaces and misreadings in W^2 are best explained as deriving from the intervening shorthand transcript, whose known text for 1–50 agrees with the draft against W^2 in 12 and 22 but omits "old" in 40 and all of 45 (with a sign marking the omission of the line), and in 49 has neither "to" nor " 'gainst" but apparently "by." Several W^2 misreadings ("About" for "Above" in 62, "fell" for "fall" in 65, "Angola" for "angora" in 82, "eye had" for "eyelids" in 115) can probably be attributed to the ambiguity of Woodhouse's shorthand notations.

Keats's September 1819 letter version omits 115–119 (and also 98-*a–p*), has unique substantive variants in 2, 8, 13, 20, 27, 56 ("All" for "And"), 64 ("their" for "its"), 70, and 85, and further varies from the British Museum MS in 59 ("homewards") and 100 ("waken"). From the variant in 59 it might be thought that Keats made his copy from Brown's transcript, but his text agrees with his earlier holograph against the transcript in 22, 33, 53, and 66, and he did not anywhere correct Brown's text, as he might have done (especially in 33) had he been working from it. His omission of the sixteen-line Morgan fragment is not particularly significant, because it had never actually been part of the text of the poem (H. B. Forman was the first to incorporate the lines into the poem).

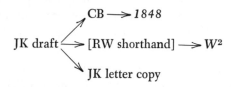

Though both the earlier and later holographs have claims to be the basis for a standard text, I would propose—mainly because the letter copy appears to have been written out casually (it occurs in the letter shortly after Keats's copy of *Not Aladdin magian,* in which he omitted a couplet and the rest of the poem after 44)—that the British Museum MS is the better choice. In any event, the sixteen-line Morgan fragment and Woodhouse's two lines following 68 (which Keats deleted in his MS when he wrote the present 69–70) do not belong in the poem.

Garrod bases his text on *1848,* making small changes in spelling and punctuation in 8, 40, 77, 101, 109, and 110, correcting Brown-*1848* substantive errors in 33 and 66, and incorporating the Morgan fragment after 98. He has, therefore (apart from 98*a–p*), the draft text generally, Brown-*1848* variants from both holographs in "organ" (22) and "plaited" (53), and Brown's and the letter copy's "homewards" (59); his "in" in 32 does not appear in any MS (the MSS read "mid" while *1848* has "and"). His apparatus omits substantive variants from the MSS to 12, 56, 59, 64, 65, and 74. Allott takes her text from W^2 but departs substantively from it in 12, 40, 59 (W^2 has "townwards"), 62, 65, 68, 82 (this and subsequent references use Garrod's line numbering), 88, 92, and 100, in effect producing a mixture of several texts (partly on the basis of faulty information in Garrod's apparatus) and retaining Woodhouse's distinctive errors in 74 and 115. She includes the canceled couplet following 68, and like Garrod incorporates the Morgan fragment after 98. Her selection of W^2 as a base-text is an especially curious one, since we have two holographs, one of which was the source (via shorthand) for the text that she chooses.

Why did I laugh tonight? No voice will tell

Written in March 1819 (before the 19th, when Keats copied the poem in a letter to his brother and sister-in-law). First published in *1848,* II, 301. Garrod, p. 470; Allott, pp. 488–489.

We have a holograph fair copy in the letter to George and Georgiana Keats of 14 February–3 May 1819 (MS at Harvard, text in *Letters*, II, 81) and transcripts by John Jeffrey (in his copy of the letter) and Milnes. Jeffrey's text varies substantively from the holograph letter only in 6— "I say wherefore" for Keats's "Say, wherefore." Milnes made his copy from Jeffrey's transcript, the only source available to him, again changing 6 (correcting the meter) to read "I say, why." The *1848* printer set the poem from Milnes's transcript, like Garrod misreading Milnes's "could" in 11 as "would."

[JK draft] ⟶ JK letter copy ➤ JJ ➤ RMM ➤ *1848*

Obviously the holograph letter copy is the proper basis for a standard text. Garrod reproduces *1848* exactly, thus retaining Milnes's revision in 6 and the *1848* printer's mistake in 11. Allott follows the letter text accurately.

When they were come unto the Fairy's court

Written on 15 April 1819 ("a little extempore" in Keats's letter to George and Georgiana under that date). Lines 1–17 first published by Colvin in *Macmillan's Magazine*, 58 (1888), 317–318, and a complete text first in H. B. Forman's *Poetry and Prose by John Keats: A Book of Fresh Verses and New Readings* (1890), pp. 31–34. Garrod, pp. 563–566; Allott, pp. 491–495.

Keats's draft in the 14 February–3 May 1819 journal letter (MS at Harvard, text in *Letters*, II, 85–88) is our sole source for these lines. Forman made a few changes when he published them, reading "into" for Keats's "unto" in 1 and emending "A quavering . . . thee" to "And quaver'd . . . the" in 46, "and" to "and then" in 53, "prick" to "prick'd" in 76, and "rub" to "rub'd" in 85. Garrod follows Forman in these except that he prints "Quavering" in 46; he further emends "Sham'd" to "Shamm'd" in 93. Allott gives the letter text more accurately in 1 and the beginning of 46, and accepts Forman's emendations in 53, 76, and 85, and Garrod's in 93. She changes Keats's "thee" in 46 to "three," which I think is a better choice than Forman's "the."

Character of C. B.

Written on 16 April 1819 (drafted in a letter to George and Georgiana on that day). First published in *1848*, I, 269–270. Garrod, p. 498; Allott, pp. 496–498.

In addition to the holograph draft in the 14 February–3 May 1819 letter to George and Georgiana (MS at Harvard, text in *Letters,* II, 89–90), there are transcripts by Brown, Woodhouse (W^2), and John Jeffrey (in his transcript of the letter).

As frequently in these histories, we have two basic texts—the earlier represented by Keats's untitled draft in the letter, with "is" (1), "feast" (18), and "cheery" (22), and the later represented by Brown's and Woodhouse's transcripts (both titled "Character of C. B."), with "was" (1), "feed" (18), and "cherry" (22). Unfortunately we do not know Brown's source, though it was certainly either the letter draft (with Keats's dictated revisions or Brown's corrections and/or errors in the three variants) or a slightly revised lost copy by Keats. Because we have no Brown transcripts for the two preceding pieces, which were also in the same letter, it is perhaps more likely that Brown transcribed a lost holograph. Woodhouse took his date from Brown ("1819 C.B."), and could have taken his text as well, which does not vary substantively from Brown's; but again I think it is a safer bet that Woodhouse copied the same lost holograph from which Brown worked. Jeffrey transcribed the letter text, changing "cheery" to "cherry" in 22 and "hoarse" to "brave" in 23, but otherwise copying accurately. Milnes printed the stanzas as part of the letter from an amanuensis' copy of Jeffrey's transcript. The *1848* text has Jeffrey's "cherry" and "brave" in 22 and 23, and further substantive changes in 3–4 ("a parle / It holds with" for "in parle / It holds the") and 13 ("-head" for "herd"—in both Keats's letter and Jeffrey's copy the word is written "heard" with the "a" deleted).

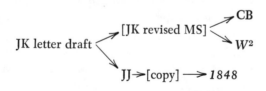

The question of a base-text—Keats's letter or Brown's and Woodhouse's transcripts—depends on whether the transcripts' variants in 1, 18, and 22 represent authoritative revisions or corruptions of the text. In the face of ignorance, I suggest that we arbitrarily consider the changes authoritative and take one or the other transcript as the standard. Both Garrod and Allott follow Keats's letter (Garrod with the heading "Character of Charles Brown" and an intermixture of *1848*'s accidentals), but both have *1848*'s "swine-head" in 13. Garrod prints "cherry-" and Allott "cheery-" in 22.

Ode on Indolence

Written in the spring of 1819 (probably after Keats described to his brother and sister-in-law on 19 March a mood of indolence in which "Poetry . . . Ambition . . . Love . . . pass by me . . . like three figures on a greek vase," and certainly before he mentioned the poem in a letter to Sarah Jeffrey of 9 June—*Letters,* II, 78–79, 116). First published in *1848,* II, 276–278. Garrod, pp. 447–449; Allott, pp. 541–544.

The two extant MSS are transcripts by Brown and Woodhouse (W^2). Brown copied a lost holograph that apparently consisted of several separate sheets, for he initially got the stanzas in the wrong order (Gittings, *John Keats,* p. 311 n., and *Odes,* p. 65, suggests that Brown was thinking of the MS of *Indolence* when he recalled in his "Life" of Keats how he rescued the text of *Nightingale* from "some scraps of paper . . . four or five in number"—*KC,* II, 65). His transcript gives the stanzas as follows (the angle brackets indicate deleted stanza numbers):

1		One morn before me were three figures seen . . .
2		How is it, Shadows, that I knew ye not? . . .
<3>	4	They faded, and, forsooth! I wanted wings . . .
<4>	6	So, ye three Ghosts, adieu! Ye cannot raise . . .
<5>	3	A third time pass'd they by, and, passing, turn'd . . .
5		A third time came they by;—alas! wherefore? . . .

The uncorrected "5" at the head of this final stanza shows that Brown discovered his mistake and, possibly in consultation with Keats, corrected the numbering of the preceding three stanzas before he wrote out the last stanza. His corrected order is thus the following:

1	One morn before me . . .
2	How is it, Shadows . . .
3	A third time pass'd they by . . .
4	They faded, and, forsooth! . . .
5	A third time came they by . . .
6	So, ye three Ghosts, adieu! . . .

Woodhouse transcribed the stanzas in this order "from C.B." (there are no substantive differences between the two texts), and Milnes used Brown's MS as printer's copy for *1848,* changing "A third time" at the beginning of the fifth stanza in proofs to read "And once more."

$$[\text{JK MS}] \longrightarrow \text{CB} \underset{\searrow 1848}{\overset{\nearrow W^2}{}}$$

Brown's transcript, the only version deriving directly from a holograph MS, is the proper basis for a standard text. Garrod prints *1848's* wording and accidentals (except for restoring Brown's text at the beginning of stanza 5 and making five minor changes in punctuation and spelling), but, under the mistaken impression that Milnes changed the order of the stanzas, moves the fifth stanza up to come after stanza 2. (For a fuller discussion of the textual history and Garrod's rearrangement of stanzas see my article in *SB,* 22 [1969], 255–258, reprinted in *Hoodwinking,* pp. 174–178.) Allott, following W^2, has the same substantive text as Brown's except for a misprint, "while" for "whiles," in 22.

As Hermes once took to his feathers light

Written in April 1819 (on or before the 16th, when Keats copied the poem in a letter to his brother and sister-in-law). First published in the *Indicator,* 28 June 1820, p. 304, and then in the *London Magazine,* 4 (November 1821), 526, the *Ladies' Companion,* 7 (August 1837), 186, and *1848,* II, 302. The text in the *Ladies' Pocket Magazine,* Part I (1838), pp. 228–229, is a reprint from the *Ladies' Companion.* Garrod, p. 471; Allott, pp. 498–500.

In addition to the early printed versions, there are two holograph MSS —one written on a blank leaf at the end of Volume I of H. F. Cary's 1814 translation, *The Vision; or, Hell, Purgatory, and Paradise, of Dante Alighieri* (Yale—facsimile in *Rare Books, Original Drawings, Autograph Letters and Manuscripts Collected by the Late A. Edward Newton,* Parke-Bernet sale catalogue, New York, 1941, Part Two, p. 157), the other a fair copy in Keats's letter to George and Georgiana of 14 February–3 May 1819 (MS at Harvard, text in *Letters,* II, 91)—and no fewer than seven transcripts, by Brown, Dilke, Woodhouse (two copies, W^2 and W^1), J. A. Hessey (Garrod's W^3), John Howard Payne, and John Jeffrey (in his transcript of the letter). The copy made from the *Indicator* that C. C. Clarke sent to Milnes via Severn in 1846 (*KC,* II, 155) has not survived.

Most of the MSS are untitled; Brown and Dilke head the poem "Sonnet, On a Dream," while Hessey has "Sonnet after reading Dante." There is a slip of the pen ("look") in the first line of W^1, and Jeffrey omitted the entire first line and copied "pure" as "pine" in 7, but otherwise the MSS do not differ among themselves as originally written. Brown's transcript shows "that" altered to "a" in 8, and this is the only significant variant among the texts. The *Indicator* text also has "a" in 8, and unique variants that almost surely ought to be disregarded in 7 ("Not unto" for

"Not to pure") and 10 (" 'mid" for "in" and "world-wind" for "whirl-wind").

With so little internal evidence it is difficult to be certain about the relationships among the MSS. The holograph in the Dante volume is pretty clearly Keats's original draft (even though it shows alterations and revisions only in 7, 10, and 11), and we may assume that his letter copy followed soon after, though whether from the extant draft or a lost holograph in his "book" (see *Letters,* II, 104) is not known. Brown probably transcribed a lost holograph rather than the draft or the letter copy (this simply on the basis of what seems to have been his practice with other short poems of about the same time). Dilke copied Brown's text exactly, and before Brown changed "that" to "a" in 8. I should guess that Woodhouse's source in W^2 was the same lost MS that I have posited as Brown's. W^2 has "baffled" in parentheses in 2, a date at the end (April 1819), and a note on the opposite page recording Brown's title and citing some illustrative passages from Cary's Dante; at some later time Woodhouse tried his hand (in pencil) at revising 12, producing "Pale was the sweet cheek I saw" to avoid the repetition of "lips" in the next line. I suppose that W^1 was taken from W^2 (the penciled corrections in W^1—"took" for "look" in 1 and "a" for "that" in 8—may have been made by a later hand, on the basis of *1848* or some subsequent text). Hessey's transcript, certainly deriving from Woodhouse but not necessarily directly from W^2 or W^1, apparently was printer's copy for his *London Magazine*'s version (capital letters are underlined thrice in his transcript, and there is a penciled direction at the bottom, "to follow the 'Lawyer,' " referring to a poem that appeared in the *London* in August 1821); in a footnote to 9 the *London* prints some of the Dante lines that Woodhouse had quoted in his note in W^2.

Keats presumably supplied copy for the *Indicator* version—he was living at Hunt's at the time the poem was published—and possibly by dictation, since the erroneous "world-wind" sounds much like Keats's "whirlwind." The *Indicator*'s variants in 7 and 10 are almost certainly corruptions (" 'mid" perhaps an editorial change by Hunt). Payne's transcript, which he sent Milnes in 1847, derives from a lost copy of the poem made by George Keats from the journal letter (see *KC,* II, 224). The same George Keats copy was the basis for the version included in Payne's article in the *Ladies' Companion* (which printed "it" for "so" in 6, an independent error). Jeffrey of course also copied the letter. Brown's transcript was printer's copy for *1848,* and Milnes struck out "Sonnet" in the title and added the reference to his Volume I, page 270, on the transcript.

[JHP] → *Ladies'*
Companion

[GK]
JK letter ↗   ↘ JHP
copy ↘ JJ

CWD
CB ↗
↘ 1848

JK draft → [JK MS]

W¹
W² ↗
↘ JAH → *London Magazine*

Indicator

Since there is only the substantive variant in 8 to worry about, Keats's letter copy and Brown's and Woodhouse's transcripts all have claims to be the basis for a standard text. I think, however, that we should regard Brown's change in 8 as authoritative, and print "a" rather than "that" of the draft, the letter copy, and the lost MS hypothesized as Brown's and Woodhouse's source. If Brown and Woodhouse did copy the same MS, then (since W^2 is untitled) Brown's heading may be one of his own devising. Garrod takes his text from *1848,* changing punctuation in 3 and 6, lowercasing "Hell" in 9, and emending substantively (to restore the draft's and the letter copy's "that") in 8. Allott follows the letter copy accurately.

Bright star, would I were steadfast as thou art

Written in 1819 (so dated in Brown's transcript; a more precise dating is not possible, though critics have vigorously debated in favor of various specific months and even specific days between October 1818 and the end of 1819). First published in *PDWJ,* 27 September 1838, and then in the *Union Magazine,* 1 (February 1846), 156 (a facsimile of the extant holograph), and *1848,* II, 306. Garrod, p. 475; Allott, pp. 736–739.

We have a holograph copy written on a blank page of the 1806 *Poetical Works of William Shakespeare* at Keats House, Hampstead (facsimiles in the *Union Magazine* [see above]; Forman [1883], facing II, 361; Williamson, plate VI; *The John Keats Memorial Volume,* 1921, facing p. 202; Caroline F. E. Spurgeon, *Keats's Shakespeare,* 1928, facing p. 42; Joanna

Richardson, *Fanny Brawne: A Biography,* 1952, p. 77; Gittings, *John Keats,* following p. 400; Dorothy Hewlett, *A Life of John Keats,* 3rd ed., 1970, p. 352; and other places), and transcripts by Brown and Fanny Brawne (the latter written on a flyleaf of Volume I of H. F. Cary's 1814 translation of Dante's *Vision* at Yale—facsimiles in Gittings' *The Mask of Keats,* 1956, facing p. 8, and *John Keats,* following p. 400).

There are two quite different versions of this poem, the earlier represented by Brown's transcript (from a lost holograph, possibly the original draft) and the later represented by Keats's copy in the Shakespeare volume and Fanny Brawne's transcript. Brown varies substantively from the other two MS texts (which themselves agree substantively throughout) in 2 ("amid" for the later MSS' "aloft"), 3 ("Not" for "And"), 4 ("devout" for "patient"), 5 ("morning" for "moving," possibly a simple copying error, though it is defended by David Mackay in *TLS,* 3 July 1969, p. 731), 10 ("Cheek-pillow'd on my Love's white" for "Pillow'd upon my fair love's"), 11 ("touch . . . warm sink and swell" for "feel . . . soft swell and fall"), 13 ("To hear, to feel" for "Still, still to hear"), and 14 ("Half passionless, and so swoon on" for "And so live ever—or else swoon").

Keats made the extant holograph copy aboard ship on his way to Italy (if we can believe Severn's well-known account), at the end of September or the beginning of October 1820. Fanny Brawne most likely took her text from this MS after Keats's death, though it is also possible that she transcribed another holograph now unknown (Sharp, p. 55, seems to say that Severn got another copy from Keats besides the one in the Shakespeare volume). The *PDWJ* version derives from Brown's transcript, and the *Union Magazine* printed a facsimile of the extant holograph, sent in by Severn. The *1848* text (headed "Keats's Last Sonnet") is also based on the holograph, but whether from a Severn transcript, the *Union Magazine*'s facsimile, or examination of the MS itself is not certain. Milnes introduced a single substantive change, printing "fall and swell" in 11 rather than the holograph's and Fanny Brawne's "swell and fall" (he also, in a footnote, gives the final line of Brown's transcript as "Another reading").

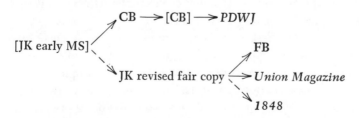

The extant holograph is the proper basis for a standard text. Garrod reproduces *1848* exactly except for omitting Milnes's title and making two minor changes in 4. Allott takes her text from the holograph, but nevertheless has, like Garrod, Milnes's "fall and swell" in 11. Milnes's revision may make a better rhyme and possibly a more attractive image, but surely we should print the words as Keats wrote them.

Hyperion: A Fragment

Begun in the closing months of 1818 (Keats refers to the poem on 27 October—*Letters,* I, 387) and abandoned in April 1819 (Woodhouse copied the fragment on 20 April). First published in *1820.* Garrod, pp. 276–305; Allott, pp. 394–441.

A holograph MS lacking only II.116–127 and 292–293 is in the British Museum (facsimiles of the whole in de Selincourt, *Hyperion,* and of the first page in Gittings, *The Mask of Keats,* 1956, facing p. 20). The partial leaf containing II.116–127, which was given away by Hunt, who had possession of the complete MS during his lifetime, is in the Morgan Library. There are transcripts by Woodhouse (W^2) and one of his clerks (W^1). The "copy of Hyperion" that E. L. Lushington wrote to Milnes about in 1856 (*KC,* II, 316–317) has not been identified; it seems unlikely that it was any of the extant MSS of either *Hyperion* or *The Fall of Hyperion.*

Though various writers have described the British Museum holograph as a fair copy or second draft (e.g., de Selincourt, *Hyperion,* p. 5; Ridley, p. 67; Ward, p. 430, n. 8), according to Woodhouse the MS was "the original & only copy . . . composed & written down at once as it now stands" (see just below). Perhaps Woodhouse was mistaken; in any case it has always seemed difficult to believe that Keats could *draft* two books and part of a third of a long narrative poem in as finished a form as the extant holograph shows. But Woodhouse's "composed & written down at once as it now stands" sounds like information (whether or not true) from the poet himself, and I think we must, without better evidence to the contrary, accept Woodhouse's statement that the MS we have is the only holograph of the poem that ever existed.

From this to the first published version the way is clear and unmistakable. Woodhouse copied the holograph in W^2, adding after the last line "Thus the M.S. copy Ends," and below this "Copied 20 Ap^1 1819 from J.K's Manuscript written in 1818/9" and "The Copy from which I took the above was the original & only copy—The alterations are noted in the margin—With the exception of these, it was composed & written down at once as it now stands." It is a very painstaking copy, with many marginal notes describing canceled readings in the holograph. Woodhouse's clerk (W^1) made his transcript from W^2 (the evidences for this, mainly in places where the clerk miscopied or could not read Woodhouse's handwriting, and where Woodhouse later corrected errors and filled in blanks, are too numerous to detail). W^1 was printer's copy for *1820* (for this also there is abundant evidence, from H. B. Forman's observation of remnants of sealing wax used to hold the rest of the W^1 book together while leaving *Hyperion* free for the compositor—see Hampstead Keats, III, 190—to the printer's marking of *1820* page and signature in the MS at II.29 and III.29). The progress is thus quite plain and straightforward:

$$\text{JK MS} \longrightarrow W^2 \longrightarrow \text{RW's clerk } (W^1) \longrightarrow 1820$$

Of the principal changes between the holograph text and *1820*, those recorded in Garrod's apparatus for the following lines first appear in W^2: I.9 (though the *1820* text penciled above the line in W^2 may have been entered after *1820* was published; that it is in Keats's hand is very doubtful), 16, 21/22 (the four lines are bracketed in W^2, deleted in W^1), 46 ("hollow" is underlined in pencil in W^2, deleted in W^1), 81 (both W^2 and W^1 have "falling"), 147, 283 (the insertion of "Two"), 306, 345; II.1, 91, 128 (the alteration of "vibrated" to "vibrating"), 231, 232 (both W^2 and W^1 have "of"); III.58, 102. Changes in the following lines first appear in W^1: I.6 (a copying error), 76 (the penciled "gradual" may be by a late hand, however, after *1820* was published), 102 (the deletion of two half-lines), 189 (the alteration appears to be in Woodhouse's hand), 200 (again probably Woodhouse's hand), 217 ("s" is marginally added to "dove-wing" in pencil); II.21 ("in"), 134 ("starr'd" is changed to "starry" and "his" deleted, both changes in pencil); III.125/ 126 (three lines deleted in pencil). New readings appear for the first time in *1820* in I.30, 48, 65, 116, 156, 199, 205/206 (a line omitted), 209, 268; II.60 (the penciled *1820* reading "sacred" in W^1 is probably by a late hand), 124, 167, 312, 313; III.49, 81, 126, 132.

These lists do not include several corrections of Keats's slips of the pen and faulty grammar, nor do they indicate responsibility for the various changes. Some of the pencilings in W^1, especially those that simply delete words or lines, cannot be attributed with certainty to any specific person, though one may guess that, as with the other long poems in *1820,* Woodhouse was the main editor and reviser. (Woodhouse's pencilings in the holograph at II.366, 369, 370, and a few other places are easier to identify.) There is no real evidence that Keats read or marked the poem in either W^2 or W^1, and even the well-known final line completed in pencil by Woodhouse at the end of W^1 ("Celestial Glory dawn'd: he was a god!") is probably, where it adds to the canceled text at the conclusion of the British Museum holograph, Woodhouse's own invention rather than Keats's. Nevertheless, as with *1820* more generally, we must in theory accept the idea that Keats at least saw and approved whatever changes he did not himself actually initiate, and continue to regard *1820* as the proper basis for a standard text.

Garrod emends *1820* twice substantively—"above" for "about" in I.6 and "fallen" for "falling" in I.81—and departs intentionally from *1820* capitalization, punctuation, and spelling in I.145, 168, 249, 344; II.78, 191, 195, 197, 200, 310, 324 (the change at II.78 seems ill-advised, and Garrod does not treat capitalization consistently). He errs in omitting *1820* end punctuation in I.241, 285, 298, and III.89, and in printing a period instead of a comma at the end of II.145. Allott does not emend I.6 and 81, nor does she otherwise depart substantively from *1820*. She follows the holograph in breaking I.112 into two half-lines and in omitting *1820*'s paragraph division after I.149.

La Belle Dame sans Merci: A Ballad

Written on 21 or 28 April 1819 (21 April is the date given by Rollins to the section of the journal letter in which Keats drafted the poem, but the dating is based on Keats's mention of Daniel Terry's "new dull and half damnd opera call'd 'the heart of Mid Lothian' that was on Saturday," which Rollins takes as a reference to the opening performance on 17 April; *The Heart of Midlothian* also played on the following Saturday, 24 April, however, when it was still "new," and Keats's "Wednesday Evening" just before the poem could as easily refer to 28 April—*Letters*, II, 94–95). First published in the *Indicator*, 10 May 1820, p. 248, and then in *1848*, II, 268–270. The text in *Arcturus*, 3 (January 1842), 158–159, is a reprint from the *Indicator*. Garrod, pp. 441–443; Allott, pp. 500–506.

In addition to Keats's draft in the letter to George and Georgiana (MS at Harvard, text in *Letters*, II, 95–96), we have a transcript by Brown and two by Woodhouse (W^2, W^1). The letter version and the transcripts differ very little substantively among themselves. The letter has "hill" in 36 where the transcripts read "hill's" (Brown added " 's" to "hill" in his

MS) and "Thee hath" in 40 for the transcripts' "Hath thee" (the letter also has "dreamt" in 35, which might be considered semisubstantive, for the transcripts' "dream'd"). Both Brown and Woodhouse add "A Ballad" after the main title. We do not know the source of either transcript, but may suppose that Brown copied the poem from a lost holograph and that Woodhouse copied either Brown (from whom he took at least the date, "C.B.—1819"—and his text is closer than usual to Brown's in minor details) or the same lost holograph. W^1 was probably made from W^2, and Brown's transcript was printer's copy for *1848*. My diagram for this earlier state of text arbitrarily shows W^2 deriving from the lost holograph.

The other state is that in Hunt's *Indicator,* for which copy was presumably supplied by Keats himself, perhaps on the basis of Brown's transcript. The *Indicator* text varies substantively from the letter and the transcripts in 1, 3, 11, 23, 30, 31, 32, 33, 36 (here, however, agreeing with the letter text), 39, 41, and 44, and in the transposition of the fifth and sixth stanzas. Such extensive changes are difficult to explain, and some writers have been tempted to attribute some or all of them to Hunt's influence or even to his actual editing of the poem. In 1845 John Jeffrey had in his possession a holograph beginning "Ah what can ail thee, wretched wight" (*KC,* II, 120); this agreement with the *Indicator's* first line does not necessarily mean that Jeffrey's holograph had the *Indicator* readings throughout, or that Hunt had no influence in the alterations, but it does suggest that Keats had a hand in some version differing from that represented by the letter draft and the transcripts.

Two editorial problems, a large one and a small one, obviously result from the above details—first, whether to choose the *Indicator* or the earlier version as the basis for a standard text, and, second, if the earlier version is chosen, whether or not the Brown-Woodhouse readings in 36 and 40 are to be considered authoritative. Critics have always (sometimes eloquently and occasionally even vehemently) preferred the earlier version, and perhaps some theoretical justification for their choice can be based on the frequency with which unique variants appear in the periodical and annual texts of other poems by Keats (see Section III.2). In the face of ignorance concerning the second matter, I suggest that we arbitrarily consider the Brown-Woodhouse readings in 36 and 40 as authoritative.

Garrod reproduces *1848* exactly except for a change in punctuation at the end of 5 (*1848* has an exclamation), "hill" in 36 (from the letter text, which he does not, however, follow in 40), and "has" in 47 (the MSS, *Indicator,* and *1848* all have "is"). Allott takes her text from the letter, but prints the transcripts' and *1848*'s "Hath thee" in 40 and the *Indicator*'s "hill" in 44 (she also has "dreamed" for the letter's "dreamt" in 35).

Song of Four Fairies

Written on 21 or 28 April 1819 (dating the same as for the preceding poem). First published in *1848,* II, 271–275. Garrod, pp. 443–447; Allott, pp. 506–510.

We have two holograph MSS—Keats's draft in the 21 or 28 April section of the letter to George and Georgiana Keats of 14 February–3 May 1819 (MS at Harvard, text in *Letters,* II, 97–100) and a fair copy (also Harvard)—and transcripts by Brown and Woodhouse (W^2).

The letter draft differs substantively from later MSS in 9, 19, 26 (Brown also has "all"), 32, 44 ("sometime," as in the fair copy), 46, 47 (Brown also has "browed"), 55, 60 ("Of," as in Brown and W^2—the fair copy has "From"), 71 ("is," as in the fair copy), 77 (Brown also has "Frost and"), 93 ("tongued," as in the fair copy), and 98 ("where"). Brown may have taken his copy from the letter draft—for "wrought" in 16 he originally wrote "wrangle," which is what Keats's word looks like in the letter, and his "when" in 98 appears to have been first written "where"—but his substantive variants from the draft (9, 19, 32, 44, 46, 55, 71, and 93) seem too numerous to explain either as his own alterations or as revisions requested by Keats, and I think we should assume that he followed some lost revised holograph. His transcript was printer's copy for *1848,* which reproduced it substantively (adding italics to "will" in 38).

Woodhouse made his transcript either from Brown (from whom he at least took the date, "C.B. 1819") or, what is perhaps more likely, from the same MS that Brown copied; W^2 also originally had a word that resembles "wrangle" in 16 and had "where" in 98, and its initial text does not otherwise vary substantively from Brown's, though Woodhouse left a space for a rhyming line after 47 in which he later penciled "When his arched course is run," interlining "done" above "run." Subsequently Woodhouse saw the holograph fair copy and altered W^2 according to its readings (see below) in 9, 26, 44, 47, 71, 77, 93, and 98 (but not 60), noting at the end, "Corrected, by Keats's copy for the press."

The Harvard fair copy is a further revised version based either on the lost MS that Brown (and Woodhouse?) transcribed or, more probably, on Brown's transcript itself (the fair copy and Brown's transcript have many likenesses in minor details, and if one came from the other it was certainly, because of the substantive differences between them, Keats's from Brown's rather than vice versa). Woodhouse's identification of this MS as "Keats's copy for the press" tells us that the poem was once intended for inclusion in *1820,* and thus we have an example of what printer's copy for the shorter poems in *1820* looked like. My diagram supposes that Woodhouse transcribed the same MS Brown worked from and that Keats made his fair copy from Brown's transcript.

JK letter draft ⟶ [JK revised MS] ⟨ CB ⟨ JK fair copy / 1848 / W²

Keats's fair copy—the version that he once intended to publish, and therefore clearly the proper basis for a standard text—reads "Nimbly" in 9, "and" in 26, "sometime" in 44, "-presenc'd" in 47, "From" in 60, "is" in 71, "Frost or" in 77, "tongued" in 93, and "when" in 98. Garrod takes his text from *1848,* changing the arrangement of speaker-headings (they are at the left margin in the MSS and *1848*), altering *1848*'s italics, spelling, and punctuation in 38 and 39, and emending substantively according to the fair copy in 47 ("-presenc'd") and 93 ("tongued-"). He does not emend 9, 26, 44, 60 (wrong in his apparatus), 71, or 77. Allott, following the fair copy, nevertheless has draft readings in 26 ("all"), 60 ("Of"), and 77 ("Frost and"), and the Brown-Woodhouse-*1848* 71 ("are").

To Sleep

Written in April 1819 ("lately written" when Keats copied the poem into a letter to his brother and sister-in-law on 30 April—*Letters,* II, 104). First published in *PDWJ,* 11 October 1838, and then in *1848,* II, 298. Garrod, p. 467; Allott, pp. 510–512.

There are three extant holographs—a draft written on a flyleaf of Volume II of the 1807 *Paradise Lost* that Keats gave to Mrs. Dilke (Keats House, Hampstead—facsimile in Williamson, plate VIII), a fair copy in the 14 February–3 May 1819 letter to George and Georgiana Keats (MS at Harvard, text in *Letters,* II, 105), and a fair copy signed and dated June 1820 that was once in a lady's album subsequently owned by Sir John Bowring (Berg Collection, New York Public Library, a MS not seen by Garrod or Allott). We have transcripts by Brown, Dilke, and Woodhouse (two copies, W^2 and W^1).

The earliest version is the twelve-line original draft in the Hampstead Milton, which varies from all other MSS in 4, 6, and 8–12. The principal substantive differences among the MSS following this draft occur in 8, where Keats's letter copy, Brown, Dilke, W^1, and initially W^2 read "dewy" and the Berg MS has "lulling"; 11, where the letter, Brown, Dilke, and initially W^2 read "lords" and the Berg MS and W^1 have "hoards"; and 12, where the letter, Brown, Dilke, W^2, and W^1 read "a" ("the" altered to "a" in the letter) and the Berg MS has "the." (The letter also has a unique "borrowing" in 12, presumably a copying error for the other MSS' "burrowing.") Subsequently Keats substituted "lulling" for "dewy" in the margin of W^2 (the same word is inserted above the line in Brown's MS— see below), and Woodhouse interlined "hoards" in pencil above "lords" in W^2.

Just as for the other sonnets that Keats copied at the end of his longest journal letter, we must hypothesize a lost holograph (in Keats's "book"— *Letters,* II, 104) as the source of at least Keats's letter copy and Brown's transcript. Dilke followed Brown's copy exactly in every detail. Woodhouse took his text in W^2 either from the lost holograph or from Brown's copy (from which he got at least the date, "C.B. 1819"). Since this and the next three sonnets appear together in the W^2 book (fols. 151–154), I should guess that the evidence for one of them (the second sonnet *On Fame*)—that Woodhouse copied the same lost MS that Brown worked from—would apply to the others as well. In June 1820 Keats read over W^2 and changed "dewy" to "lulling" in circumstances that Woodhouse explains in a note opposite his transcript: "This word '*lulling*' is in K's handwriting. The correction was made when he borrowed this book to select a small poem to write in an Album, intended to consist of original Poetry, for a lady." Obviously the Berg MS is the album copy that Keats made. Still later someone—almost surely Woodhouse—penciled "lulling" over "dewy" in Brown's transcript. If the handwriting there could be definitely identified as Woodhouse's we would have further evidence that Woodhouse already possessed a text of the poem before he saw Brown's MS.

There has been a great deal of controversy over "lords" vs. "hoards" in

11 (see *TLS,* 8, 29 March, 12, 19 April, 3 May 1941, pp. 117, 151, 179, 191, 215; Garrod's Oxford Standard Authors edition, 1956, p. 467; and R. W. King's review of Allott in *Review of English Studies,* n.s. 22 [1971], 505). In the extant MSS, "hoards" first appears in W^2, where it is penciled above a deleted "lords" in Woodhouse's hand. Because W^1, which was almost certainly made from W^2, has "hoards" but also "dewy" (with no sign of the change to "lulling"), we have to think that Woodhouse inserted "hoards" in W^2, and then copied it into W^1, *before* Keats saw W^2 and substituted "lulling" for "dewy." It seems likely, as a consequence, that "hoards" is Woodhouse's own invention. The Berg MS, however, has "hoards," and Garrod's triumphant conclusion—"Keats, then, wrote 'lords.' Brown, under his eye, copied it as 'lords.' Woodhouse . . . wrote 'lords' in W^2. Keats himself found 'lords' in W^2, and let it stand" (*TLS,* 12 April 1941, p. 179)—has to be modified by the evidence that Keats found a penciled "hoards" in W^2 and copied it into the lady's album. Whether or not we incorporate the word into our texts, we must allow that Keats's choice of "hoards" in the Berg MS signifies an acceptance of Woodhouse's alteration.

Brown's transcript was the basis of the *PDWJ* version (which has "lulling" in 8 and two unique variants, "head" for "bed" in 8 and "rise"— possibly to rhyme with "eyes" and "charities"—for "shine" in 9), and was printer's copy for *1848* (which follows the transcript substantively, including "lulling" in 8).

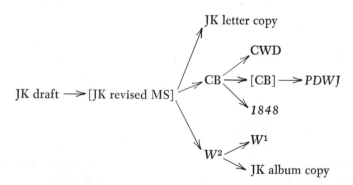

Each of four MSS has a claim to be the basis for a standard text—Keats's letter copy, Brown's and Woodhouse's transcripts, and Keats's late album copy (the Berg MS). Since album-copying constitutes publication of a sort, I suggest that we prefer the Berg MS and print not only "lulling" in 8 but also "hoards" in 11 and "the" in 12. Garrod takes his text from *1848,* altering punctuation three times in 1 and 12 and spelling in 3,

and thus has "lulling," "lords," and "a" in the lines at issue. Allott follows
W^2, reading "lulling," "hoards," and "a."

Ode to Psyche

Written toward the end of April 1819 ("the last I have written," Keats
says on 30 April, forgetting for the moment the two sonnets *On Fame,*
which he obviously had composed more recently than the ode—*Letters,*
II, 104–105). First published in *1820.* Garrod, pp. 262–264; Allott,
pp. 514–521.

In addition to the *1820* text, we have two holographs—Keats's draft
in the Morgan Library (facsimile and transcription in Gittings, *Odes,* pp.
50–55) and his copy in the 30 April section of his longest journal letter
to George and Georgiana (MS at Harvard, text in *Letters,* II, 106–108)
—and transcripts by Brown and Woodhouse (W^2).

According to a note in W^2 (see below), Keats gave a MS of the poem
to Reynolds on 4 May. This has to be the Morgan draft, which remained
with Reynolds and his relatives and their descendants until 1901, when
it was sold with three other Keats MSS at Sotheby's (two of the others,
which on the evidence of a marked copy of the sale catalogue in the Uni-
versity of Illinois Library were acquired by the same dealer who purchased
Psyche, have similarly ended up in the Morgan); Reynolds lent it to
Milnes in 1847 as "the *original*" MS (*KC,* II, 227). There ought to be
no question about its chronological priority over the letter text, which is
straightforwardly written out and incorporates in its text among other
things two words in 14 that Keats added tentatively in the margin of the
Morgan MS. The letter version also shows changes in 28 and 30; I take
"awaked" in 6 and "lastest" in 24 to be copying errors, and the deletions
and revisions in 57 and 62 (the replacement of "charmd" by "lull'd" and
"frame" by "feign") to be instances in which Keats tried out revisions and
then reverted to his original wording.

If Brown copied one or the other of the two known holographs, as I
think he did, then it was the Morgan MS, from which his transcript varies
significantly only in 15, "soft" for "calm," an alteration for which Keats
may have been responsible at the time Brown made his copy. Keats sub-
sequently read over this transcript, changing "fan" to "roof" (10) and cor-
recting "by own" to "by my own" (43). Woodhouse's source is less easily
determined. His note at the end of the text, "Given by J.K. to J.H.R. 4
May 1819," might suggest that he copied the Morgan draft, but the sub-
stantive variants in his transcript rule out this possibility. W^2 differs from

the draft in 13, in 14, and most notably in 67, and Woodhouse does not record, as he almost surely would have, had he seen the draft, the various cancellations and revisions in the draft, including eight changes of "nor" to "no" in 32 and 34; the one hint of the draft—a notation in the margin of W^2 that corresponds to an alternative reading for 14 in the draft—must have come via an intervening source: the draft reads "Blue, silver-white," with "freckle pink" in the margin, while W^2 has "Blue, freckled, pink" in its text and the note "originally freckle" in the margin. The best explanation is that Woodhouse transcribed not a holograph but a copy of the Morgan draft made (and slightly revised in the process) by Reynolds.

Various pencilings above the lines and in the margins of W^2 give *1820* readings for 14, 17, 30, 44, and 67; some, but not all, of these could have been taken from Brown's transcript, which Woodhouse undoubtedly saw (his penciled "a" over "to" in 57 very likely was based on Brown's MS, in which "asleep," perhaps just a copying error, was altered to "to sleep"). Perhaps Woodhouse entered these variants before the poem was published, since he does not notice other readings (in 14 and 36) that first appeared in *1820*.

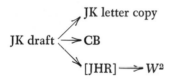

The text of *1820*, set from a lost copy by Keats or Brown, is quite close to that of Brown's transcript, but varies in 14 ("Tyrian," not in any MS), 15 ("calm," as in the two holographs and W^2), 30 ("delicious," the reading of Keats's letter copy), 36 ("brightest," not in any MS), and 44 ("So," occurring elsewhere only as a marginal penciling in W^2). It is the final authoritative version (whether or not its new readings originated with Woodhouse and/or the publishers), and should continue to be the basis for a standard text. Garrod follows *1820* exactly except for emending 17 ("bid" for Brown's and *1820*'s "bade"). Allott reproduces the *1820* wording, but inadvertently omits the stanza division after 23.

On Fame ("Fame, like a wayward girl")

Written on 30 April 1819 ("just written" before Keats copied the poem under that date in a letter to George and Georgiana—*Letters*, II, 104). First published in the *Ladies' Companion*, 7 (August 1837), 186, and then in *1848*, II, 299. The text in the *Ladies' Pocket Magazine*, Part I

(1838), p. 228, is a reprint from the *Ladies' Companion,* and that in the *Odd Fellow,* 8 January 1842, is a reprint from one or the other of these. Garrod, p. 468; Allott, pp. 512–513.

In addition to Keats's copy in the 14 February–3 May 1819 journal letter (MS at Harvard, text in *Letters,* II, 105), we have a transcript each by Brown, Dilke, and John Howard Payne, and two transcripts by Woodhouse (W^2, W^1). There are no substantive differences among the MSS except for the transposition of "Artists" and "lovelorn" (12) in Keats's letter copy and Payne's transcript.

Brown transcribed the poem (on the same day that Keats wrote it) from the same source that Keats copied in the letter, a lost MS in Keats's "book" (*Letters,* II, 104). Dilke's transcript follows Brown's exactly except for spelling errors in 8 and 10 ("scandel" and "jeaulous"). Woodhouse, who took his date in W^2 from Brown, probably copied the same lost holograph (see the discussion of *To Sleep*) and presumably made W^1 from W^2. Payne's transcript, which he sent Milnes in 1847, came from a lost copy made by George Keats from the letter (*KC,* II, 224); the same George Keats copy was also the basis for the text included in Payne's article in the *Ladies' Companion.* Brown's transcript was printer's copy for *1848.*

```
                         ,CWD
                 CB <
             ,            >1848
                                           ,[JHP]—> Ladies'
   [JK MS]<—>JK letter copy —>[GK]<          Companion
             \                             >JHP
              >W² —> W¹
```

Because the lost holograph, represented by Brown's and Woodhouse's transcripts, was probably a more considered version than that in the letter (Keats did not always take his letter-copying seriously), I think we should base our standard text on one of the transcripts, with "Artists lovelorn" rather than the letter's "lovelorn Artists" in 12. Garrod reproduces *1848* (and "Artists lovelorn"), varying only in the omission of a dash in 5. Allott follows Keats's letter copy.

On Fame ("How fever'd is the man")

Written on 30 April 1819 (drafted under that date in a letter to George and Georgiana Keats). First published in *1848,* II, 300. Garrod, p. 469; Allott, pp. 513–514.

We have Keats's draft in the 14 February–3 May journal letter (MS at Harvard, text in *Letters,* II, 104–105) and transcripts by Brown, Dilke, and Woodhouse (W^2). Brown's copy, which initially had the same substantive text as the draft except for "the" in 1 and "for" in 14 (Rollins' reading of "leasing" in 13 of the draft is probably a mistake, since uncrossed "t" is fairly common in Keats's MSS), almost surely came from a slightly altered holograph copy in Keats's "book" (see the preceding poem). Subsequently Keats rewrote 7–8, and Brown deleted the original text and entered the new lines accordingly in his transcript. Dilke copied Brown's MS in this revised state (lowercasing eight capitalized words and omitting the comma in 11, but otherwise following Brown exactly). Woodhouse has the same text as Brown's revised MS (except in his title, "Sonnet. / To Fame," where Brown has "Sonnet. / on Fame") and also records the earlier version of 7–8, with a note pointing out that Keats's revision of these lines "left an allusion in the 12th line to those thus erased." Like Brown's transcript, W^2 shows "itself" in 5 altered to "herself," and in 12, where Brown had written "chrystal" and subsequently crossed out the "h," Woodhouse began "chr" and then deleted the letters and wrote "crystal." Because of these peculiarities, I suggest that Woodhouse's text (dated "C.B. 1819") came from the same lost holograph that Brown copied. Brown's transcript was printer's copy for *1848.*

$$\text{JK letter draft} \longrightarrow \text{[JK copy]} \underset{\searrow W^2}{\overset{\nearrow \text{CB} \overset{\nearrow \text{CWD}}{\searrow 1848}}{}}$$

The consensus of Brown's and Woodhouse's transcripts is the proper basis for a standard text. Garrod reproduces *1848* exactly, and Allott, following W^2, has the same substantive text as Garrod.

If by dull rhymes our English must be chain'd

Written toward the end of April or at the beginning of May 1819 (copied out in a letter to George and Georgiana Keats on or before 3 May —it is not clear, especially since the end of the letter is known only through Jeffrey's transcript, where the 3 May section actually begins). First published in the *Plymouth, Devonport, and Stonehouse News,* 15 October 1836, and then in *1848,* II, 303. Garrod, p. 472; Allott, pp. 521–522.

We have a holograph version of 1–4 in Keats's journal letter of 14

February–3 May 1819 (MS at Harvard, text in *Letters,* II, 108; the holograph of the remainder of the letter is extant but in private ownership and unavailable) and transcripts by Brown, Dilke, Woodhouse (two copies, W^2 and W^1), and John Jeffrey (in his copy of the letter—text of 5–14 in *Letters,* II, 108).

There are no substantive differences among the MSS except in title (Brown, Dilke, and W^2 head the poem "Sonnet"; W^1 has "On the Sonnet," and both W^2 and W^1 add "Irregular" in parentheses beside the title). I suppose that Keats's letter copy and Brown's transcript both derive from a lost holograph (see the first sonnet *On Fame*), and that Woodhouse probably also took his text of W^2 from the same source (though he saw Brown's transcript and dates the poem "C.B. 1819"). W^1 presumably came from W^2. Dilke followed Brown's transcript exactly in every detail, and Jeffrey of course copied Keats's letter. Brown's transcript was the source of the version in the *Plymouth News* (which has "will" for "may" in 13, a copying or printing error) and was printer's copy for *1848*.

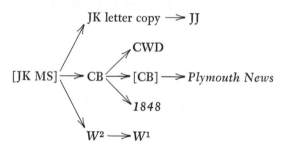

In principle (since there are no substantive variants), the consensus of Brown's transcript and W^2 should be the basis for a standard text—at least until the rest of the holograph of Keats's letter becomes public. Garrod reproduces *1848* exactly except in indentions and in his punctuation at the end of 6 (where *1848* has a semicolon). Allott follows the letter copy for 1–4 and Jeffrey for 5–14.

Two or three posies

Written probably on 1 May 1819 (Rollins' conjectural dating of the letter in which it was drafted—see *Letters,* II, 55 n.). First published in Forman (1883), III, 298–299. Garrod, pp. 566–567; Allott, pp. 522–523.

Keats's draft in the letter to Fanny Keats (MS at Harvard, text in *Letters,* II, 56–57) is our sole source. In the next-to-last line Keats wrote a word that can be read as either "dove" or "doves" (in any event there is no apostrophe). Forman, giving the lines as part of the letter, chose "dove," and Garrod reproduces Forman's text exactly. Allott follows Rollins' text in reading "dove's."

Ode to a Nightingale

Written in May 1819 (the date in Brown's lost copy, recorded in Dilke's and both of Woodhouse's transcripts). First published in *Annals of the Fine Arts,* 4 (July 1819), 354–356, and then in *1820.* Garrod, pp. 257–260; Allott, pp. 523–532.

Keats's draft has survived (Fitzwilliam Museum, Cambridge—facsimiles in the *Monthly Review,* 10 [1903], after p. 134; *The John Keats Memorial Volume,* 1921, after p. 68; *English Poetical Autographs,* ed. Desmond Flower and A. N. L. Munby, 1938, plates 26–26[4]; *Hampstead Keats,* after III, 144; and, with transcription, Gittings, *Odes,* pp. 36–43), and we have transcripts by Woodhouse (two copies, W^2 and W^1), Dilke, and George Keats. Brown's transcript, from which Woodhouse noted the date and a variant in W^2, has disappeared.

There has been considerable debate over whether the Cambridge MS is Keats's original draft (see, e.g., Robert N. Roth, *Papers of the Bibliographical Society of America,* 48 [1954], 91–95, also the references there, and Gittings, *John Keats,* p. 311 n., and *Odes,* p. 65). In his "Life" of Keats, Brown's account of how he "rescued" the ode by copying "some scraps of paper . . . four or five in number" (*KC,* II, 65) does not square with the fact that the Cambridge MS consists of two sheets, and neither of them "scraps." But the Cambridge MS has very much the appearance of other original drafts by Keats, and Gittings' suggestion that Brown was remembering not the Nightingale ode but the draft of *Ode on Indolence,* which probably *was* on several scraps of paper, is a good one. (In any event, Brown's lost transcript, which we can reconstruct from Dilke's and George Keats's copies and a note in W^2, was not taken from the extant holograph.) Keats gave the Cambridge MS to Reynolds probably not long after he wrote the poem, and it remained with Reynolds and his relatives and their descendants through the rest of the century; Reynolds lent it to Milnes in 1847, calling it "the *original*" MS (*KC,* II, 227).

Except for W^2, each of the texts before *1820* has one or more unique substantive variants—the Cambridge MS in 17, 54, 59, and 79; Dilke's transcript in 22 and 66; George Keats's transcript in 16; W^1 in 41 (I take all these variants in the transcripts to be copying errors); and *Annals* in 44 (a misreading or a printer's error). *1820* has readings that occur earlier solely in the Cambridge MS in 20 and 60, as well as several unique variants. In general terms, three states of text are discernible, represented by the Cambridge draft, the transcripts and *Annals,* and *1820.* The principal deviations from this scheme of groupings occur in 24, where the Cambridge MS, W^1, *Annals,* and *1820* read "other" while Dilke and George Keats have "other's" (W^2 has "other's" altered to "other"), and in 72, where the Cambridge MS, W^2, and W^1 read "unto myself" while Dilke, George Keats, *Annals,* and *1820* show "to my sole self."

Aside from copying errors, Dilke's and George Keats's transcripts are substantively the same, and they agree against the Cambridge MS in 17 ("beaded" for the holograph's "cluster'd"), 20 ("fade" for "fade away"), 24 ("other's" for "other"), 54 ("quiet" for "painless"), 59 ("wouldst" for "would"), 60 ("For" for "To"), 72 ("to my sole self" for "unto myself"), and 79 ("or a" for "real or"). Dilke took his text from Brown's lost transcript (he has the "CB" flourish at the end), and George Keats almost certainly also copied Brown (as he did for his texts of *Ode on a Grecian Urn, Ode on Melancholy,* and *To Autumn*), making his transcript specifically on 15 January 1820 (*Letters,* II, 243). I suppose that Brown copied some revised holograph that Keats subsequently destroyed or gave away (possibly again to Reynolds—see below). Keats, writing out the poem for James Elmes, the editor of *Annals of the Fine Arts,* probably copied either this same lost holograph or else Brown's transcript; in a note to Elmes of 12 June 1819 he mentions having "just received the Book which contains the only copy of the verses in question" (*Letters,* II, 118–120), and, since Brown at this time seems regularly to have made his transcripts of poems fairly soon after Keats composed them, I should guess that Keats was referring to Brown's copy rather than to any MS of his own. The *Annals* text varies significantly from the Dilke–George Keats agreement only in 24 ("other" for the transcripts' "other's").

W^2 is a sort of variorum text of the poem. In its initial state it differed substantively from Brown's text (the Dilke–George Keats agreement) only in 72, where it reads "unto myself," as in the Cambridge MS, for Dilke's and George's "to my sole self." Subsequently Woodhouse noted a variant to 74 and commented on a punctuation reading in "JHR's copy," added the date and the variant to 72 from "C.B.," and in a series of notations, all but one in shorthand, entered variants (in 17, 20, 54, 79) and deleted readings (in 1, 4, 12, 26, 31, 40, 42, 65, 69, 70, 74) from the Cambridge MS. He also, either before or after *1820* was published, wrote in *1820* readings above his own text in the title ("a" over "the"), 16 ("the" over "and"), and 49 ("dewy" over "sweetest," in this instance deleting the original word), and changed "other's" to "other" in 24.

Woodhouse's initial source for W^2 is unknown, though it was obviously a text closely related to that represented by Dilke's and George Keats's transcripts. One possibility is that he originally took the poem from a lost copy made by Reynolds from the same holograph that Brown transcribed. Woodhouse's insertion of "(feigned) JHR" above "famed" in 74—apparently Reynolds had written down, suggested, or queried "feigned"—and his note opposite the last line, referring to his question mark after "music," "JHR's copy has this Note of Interrog^n—It is left out of the Printed Copy [1820]—(Why?),", are clear evidence that he at least saw a Reynolds copy, and that this copy was virtually identical with the Dilke–George Keats agreement (were it not, Woodhouse would of course have noted other variants). The better likelihood, however, is that he copied the same lost holograph that Brown worked from, and that Keats revised 72 on Brown's transcript. W^1 was fairly certainly made from W^2, and after Woodhouse altered "other's" in 24 to "other."

$$JK\ draft \longrightarrow [JK\ revised\ MS] \begin{cases} [CB] \begin{cases} CWD \\ [JK\ copy] \longrightarrow Annals \\ GK \end{cases} \\ [JHR] \\ W^2 \longrightarrow W^1 \end{cases}$$

1820, printed from a lost copy by Keats or Brown, returns to the wording of the Cambridge MS in 20 and 60 and has readings not in any MS in the title and in 11, 16, 49, and 57 (though some of these are entered above the line in W^2). While the publishers may have been responsible for some or all of these new readings, we must, lacking evidence to the contrary, assume that Keats himself made—or was an assenting party to —the changes, and must continue to take *1820* as the basis for a standard text. Garrod reproduces *1820* exactly, and Allott does not depart substantively.

Ode on a Grecian Urn

Written in 1819 (the date in Brown's transcript, repeated in Dilke's, Woodhouse's, and George Keats's copies), perhaps in the spring. The dating is difficult to consider objectively, because virtually all writers in the twentieth century have assigned the poem specifically to May (usually without question or qualification), and this tradition has been given the status of fact by Garrod's mistaken report of "May 1819" in Dilke's transcript. First published in *Annals of the Fine Arts,* 4 (January 1820), 638–639, and then in *1820.* Garrod, pp. 260–262; Allott, pp. 532–538.

In addition to the two early printings, we have transcripts by Brown, Dilke, George Keats (facsimile and transcription in Gittings, *Odes,* pp. 44–49), and Woodhouse (W^2). There is no extant holograph of the poem.

On the significance and relationships of the transcripts see Alvin Whitley, *Keats-Shelley Memorial Bulletin,* 5 (1953), 1–3; my note in *PMLA,* 73 (1958), 447–448 (reprinted in *Hoodwinking,* pp. 167–171); and the review of Gittings' *Odes* in *Journal of English and Germanic Philology,* 71 (1972), 263–267. Brown's is the one transcript made directly from a holograph MS. Dilke's transcript, the next written, lowercases twenty-one words that are capitalized in Brown's copy, but otherwise follows Brown almost exactly (there is but a single difference in punctuation), and has the "CB" flourish at the end. Dilke copied the poem before Brown's "ne'er" in 40 was altered by erasure to "e'er." George Keats's transcript, made in January 1820, varies from Brown's text in twelve details of capitalization, three of punctuation, and one of hyphenation, but nevertheless also clearly derives from Brown; following his source mechanically, George left some extra space before "e'er" in 40 where Brown's transcript, after the erasure of the initial letter in "ne'er," also has extra space. Woodhouse likewise took his copy "from C.B."; W^2 shows an unrecorded variant in 40 ("will" for "can") and also "e'er" in the same line.

The *Annals* text, which most likely was printed from a Keats copy transmitted by Haydon (see *Letters,* II, 118–120, and W. Roberts, *TLS,* 20 August 1938, p. 544), has new readings in 34 and 48 and unique variants that represent copying and/or printing errors in 8, 16, and 22. My diagram supposes that Keats made his copy for the *Annals* from Brown's transcript rather than from a MS of his own (see the discussion of the preceding poem).

CWD

[JK copy] ⟶ *Annals*

[JK MS] ⟶ CB

GK

W^2

The *1820* text, printed from a lost MS by Keats or Brown, has substantive readings that do not appear in any extant MS in 9, 18, 34 (though *Annals* has "flanks"), 47, and 48 (though *Annals* has "a"), and of course the controversial quotation marks in 49, which, because of their importance in the interpretation of the poem, take on the character of a substantive reading (see *Hoodwinking,* pp. 171–173, and Allott, pp. 537–538 n., on critics' and editors' attempts to resolve the problems caused by these). As with new *1820* readings in other poems, we must assume that Keats was responsible for the changes and continue to base our standard text on *1820.* Garrod reproduces *1820* exactly except for dropping the quotation marks in 49, and Allott (retaining the quotes) does not depart substantively.

Ode on Melancholy

Written in 1819 (so dated in Brown's transcript), perhaps in the spring. A more precise dating is not possible, though most writers routinely assign the poem to May. First published in *1820.* Garrod, pp. 274–275; Allott, pp. 538–541.

The first sheet of the single extant holograph, containing stanzas 1 and 2, is in the Robert H. Taylor Collection, Princeton University Library, and the second sheet, containing stanza 3, is in the Berg Collection, New York Public Library (facsimiles of stanzas 1 and 2 in Thomas Wentworth Higginson's article in the *Forum,* 21 [1896], 422, reprinted in Higginson's *Book and Heart: Essays on Literature and Life,* New York, 1897, p. 19; of stanza 3 in the Sotheby sale catalogue for 25 July 1932; of the complete MS, with transcription, in Gittings, *Odes,* pp. 60–63). There are transcripts by Brown, George Keats, and Woodhouse (W^2).

The Taylor-Berg MS, with cancellations and additions in eight of its thirty lines, is probably Keats's original draft of the poem, though Keats's interlineation of "taste" in 29 might suggest that he was copying from an earlier MS. This earliest known version, titled "On Melancholy," differs substantively from *1820* in 6 ("or" for *1820*'s "nor"), 14 ("hills"), 21 ("lives in"), 27 ("but"), and 29 ("anguish"). Brown's transcript varies from the draft in 6 ("nor"), 27 ("save"), and 29 ("sadness"), and in addition has the canceled opening stanza (lightly crossed out in the transcript) that was first printed by Milnes in *1848,* I, 287 (in Garrod, pp. 503–504). Brown may have copied the Taylor-Berg MS, taking the additional opening stanza from a separate now-lost sheet provided by Keats as an afterthought and making changes in 6, 27, and 29 according to Keats's direction as he copied, or he may have transcribed a later, revised MS containing the additional opening stanza. The one certainty in the matter (contrary to Gittings, *Odes,* p. 77) is that Brown did not take his text from an *earlier* version than the extant holograph, for his transcript has half a dozen readings that Keats arrived at by revisions in the Taylor-Berg MS (e.g., Keats wrote "heavily" in 9, altered it to "sleepily" and finally to "drowsily," while Brown simply gives "drowsily"), and Brown could not have copied these final-text readings had he been working from an earlier version.

George Keats's transcript derives from Brown's (George has thirty-four of Brown's thirty-eight marks of punctuation, omitting four commas but otherwise varying mainly in the reduction of seven capitals to lowercase). Since George includes only the three stanzas that were published in *1820,* the decision to delete the opening stanza in Brown's transcript must have been reached in or before January 1820, when George made his copy. Woodhouse also took his text "from C.B.," following Brown's minor details with an unusual fidelity and including the canceled opening stanza without any comment on its status. (In spite of the presence of this stanza, Woodhouse's transcript is almost certainly later than George's. Occasionally elsewhere—e.g., in *The Eve of St. Mark* following 68— Woodhouse copied lines that were clearly deleted in his source.) Both Brown's and Woodhouse's transcripts show "shrouds" penciled above or opposite "creeds" in the third line of the canceled opening stanza. The handwriting appears to be the same in both transcripts, and is probably Woodhouse's (cf. Woodhouse's insertion of "I swear" in various MSS of *Lines on Seeing a Lock of Milton's Hair*). The *1848* text of the stanza, again deriving from Brown's transcript, has "shrouds." In my diagram, the hypothesized revised holograph may have been no more than the addition of the subsequently canceled opening stanza on a separate sheet.

$$\text{JK draft} \longrightarrow \text{[JK revised MS]} \longrightarrow \text{CB} \begin{cases} \nearrow \text{GK} \\ \searrow \text{W}^2 \end{cases}$$

The *1820* text, set from a lost copy by Keats or Brown, has Brown's wording in 6, 27, and 29, and two readings that do not appear in any MS—"hill" in 14 and "dwells with" in 21. It is as usual the proper basis for a standard text. Garrod reproduces *1820* exactly, and Allott does not depart substantively.

Shed no tear—O shed no tear

Written probably in 1819 (but the dating is highly conjectural, since we cannot date Brown's fairy tale for which the poem was composed—see below). First published in *PDWJ,* 18 October 1838, and then in *1848,* II, 261. Garrod, p. 436; Allott, pp. 489–490.

In addition to the single extant holograph (Harvard—facsimile in *1848,* facing the title page of Volume II), which is endorsed by Brown "A faery Song written for a particular purpose at the request of CB," we have a text by Brown included in his unfinished MS "The Fairies' Triumph" (Keats House, Hampstead—see *K-SJ,* 10 [1961], 6–8, for transcription and context) and a transcript by Milnes. Frederick Locker-Lampson's transcript in a copy of the 1841 *Poetical Works of John Keats* in the Berg Collection, New York Public Library, was made from the text (not the facsimile) in *1848,* and can be ignored.

Apart from their titles—"The Faery Bird's Song" in *PDWJ,* "Fairy's Song" in Milnes's transcript, "Faery Song" in *1848* (the holograph and Brown's copy in his fairy tale are untitled)—the texts differ very little substantively. Brown's fairy-tale MS at Hampstead has "the heart in" for the holograph's "my breast of" in 7 and "heavens" for the holograph's "heaven's" in 18. The *PDWJ* text, which derives from a lost copy by Brown, shows "birds" (either a misprint or a misreading of Brown's hand) for "buds" in 4 and "heavens" again in 18. Milnes's MS varies from the holograph, which was almost surely his source, only in "the" for "this" in 13. *1848,* printed from Milnes's copy, restores "this" in 13.

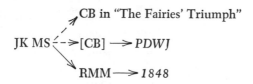

In this case, because the precise relationships between the extant holograph and Brown's transcripts are not clear, I think the holograph is the soundest basis for a standard text, and probably we should head the poem by its first line, since the authority of the *PDWJ* title is questionable (Brown frequently made up special titles for *PDWJ* printings) and the other titles are plainly not authoritative. Garrod reproduces *1848* exactly except for his title, which he takes from Milnes's transcript, and two marks of punctuation in 1 and 5. Allott, following Keats's MS and using the poem's first line as a title, has the same substantive text as Garrod.

Otho the Great

Written by Keats and Brown in July–August 1819 (*Letters*, II, 128, 139, 143, 149), with further slight revisions in December 1819 and January 1820 (*Letters*, II, 237, 241). First published in *1848*, II, 111–203. Garrod, pp. 309–381; Allott, pp. 544–613.

Generally speaking, we have two MSS of the play, a draft and a revised fair copy, neither of which is quite complete. The earlier MS, almost entirely in Keats's hand, is divided between the University of Texas (Acts I–III and the first scene of IV minus the leaf containing IV.i.71–90) and the Huntington Library (the remainder minus leaves containing IV.ii.-118–140, V.v.11–58, 142–162), with interstitial and additional fragments, mainly the result of Severn's good-natured generosity and busy scissors, in the Robert H. Taylor Collection, Princeton University Library (I.i.6–7, "is sav'd . . . axe," plus nine lines subsequently discarded and, on the verso, in Brown's hand, part of the Dramatis Personae), at Harvard (I.i.16–22, 32–42, IV.i.76–85, IV.ii.122–140, V.i.18–32, V.ii.8–15, V.v.149–162, 171–172—facsimile of V.v.149–162 in Sotheby sale catalogue, 12 November 1963), at the University of Texas (I.i.53–58, 64–66, 142–149—facsimiles of 53–58 in Maggs Bros. sale catalogue, August 1915, and American Art Association sale catalogue, 8 February 1927), in the British Museum (I.i.138–141 in Brown's hand), and in the Berg Collection, New York Public Library (V.v.138, 142–149, 178–180). A facsimile of I.iii.117–123 followed by I.i.2–20, clipped from an unidentified sale catalogue, is among Louis A. Holman's papers at Harvard, and Garrod knew of, but was not allowed to see, some lines beginning at I.i.138 in the possession of W. T. Spencer. Doubtless there are other fragments in existence. Most of this MS appears to be the original draft, but a few sheets and fragments, especially some of those for I.i, represent intermediate text—revisions, insertions, and occasional recopying by Keats to make "the whole . . . perfect" when George Keats took the MS back to America in January 1820 (it was not, however, complete—see *KC*, II, 15–16, 23, 117, 120—and clearly some parts of it were in the possession of Severn, who inscribed the various fragments that he gave away). Keats quotes I.iii.24–29 from this MS at the end of his 17–27 September 1819 journal letter to George and Georgiana (MS in the Morgan Library, text of the excerpt in *Letters*, II, 217–218).

The revised fair copy, mostly in Brown's hand, is at Harvard, complete except for I.i.1–18, IV.ii.3–45, and V.i.30–ii.27 (five leaves apparently lost by Milnes or his printer). This MS was the source of twelve extracts amounting to thirty-one lines that Brown gave E. J. Trelawny to be used as chapter epigraphs in his *Adventures of a Younger Son* (1831), and was printer's copy for *1848*. According to both Dilke (in his notes at the end of his copy of *1818* at Keats House, Hampstead) and Severn (Sharp, p. 166), Woodhouse had a copy made of this MS, but the transcript has not survived; it is possible that he destroyed it after Brown wrote to Taylor in March 1820, "Don't let any one take a Copy of Otho" (*Letters,* II, 276).

Though there are passages in which the MS in Keats's hand is not the first draft, and passages in which Brown's MS derives from some other source than the earlier extant MS, my diagram generally describes the relationships between the two and *1848*.

JK draft ⟶ CB revised fair copy ⟶ *1848*

The *1848* text is a fairly accurate printing of Brown's MS, with substantive errors and alterations in I.i.81 ("ration" for Brown's "ratio"), I.ii.81 (the omission of a fourth "no"), 172 ("-cakes" for "-cates"), I.iii.51 ("the" for "a"), II.ii.55 (*"reading"* for *"reads it"*), 58 (*"Speaks to himself"* for "aside"), 59 (the addition of *"Reads"*), 81 (*"Enter Gersa"* for *"enters"*), 128 ("I' . . . demand" for "In . . . demand of you"), III.i.8 ("white limbs" for "limbo"), 33 (the omission of a third "ha!"), 64 ("To" for "Is"), III.ii.15 ("recipe" for "receipt"), 59 ("hangman" for "hangmen"), 128 (the omission of a second "whither"—deleted in Brown's MS probably by Milnes), 153 ("jaw" for "jaws"), 160 ("hideous" for "tedious"), 204 ("Bold" for "Bald"), 279 ("more" for "mere"), IV.i.61 ("Tho' " for "Thou," correcting Brown's slip of the pen), 168 ("prudence" for "prudence' "), 184 (the omission of "Oh! Oh! Oh!"), IV.ii.103 ("last new" for "fresh"—the *1848* reading is inserted in pencil in Brown's MS, but not in Keats's or Brown's hand), 128 ("answers" for "answer"), V.i.27 ("dreamy" for "dreary"), 32 ("How"—Brown's MS is lost for this and the next three items, but Keats's draft has "Now," and this was almost surely the word in Brown's MS, which *1848* misread or misprinted), V.ii.4 ("thee"—Keats's draft has "you"; in this instance it is not clear whether "thee" is an authoritative revision or an emendation by Milnes), 10 ("Shrine"—the draft has "Shrive"), 25 ("white"—the draft has "mild"; as with "thee" in V.ii.4, it is not clear whether "white" is a revision or a corruption), V.iii.1, 3, 9, 13, 14 ("1st *Knight*" in all five of these lines—so also Brown, who, however, changed "1st *Knight*" in the opening stage direction to "*Theodore*"), V.iv.4 ("to" for "can"), and 56 (the omission of "the").

I list these details primarily because *1848*, though the first published version, is still the best text so far printed. Brown's MS, which both Keats and Brown went over and several times revised (Keats's hand appears in twenty-six passages in the MS), is clearly the authorially approved version that should be the basis for a standard text, and this is the sole source that *1848* printed from. By comparison, the modern editing of the play has not been nearly so good—mainly, I think, because the draft in Keats's hand became publicly available to scholars earlier than Brown's MS. In the later nineteenth century and on into the twentieth, faced with a choice between readings in Keats's draft and those in *1848*, editors tended to prefer the seemingly more authoritative readings of the draft; and this had an effect that the later accessibility of Brown's MS, with its clear evidence of Keats's participation throughout the revised version, has not countered. The result is that all recent editors, whether or not intentionally, have incorporated readings from both MSS and thus have produced mixtures of the two basic states of text, original and revised.

Garrod says of his text (p. xlv) that he has regularly chosen Keats's revisions in Brown's MS over readings of the original draft but otherwise has "consistently preferred the readings of [Keats's draft] to any other variants found in [Brown's MS]." His preference for the draft readings of course does Keats and Brown an injustice (some of them break up the meter, others impair the grammar), and Garrod does not usually elsewhere print a rough draft text instead of a known revised version. But Garrod's claim to consistency does not hold up: there are many places where Brown and/or *1848* readings appear in his text rather than those of the original draft. He is not consistent in his preference for the draft or in anything else in this particular work—punctuation, spelling, grammar, stage directions, emendation procedures, and so on. It is perhaps characteristic of his editing of the play generally that, in incorporating into his text an extra line that Keats wrote for Ludolph's final speech, he prints the line *after* the stage direction telling us that Ludolph "*Dies.*" (In a similar practical mistake, Allott has Albert entering at IV.i.103, two lines before Auranthe opens the door for him.)

The following account is necessarily selective. Starting with *1848* wording and accidentals, Garrod restores substantive readings of Keats's draft in I.i.41, 136, I.ii.6, 51, 81 (correcting *1848*'s error), 88, 134,

137, 172 (correcting *1848*), 179, 193, I.iii.2, 51 (correcting *1848*), 52, II.i.24, 56, 97, 108, 125, II.ii.7, 12, 16, 63, 66, 82, 88, 128 (correcting *1848*), III.i.8 (correcting *1848*), 21, 33 (correcting *1848*), 42, 43, 53, III.ii.15 (correcting *1848*), 17*a*, 49, 49*a*, 59*a*, 64, 76, 77, 83, 153 (correcting *1848*), 160 (correcting *1848*), 204 (correcting *1848*), 220, 221, 227, 238, 245, 246, 247, 272*a*–*b*, 273, 274, 276, 277, 278 (the reversal of five speaker-headings), 279 (correcting *1848*), IV.i.69, 99, 101, 102, 118, 164, 166, 168 (correcting *1848*), 184 (correcting *1848*), IV.ii.2, 45, 98 (Brown and *1848* have " 'e" for the draft's "ye"), 103 (correcting *1848*), 114/115, 128 (correcting *1848*), 138*a*, V.i.8, 11, 12, 13 (Brown and *1848* have "o' " for the draft's "of"), 25, 27 (correcting *1848*), 32 (correcting *1848*), V.ii.4 (perhaps correcting *1848*), 7/8, 10 (correcting *1848*), 25 (perhaps correcting *1848*), 29, 45, 48, V.iii.1, 3, 9, 13, 14 (in all five places correcting *1848* speaker-headings), V.iv.3, 4 (correcting *1848*), 34, 37, 38 (Brown and *1848* read "Fill, fill" and present "Fill . . . health!" as a single line), 39, 44 (Garrod's apparatus is wrong concerning Brown's MS and *1848*), 59, V.v.3, 4, 59–60 (the position of the lines), 111, 117, 182, 188. In all of these not specifically indicated as corrections of *1848* Garrod is discarding Keats's and Brown's considered revisions in favor of earlier, rejected text ("it is interesting to have Keats' first draft," he remarks on p. xlvi). On the basis of the revised MS, he further corrects *1848* errors in I.i.81 and III.i.64.

Garrod incorporates stage directions from *1848* in II.ii.55, 58, 59, 81; *1848* corruptions in III.ii.59, 128, and V.iv.56; two emendations suggested by H. B. Forman in III.ii.15 and 20, and an error from Forman in V.v.36 ("Hanging" for Brown's and *1848*'s "Hangings"); Keats's revised text of IV.i.141–142 (an intermediate version subsequently canceled and rewritten in Brown's hand); and Keats's extra line in the final speech of the play (printed as V.v.193). What remains is the substantive text more or less as Keats and Brown left it, though there are further errors in the omission of end punctuation in I.i.40 and 66, a misprint in III.ii.53 ("rech" for "reach"), and some odd spellings based on Keats's MS (e.g., "clog'd" in IV.ii.33 and "sin'd" in V.ii.24).

Allott more wisely chooses Brown's MS as her base-text. Oddly, however, she takes I.i.1–18, the lines of the missing first leaf of Brown's MS, from Keats's draft, and thus has readings in I.i.5 ("struck"), 6 ("sail" and "safe"), 9 ("petars"), and 13 ("sweet") that vary from the revised text as represented by *1848*. What is more curious still is her inclusion of readings from Keats's draft (where they differ from Brown's MS) in

I.i.41, I.ii.88, 134, II.ii.7, 16, 88, III.i.21, 53, III.ii.49, 64, 83, 220, 238, 247, IV.i.101, 164, 166, IV.ii.2, 45, 98, 114/115, V.i.8, 13, V.ii.7/8, 29, 45, 48, V.iv.3, 34, 37, 38, 39, 44, 59, V.v.3, 4, 117, and 182 (about twenty of these may be blamed on Garrod's apparatus, where the readings of Brown's MS are either omitted or wrongly recorded). She incorporates or retains *1848* substantive mistakes and variants from both MSS (where both are extant) in I.i.81, I.iii.51, II.ii.55, 58, 59 (three stage directions), III.i.33, III.ii.15, 59, 128, IV.i.184, IV.ii.103, V.i.27, V.ii.10, and V.iv.56; takes over mistakes from one of H. B. Forman's texts in I.i.31 ("to" for "in"), I.ii.150 ("mine" for "my"), IV.i.17 ("council" for "counsel"), IV.ii.6 ("bid" for "bade"), 19 (the omission of the stage direction), and V.v.36 ("Hanging" for "Hangings"); and has independent errors in I.ii.84/85 (*"fastened"* for *"hastened"* in the stage direction), III.i.5 ("hurdled" for "hurl'd"), IV.i.11 ("Ay," her systematic spelling for the word meaning "ever," where the affirmative "Aye" is called for), 105 (the omission of the short line "Who knocks?"), 105/106 (the stage direction is mistakenly printed after 103), and V.i.27 ("Suckled" for "Suck'd"). She accepts Forman's emendation in III.ii.20, but not that suggested for III.ii.15. Her modernizing produces further changes in I.ii.18 ("feel it" for "feel't"), I.iii.62 ("taken" for "ta'en"), II.i.43 ("on it" for "on't"), and IV.ii.22 ("even" for "e'en"). On the positive side, she introduces the extra line for Ludolph's final speech after V.v.190, which is obviously the best position for it, if it is to be included at all.

Possibly the play deserves this sort of editorial treatment. Still it is strange that *1848,* with some thirty substantive differences from Keats's and Brown's revised text, is two or three times more accurate and consistent a text than those of the modern editions.

Lamia

Written mainly in July and August 1819 (perhaps begun at the end of June, after Keats arrived at Shanklin on the 28th, and completed in the first few days of September—see *Letters,* II, 128, 139, 157). First published in *1820.* Garrod, pp. 191–214; Allott, pp. 613–648.

For this poem we have a virtually complete sequence of documents, from Keats's first draft to the earliest printed text. What has survived or been recorded of the original draft, which was once in the possession of Severn (or perhaps shared by Severn and Brown) and like *Isabella* and some others was given away in fragments, can be listed as follows:

I.185	Two and a half lines (same wording as the fair copy text through "Lycius the happy," Garrod, p. 196 n.) at the University of Texas
I.185–190	Keats-Shelley Memorial House, Rome (facsimile of this and II.67–74 in *Keats-Shelley Memorial Bulletin,* 2 [1913], facing p. 92)
I.324–329	Berg Collection, New York Public Library
I.386–397	Seen by H. B. Forman and since disappeared (transcription in Hampstead Keats, III, 29–31 n.)
II. 26–49	Harvard
II. 50–67	Robert H. Taylor Collection, Princeton University Library (facsimile and transcription of II.50–61 in Sotheby sale catalogue, 6 May 1936)
II. 67–74	Keats-Shelley Memorial House, Rome
II. 85–92	Harvard (plus twelve lines subsequently discarded)
II.122–147	Harvard
II.191–198	Harvard

(The fragment that Brown sent Milnes in 1840—*KC*, II, 37—has not been identified.) There is an intermediate draft version of II.122–162, plus eighteen lines subsequently discarded, in Keats's letter to Taylor of 5 September 1819 (MS at Harvard—text in *Letters,* II, 157–159, with facsimile of the first twenty-two lines facing II, 208; there is also a transcript by Woodhouse in his letterbook). Keats's revised fair copy, from which the poem was printed in *1820,* and a set of proof-sheets (facsimile of one page in Gittings, *John Keats,* facing p. 400) are also at Harvard. The materials produce one of the simpler diagrams of the present study.

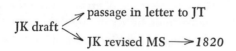

The fair copy, made sometime between September 1819 and March 1820 and showing revisions and corrections that Brown may be referring to in his note tentatively dated 13 March 1820 (*Letters,* II, 276), is especially neatly written and well punctuated. It was clearly printer's copy for *1820* (the printer has marked the *1820* signature and page number on one leaf), and except for capitals and "-ed" vs. "-'d" verb endings the printer followed its accidental details quite closely. There are substantive differences between the MS and *1820* in some fifty lines—see Garrod's apparatus for I.69, 78, 104, 114, 115, 116, 123, 132 ("languid" in *1820*), 167–168, 173, 174, 176, 185, 192, 196, 212, 225, 236, 260/261, 272, 287, 320, 322, 363, 371, 373 (two variants), 379, 383, 393; II.10, 45/46 (Garrod misprints "44/45"), 53, 89 (the penciled cancellations in 88, 89, 90, and other places are almost certainly not by Keats), 134, 150, 177, 178, 218–219, 239, 246, 247, 254, 255, 293, 294, and 296–298.

The extant proof-sheets, a set read and marked by both Woodhouse and Keats (see William Allan Coles, *HLB,* 8 [1954], 114–119, and the comments by Gittings, *John Keats,* pp. 395–398), are especially valuable in showing at what stage, and in many instances by whom, the changes were made between the MS and the printed text. (*Lamia* is the only *1820* poem for which we have no Woodhouse transcript. Woodhouse preserved these proofs in lieu of a transcript, recording variants from the draft passage in Keats's letter to Taylor in the same manner in which he recorded alternative readings from other sources in his W² transcripts.) In almost all of the lines listed above, the text of Keats's MS was set in type; only in I.132 (where the printer read "languid" for Keats's "langrous"), I.287 (where the text was changed in the MS apparently by Taylor), and II.89 (where "silver" was canceled in pencil in the MS, probably also by Taylor) was Keats's text altered *before* it was set in type (Coles is misleading in failing to mention the proof variants from *1820* at I.115, 260/261, 371, 373; II.10, 53, 134, 177, 178, 218–219, 239, 246–247, 254, 255, 293–294—in every instance the proofs show the same text as Keats's MS—and Coles also does not distinguish between actual proof corrections and Woodhouse's transcript-like record of variants in the proofs).

With just a few exceptions, then, the substantive changes were made in proof stage. One of them, the revision of II.293–294, was done by Keats in Taylor's office (see Garrod, p. xxxv). A great many others were marked in the surviving proofs, sometimes by Keats, sometimes by Woodhouse. In particular, Woodhouse made changes in I.114, 123, 173–174, 176, 192, 196, 236, 272, 320, 322, 363, 379, 383, and 393; and he undoubtedly was responsible for some of the others (where we cannot identify the hand, or where—for example, by pointing out metrical defects— he prompted the corrections made by Keats; see also *KC,* I, 112–113, for a note to Taylor in which Woodhouse suggests a revision for I.167–168, a couplet that was subsequently rewritten in a different way). In a note to his letterbook transcript of Keats's 5 September 1819 letter to Taylor, Woodhouse mentions "my revise of Lamia" (*Letters,* II, 158 n.); whether he actually meant "revision" (as Gittings thinks, *John Keats,* p. 394) or, as is much more likely, was merely using the term to refer to the extant proof-sheets, his help in getting the poem to its final form was fairly extensive.

It is not possible to give here a complete account of the changes made by Woodhouse and Keats. At least seven of them have to do with the correct accenting of proper names (I.78, 115, 174, 176, 225, 272, 371), and are surely related to Keats's jottings of Greek names on the half title of the proofs (Coles, p. 115 n.), possibly the result of Woodhouse's instructions in Greek pronunciation. Three of the alterations involve the striking out of "silver" and "Silverly" (I.69; II.89, 134). A number of others correct the meter or grammar, sharpen passages that originally were syntactically confusing or otherwise unclear, and tone down sensational elements (e.g., the MS's II.294, and "stark" in the passage rewritten as II.297–298—see *KC*, I, 113 and n.). Presumably Keats approved all of these changes (save perhaps that in I.132, which he may not have noticed); at least in theory we must think that he did, and there is no evidence that he did not. *1820* must continue to be the proper basis for a standard text, even where we have documentary evidence that changes from Keats's MS apparently originated with someone else.

Garrod adds closing quotation marks in I.377 and II.298 (in the latter instance without a note), emends *1820*'s "a thought, a buzzing" to "a thought a-buzzing" in II.29 (this on the basis of the draft's and the fair copy's "a thought a buzzing" and Keats's original wording in the draft, "a thought at work"), and errs in printing a comma for a semicolon in I.158 and omitting commas at the end of I.394 and II.72. Allott also emends II.29, follows one of H. B. Forman's texts in making a paragraph division after I.26 (I.27 is indented in the fair copy but not in *1820*) and in substantive mistakes in I.260 ("shall I" for "I shall"), 316 ("lent" for "leant"), and II.11 ("Beside" for "Besides"), and has an independent error in I.329 ("sweet" for "sweets of").

Pensive they sit and roll their languid eyes

Written on 17 September 1819 (in the opening section of Keats's 17–27 September journal letter to George and Georgiana). First published (with extracts from the letter) in the New York *World,* 25 June 1877, p. 2. Garrod, p. 568; Allott, pp. 649–650.

Keats's draft in the letter (MS in the Morgan Library, text in *Letters,* II, 188) is our sole source of text. Garrod reproduces the letter substantively, with "toasts" in 2 (Rollins prints "tosts" and says that the word may also be read as "toste"). His colon in 20 is an error (there should be no punctuation), and his paragraph space between 13 and 14 derives from Forman's 1883 edition, where 14 begins with an indention on a new page. Allott also takes her text from the letter, but has "toast" in 2, "Inserts" for "Inverts" in 11, and "straggler" for "struggler" in 12—all of which come from the *World*'s text by way of Forman—and also a paragraph indention at 14.

To Autumn

Written on 19 September 1819 (*Letters,* II, 167). First published in *1820*. Garrod, pp. 273–274; Allott, pp. 650–655.

The two extant holographs, both at Harvard, are an early draft (facsimiles in the *Century Magazine,* 69 [1904], 84, 89, Finney, after II, 706, Rollins, *Keats' Reputation in America to 1848,* Cambridge, Mass., 1946, after p. 50, and, with transcriptions, Gittings, *Odes,* pp. 56–59, and P. J. Croft, *Autograph Poetry in the English Language,* 1973, Nos. 108–109; facsimile of the first two stanzas in Allott, facing p. 645) and a fair copy sent in a letter to Woodhouse of 21, 22 September (text in *Letters,* II, 170–171). There are transcripts by Brown, George Keats, and Woodhouse (W^2). Garrod's *H* transcript does not exist, and I have ignored his *Ch.,* an unidentified copy in a scrapbook owned by R. W. Chapman that Garrod thinks was made from *1820*.

The earlier Harvard MS is probably the original draft. Brown's transcript, which initially varied substantively from it in 8 ("sweet" for the draft's "white"), 17 ("Dosed" for "Das'd"), 18 ("sheath" for "swath" and "honied" for "twined"), 20 ("leaden" for "laden"), and 29 ("or" for "and"), was almost certainly made from this draft. The variants in 17 and 18 are easily seen as misreadings of Keats's handwriting, and that in 20 is a slip of the pen. Those in 8 and 29 are more difficult to account for, but since Brown (unlike Woodhouse) rarely undertook to improve Keats's texts on his own initiative I think we must view the changes as authoritative, perhaps requested by Keats at the time Brown made his copy. Keats later read over Brown's transcript and corrected "sheath" to "swath" and "honied" to "twined" in 18. Brown's MS shows further corrections in 17 ("Dosed" to "Dased") and 20 ("leaden" to "laden"), and the alteration of "the" to "a" in 20; at least the first two of these (initially marked in pencil) were probably made by Woodhouse when he collated his W^2 text with Brown's. George Keats copied Brown's transcript, incorporating Brown's distinctive errors in 17, 18, and 20 and writing a unique "a" for "the" in 17. Since we know that George made his transcript in January

1820, we have an approximate date after which the corrections to 17, 18, and 20 were entered in Brown's MS.

Keats's letter copy for Woodhouse, written very shortly after the initial composition of the poem, varies from the draft in 6 ("fruit" for the draft's "fruits" and "ripeness" for "swee[t]ness"), 12 ("stores" for "store"), 20 ("a" for "the"), 22 ("oozings" for "oozing"), 31 ("with treble" for "again full"), and 33 ("gather'd" for "Gathering"). Woodhouse transcribed the letter text in W^2, with "yet" for Keats's "still" in 9 and "When" for "While" in 25. He later entered in red ink variants from Brown's transcript to 6 (Brown's "sweetness"—Woodhouse did not notice "fruits" in the same line), 8, 9 (Woodhouse here in effect correcting his own copying error), 17, 20, 22, 29, 31, and 33, and altered "stores" to "store" in 12.

$$\text{JK draft} \begin{cases} \text{JK letter copy} \longrightarrow W^2 \\ \text{CB} \longrightarrow \text{GK} \end{cases}$$

The *1820* text, set from a lost MS by Keats or Brown, is closer to Keats's letter copy than to the draft (it incorporates letter readings in 6, 20, 22, and 31), but has Brown's wording in 8 ("sweet") and 29 ("or"), a new inversion in 4 ("With fruit the vines"), and a new word in 17 ("Drows'd"). *1820* is of course the proper basis for a standard text. Garrod follows it exactly (except for a misprint—"shallows" for "sallows"—in 28), and Allott does not depart substantively.

The Fall of Hyperion: A Dream

Begun as a revision of *Hyperion* probably in July 1819 and given up on 21 September (*Letters,* II, 132, 139, 167; the possibility of still later work on the poem has been suggested on the basis of Brown's remark that Keats was "remodelling" *Hyperion* at the same time that he wrote *The Jealousies—KC,* II, 72—but unfortunately we do not have a definite date for the latter poem). First published by Milnes in *1857*—"Another Version of Keats's 'Hyperion,' " in *Miscellanies of the Philobiblon Society,* 3 (1856–57, with the spine date *1857*)—and about the same time privately issued by Milnes as a separate pamphlet (see Garrod, pp. xxvii–xxviii). The two publications are on the same paper and except for the manner of issue are bibliographically identical; it is not clear whether the pamphlet should be taken to represent a small batch of offprints from the *Miscellanies,* or the *Miscellanies* (in which each item is separately paged) a binding-up of copies of the pamphlet. Milnes reprinted the work with a few corrections in an appendix in his one-volume *Life* of 1867. Garrod, pp. 507–523; Allott, pp. 655–685.

In Keats's own hand we have only I.1–11, 61–86, II.1–4, 6 copied out in a letter to Woodhouse of 21, 22 September 1819 (MS at Harvard, text of the extracts in *Letters,* II, 171–172), but there exist complete transcripts by Woodhouse (W^2) and two of his clerks (Garrod's T—transcription in de Selincourt, *Hyperion,* pp. 33–50) and a partial transcript by Charlotte Reynolds (I.1–326 only). On E. L. Lushington's "copy of Hyperion" in 1856 see the discussion of *Hyperion,* above.

The lines quoted by Keats in his letter to Woodhouse vary substantively from all other texts in I.10, 64, 65, 70, 83, and 85 (it is odd that Woodhouse did not record these variants, especially since he conjectured the first of them in a note opposite the text in W^2). These unique readings suggest that there was a draft of at least part of the poem prior to the lost holograph from which all subsequent texts derive. Following that lost holograph, the relationships among the existing MSS and the first printed version are fairly easy to work out. The W^2 transcript, headed "The Fall of Hyperion—A Dream," has neither date nor any indication of source, but there is clear evidence that it was made from a MS in Keats's own hand—e.g., in Woodhouse's "cham" in I.10, with the penciled note "probably *charm*"; in his note recording a canceled reading in his source in I.48; in his marking and emending of I.167–168, with the indication "The M.S is as here"; in his marginally penciled "euewhie" beside I.179, to show how Keats wrote "erewhile"; in his note telling that Keats originally wrote "Degraged" in I.322. There is no basis for the fiction (begun by de Selincourt, *Hyperion,* p. 21, and continued by H. B. Forman, e.g. in the Hampstead Keats, III, 259, and Finney, II, 455) that Woodhouse received a holograph MS from Brown in the 1830's; it was in fact Woodhouse who supplied Brown with a copy of the poem.

Charlotte Reynolds' transcript of I.1–326 differs substantively from W^2 only in 7 ("the" for "they," like several of the other variants a simple copying error), 10 ("chain"), 19 ("were" for "where"), 51 ("wrapt"—W^2 has "wrapt" with the "w" deleted), 69 (the same words as in W^2 but without Woodhouse's transposition marks), 75 (the omission of the line), 147 ("the" for "that"), 165–166 (the omission of two half-lines), 185 (the omission of "love of"), 188 ("in" for "into"), 234 ("painted"), 259 ("I" for "It"), 298 ("what"—W^2 has "was" with a penciled "what?" in the margin), 299 ("on"), and 319 ("footmark"). The two transcripts are strikingly close in minor details—both, for example, omit the opening quotation mark at I.156, and there are substantial passages (e.g., I.155–185, 241–255, 266–279, 307–326) where their punctuation is exactly the same in every particular—and the situation is such that one of them almost surely had to have come from the other. It is not possible that Woodhouse copied Charlotte, since she has only the first 326 lines (and also some omissions within those); the conclusion, then, is that she took her lines from W^2 (see also Section II.5).

Toward the end of his life (on paper watermarked 1833) Woodhouse had W^2 copied for Brown by two of his clerks, the one writing Canto I, the other Canto II, and Woodhouse going over and correcting the whole. There are a number of errors in the clerks' transcript that can be seen as misreadings of W^2 (e.g., "-paid" in I.93, where Woodhouse had written "-pac'd" in such a way, with the apostrophe over a not very well-rounded "c," that the word looks like "-paid"), but the simplest evidence for the relationship between W^2 and the later transcript is the fact that the first clerk, in numbering the lines by tens as he copied, skipped from "140" to "160" (omitting "150") just as Woodhouse did in W^2.

Though Brown gave the clerks' transcript to Milnes with the rest of his MSS in 1841, Milnes did not include *The Fall of Hyperion* in *1848,* apparently thinking it was not worth presenting as an independent work. Even when he decided to publish it in *1857,* he was uncertain, as he says in his prefatory note, whether it was "the original sketch . . . or . . . the commencement of a reconstruction of the whole." That the *1857* text derives from the clerks' transcript is plain from several variants in which Milnes or a copyist misread the clerks' handwriting (e.g., "Twining" in I.24, where the clerk's "Turning" could be read as "Twining," and "curved" in I.61, where the clerk's word appears as "curved" corrected to "carved"). Perhaps the clincher is the fact that *1857*'s distinctive punctuation in 22–24—"In neighbourhood of fountains (by the noise / Soft-showering in mine ears), and (by the touch / Of scent) not far from roses"—came from parentheses that were added in pencil to the clerks' transcript. The transcript shows no signs of having been handled by a printer, and some of the variants in *1857*—e.g., Milnes's introduction of readings from *Hyperion*—are further evidence that the printed text was set from an intervening copy rather than directly from the transcript.

There is not room here for a full account of the sixty or more substantive differences between *1857* and W^2. Five of *1857*'s variants represent errors in the clerks' transcript, a half-dozen are clearly misreadings of the first clerk's handwriting, thirteen more come from Milnes's substitution of *Hyperion* readings for those of *The Fall,* and the rest are a mixture of corrections and emendations by Milnes and a sizable number of copyist's and/or printer's errors. On the basis of Woodhouse's note in the clerks' transcript (see below), Milnes omitted I.187–210. His title—"Hyperion, A Vision"—is apparently based on his own words in *1848* (". . . still later re-cast it into the shape of a Vision," I, 244), which he undoubtedly took from the MS of Brown's "Life" of Keats (". . . remodelling . . . 'Hyperion' into a 'Vision,'" *KC*, II, 72).

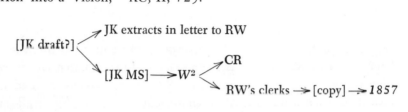

Obviously W^2 is the proper basis for a standard text. The main textual problem has to do with the so-called "disputed lines" of the poem (see Ridley, p. 273; Brian Wicker, *Essays in Criticism,* 7 [1957], 28–41; and the references in Irene H. Chayes, *Philological Quarterly,* 46 [1967], 499 n.). In W^2 and the clerks' transcript, 187–202 (through "vexes it") and 205–210 are marked with a penciled line—in the margin of W^2 and vertically through the text in the clerks' copy—and there are notes by Woodhouse in both MSS to the effect that "Keats seems to have intended to erase this & the 21 follow^g verses" (W^2). The fact that the lines were copied currently in the transcripts and the wording of Woodhouse's notes ("*seems* to have intended") make virtually certain that the lines were not actually marked for deletion or revision by Keats, and that Woodhouse's notes represent a critical conjecture (most probably based on the duplication of 187, 194–198 in 211, 216–220) rather than a piece of textual information. The fact that Woodhouse added the present 202–204 (from "Then shouted I") on a verso page in W^2 and in the top margin of his clerks' transcript, and did not include them in his count of "this & the 21 follow^g verses," suggests that Keats may have later expanded the section that Woodhouse thought he "intended to erase"—though it is also possible that Keats had already inserted the lines in his MS and that Woodhouse, intent on making an unusually faithful transcript, entered them as an addition in imitation of the appearance of the holograph. Charlotte Reynolds copied 187–210 straight out, either ignoring Woodhouse's note in W^2 or else making her transcript before Woodhouse wrote the note.

Both Garrod and Allott rightly include the "disputed lines." Garrod, whose "version . . . is unless otherwise indicated that of W^2, in text, punctuation, and orthography," actually departs from W^2 in favor of *1857*'s variant punctuation, spelling, and capitalization in some seventy places, but has only six errors—the omission of a period at the end of I.15, "Amongst" for "Among" in 52, "spoke" for "spake" in 349, "The" for "And" in 359 (this and the preceding error derive from *1857*), and "winding" for "windings" and "holes" for "hole" in 409. He adds opening quotation marks in I.148 and 156, and emends "cham" to "charm" in I.10 (following Keats's letter extract and Woodhouse's conjecture), "mid-way" to "mid-May" in 97 (accepting A. E. Housman's suggestion in *TLS,* 8 May 1924, p. 286), "was" to "what" in 298 (in answer to Woodhouse's query), and "every" to "ever" in 395 (J. C. Maxwell's suggestion).

Allott, also following W^2, similarly adds quotation marks in I.148 and 156 and emends the wording in I.10, 97, 298, and 395. She fails to mark a new paragraph at I.81, and she has several errors taken over from *1857* via one of H. B. Forman's texts: "Those" for "They" in I.161, an unwarranted paragraph division after 215, "Spoke" for "Spake" in 217, "these" for "those" in 247 and again in 382, "of" for "in" in 409, "an aching" for "a shaking" in 426, and "there shall" for "let there" in 436.

The day is gone, and all its sweets are gone

Written in 1819 (so dated in Brown's transcript and Woodhouse's last transcript), possibly toward the end of the year (but the specific October datings by almost all writers are not well grounded). First published in *PDWJ,* 4 October 1838, and then in *1848,* II, 304. Garrod, p. 473; Allott, pp. 685–686.

A holograph draft is extant in the Morgan Library (facsimile in the *Bookman,* 31 [1906], 16), and we have three transcripts by Woodhouse (W^3, W^2, and the Harvard copy that Garrod refers to as T) and a transcript by Brown.

The earlier of two recoverable states of text is that of the extant draft. All of Woodhouse's transcripts reproduce this draft text. In the margins and between the lines of W^3 he noted canceled readings from the draft's 8–10 (and also provisionally revised 13 in pencil to correct the meter, altering "But as I" to "As I"), and after the text in W^2 he added an exact representation of the draft's 8–12, with all of Keats's cancellations and revisions. Since W^3 has the appearance of a more hurried copying, and W^2 has details that could not have come from W^3, I should guess that both transcripts were made independently from the draft. Much later Woodhouse wrote out the T transcript from W^2.

The later state of text is represented by Brown's transcript, which has "light" for the draft's and Woodhouse's "tranc'd" in 3 and "I've" for "I have" in 13, and transposes the earlier version's second and third quatrains. Brown's source is not known, but there is a good possibility that this is one of the poems that he took from MSS in Fanny Brawne's possession (see *The Letters of Charles Armitage Brown,* Cambridge, Mass., 1966, p. 295—some or all of the next three poems in the present study also may have come from Fanny Brawne). Brown's transcript was the source of the *PDWJ* text (which has "shade" for "shape" in 7 and "roof" for "woof" in 12, both copying or printing errors), and was printer's copy for *1848.*

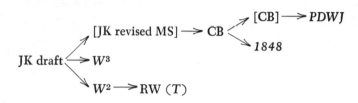

Brown's transcript is the proper basis for a standard text. Garrod reproduces *1848* exactly, and Allott, following Brown, has the same substantive text as Garrod.

I cry your mercy—pity—love!—aye, love

Written in 1819 (so dated in Brown's transcript), perhaps toward the end of the year. First published in *1848,* II, 305. Garrod, p. 474; Allott, pp. 689–690.

The single extant MS is a transcript by Brown headed "Sonnet. 1819." This is probably one of the transcripts that Brown made from MSS in Fanny Brawne's possession (see the discussion of the preceding poem). His transcript was printer's copy for *1848.* Both Garrod and Allott follow *1848,* Garrod exactly except for a misprint ("Without" for "Withhold") in 10.

What can I do to drive away

Written probably in 1819 (Milnes, after quoting Keats's letter to Dilke of 1 October 1819, gives these lines as "a fragment written about this date," and H. B. Forman, Lowell, and Garrod have turned this into a specific fact represented by Garrod's headnote, "Dated: Oct. 1819 *1848*"; subsequent writers, accepting October and even trying to determine *when* in October Keats composed the lines, overlook the fact that Milnes's approximate dating in the first place was a mere guess). First published in *1848*, II, 34–35. Garrod, pp. 504–505; Allott, pp. 686–689.

There are no extant MSS, and *1848* (headed "To _____") is the sole source of text. I should guess that this is another of the poems that Brown copied from MSS in Fanny Brawne's possession (see *The day is gone*), and that Milnes took his text from a lost Brown transcript. Garrod reproduces *1848* exactly except in indentions and a single change of spelling, "herbaged" to "herbag'd" in 40. Allott also follows *1848* but with the heading "To [Fanny]" and two readings proposed by H. B. Forman— "wretched" for "wrecked" in 33 and "bud" for "bad" in 42 (she does not accept Forman's further suggestions of "Aye, and [*or* but] an" in 3 and "Even" in 35).

To Fanny ("Physician Nature")

Written probably toward the end of 1819 or during the early months of 1820 (a more precise dating is not possible). First published in *1848*, II, 284–286. Garrod, pp. 454–456; Allott, pp. 739–742.

We have Keats's fragmentary draft at Harvard (lacking a title and the first and fourth stanzas) and a transcript by Milnes. The transcript differs substantively from the draft in 12 ("smile of such" for the draft's "smiling"), 45 ("Dare" for "Can"), and 49 ("soul" for "heart"). Milnes did not, I think, take his text from the extant draft. We may conjecture that this is another of the poems that Fanny Brawne permitted Brown to transcribe (see *The day is gone*), and that Milnes copied it from a lost Brown transcript. Milnes's MS, headed "To Fanny," was printer's copy for *1848*, which varies from it, generally misreading Milnes's handwriting, in 8 ("not" for Milnes's "out"), 15 (the omission of "a"), 46 ("his" for "has"), and 56 ("lost" for "last").

JK draft ⟶ [JK revised MS] ⟶ [CB] ⟶ RMM ⟶ *1848*

Milnes's transcript, representing a slightly revised version, is the proper basis for a standard text. Garrod takes his text from *1848*, adding stanza numbers, altering indentions, changing capitalization, punctuation, and spelling in 5, 26, 43, and 46, and correcting *1848* substantively in 8, 46, and 56—in effect producing Milnes's MS text except in title (Garrod prints "Ode to Fanny," which he thinks is in the extant draft) and 15 (his apparatus is wrong—"a soft" appears in both the draft and Milnes's transcript). Allott also follows *1848,* correcting 8, 46, and 56 (but not 15) and preferring Garrod's heading to Milnes's.

King Stephen: A Fragment of a Tragedy

Begun late in August 1819 (just after the completion of *Otho—KC,* II, 67) and given up probably in November (the date after the title in Brown's partial transcript). First published in *1848,* II, 204–214. Garrod, pp. 383–392; Allott, pp. 690–700.

The two extant MSS, Brown's transcript of I.i.1–ii.19 and Keats's draft of I.ii.19–iv.58 (at Harvard), together constitute our sole source of text for this work (they overlap only in "Now our dreaded Queen" in I.ii.19). From these two MSS Brown supplied the four extracts amounting to thirteen lines that were used as chapter epigraphs in Trelawny's *Adventures of a Younger Son* (1831). There is ample evidence, mainly in various peculiarities of accidentals and the understandable misreading of Keats's "mars" in I.ii.51, that both MSS together were the source of *1848's* text. Since neither MS shows signs of having been directly used by the printer, I take it that the work was set in type from Milnes's or an amanuensis' copy made from the two MSS.

$$\text{JK draft} \quad \overset{\nearrow \text{CB (I.i.1–ii.19)} \searrow}{\xrightarrow{\hspace{5cm}}} \text{[copy]} \longrightarrow \textit{1848}$$

1848 shows substantive variants from Brown's MS in the stage direction at I.i.36 ("*Alarum*" for Brown's "*Alarums*") and from Keats's MS in I.ii.50 ("hilt" for Keats's "hilts"), 51 ("man" for "mars"), I.iii.5 ("come" for "comes"), 16 ("dips" for "dip"), 45 ("hilt" for "hilts"), 47 ("you" for "ye"), I.iv.9 ("I will" for "will I"), and 20 ("as" for "as a"). *1848* also corrects Brown's "Earl of Chesters" to "Earls of Chester" in I.i.35 and emends Keats's "Knight" to "*2nd Knight*" in the stage direction and speaker-headings at I.ii.28, 29, 31, 35, and 45.

Garrod takes his text from *1848,* including the correction in I.i.35 and the stage directions at I.i.36 and I.ii.28–45, but emends to the readings of Keats's MS in I.ii.50, 51, I.iii.5, 16, 45, 47, I.iv.9, 20. He generally follows *1848's* "Glocester" but oddly prints "Gloucester" in I.i.9 (where Brown had written "Gloucester" and then struck through the "u") and "Gloster" in I.ii.24 (Keats's spelling there). He inadvertently omits a period at the end of I.iii.8. Allott, following Brown's and Keats's MSS but also accepting *1848*'s correction of I.i.35 and the emended stage directions, has "be it" for Brown's "be't" in I.i.32, "came" for Keats's "come" in I.ii.28, "anointed" for " 'nointed" in I.ii.32, and the three *1848* variants listed above for I.iii.5, I.iv.9, and I.iv.20. No text has ever included Brown's Dramatis Personae on the verso of the first leaf of his transcript, though Forman (1883), II, 474, printed a list of his own devising.

This living hand, now warm and capable

Written probably toward the end of 1819 (in the draft MS of *The Jealousies*; it appears on the page containing 451–459, but could of course have been written there earlier or jotted down sometime after Keats was working on the longer poem). First published in H. B. Forman's one-volume *Poetical Works of John Keats,* 6th ed. (1898), p. 417. Garrod, p. 553; Allott, pp. 700–701.

The holograph MS is at Harvard (facsimiles in William Harris Arnold, *First Report of a Book-Collector,* New York, 1898, p. 105, and Finney, facing II, 740). Garrod reproduces Forman's text, which emends "would" to "wouldst" in 5 and makes other slight changes and corrections. Allott follows the MS, retaining "would" in 5.

The Jealousies: A Fairy Tale

Written probably toward the end of 1819 (Brown's reference in *KC,* II, 71–72, cannot be dated more precisely, and there is no other evidence for dating). Lines 217–256 first published in the *Indicator,* 23 August 1820, p. 368, and a complete text (except for 793–794) first in *1848,* II, 215–251. Garrod, pp. 393–428; Allott, pp. 701–736.

Keats's original draft of 1–729 is extant in three places—the Morgan Library (1–72, 145–398, 460–729), the Huntington Library (73–108), and Harvard (109–144, 397–459—facsimiles of 451–459 in William Harris Arnold, *First Report of a Book-Collector,* New York, 1898, p. 105, and Finney, facing II, 740). We have a complete transcript by Woodhouse (W²).

What is lacking is a very important transcript by Brown. "I copied as he wrote," Brown tells in his "Life" of Keats (*KC,* II, 72), and there are various evidences of his transcript in the years after Keats's death: Brown provided two excerpts amounting to sixteen lines (390–396, 415–423) for Trelawny to use as chapter epigraphs in *Adventures of a Younger Son*

(1831); he specifically refers to the poem among the "parcel containing all Keats's poems in my possession" that he sent Milnes in 1841 (*KC,* II, 98–99); and Milnes published the poem with a note on its incompleteness and lack of plan signed "Charles Brown." It is virtually certain that Brown's lost transcript was either printer's copy or the source of printer's copy for *1848*; and it is also likely that, when Keats gave Hunt the stanzas for the *Indicator* (at a time when Brown was in Scotland), he did so from Brown's copy, since the *Indicator* and *1848* agree substantively in seven lines against readings of Keats's draft.

Woodhouse's transcript, which is headed "The jealousies. A faery Tale, by Lucy Vaughan Lloyd of China Walk, Lambeth" and has no indication of date or source, agrees substantively with *1848* against Keats's draft in fifty-six lines—23, 34, 78, 112, 135, 148, 159, 161, 170, 177, 192, 207, 208, 211, 214, 215, 216, 223, 225, 231, 241, 242, 246, 265, 304, 323, 365, 387, 393, 407, 409, 415, 416, 419, 480, 491, 508, 509, 521, 522, 526, 531, 540, 549, 551, 562, 564, 597, 613, 634, 641, 658, 666, 673, 707, 708 (these do not include differences owing to Keats's obvious slips of the pen)—and in such peculiarities as the copying error "dealers" in 208, the incompleteness of 522, and the inclusion of the notes to 365 and 403 (which are not present in the draft). The fourteen unique substantive variants in W^2 (in 32, 61, 91, 107, 286, 293, 307, 437, 468, 477, 492, 527, 565, 582) can in every instance be seen as a copying error or Woodhouse's attempt to correct or improve the text. The thirteen unique substantive variants in *1848* (in 107, 180, 214, 297, 347, 355, 422, 505, 544, 568, 569, 575, 719) can also, except in perhaps two instances (107, 422), be seen as either Milnes's emendations or printer's errors. With the likenesses between *1848* and W^2 so extensive, and their relatively few differences explainable in these ways, it would seem highly probable that Woodhouse copied the poem from *1848*'s source, Brown's lost transcript. The principal difficulty with this view occurs in 422, where Keats's draft and W^2 read "save 'the creature'" (the draft, however, without the quotation marks) while Trelawny's chapter epigraph and *1848* (and therefore Brown's transcript) read "catch the treasure." I should conjecture that Brown's transcript originally had "save 'the creature,'" and then "catch the treasure" substituted above it, and that Woodhouse, preferring the earlier reading (as he did occasionally elsewhere in his transcripts), copied the original instead of the revised text. While this may seem farfetched, it is easier to accept than the idea that Woodhouse copied from some other source that we know nothing about. I do not think there was any other holograph version than the draft we have.

If, as seems highly likely on a probability basis, both W^2 and *1848* (as well as the *Indicator* and Trelawny extracts) came from the lost Brown transcript, then we have two basic texts of the poem, that of the original draft and that of Brown's transcript as represented by the agreement of the various texts deriving from it. The next problem is to explain the relationship between the two, and especially their substantive differences in some fifty-six or more lines not accountable in terms of Woodhouse's or Milnes's or the *1848* printer's alterations. It is unlikely that Brown invented the changes himself (because he did not elsewhere alter Keats's lines extensively), and it is also unlikely that the lost transcript was a different MS from the copy that Brown made "as [Keats] wrote" (because, except for two or three short poems—*Not Aladdin magian, In after time a sage of mickle lore,* and perhaps *Shed no tear*—and probably some lost copies written out for the *1820* and *PDWJ* printers, there is no evidence that Brown made more than a single transcript of a poem). One has to suppose, as a consequence, that Brown did what he said—"copied as [Keats] wrote"—and that the differences between the original draft and Brown's text as represented by W^2 and *1848* are the result of Keats's revisions, either in his own hand or by his request, in the lost transcript. I think it would be best to take this view until some new evidence turns up to change it.

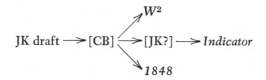

Where they agree, W^2 and *1848* together should be the basis for a standard text except perhaps in five places: 207 (where Keats seems to have changed his draft to read "for shortest" after Brown took his copy), 208 (where W^2's and *1848*'s "dealers" is probably the result of a copying error by Brown), 419 (where Keats later changed "the" to "one" in the draft), 521 (where Keats later altered "But lift" to "Up lift"), and 522 (where Keats completed the line after Brown made his copy). Another instance of a later change may occur in 234, where the *Indicator* reads "vile no-use" for the other texts' "modern use"—but this may have been Hunt's alteration rather than Keats's. Where W^2 and *1848* disagree,

1848's 107 ("seems") and 422 ("catch the treasure") are preferable, and Milnes's emendations to present-tense verbs in 568, 569, and 575 seem worth retaining (though they should of course be viewed as emendations). The rest of the W^2 and *1848* unique variants can be scrapped on the theory that they represent Woodhouse's or Milnes's or the printer's departures from the lost Brown transcript. As to title, *1848* printed the poem as "The Cap and Bells; Or, the Jealousies. A Faëry Tale. Unfinished," and Woodhouse headed it "The jealousies. A faery Tale . . ." (see above). Probably Woodhouse's title, representing that in the lost Brown transcript, should be adopted, especially since Brown says that the poem "was to be published under the feigned authorship of Lucy Vaughan Lloyd, and to bear the title of *The Cap and Bells,* or, which [Keats] preferred, *The Jealousies*" (*KC,* II, 72). Pretty clearly it was Milnes who preferred "The Cap and Bells," taking the title from Brown's "Life" just as he later based another title, "Hyperion, A Vision," on the same source.

Garrod follows *1848* in title and generally in wording and accidentals. He corrects *1848* substantively according to Keats's draft in 180, 208, 297, 347, 355, 505, 544, and 719 (but not in 214), incorporates Keats's later revisions and completion of draft text in 419, 521, and 522 (but not in 207), and adds 793–794 from W^2 (the only source for these lines). More questionably, he accepts H. B. Forman's emendation, "yelping," in 314 (the MSS and *1848* have "whelping"), and prefers draft readings against the agreement of W^2 and *1848* in 223, 323, 416, 509, 564, and 658 (also draft punctuation of substantive significance in 383 —"Bertha Pearl what makes . . ." for "Bertha Pearl! What makes . . ." in W^2 and *1848*). In 422 he prints the draft's and W^2's "save 'the creature.'" His "oped" in 396 may be a misreading of the draft (which I think has either "open" altered to "ope" or "ope" altered to "open"—W^2, Trelawny's chapter epigraph, and *1848* all read "ope"), and "this" in 523 is an error for "that" (the reading of all texts). "Sin'd" in 15 is a misprint for "sinn'd," and *1848* punctuation is inadvertently omitted in 92, 181, 233, 550, and 700.

Allott takes her text (but not her title) from W^2, and has unique readings from that source in 32, 91, 107, 437, 468, 527, 565, and 582. She notes departures from W^2 in 208 (in favor of Keats's draft), 286 (in favor of the draft and *1848*), 314 (Forman's "yelping"), and 522 (the full line in Keats's draft), and has unnoted differences from her source in 61, 148, 170, 214, 223, 293, 307, 323, 396, 416, 419, 422, 477, 492, 508, 509, 521, 523, 551, 568, 569, 575, 658, and 666.

Most of these represent a return to Keats's draft or a preference for the agreement of the draft and *1848,* but 214, 568, 569, and 575 derive uniquely from *1848,* "oped" in 396 and "this" in 523 derive from Garrod or one of H. B. Forman's texts, and "catch 'the creature' " in 422 is a combination of readings in *1848* ("catch") and the draft and W^2 ("the creature").

In after time a sage of mickle lore

Written in 1820 (so dated in Brown's extant transcript; "the last stanza, of any kind, that he wrote before his lamented death" in *PDWJ*). First published in *PDWJ,* 4 July 1839, and then in *1848,* I, 281. Garrod, p. 499; Allott, pp. 742–743.

Keats wrote the stanza (at the end of *The Faerie Queene* V.ii) in a copy of Spenser that he gave to Fanny Brawne. The volume was lent to Fanny Keats in 1823, and subsequently "was lost in Germany" (see *Letters,* II, 302, and *Letters of Fanny Brawne to Fanny Keats,* ed. Fred Edgcumbe, New York, 1937, pp. 84, 86 n.). The only extant MS is a transcript by Brown also after *F.Q.* V.ii in his own copy of Spenser now at Keats House, Hampstead. The text there is substantively the same as that of the two earliest printings (originally Brown wrote "Talus slim" in 8, and then added "grim" above "slim"—perhaps just as in the lost holograph). Brown quoted the stanza in a political article in *PDWJ,* and gave Milnes the text that was printed in *1848.*

$$[\text{JK in Spenser}] \longrightarrow \text{CB in Spenser} \begin{cases} [\text{CB}] \longrightarrow PDWJ \\ [\text{CB}] \longrightarrow 1848 \end{cases}$$

Brown's extant transcript is of course the proper basis for a standard text. Both Garrod and Allott reproduce *1848* (Garrod exactly except for indenting 1–8 in the usual manner of a Spenserian stanza).

3   QUESTIONABLE ATTRIBUTIONS

On Death

This eight-line poem, first published by Forman (1883), II, 201, exists in a transcript (dated 1814) by Georgiana Wylie in the Keats-

Wylie Scrapbook. No author's name is given there, and Garrod is right (pp. xlix–l) that we have no reason for assigning it to Keats. Both Garrod (p. 539) and Allott (p. 744, among "Doubtful Attributions and Trivia") include the poem from Forman's text.

See, the ship in the bay is riding

For this, first published by Garrod in his 1939 edition, there are two transcripts by Woodhouse in the Morgan Library. One of them, with "F" at the end, indicating that Woodhouse got the poem from a Kirkman copy in Mary Frogley's album, was originally written on fol. 3 of the W^2 book of transcripts, and was later transferred by Woodhouse to the W^3 scrapbook. The second has "from Mary Frogley" in shorthand at the end. The transcripts are substantively the same, and both have spaces for a line between 5 and 6, in the first of which Woodhouse penciled in the rhyming comment, "A line seems here omitted to be." Woodhouse subsequently added a note opposite the first transcript, "This piece K. said had not been written by him. He did not see it: but I repeated the first 4 lines to him."

Keats's disavowal of the poem does not necessarily mean that he did not write it (one wonders how many other early poems he would have disowned if Woodhouse had read their opening lines to him), but it does of course cast considerable doubt on his authorship of it. Finney, I, 47, thinks it was "composed probably either by [G. F.] Mathew or by some member of his coterie." Garrod includes it (p. 539, from the second of the transcripts above) "with no belief in its authenticity" (p. lxxii). Allott places it among "Doubtful Attributions and Trivia" (pp. 745–746, "Text from *Woodhouse* 3"). Both err in printing "Bends" for the transcripts' "Blends" in 11.

To Woman (from the Greek)

This poem, unassigned not only in the transcript by Woodhouse in the Morgan Library but also in two copies in Mary Strange Mathew's album and in a printed version clipped and pasted into the Keats-Wylie Scrapbook, was first published as possibly Keats's by Garrod in his 1939 edition, and is included (from Woodhouse's transcript, with a mistaken "to" for "at" in 5) in his 1958 edition on p. lxxiv. As Garrod learned while his 1958 edition was in press—see his Postscript, p. x—the lines are from Edward William Barnard's anonymous *Trifles Imitative of the Chaster Style of Meleager* (1818). Allott, overlooking Garrod's last-minute note, prints the poem among "Doubtful Attributions and Trivia" (pp. 747–748, "Text from *Woodhouse* 3" but with Garrod's "to" in 5).

To A. G. S.

The full title of this sonnet, first published by Garrod in *TLS*, 27 November 1937, p. 906, from a Woodhouse MS in the Morgan Library (the only known source), is "Sonnet / To A. G. S. on reading his admirable Verses, written in this (Miss Reynolds') Album, on either Side of the follow^g attempt to pay Small tribute thereto" (the parenthetical "Miss Reynolds' " is in shorthand). Though the heading may have been added afterward on the MS, both the heading and the text appear to be in the same hand, that of Woodhouse, who, as Finney suggests (II, 751), may be the author of the poem.

No author's name is given in the MS, and the sonnet therefore has the same status as *"The House of Mourning" written by Mr. Scott* and *Gripus* (and also that of *To Woman* before Garrod learned that E. W. Barnard wrote it, and of *The Poet* before Mabel Steele discovered Hessey's attribution to Taylor)—that is, it is one of several lately discovered poems among Woodhouse's papers in the Morgan Library, with no name attached to any of them, that have been assigned to Keats by Lowell, Finney, or Garrod on the basis of Woodhouse's note on a leaf that once served as the title page of the W^3 scrapbook: "All that are not by Keats, have the names of the Authors added." But Steele has shown that this leaf was originally the title page of the W^2 book of transcripts, and was later cut out and transferred to the W^3 scrapbook, and that the note almost surely was intended to refer to the W^2 transcripts rather than to those in W^3 (see *HLB*, 3 [1949], 232–256, and especially *K-SJ*, 5 [1956], 74 n.). If we discount Woodhouse's note, then the only evidence for Keats's authorship is removed and the poems thus attributed to him once again become unassigned. It is not necessary to find another author (as Garrod did for *To Woman* and Steele did for *The Poet*) to demonstrate that Keats did not write them; rather, the burden of proof falls on those who wish to argue *for* Keats's authorship. I am not especially anxious to banish these poems from the canon, but they are clearly of questionable or doubtful status.

Both Garrod (p. 538) and Allott (p. 291), accepting the poem as Keats's, take their text from Woodhouse's MS, and both substitute Woodhouse's marginal "And" for his text's "Yea" at the beginning of 14. Allott emends "muses" in 12 to "muse's"; either word causes a problem, but

Garrod's explanation ("drank to thy muses") is probably preferable to Allott's ("drank to thy muse's health").

Love and Folly

This poem of eleven Spenserian stanzas appeared in *NMM,* 5 (July 1822), 47–48, over the signature "S.Y."—the same initials used to sign Brown's and Keats's *On Some Skulls in Beauley Abbey* when it was published in the same magazine earlier in the same year. Walter E. Peck, *N&Q,* 25 February 1939, pp. 129–131, reprints the poem and assigns it to Brown and Keats on this circumstantial evidence. J. R. MacGillivray, *Keats: A Bibliography and Reference Guide* (Toronto, 1949), p. 76, thinks the attribution "probable," but neither Garrod nor Allott includes or mentions the poem.

"The House of Mourning" written by Mr. Scott

First published by Finney, II, 652, from a Woodhouse MS in the Morgan Library (facsimile facing the text in Finney), this sonnet is unassigned and has the same questionable status as *To A. G. S.* (see the discussion under that title). Possibly it is by Woodhouse himself. Both Garrod (p. 537) and Allott (pp. 495–496), accepting the poem as Keats's, take their text from Woodhouse's MS, the only known source.

Gripus

This unassigned fragment among Woodhouse's papers in the Morgan Library was first published by Lowell, II, 535–544, who took it to be Keats's on the grounds that all poems in the Morgan Woodhouse collection were Keats's except those specifically attributed to another author (see the discussion of *To A. G. S.*). The handwriting appears to be Woodhouse's, but it is a very uncharacteristic piece of copying—not only is the MS almost entirely lacking in punctuation, but speaker-headings and most of the apostrophes in possessives and verb endings are omitted as well. At present there does not seem to be any reason for thinking that Keats wrote the lines.

Garrod, who gives the lines in an appendix (pp. 570–574), adds speaker-headings and punctuation (though he is not very consistent in his practice), and errs substantively in 4 ("has" for the MS's "hast"), 97 ("tiptoe" for "tiptoes"), 105 ("my" for "thy"), and 135 ("Heav'n" for

"Heavn's"). Allott, including the fragment among "Doubtful Attributions and Trivia" (pp. 748–752), takes her text from Garrod, correcting "my" to "thy" in 105.

The Poet

This sonnet, first published in the *London Magazine,* 4 (October 1821), 417, was in the Keats canon for three decades after Lowell, I, 163–164, first assigned it to Keats and printed it from a Woodhouse transcript in the Morgan Library. In the 1950's Mabel Steele discovered a copy by J. A. Hessey that dates the poem 1821 and unequivocally assigns it to John Taylor, and since that time it has generally been accepted as Taylor's. See the articles by E. L. Brooks, *Modern Language Notes,* 67 (1952), 450–454, Earl R. Wasserman, *Modern Language Notes,* 67 (1952), 454–456, and Steele, *K-SJ,* 5 (1956), 69–80; the letter by Bernard Blackstone, *TLS,* 13 November 1959, p. 661; and the footnote in *Journal of English and Germanic Philology,* 62 (1963), 692.

Garrod (who is uncertain about the authorship and appears, from various errors on pp. vii, lxxiii, 528, not to have actually read Steele's article) prints the poem from Woodhouse's transcript (p. 528). Allott includes it among "Doubtful Attributions and Trivia" (pp. 746–747), choosing the *London* text but constructing it from Garrod's apparatus, which does not record the *London*'s "wise" for "see" in 8. Woodhouse's transcript differs substantively from the *London* version in eight of the fourteen lines. Some of his changes (e.g., the substitution of "ball" for "earth" in 10, and the further addition of "sphere" in parentheses before "ball") are the sort that one makes in original composition rather than in copying, and it may be that at least some, and possibly all, of the variants in the transcript are his work instead of Taylor's.

V

Final Comments

If we set aside occasional variances in titles, Garrod's and Allott's texts happen to be substantively identical for seventy-five of Keats's 150 poems and substantively different for the other seventy five. The figures are misleading, however, in at least two ways. On the one hand, were we to count individual lines rather than poems, the proportion of agreement between them would be vastly increased: thousands of Keats's lines are substantively the same in both editions. On the other hand, their substantive agreement in eleven of the poems involves conformity in errors (the most extreme instance is *On Some Skulls in Beauley Abbey,* in which they have the same five wrong words in as many lines); in a twelfth poem, *Think not of it,* they agree in preferring the rough draft text over the revised. If we take away these twelve, they can be said to agree substantively in satisfactory texts of no more than sixty-three of the 150 pieces.

There are of course a number of poems in which it is perfectly proper to disagree over a reading, or an emendation, or the choice of a base-text, but not nearly so many as are represented by Garrod's and Allott's substantive differences from one another. Our standard texts ought to have a larger proportion of agreement than they do—or else more of the differences between them ought to represent improvement in the texts rather than the reviving of old errors and the making of new ones. Had the modern editors published their texts in 1848 we should, at this distance, have only the highest praise for their care and accuracy. But, to take a special group of poems for illustration, where Milnes and his helpers introduced substantive corruptions in at least thirty-seven of the sixty-odd poems that he included in *1848*, Garrod's texts are faulty for thirty-four of the same poems and Allott's for twenty-five. The degree of improvement over Milnes, 110 and 122 years later, respectively, is not very impressive.

I think the present study, with the new information that it gives about the order of states of text for various poems, the sources and significance of MS and early printed versions, and the relative authoritativeness of some texts over others, would be justified even if there were nothing wrong with any of the texts in the current standard editions. But since it was undertaken in the first place out of a feeling that there were too many mistakes in those editions, one very practical conclusion ought to be a summary account of the errors needing correction. Garrod has what I consider clear mistakes and inconsistencies—the latter most often the mixing of two or more discrete states of text—in the following fifty-seven poems (see the histories in Section IV.2 for more specific details):

> Lines Written on 29 May, the Anniversary of Charles's Restoration, on Hearing the Bells Ringing (misreading in 4)
>
> Stay, ruby-breasted warbler, stay (Georgiana–George Keats text with a Woodhouse reading in 22)
>
> Fill for me the brimming bowl (Woodhouse's clerk's unique reading in 4 and Woodhouse's mixture of states of text in several other lines)
>
> To Lord Byron (*1848* corruption in 9)
>
> O Chatterton! how very sad thy fate (*1848* corruptions in 6 and 8)
>
> Ode to Apollo ("In thy western halls"—*1848* corruption in 7)
>
> To Some Ladies (mistaken emendation in 27)
>
> O come, dearest Emma! the rose is full blown (W^2 text with a George Keats–W^3 reading in 4)
>
> Specimen of an Induction to a Poem (misprint in 12)
>
> To Charles Cowden Clarke (word omitted in 106)
>
> After dark vapours have oppress'd our plains (Woodhouse-*1848* text with the *Examiner*'s unique variant in 9)
>
> To a Young Lady Who Sent Me a Laurel Crown (reading originating with Milnes in 11)
>
> God of the golden bow (mixture of draft readings in 6 and 11, fair copy readings in 27 and 32, with Woodhouse's title)
>
> On a Leander Which Miss Reynolds, My Kind Friend, Gave Me (*Gem* corruption in 5)
>
> On the Sea (*Champion* variant, probably a corruption, in 7)
>
> Hither, hither, love (misreading in 22)
>
> You say you love, but with a voice (misreading from Colvin in 19)
>
> Before he went to live with owls and bats (mixture of draft readings in 1, 3, and 6 and Brown readings in 7, 8, 10, and 14, with a nonauthoritative title)

The Gothic looks solemn (Woodhouse text with a Brown variant in 6)

Endymion (misprints and errors from various sources, including Notcutt's type-facsimile of *1818,* in I.511, 520, 591; II.28, 461; III.279, 359, 486, 652; IV.97, 411, and 529)

Lines on Seeing a Lock of Milton's Hair (Brown-*1848*-Forman text with a holograph variant in 20 and an *1848* corruption in 42)

O blush not so! O blush not so (mixture of Woodhouse readings in 2, 9, 15, and 17, Brown readings in 3 and 13, and a reading from Forman in 11)

Welcome joy and welcome sorrow (Clarke-*1848* corruption in 17)

Time's sea hath been five years at its slow ebb (Patmore's alteration in 4)

To the Nile (Brown-*1848* text with readings of an earlier state in 2 and 8)

Blue! 'Tis the life of heaven—the domain (corruptions originating with Patmore in the epigraph and 9)

Extracts from an Opera (transposition of two words in "Folly's Song" 13 and 15)

Where be ye going, you Devon maid (misreadings from Tom Taylor via Forman in 2 and 14)

Mother of Hermes! and still youthful Maia (*1848* corruption in 7)

To Homer (*1848* corruption in 5)

Give me your patience, Sister, while I frame (mistaken emendation in 12)

On Visiting the Tomb of Burns (*1848* corruption in 13 and perhaps in one or two other lines)

Old Meg she was a gipsy (letter text with a Brown variant in 7)

Ah, ken ye what I met the day (misreading from Forman in 30)

All gentle folks who owe a grudge (misprint in 1 and a mistaken emendation from Forman in 44)

Not Aladdin magian (earlier letter text with a W^1 reading in 49f)

On Some Skulls in Beauley Abbey, near Inverness (misreadings, partly from Woodhouse or Colvin, in 29, 30, 65, 80, and 85)

Fragment of Castle-builder (combination of W^2 and *1848* readings in 29)

And what is love? It is a doll dress'd up (*1848* text with a Woodhouse reading in 9)

'Tis the "witching time of night" (*1848* corruptions in 1 and 20)

I had a dove and the sweet dove died (mixture of letter text in 3, 5, and 6 and Woodhouse readings in 3 and 9)

The Eve of St. Agnes (misprint in 82)

The Eve of St. Mark (draft text with Brown-*1848* variants in 22 and 53, a Brown–*1848*–fair copy reading in 59, an independent error in 32, and the unwarranted inclusion of 98a–p)

Why did I laugh tonight? No voice will tell (Milnes's alteration in 6 and an *1848* corruption in 11)

When they were come unto the Fairy's court (misreading from Forman
   in 1 and an independent error in 46)
Character of C. B. (*1848* corruption in 13)
Ode on Indolence (stanzas in the wrong order)
Bright star, would I were steadfast as thou art (*1848* corruption in 11)
La Belle Dame sans Merci (Brown-Woodhouse-*1848* text with a letter
   reading in 36 and an independent error in 47)
Song of Four Fairies (mixture of three states—fair copy readings
   generally with draft readings in 26, 60, and 77 and Brown-*1848*
   readings in 9, 44, and 71)
Shed no tear—O shed no tear (nonauthoritative title)
Otho the Great (mixture of Keats's draft and Brown's fair copy, plus
   1848 corruptions—see the discussion in Section IV.2, above)
To Autumn (misprint in 28)
The Fall of Hyperion (errors from *1857* in I.349 and 359 and inde-
   pendent errors in I.52 and 409)
I cry your mercy—pity—love!—aye, love (misprint in 10)
To Fanny ("Physician Nature"—nonauthoritative title and *1848*'s
   omission of a word in 15)
The Jealousies (mixture of *1848* text, including some corruptions,
   with readings of Keats's draft and W^2, an emendation by Forman,
   and at least one independent error in 523—see the discussion in
   Section IV.2)

Allott has the same kinds of error and inconsistency in forty-seven
poems:

Lines Written on 29 May, the Anniversary of Charles's Restoration, on
   Hearing the Bells Ringing (misreading in 4)
Stay, ruby-breasted warbler, stay (Georgiana—George Keats text with a
   Woodhouse reading in 22)
Fill for me the brimming bowl (holograph text with a Woodhouse
   variant in 8 and an error from Forman in 25)
O Chatterton! how very sad thy fate (*1848* corruption in 8)
O come, dearest Emma! the rose is full blown (holograph text with a
   questionable title and part of a Woodhouse variant in 17)
To Charles Cowden Clarke (misprint in 121)
Sleep and Poetry (an error based on Forman in 134 and misprints in
   51, 218, and 222)
I stood tip-toe upon a little hill (mistaken emendations and/or mis-
   prints in 112, 129, and 173)
After dark vapours have oppress'd our plains (Woodhouse-*1848* text
   with an *1848* corruption in 5 and the *Examiner*'s unique variants
   in 5 and 9)
God of the golden bow (revised fair copy text with a draft variant in 6)
On a Leander Which Miss Reynolds, My Kind Friend, Gave Me (mis-
   reading in 2 and possibly also in 5)

On the Sea (*Champion* variant, probably a corruption, in 7)

Hither, hither, love (misreading in 22)

You say you love, but with a voice (John Taylor's text with Charlotte Reynolds–Woodhouse variants in 3 and 22 and a misreading from Colvin in 19)

Before he went to live with owls and bats (draft text with a Brown reading in 3, Stephens' copying error in 6, mistakes from Garrod's apparatus in 8 and 13, and a nonauthoritative title)

Endymion (misprints, misreadings, and mistaken emendations in I.33, 39, 78, 115, 120, 150; II.523, 733, 958, 985; III.515, 663, 785; and IV.663—and the omission of IV.234)

Apollo to the Graces (misreadings partly from Colvin in 3 and 6)

Lines on Seeing a Lock of Milton's Hair (letter text with a misreading from Forman in 33 and a draft–fair copy variant in 39)

O blush not so! O blush not so (Woodhouse's clerk's text with Brown variants in 5 and 13)

Welcome joy and welcome sorrow (Clarke-*1848* corruption in 17 and the inadvertent transposition of 22–23 and 24–25)

Time's sea hath been five years at its slow ebb (Patmore's alteration in 4)

Blue! 'Tis the life of heaven—the domain (corruptions originating with Patmore in the epigraph and 9)

For there's Bishop's teign (misreading from Tom Taylor via Forman in 34–35)

Where be ye going, you Devon maid (misreading from Tom Taylor via Forman in 14)

Old Meg she was a gipsy (letter text with a Brown variant in 7)

There was a naughty boy (nonauthoritative title and a misreading from Forman in 96 [Allott's line 98])

To Ailsa Rock (letter text with a *Literary Pocket-Book* variant in 2 and a misreading or mistaken modernization in 5)

There is a joy in footing slow across a silent plain (letter text with a Brown-*1848* variant in 2)

Upon my life, Sir Nevis, I am piqu'd (omission of Keats's note to 53 and a misreading from Forman in 58)

On Some Skulls in Beauley Abbey, near Inverness (misreadings taken over from Garrod in 29, 30, 65, 80, and 85)

Nature withheld Cassandra in the skies (Woodhouse text with an *1848* reading in 3)

Fragment of Castle-builder (Woodhouse text with *1848* readings in title and 29)

And what is love? It is a doll dress'd up (Woodhouse text with an *1848* reading in 9)

I had a dove and the sweet dove died (letter text with a Woodhouse reading in 3 and a Milnes-*1848* corruption in 5)

The Eve of St. Mark (W^2 text, including Woodhouse's distinctive errors in 74 and 115 [Allott's lines 76 and 133], with readings of the draft, the letter text, and Brown's transcript in 12, 40, 59, 62, 65, 68, 82, 88, 92, and 100 [her 84, 90, 94, and 118 for the last four], plus the unwarranted inclusion of 98*a–p* and a canceled couplet following 68 [her 101–116, 69–70])

Character of C. B. (*1848* corruption in 13)

Ode on Indolence (misprint in 22)

Bright star, would I were steadfast as thou art (*1848* corruption in 11)

La Belle Dame sans Merci (letter text with a Brown-Woodhouse-*1848* variant in 40 and an *Indicator* variant in 44)

Song of Four Fairies (fair copy text with draft readings in 26, 60, and 77 and a Brown-Woodhouse-*1848* variant in 71)

Otho the Great (mixture of Brown's fair copy and Keats's draft, plus *1848* corruptions, Forman's mistakes, independent errors and misprints, and the omission of IV.i.105—see the discussion in Section IV.2, above)

Lamia (errors originating with Forman in I.260, 316, and II.11, and an independent error in I.329)

Pensive they sit and roll their languid eyes (misreadings from the New York *World* via Forman in 11 and 12)

The Fall of Hyperion (errors from *1857* via Forman in I.161, 217, 247, 382, 409, 426, and 436)

To Fanny ("Physician Nature"—nonauthoritative title and *1848's* omission of a word in 15)

King Stephen (*1848* corruptions in I.iii.5, I.iv.9 and 20, and independent errors or mistaken modernizations in I.i.32, I.ii.28 and 32)

The Jealousies (mixture of W^2 text, readings of Keats's draft, *1848* corruptions, an emendation by Forman, and at least one misreading from Garrod—see the discussion in Section IV.2)

These lists account for some of the substantive differences (and also for the agreements in error) between Garrod's and Allott's texts. A number of other variances result simply from the two editors' choices of different base-texts, as in the following:

Fill for me the brimming bowl
As from the darkening gloom a silver dove
O come, dearest Emma! the rose is full blown
Written in Disgust of Vulgar Superstition
God of the golden bow
You say you love, but with a voice
The Gothic looks solemn
In drear-nighted December
Apollo to the Graces
Lines on Seeing a Lock of Milton's Hair
O blush not so! O blush not so

Hence burgundy, claret, and port
There is a joy in footing slow across a silent plain
Not Aladdin magian
And what is love? It is a doll dress'd up
The Eve of St. Mark
Song of Four Fairies
To Sleep
On Fame ("Fame, like a wayward girl")
Otho the Great
The Jealousies

There are also several differences owing to one or the other editor's individual emendations. For example, Garrod emends—and Allott leaves unemended—*Imitation of Spenser* 12 and 29; *Endymion* II.340, 524, 749, 782, III.752, and IV.151; *Welcome joy and welcome sorrow* 13; *Isabella* 485; *Character of C. B.* 22; *Hyperion* I.6 and 81; *Ode to Psyche* 17; and *This living hand* 5. Allott emends—and Garrod does not emend—*Endymion* I.661 and 762; *Dear Reynolds, as last night I lay in bed* 14; *This mortal body of a thousand days* 5; *Upon my life, Sir Nevis* 9; and *What can I do to drive away* 33 and 42. Both editors emend, but in different ways, *To Kosciusko* 7, *Endymion* I.182, and *When they were come unto the Fairy's court* 46; they disagree in their readings of Keats's handwriting in *On Receiving a Laurel Crown from Leigh Hunt* 4, *Two or three posies* 27, and *Pensive they sit* 2; and they differ in the extent to which they accept Milnes's and others' changes in *On Visiting the Tomb of Burns* and *'Tis the "witching time of night."* These details are necessarily selective, but they will serve again to emphasize the degree of variation in the two editions. Many of the differences represent Allott's improvement over Garrod's texts, and this is all to the good; but a sizable number also result from Allott's independent errors in poems for which Garrod's versions, as a consequence, are still superior—and this, on the other hand, is regrettable.

Keats's texts can to an extent be repaired simply by correction of the most obvious mistakes in the current standard editions. I have not very often, in Section IV.2, concerned myself with errors in Garrod's headnotes and apparatus (of which there are a great many, perhaps a thousand or fifteen hundred in the recording of variants in the fine print of the apparatus) or with mistakes in Allott's textual notes (which too frequently are based on Garrod's misinformation). My focus has been the texts themselves, and these can be rid of at least most of the errors and inconsistencies in new issues of Garrod's and Allott's editions, revised according to

the lists given at the beginning of this section. I would not trust my col-
lations, and the details of the histories in Section IV.2, as a basis for a
fresh editing of the poems, but they should serve in the interim as a basis
for correction.

I think, however, that a fresh editing is in order. Texts aside, Garrod's
arrangement of the poems makes no sense, his introduction and headnotes
are considerably out of date, and his cumbersome and error-filled appa-
ratus does as much harm as good. Allott's chronological arrangement is
much to be preferred, and her critical annotations, which would amount
to some four hundred pages in small type if they were printed all together,
are excellent; but she modernizes spelling, punctuation, and the like in-
consistently, and she provides too little textual information to serve the
requirements of serious scholars and critics. "What is needed now," wrote
Sperry in 1967 (p. 138), "is a full-scale re-editing of the poetry in the
light of all available evidence bearing on text, dating, and allusion . . . a
modern edition—something akin to the so-called variorum—that accu-
rately provides for any given poem all known readings of any textual
authority together with all available facts bearing on dating, allusion, and
contemporary criticism." For some of these latter matters—the historical
background and critical annotations—Allott's edition answers the need
quite nicely. But the textual work still needs to be done.

I would offer the next serious editor of Keats's poems a few suggestions.
First, I think there are only two possible arrangements of the poems to
choose from. The more obvious is a straight chronological ordering, as in
Allott and in the histories in Section IV.2 of the present work, beginning
with *Imitation of Spenser* and ending with *In after time a sage of mickle
lore,* which on Brown's information in both cases were Keats's "earliest
attempt" and "the last stanza, of any kind, that he wrote before his la-
mented death." Chronological ordering sometimes brings together the
memorable with the much less memorable pieces and the serious with the
light-hearted, but these juxtapositions do not falsify Keats's development
or his temperament. Such an arrangement is vastly superior to Garrod's,
which in general follows the order in which the poems became public
(but nevertheless presents the poems of Milnes's second volume before
those of his first, and sometimes separates poems written in a single letter),
and also to that of Ernest de Selincourt, which, after the poems of the
three original volumes, groups the poems roughly by type.

The other possible method would be to give the contents of *1817,
1818,* and *1820* in order, just as in the original volumes, and then the
rest of the poems chronologically. The basis for this latter procedure is

the notion that each of Keats's volumes constitutes a separate literary work in which the arrangement of the pieces within the volume in a sense represents one more stage of composition, and consequently that we ought to read the poems of each volume together in the order in which Keats put them. This does not of course apply to *1818,* which consists of a single poem; but the individual poems of *1817* and *1820* do take on additional meanings by their relationships with the poems that precede and follow them in the original volumes, and Keats, like other poets, must have been aware of the fact. The arrangements of poems in both *1817* and *1820* have been discussed critically, and interpretations of Keats's career to an extent based on them (see *Hoodwinking,* pp. 1–13, 116–117). It seems to me that either of these ways of presenting the poems is reasonable, and that no other will do as well. If the editor chooses straight chronology, then he must, as Allott does, somewhere include lists of the original contents of *1817* and *1820.*

As to the texts themselves—substantively they should follow the most authoritative versions available, so far as possible using words that Keats actually wrote (this perhaps cannot be done in *On Peace* 13 and *To a Young Lady Who Sent Me a Laurel Crown* 11, and certainly cannot be done in *On Visiting the Tomb of Burns* 12, where Jeffrey left a blank space and noted that "An illegible word occurs here") and, except for the correction of obvious errors, *all* the words of some single version. As Section IV.2 and the summary lists of the present section have indicated, a recurrent fault in the modern editions has been the combining of words from two or more discrete texts so as to produce versions that never existed in any MS or in the poet's mind. As I hope I have made clear from the beginning, I consider it desirable to reproduce *a* version, whole and intact, that has the poet's authority behind it. Where we have differing versions whose relative degrees of authoritativeness are unsettled, or two or more equally authoritative versions but no clear indications of chronological priority or of Keats's intentions in the texts, the editor will have some subjective choices to make. For this reason we can never have a thoroughly definitive edition of all the poems. But such cases are relatively few, and further research may yet clear up some of the remaining problems.

In the treatment of accidentals I favor at least a degree of normalizing, on the grounds that Keats's own practices in his MSS are frequently erratic, inadequate, and a hindrance to the reading and understanding of his poems, and that anyone else's punctuation, spelling, and capitalization— the early printers', Milnes's, or Forman's, for example—are, except perhaps in the three original volumes, no more authoritative than any that we would substitute in their place. Keats was not always so casual, of course: he took considerable care with the MSS of *Lamia* and a handful of other poems, and he made note of and tried to get Taylor to correct some errors in the accidentals of *Endymion*. But in general he was concerned principally with the words of his poems, and he relied on others to fuss over the minor details necessary to make them presentable to the public. I think we can help him along in this respect better than his contemporaries and the early editors did. Allott's modernizing would seem to be a step in the right direction, and her spelling and punctuation in particular make more sense than those of any previous edition. I have commented elsewhere on her practices, which are blamable mainly in their lack of consistency (see *K-SJ,* 20 [1971], 122–129). A more standard and somewhat more conservative practice would be a further improvement, but the future editor must consider both her principles and her procedures seriously.

As to textual annotation, the main rule ought to be the inclusion only of variants that have some positive degree of authority. A large fault of Garrod's apparatus, quite apart from its numerous errors, is the treatment of all MS and printed texts as having equal authority—Mary Strange Mathew's miscopying of a line from *1817* and Dilke's miscopying of a word from a Brown transcript are given the same status as a variant in Keats's own hand. Except for historical purposes (for which a separate account of nonauthoritative variants might be included at the back of an edition), only variants from authorial versions, or from the closest representatives that we have of such versions, should be given. The readings of Dilke's, George Keats's, and Woodhouse's transcripts known to have been copied from Brown's extant transcripts, the various MSS written out from printed sources, all of *1848's* texts for which we have Milnes's sources, and a number of similarly derivative texts should be scrapped or relegated to a separate section at the end. Again except for historical purposes, all accidental variants should be ignored save in those relatively few instances in which the accidentals are of importance to the interpretation (the most obvious example would be the quotation marks in *Ode on a Grecian Urn* 49). In these ways the textual apparatus would be greatly simplified and made much more useful to scholars and critics who lack the time or access to the MSS necessary in order to do their own collating and deciding. Allott's textual annotation is fairly discriminating in its selection but, as I have said before, depends too much on Garrod's apparatus and repeats too many of his mistakes. The business can be carried out more efficiently and judiciously.

Finally, since a number of mistakes in the current standard editions are printer's errors, I suppose I should advocate more rigorous proofreading. I do not think it is possible to produce a book the size of a Keats edition that is free of errors, but the number can be reduced, and then further reduced. The simplest conclusion of my study would be that if the suggestions of this final section were carried out, and the misprints were confined to obvious errors like Garrod's "Phœbuts" (*Endymion* IV.411), then Keats's texts would be in a healthier condition than they are at present.

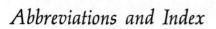

Abbreviations and Index

Abbreviations

1817	John Keats, *Poems*, 1817
1818	John Keats, *Endymion: A Poetic Romance*, 1818
1820	John Keats, *Lamia, Isabella, The Eve of St. Agnes, and Other Poems,* 1820
1848	*Life, Letters, and Literary Remains, of John Keats,* ed. Richard Monckton Milnes, 2 vols., 1848
1857	R. M. Milnes, "Another Version of Keats's 'Hyperion,'" *Miscellanies of the Philobiblon Society,* 3 (1856–57)
1876	*The Poetical Works of John Keats*, ed. Lord Houghton [R. M. Milnes], 1876
Allott	*The Poems of John Keats*, ed. Miriam Allott, 1970
Bate	Walter Jackson Bate, *John Keats*, Cambridge, Mass., 1963
Clarke, *Recollections*	Charles and Mary Cowden Clarke, *Recollections of Writers,* 1878
Colvin	Sidney Colvin, *John Keats: His Life and Poetry, His Friends, Critics, and After-Fame,* 1917
de Selincourt, *Hyperion*	*"Hyperion": A Facsimile of Keats's Autograph Manuscript, with a Transliteration of the Manuscript of "The Fall of Hyperion: A Dream,"* with introductions and notes by Ernest de Selincourt, Oxford, 1905
Finney	Claude Lee Finney, *The Evolution of Keats's Poetry*, 2 vols., Cambridge, Mass., 1936
Forman (1883)	*The Poetical Works and Other Writings of John Keats*, ed. Harry Buxton Forman, 4 vols., 1883
Galignani (1829)	*The Poetical Works of Coleridge, Shelley, and Keats,* Paris, 1829
Garrod	*The Poetical Works of John Keats*, ed. H. W. Garrod, 2nd ed., Oxford, 1958
Gittings, *John Keats*	Robert Gittings, *John Keats*, Boston, 1968
Gittings, *Odes*	*The Odes of Keats and Their Earliest Known Manuscripts,* introduced with notes by Robert Gittings, Kent, Ohio, 1970

Hampstead Keats	*The Poetical Works and Other Writings of John Keats*, ed. H. Buxton Forman, rev. by Maurice Buxton Forman, 8 vols., New York, 1938–39
HLB	*Harvard Library Bulletin*
Hoodwinking	Jack Stillinger, *The Hoodwinking of Madeline and Other Essays on Keats's Poems*, Urbana, 1971
KC	*The Keats Circle: Letters and Papers, 1816–1878*, ed. Hyder Edward Rollins, 2 vols., Cambridge, Mass., 1948
K-SJ	*Keats-Shelley Journal*
Letters	*The Letters of John Keats, 1814–1821*, ed. Hyder Edward Rollins, 2 vols., Cambridge, Mass., 1958
Lowell	Amy Lowell, *John Keats*, 2 vols., Boston, 1925
N&Q	*Notes and Queries*
NMM	*The New Monthly Magazine*
PDWJ	*The Plymouth and Devonport Weekly Journal*
Ridley	M. R. Ridley, *Keats' Craftsmanship: A Study in Poetic Development*, Oxford, 1933
SB	*Studies in Bibliography*
Sharp	William Sharp, *The Life and Letters of Joseph Severn*, 1892
Sperry	Stuart M. Sperry, Jr., "Richard Woodhouse's Interleaved and Annotated Copy of Keats's *Poems* (1817)," *Literary Monographs*, 1 (Madison, 1967), 101–164, 308–311
TLS	*The Times Literary Supplement*
W¹	Transcripts in the smaller of two volumes of Woodhouse copies of poems at Harvard (on this and the next two items see Section II.4)
W²	Transcripts in the larger of two volumes of Woodhouse copies of poems at Harvard
W³	Woodhouse transcripts in the Morgan Library (in Garrod's and Allott's use, "W³" and "*Woodhouse 3*" also refer to transcripts by other copyists in the same collection)
Ward	Aileen Ward, *John Keats: The Making of a Poet*, New York, 1963
Williamson	*The Keats Letters, Papers, and Other Relics Forming the Dilke Bequest in the Hampstead Public Library*, ed. George C. Williamson, 1914

Index of Titles and First Lines